Two Days in June

Two Days in June

John F. Kennedy
and the 48 Hours *that* Made History

ANDREW COHEN

Library and Archives of Canada Cataloguing in Publication data is available upon request

ISBN 978-0-7710-2387-3

Published simultaneously in the United States of America by McClelland & Stewart, a division of Random House of Canada Limited

Library of Congress Control Number: 2014944155

Printed and bound in USA

McClelland & Stewart,
a division of Random House of Canada Limited,
a Penguin Random House Company
www.randomhouse.ca

1 2 3 4 5   18 17 16 15 14

In memory of Zachary Goodyear –
teacher, housemaster, coach, counselor, and friend
at Choate Rosemary Hall for forty-four years.
He introduced a generation of students to Washington
and explained its mysteries. We are all in his debt.

CONTENTS

"But wherever we are, we must all, in our daily lives, live up to the age-old faith that peace and freedom walk together. In too many of our cities today, the peace is not secure because the freedom is incomplete."

JOHN F. KENNEDY

JUNE 10, 1963

"We preach freedom around the world, and we mean it, and we cherish our freedom here at home, but are we to say to the world, and much more importantly, to each other that this is the land of the free except for the Negroes . . . ?"

JOHN F. KENNEDY

JUNE 11, 1963

ACKNOWLEDGEMENTS

If you're going to write another book on John Fitzgerald Kennedy, a literary critic warned recently, you better have a damn good reason. In writing *Two Days in June*, I think I have a good reason: to tell the story of a president who pivoted decisively on the two biggest issues of his time. To tell the story over two days, in granular detail, from sources previously unavailable or unexamined. And to observe the president up close – hour-by-hour, moment-by-moment – as he conducts ordinary business amid extraordinary circumstances.

In a sense, I have been thinking about JFK since I learned of his assassination as a third grader in Aphrodite Christie's class at Roslyn School in Montreal. I have looked for him ever since – at Choate Rosemary Hall in Connecticut, at McGill and Cambridge Universities, as a reporter with *United Press International* and the *Globe and Mail* in Washington, as a columnist, a professor, and an author. I did not know my search would lead to this book and I do not claim to have found him. I can say, though, that the journey has been the joy of a lifetime.

On this journey – which has taken me into libraries, museums, private collections, and other places of interest around North America and beyond – I have had wise and sure-footed guides at every turn.

They include Tal Nadan, Reference Archivist, and Laura Slezak Karas, Manuscripts Specialist, in the papers of Arthur M. Schlesinger

Jr. in the Brooke Russell Astor Reading Room of the New York Public Library; Nelson D. Lankford, biographer of David Bruce, and Frances S. Pollard, Chief Librarian, in the papers of David Bruce at the Virginia Historical Society; Jennifer Toews, Librarian, in the papers of Charles Ritchie at the Thomas Fisher Rare Book Library at the University of Toronto; and Harry Miller, Reference Archivist, and David L. Williams, historian and retired librarian, in the papers of William Attwood at the Wisconsin Historical Society. My thanks to them all.

Cathy Andreen, Director of Media Relations at the University of Alabama in Tuscaloosa, and Laura Drake Davis, Associate Archivist at American University in Washington, D.C., greatly helped in my visits to their fine institutions, which play a leading role in this story.

Dr. Jeffrey S. Underwood kindly showed me around Kennedy's Air Force One at Wright-Patterson Air Force Base in Ohio, explaining the context and symbolism of the airplane. Charles and Martha Bartlett, who introduced Jack and Jackie Kennedy, reflected frankly on the couple in their lovely garden in Washington a half century later, as did Ben Bradlee, the former editor of the *Washington Post*, some years earlier. The late Lansing Lamont, who was our neighbor on North Haven Island, Maine, across the Thoroughfare, discussed Kennedy's Washington with a critical eye. He was always kind and gracious. The late Thomas Delworth of Ottawa evoked Saigon in 1963. We talked in the last months of his long, extraordinary life, when he was ill and nearly blind, and I was struck by his elegance and vivid recall. Michael Shenstone, another former Canadian diplomat, shared his good fortune working for Charles Ritchie in Washington.

I owe particular thanks to Lady Antonia Fraser, who welcomed me into her drawing room in London. She retrieved her photo albums, diaries, and news clippings from her visits to the United States in 1961 and 1963, which she said she had not examined in fifty years. Her memories, and her diaries, illuminated what JFK – and official Washington – was thinking in June of 1963.

Much of *Two Days in June* comes from hours of raw footage shot for *Crisis: Behind a Presidential Commitment*, Robert Drew's seminal cinéma vérité documentary (discussed in the *Note on Sources*). I thank him for his help. For arranging my visit, finding and screening the film from the Robert Drew Collection at the Academy Film Archive in Hollywood, I am indebted to May Haduong, Public Access Manager; Cassie Blake, Public Access Coordinator; Brian Drischell, Traffic Manager; and Andrew Bradburn, Film Archivist. They were unfailingly generous and professional.

At the Library of Congress, where I spent days reading Katie Louchheim's diaries and the papers of the Alsop brothers, the archivists were courteous and helpful. Let me thank as well, the staff of the MacOdrum Library at Carleton University in Ottawa, where I teach; the library generously arranged many books on inter-library-loan and allowed me to borrow books from its own large collection, seemingly forever.

At the John F. Kennedy Presidential Library, I was assisted by Stephen Plotkin, Reference Archivist, who introduced me to the world of novelist Richard Yates and reliably explained other mysteries. Maryrose Grossman, Audiovisual Archivist, kindly showed me Bernard Lamotte's semi-tropical murals which once adorned the walls of the White House Swimming Pool.

Laurie Coulter, my editor, was cheerful, incisive, and clear-eyed. Douglas Pepper, my gentlemanly friend and publisher of Signal Books, as well as Jenny Bradshaw, Elizabeth Kribs, Bhavna Chauhan, and Lucy Coren at Random House, were patient and accommodating under pressure.

More thanks to R.M. Doyon, Ronald I. Cohen, and Paul Torrie. All gave the manuscript a careful and constructive examination, which imposed on their time. From beginning to end, they were curious, generous, and fastidious.

Allan Rock, Peter Herrndorf, Lawrence Martin, Don Newman and David Halton, intrigued and inspired by the Kennedys, were always encouraging. So were Stephen Davis, Basil Hero, David Timberman, and Michael Ward, old classmates from Choate Rosemary Hall, where I explored the Kennedy Collection. In London, Constantine Partasides, Klearchos Kyriakides, and Jackie Donnelly Russell offered ideas; in Toronto, Marcus Gee, William Thorsell, and Martin Regg Cohn did, too.

Sally Bedell Smith was keen from the moment I told her about this project – she guessed the two days immediately – as was Thurston Clarke, with whom I shared a public platform one evening discussing JFK. David M. Shribman, winner of the Pulitzer Prize and executive editor of the *Pittsburgh Post-Gazette*, has been a friend and colleague since we covered Bill Clinton together. His generosity, over the years, is without parallel.

Jean Morin, a retired military historian, kindly translated passages from Hervé Alphand's diaries. Jordan Deagle, a graduate student, ably scoured Joe Alsop's papers in the Library of Congress for some missing pieces.

To my researcher, Kristina Roic, I owe much. This is the third book on which we have collaborated, and I could not do them without her. To every project she brings commitment, imagination, and cheerfulness. She is indispensable.

Lastly, to my children, Alexander and Rachel, who have heard more about JFK than anyone should as teenagers, and to my wife, Mary Gooderham, who, once again, brought her sharp editorial eye and discriminating ear to an unwieldy manuscript. After twenty years of marriage, she still adjusts my words, streamlines my sentences, and sweetens my world.

Andrew Cohen
Ottawa
June 11, 2014

By June 1963, John Fitzgerald Kennedy had been president of the United States for almost two-and-a-half years. His record was uneven. In his first nine months in office, he authorized a disastrous invasion of Cuba, endured a belligerent Nikita Khrushchev in Vienna, faced instability in Laos and the Congo, and watched the Wall go up in Berlin. His critics found his responses inept. A half century later, George Will, the bow-tied conservative commentator, called 1961 "the most incompetent first year of any presidency." When a journalist proposed a book on his first year, Kennedy asked ruefully: "Why would you want to write about disasters?" In 1962, though, Kennedy learned to turn crisis to his advantage. He made the steel barons of Pittsburgh roll back their price increases, he forced the governor of Mississippi to integrate its all-white state university, and, most memorably, he persuaded the premier of the Soviet Union to remove his nuclear missiles from Cuba.

Today these confrontations are signposts along the New Frontier: the Bay of Pigs, the Vienna Summit, the Berlin Crisis, the

Steel Crisis, the Cuban Missile Crisis, the Battle of Ole Miss. The pace of Kennedy's White House was dizzying; events tumbled upon one another like a tower of Sinatra LPs falling on a phonograph. Richard M. Nixon reflected on his tumultuous yet unfinished career in 1962 in a memoir titled *Six Crises*; by one count, Kennedy faced fifteen crises over his presidency alone. The youngest elected president in the country's history, Kennedy was characteristically sardonic about the job he had craved "more than life itself." Two days after his inauguration, he told journalist Charles Bartlett, his old friend, that he had slept in Lincoln's bed the night before. "Did anything strange happen or did you have any unusual dreams?" Bartlett asked. "No," replied Kennedy. "I just jumped in and hung on!"

By his third year in the White House, Kennedy was more than hanging on. He was taking charge, seizing the instruments of the office – rhetorical and real – and shaping the culture of Washington like no president had since Theodore Roosevelt. He was tempered by the "hard and bitter peace" of the postwar world (as he had called it in his Inaugural Address), but was no longer willing to be trapped by its dogma. Although his legislation languished in Congress, he had learned to use executive power when he could. He established the Alliance for Progress in Latin America, created the Peace Corps, and promised the moon. By 1963, teachers were going into the Third World and astronauts were going into Outer Space. In May of that year, Gordon Cooper orbited Earth twenty-two times, spending thirty-four hours and twenty minutes aloft. It was a record for manned space flight and it boosted the nation's confidence. In the Senate, the Democrats had increased their majority in the midterm elections of 1962, which was rare for the party of any sitting president. Although JFK's popularity had fallen from a high of 83 percent following the aborted invasion of Communist Cuba at the Bay of Pigs in April 1961, it held strong in June at 64 percent. He was optimistic about his re-election in 1964. He relished the prospect of facing the Republicans led, he hoped, by Barry Goldwater, the gnarled, unreconstructed conservative from Arizona.

On May 29, 1963, Kennedy turned forty-six years old. While he remained plagued by a bad back and a panoply of illnesses – his doleful medical history would not emerge for decades – he looked and felt better than he had in some time. His chestnut hair had touches of gray. His face was less puffy from cortisone. Some said he had aged in office, but to the country he looked vigorous. Jacqueline Bouvier Kennedy, his stylish wife, was expecting a baby that summer, and this, as well as the growth of his two children, cheered him. Having come through a rough passage, he had greater self-awareness. He was more conscious of what he should do and less cautious about what he could do. Bartlett observes today that he had never seen anyone grow as much as Kennedy did in the two years before he became president. He might have said the same of Kennedy in the two years *after* he became president. Kennedy was realizing now that he had to act. As a student of history, he could see the two great, seismic forces at play in the early 1960s: the proliferation of nuclear arms and the struggle for civil rights. He could avoid neither. Both were pressing upon him, every day, with exquisite fury. They were dictating choices to him and demanding decisions of him.

The Cold War, now eighteen years old, was simmering. The Soviets tested their first nuclear weapon in 1953, eight years after the Americans had dropped their atomic bombs on Japan. Although the danger of a nuclear attack from "the Reds" was never as great as Kennedy had claimed in 1960 when he warned of a nonexistent "missile gap" between the United States and the Soviet Union, the threat of thermonuclear war shrouded the country and shaded the Zeitgeist. Americans were digging bomb shelters while their generals stockpiled bombs. Both the United States and the Soviet Union were conducting poisonous nuclear tests in the atmosphere. In the autumn of 1961, the Soviets detonated fifty hydrogen bombs in sixty days. On October 30, 1961, they exploded a fifty-megaton bomb that was 2,500 times as great as the one dropped on Hiroshima. The United States launched some forty tests of its own. MAD – Mutual Assured Destruction – was part of the vernacular. Peace activists were stirring; on November 1, 1961, fifty thousand members of Women Strike for Peace marched in sixty cities across the United States to protest nuclear weapons.

It was the Age of Anxiety, when anxiety meant something different than it would a decade or two later. Pollution, insecticides, obesity, cancer and cholesterol were not considered public perils in 1963. Feminism, environmentalism, ageism, consumer rights, disabled rights, children's rights and gay rights were yet to come. Smog smothered industrial cities crumbling at the core as white Americans fled to the suburbs. Crime was rising. Books were banned or censored by library boards. Automobiles had no seatbelts and cigarettes had no warnings. There was asbestos in schools and lead in gasoline. More than three-fifths of Americans voted in 1960; they trusted government and respected public service. Authority – personified by the police chief, the school principal, the rabbi or minister, mother or father – commanded respect.

Americans had learned to live with the Bomb but they could never escape its shadow. It wasn't surprising that Kennedy devoted his stern Inaugural Address almost exclusively to the dangers and responsibilities of living in a divided, Manichean world, one dominated by "the long twilight struggle" against Communism. As for the home front, he made only passing mention of civil rights, as if it were an afterthought. To white America in 1961, it was. More a movement than a crusade, racial equality pricked the public consciousness but did not command it.

Negroes, as they were called in 1963, had been demanding rights in the courts and the streets for a decade. In 1957, President Dwight D. Eisenhower sent federal troops into Little Rock, Arkansas, to integrate Central High School. In the election of 1960,

Kennedy won favor among black Americans when his brother, Robert Francis Kennedy, helped free the Reverend Martin Luther King Jr. from jail in Atlanta. JFK placed a telephone call to King's wife, Coretta, to show his solidarity. In 1960, the South practiced its own kind of apartheid. Black Southerners could not vote, hold office, or serve on juries. Despite the Supreme Court's landmark ruling in 1954 in *Brown v. Board of Education*, most schools remained segregated in the South. In most cities, blacks still moved to the back of the bus, drank from separate water fountains, and sat at separate lunch counters – if they sat at all. In the South, interracial marriage was a crime. In the North, where segregation endured but was less egregious, country clubs and social clubs refused to admit blacks (as they did Jews). There were no black senators, cabinet members, or Supreme Court justices, and only four black congressmen among the 435 members of the House of Representatives. As the threat of nuclear arms seized America in 1963, so did the demand for equal rights.

✳

Two crises in the early fall of 1962 foreshadowed the events of the late spring of 1963. Between October 16 and 28, Kennedy had confronted the Soviets over their secret deployment of nuclear missiles in Cuba, ninety miles from the coast of Florida. It was the greatest crisis of the Cold War, a harrowing thirteen days that brought the world closer to Armageddon than any time before or since. Kennedy wondered how long the Cold War could remain cold and realized that there had to be a new *modus vivendi* between East and West. Having heard Khrushchev's threats in Vienna, having seen him sanction a wall to keep East Germans from fleeing to the West, having survived, barely, the nuclear saber-rattling in Cuba, he remained only slightly less pessimistic than he had been in the summer of 1961. As the Soviets murmured about seizing West

Berlin, he told Hugh Sidey, the journalist: "I think sooner or later we are going to have a nuclear exchange. I read history. Since the days of the longbow, when men began to deliver weapons, someone has built them, stockpiled them, and used them. No weapon that I know of has gone unused in warfare after it has been developed."

A little more than a fortnight before facing down the Communists, Kennedy had faced down the segregationists. Ross Barnett, the governor of Mississippi, had refused to admit a black student to the state university at Oxford known as Ole Miss. His resistance sparked the greatest insurrection in the South since Reconstruction, forcing the federal government to send in federal troops to enforce the law. On September 30 and October 1, 1962, a mob rioted for fifteen hours at Ole Miss, killing two people, injuring hundreds, and threatening to ignite a minor regional rebellion. Kennedy, who lost control of the situation, was stunned. Ultimately the University of Mississippi was integrated and the movement for equal rights accelerated. That autumn and winter brought more boycotts, more marches, more riots. In two days in the early spring of 1963, there were 162 protests across the nation. Kennedy worried "that the country could not continue to do business without facing up to the civil rights problem." He worried about its image in the world, too.

Kennedy had learned from his crises over nuclear arms and civil rights. To be a president of consequence – let alone a great one, which he yearned to be – he could not remain passive. In 1963, one should remember, there was no arms agreement with the Soviets; there had been nothing, in fact, since the Second World War. Nor was there any meaningful legislation protecting the rights of black Americans. In lily-white, Cold War America, what Kennedy was contemplating on both issues was unprecedented. Neither would be legislatively easy nor politically advantageous for him. Given the country's conservatism, it was risky to place his administration four-square on the side of arms control and civil rights. His advisors warned him to be careful; he was elected with the most slender of mandates. In embracing Uncle Vanya and spurning Jim Crow, Kennedy was as much at sea as Gordon Cooper had been in space.

All that notwithstanding, Kennedy decided to change the channel that June. Recasting the Cold War and reframing civil rights recognized what must be done. "There comes a time," he told an associate, "when a man has to take a stand and history will record that he has to meet these tough situations and ultimately make a decision." For Kennedy, this was the time. This was the situation. This was the decision.

Now, in the last months of his life, Kennedy reached a tipping point. For the past two-and-a-half years, he had spoken the language of peace and justice haltingly, without volume or fluency. He did not know the grammar, he lacked the vocabulary, he confused the tenses. What little he did say was soft, conditional, and tentative. By June, though, he was ready to speak of arms and rights in strong, declarative sentences. He saw the compelling argument in both – moral as well as practical – and articulated it with the zeal of an evangelical. He did this on two successive days in the second week of the month, in two speeches, on two issues, one domestic, one foreign.

Although his speeches are the pillars of this story, they are also the parentheses. Over this feverish forty-eight hours, there was other business inside and outside the White House. When Kennedy wasn't managing race relations or nuclear summitry, he was addressing a regime of emerging issues, from immigration to Vietnam, that would shape the country's future. The rest of the time, he was just being president. He ate, slept, bathed, read. He swam in the White House pool. He attended a private dinner party in Georgetown. He followed a menacing overseas scandal. He met visitors in the Oval Office. He saw his mistress. And for an hour one evening, he disappeared.

*

To the calendar, June 10 and June 11, 1963, was late spring; to history, it was high summer. Great forces converged and smaller ones emerged over these forty-eight hours, bracketed by two imperishable speeches. One produced an arms treaty, the first of the Cold War. The other produced a civil rights law, the most important of its time.

There were 1,036 days in the presidency of John F. Kennedy. This is the story of two of them.

Monday, June 10, 1963

CHAPTER 1

Dawn

ON THE MORNING of June 10, 1963, the president of the
United States awoke in celestial isolation and terrestrial
luxury. He was streaking through the heavens at 550 miles an hour,
30,000 feet above Earth, hurrying home from Hawaii. It was the
last stop on a five-day tour that had also taken him to Colorado,
New Mexico, Texas, and California. He had left Honolulu International Airport at 5:55 p.m. on June 9 and would land at Andrews
Air Force Base in Maryland, just outside Washington, at 8:50 a.m.
on June 10. His direct, jet-propelled flight took just under nine
hours. He awoke an hour, maybe two, before landing; he might
have stirred instinctively on his hard, horsehair mattress at 7:30
a.m., the hour his loyal valet, George Thomas, would normally
knock on his bedroom door at the White House. This morning on
Air Force One – as he had done every morning of the past two
years, four months, and twenty days – Thomas ensured Kennedy
was up, alert, and ready for the world. Whether he was or not, it
marked the beginning of two momentous days of his presidency.

Among the members of the travelling presidential party with him was Theodore C. Sorensen, Kennedy's special counsel and chief speechwriter. No one was closer, intellectually, to Kennedy. In clichéd Washington, Sorensen was called the president's "alter ego" or, in Sorensen's words, his "intellectual bloodbank." Sorensen, thirty-five, was tall and sinewy, his austere saturnine face framed by heavy horn-rimmed glasses and short-cropped black hair. He and Kennedy had worked together since 1953. Sorensen, then a brilliant, newly minted lawyer of twenty-four, had left his native Nebraska to find work in Washington. Kennedy, a three-term congressman, had left the House of Representatives to enter the Senate. After more than ten years, theirs was, perhaps, the most extraordinary collaboration in the modern presidency.

Sorensen usually did not make domestic trips; he was typically bound to Washington, producing a flood of statements, messages, and speeches in his tidy office in the West Wing down the hall from the president's. On this occasion, Sorensen had expressed rare "personal reasons" for wanting to precede the president to Hawaii. His friend, Dolores Martin, had wired him on June 5: "BRING YOUR BATHING SUIT THE SUN IS SHINING AND WE ARE WAITING ALOHA." Unfortunately, once again, Kennedy had asked Sorensen to stay behind and to join him in Honolulu at the last moment, so that the two could discuss urgent business on the flight home. Sorensen dutifully left Washington on Saturday morning, caught up with the president in Los Angeles in the afternoon, flew on with him to Hawaii that night, then boarded the plane again on Sunday evening. There was no time for a swim with Dolores. It was a long way to go, but such was Kennedy's expectation and such was Sorensen's devotion. The punishing demands never shook Sorensen's loyalty even as they ravaged his health, strained his friendships, and shattered his marriage.

On Monday, June 10, Kennedy was to speak at midmorning commencement exercises at American University in Washington.

He had given many such addresses as president, senator, and representative. Sorensen had written most of them. But this speech was different. It would address Russia, peace, and nuclear arms in language that no president had used before, with consequences unseen before. It would revisit and question the Cold War itself.

After Kennedy had retired to his bedroom on *Air Force One*, Sorensen continued to work. He was known for pushing himself all night honing speeches – adjusting the rhythm, refining the tone, polishing the prose, seeking *le mot juste*. He had sat up much of Thursday night reworking the first draft, and perhaps Friday, too. Now, in the forward passenger cabin of *Air Force One*, it would not have been surprising to learn that Sorensen had worked until dawn again, just as he did at the White House.

There had been time. It was a long way home. Sorensen and Kennedy were flying from the reaches of the republic to its seat: from the state of Hawaii, the verdant, volcanic archipelago in the Pacific Ocean, breezy and languid, to the District of Columbia, the incandescent, marbled citadel in the tidal marshlands of the Atlantic Ocean, sweltering and sticky. They were going from the most exotic, southern, western, and youngest state of the Union to its old, fractious, increasingly violent and occasionally tawdry capital. As the light faded in early evening – sunset was at 7:11 p.m. in Honolulu, darkness at 7:41 p.m. – they could not see much after the first hour aloft. For most of the flight, the ride was smooth. There was light turbulence in places, as well as patches of fog and haze, but nothing serious. Had the president been gazing out a window, as he was once photographed, he would have been in the dark as he hurtled across 2,300 miles of the Pacific. Five hours later, the coast of North America came into view and beyond it an inky continent, broken by specks and ribbons of light. By then, though, Kennedy would have been long asleep.

Below him was "the Great Republic," as Winston Churchill fondly called it. This was an America that Jack Kennedy of Boston,

Bronxville, Georgetown, Hyannis Port, and Palm Beach had come to know in the late 1950s. As a senator-in-a-hurry, hazel eyes fixed on the presidency, he had spent weekend after weekend traveling to its distant marches to advance his ambitions. In 1960, he had barnstormed across the United States in the closest of elections, promising "to get this country moving again." Since 1961, as president, he had seen it like a proconsul touring the provinces.

His route from day to night to day put him on a flight path of 4,221 nautical miles, following the great circle route. It would take him from eclectic California to arid Nevada, over the creases, heights and plains of Utah, Colorado, and Kansas, and then Missouri. He may have remembered, tough Irish chieftain that he was, that of these states, only Nevada and Missouri had voted for him. A generation later, as the population grew sharply on the country's west and east coasts, the hinterland would become known to Democrats, derisively, as "flyover country." Kennedy's route also carried him over Illinois, where Mayor Richard J. Daley of Chicago had delivered his city and the state's decisive electoral votes. He sailed over Indiana and Ohio, both Republican in 1960, and over Protestant West Virginia, where, as a Catholic, he had won a pivotal victory in the presidential primary of May 1960, clinching the nomination of the Democratic Party. Then over Virginia, the capital of the Confederacy, roiling in racial strife that spring, and into Maryland, a border state touched by the same unrest. In 1963, these were not known as Red States and Blue States, though they were as tribally loyal to Republicans and Democrats then as they would be a generation later. They made up an America of 189,241,798 souls, which was more rural, more agrarian, and more homogenous. It was less Hispanic, less Asian, less black, less rich, less educated, less healthy. It was also a country on the cusp of monumental change – spurred, in some part, by what President Kennedy would say and do in the next forty-eight hours.

✳

Kennedy loved being president. In moments of pique he might scowl and swear and tell his critics to take this lousy job, but he never meant it. The office awed him. It was why he wore a silk top hat and morning coat at his Inauguration; it was why his wife had restored the grandeur of the White House. On their visit to Paris two years before, they had admired the French sense of the ceremonial. In a more formal era, Kennedy was a formal man, maintaining a discreet distance between himself and the people. It was metaphorical more than physical, less distance than degree. That meant a correctness in public behavior (little touching, husbanded displays of affection, few details of his personal health); dress (casual or business, always appropriate, always elegant); and language (strict use of honorifics, few contractions, no jargon). He had never called his personal secretary, Evelyn Lincoln, anything other than "Mrs. Lincoln" in their twelve years together. He had never asked Mimi Beardsley, his young lover, to call him anything other than "Mr. President" in their eighteen months together. And although he did not behave toward his staff in the manner of a medieval sultan, as did other presidents, Kennedy relished power and its perquisites.

None was greater than *Air Force One*. While presidents worry about being too regal in folksy, egalitarian America, the president's plane was as much a symbol of authority to Kennedy as the royal barge had been to English monarchs. His predecessors had airplanes, of course, but none as striking as this one. The idea of Kennedy acquiring a new airplane in 1962 was to make a point. Under the septuagenarian Dwight D. Eisenhower, who had been jolted when the Soviets showed off their technological superiority in aerospace when they launched *Sputnik* in 1957, the presidential plane had looked dowdy on foreign runways. America needed something flashier. This was the jet age, after all, and this youthful president was its avatar. The impulse was new, shiny, *modern* – a new decade, a new president, a new plane.

13

Boeing designed a plane at a cost of $7.8 million. In Congress, Representative Gerald Ford of Michigan groused about the price (even though Boeing said it lost $1.5 million on the deal.) Having persuaded Ford of its value, a presidential assistant confidently declared that "this is probably the last we will hear about this from the congressman." (A little over a decade later, the congressman was president and the plane was his.) On October 10, 1962, Kennedy took possession of the modified Boeing 707, known as SAM (Special Air Mission) 26000. It was the first airplane made specifically for the president, and it could go farther and faster than its predecessors. Up to then, the president's plane had been known only informally by its code name, *Air Force One*. Kennedy adopted the name and popularized it. From then on, any airplane carrying the president was known as *Air Force One*.

How to make this chariot distinctly presidential? Kennedy engaged Raymond Loewy, the country's foremost industrial designer, who had brought panache to practical things. On October 31, 1949, the mustachioed Loewy stared out from the cover of *Time* magazine, a mélange of boats, planes, trains, automobiles, appliances, chairs, and bottles floating dreamily about him. "He streamlines the sales curve," *Time* cooed. "I was unimpressed by the gaudy red exterior markings and . . . the amateurish graphics of *Air Force One*," Loewy remembered when Kennedy showed him the design of the new plane. He and Kennedy got on the floor of the Oval Office and began cutting and pasting, like kids doing arts and crafts at summer camp. "*Air Force One* was Kennedy's baby," Loewy said.

For the plane, Loewy proposed a three-color motif: white, a traditional slate blue, and cyan, a color to represent the future. He reduced the Air Force markings and replaced the red writing with "a luminous ultramarine blue." He studied the typeface on the nation's founding documents. Now *United States of America* was emblazoned across the fuselage. On each side of the tail was the Stars and Stripes. Sitting on the runway, the aircraft's letters and legend could be seen a half mile away. *Air Force One* conveyed an idea of empire as much as the emperor it carried. It was an emblem of American technology in a time most people had never flown; jet service between Los Angeles and New York had only begun in 1959. This plane was a movable stage – and no more so than when a glamorous Jack and Jackie appeared at its rear door, smiling and waving, next to the presidential seal of office. Kennedy was so pleased with the new look of *Air Force One*, Loewy says, that he discussed extending "standards and concepts of design" to highways, cities, and federal buildings.

The plane was a marvel. On thirty minutes' notice, it could fly anywhere in the world. It could land and take off exactly – exactly – when planned, monitored by a network of tracking stations along its route. It could carry six to eight crew members and forty passengers and reach 604 miles per hour. Its range was more than six thousand miles. On board, the president was connected to the world through a classified communications system. In the nuclear age, staying in touch was critical, if not always foolproof. Once, to tease his Air Force aide and test his French, JFK asked to call General Charles de Gaulle, the president of France, in Paris. Within four minutes, the airplane operators had reached the Élysée Palace. Unfortunately, it was the hotel, not the palace. "I knew it," scoffed Kennedy. "It's no damn good." The second time, the embarrassed operators reached the general in two minutes.

The new *Air Force One* gave the president more privacy. Eisenhower had entered his plane at the front and then walked past everyone inside to reach his modest suite in the rear. Kennedy had his own entrance at the back, where he had a stateroom with a desk and four padded chairs. Oil paintings chosen by Jackie hung on the walls. There was also a bedroom with two beds, a closet, and a bathroom. (Kennedy asked Loewy to design "a pale blue rug with an American eagle in the center of an oval formed by thirteen stars.") Kennedy's bed was customized; because of his weak back, he required a special mattress ordered by Dr. Janet Travell, one of the White House physicians. It was forty inches wide and seventy-six inches long, resting on a solid wooden base. On this trip, when his back pain had flared up, bed was a relief.

A conference room seated nine and a galley with four burners served meals, especially the rich, creamy seafood chowder Kennedy favored. The forward passenger cabin had twenty-four reclining seats, two desks, and four sleeping berths. On this flight, those and other seats were filled by thirty-four members of the presidential party, which, as on most trips, included: Evelyn Lincoln; Kenneth O'Donnell, the appointments secretary; Lawrence O'Brien, the congressional liaison; Pierre Salinger, the press secretary; Salinger's two assistants, Christine Camp and Sue Mortensen Vogelsinger; Admiral George Burkley, a White House doctor; and the ubiquitous Dave Powers, First Friend. Two unexpected passengers were Mike Mansfield, the majority leader of the Senate, and Averell Harriman, the administration's diplomatic troubleshooter. Kennedy wanted to confer with both on Monday's speech. Other seats were occupied by guests, journalists, the crew, and a posse of Secret Service agents.

Among its now quaint accoutrements, the plane had a "duplicating machine" and "overhead hat racks." They disappeared when *Air Force One* was remodeled by Kennedy's successors. (Bill Clinton retired the plane in 1998.) One of the few surviving features from 1963 was a long, slender, padded bench running through the cabin on the port side. It was beige and brown to match the cabin colors. Unsurprisingly, Jackie ordered the finest glassware from Tiffany & Co., the purveyor of luxury goods in New York City. This included a dozen highball glasses, a dozen old-fashioned glasses, a dozen champagne goblets, and a dozen tulip champagne glasses. The presidential seal adorned the pillowcases, the crockery, and even the medallion of the rotary dial on each telephone – not to mention matches and napkins, which reporters pocketed as souvenirs.

On this flight, like all flights, a pool of five journalists had been designated from among the White House press corps to travel with the president: Merriman Smith of United Press International (UPI), Frank Cormier and Doug Cornell of Associated Press (AP), Sander Vanocur of NBC News, and Bill Lawrence of ABC News. The bylines of the print correspondents appeared often in the five daily newspapers and fifteen magazines provided for the president's reading on every flight. Kennedy's appetite for news was bottomless; he was notorious for filching newspapers and magazines from undefended desks in the West Wing. On *Air Force One*, Kennedy had much to read and much to ponder.

*

The president had left Hawaii too early for the bulldog editions of the next day's newspapers. Kennedy would have to wait to read Monday's *New York Times*, which reported that the government of Harold Macmillan, the British prime minister, was reeling from the recent resignation of John Profumo, the secretary of state for war. Profumo had slept with a courtesan who at the time was also sleeping with a Soviet diplomat. Monday's newspaper would also report that in Laos, where Kennedy had defused a crisis two years earlier, the neutralist leader, General Kong Le, was under new pressure from pro-Communist forces. In South Vietnam, where the United States had sent some sixteen thousand military "advisors" to support the embattled regime, relations between Buddhists and the government of President Ngo Dinh Diem were deteriorating.

At home, the story was civil rights, as it had been throughout that tumultuous spring of riots, demonstrations, and sit-ins in the South. Civil rights was the topic of the speech that Kennedy had given in Hawaii, his first visit there as president. The stop had been added belatedly to his itinerary. As the *Washington Post* reported, the speech, to the United States Conference of Mayors, which was

17

meeting in Honolulu, was "intended to be a prelude to, and to dramatize, a drive he is about to open to get a civil rights program through Congress." Kennedy's surprise visit emboldened Governor John A. Burns to issue a proclamation. Contriving a host of reasons ("that the President embodies the hopes and aspirations of all Americans . . . that the President will use this time and place to make a policy statement of major significance"), the governor declared June 9 "President's Day" in the Islands.

It had been a quick departure after a whirlwind visit. On Sunday afternoon, Kennedy spoke to the mayors at 4:49 p.m. and finished at 5:05 p.m. He left the Hilton Hawaiian Village Hotel at 5:15 p.m. and reached Honolulu International Airport, twenty minutes later, at 5:35 p.m. Governor Burns was there to say good-bye and drape one more floral lei around his neck. Another twenty minutes later, Kennedy was off. From speech to plane, from hats-off to wheels-up, in under an hour.

Representative Spark M. Matsunaga, who had not been home in six months, was thrilled to be on board. So was Representative Thomas P. Gill, the other congressman from Hawaii. An invitation to travel on *Air Force One* was one of the ways a president could confer favor on a local politician. Both had been delighted to see ten thousand Hawaiians cheering Kennedy at the airport at 9:00 p.m. on Saturday, June 8. He had flown five hours from Los Angeles to get there. The next day, Kennedy attended church and laid a wreath at the USS *Arizona* Memorial in Pearl Harbor. Some 250,000 people lined the streets of the capital to see Kennedy, wearing a narrow floral lei and a broad grin, as he swept by standing in the well of his blue Lincoln Continental. "Never in the Islands' history has there been such a reception for anyone, barring none," an exuberant Matsunaga wrote the president. The congressman was especially delighted that Kennedy had chosen to address civil rights in multiracial Hawaii, where the president noted that "there is no place from where it is more appropriately said and understood than . . . here on this island." Gill, for his part, thanked Kennedy for "the very great compliment" about "our success in achieving racial harmony."

Coverage of the president's speech to the mayors filled most of the right-hand column of the front page of the *New York Times*. In the Lawn House of the Hawaiian Village Hotel, Kennedy told them that he had come "a good many thousands of miles" because he thought it was the best opportunity to talk about a growing national problem. "The challenge is there," he said. "The cause is just. The question is whether you and I will do nothing, thereby inviting pressure and increasing tension, and inviting possible violence, or whether you will anticipate these problems and move to fulfill the rights of your Negro citizens in a peaceful and constructive manner." For two years, Kennedy had been called a laggard on civil rights. Now he was signaling a risky, personal commitment that would flower over the next two days. "It is clear to me that the time for token moves and talk is past, if we are going to meet this problem and master it, that these rights are going to be won, and that it is our responsibility, yours and mine, to see that they are won in a peaceful and constructive way, and not won in the streets."

He called on the mayors to establish biracial committees, eliminate segregation ordinances, promise equal opportunity in hiring, and create special programs to prevent high school students from dropping out. Then, a clarion call: "Justice cannot wait for too many meetings. It cannot wait for the action of the Congress or the courts. We face a moment of moral and constitutional crisis, and men of generosity and vision must make themselves heard in every section of this country. I do not say that all men are equal in their ability, their character or their motivation, but I say they should be equal in their chance to develop their character, their motivation, and their ability. They should be given a fair chance to develop all the talents that they have, which is a basic assumption and presumption of this democracy of ours."

That wasn't enough for his critics. In Monday's newspapers, the American Jewish Congress, the voice of the country's Jewry, called the administration's gradualism on racial equality "a folly and a failure." Martin Luther King Jr., whom the *New York Times* called "the Negro integrationist leader," castigated the president's caution. Both the Jews and the blacks found him too timid. Down in Alabama, though, he was too bold. There, the *Times* reported, Governor George C. Wallace of Alabama continued to denounce Kennedy's call for racial accommodation, as he had throughout that embattled spring. On Monday, June 10, Wallace was preparing to fly from the capital of Montgomery to Tuscaloosa, in central Alabama, to direct preparations to defy the federal court order desegregating the University of Alabama. The governor knew he could not stop the rule of law, which would be enforced by troops if necessary, but he was determined to honor his campaign promise to make a stand in "the schoolhouse door."

What was not news in the *Times* was communist Russia, though the newspaper reported another crackdown on Soviet Jews. There was a full-page advertisement, signed by scores of college professors alarmed by nuclear war and renewing the call for a nuclear test ban treaty. The boldface headline: "Mankind must put an end to war or war will put an end to mankind." The words were Kennedy's.

Of all that was on Kennedy's mind on his journey home from Hawaii – Laos, Vietnam, Alabama, Harold Macmillan, Martin Luther King Jr., George Wallace – what was most immediate, as he rose that morning, was the issue that had absorbed him more than any other as president: nuclear war and world peace. Now Sorensen's draft awaited him.

✳

For several weeks, the speech at American University had been closely guarded within the government. While it was not a secret, strictly speaking, only a handful of senior officials knew about it. In preparing a major address on foreign policy, the White House would usually, if reluctantly, consult the Department of State, the Department of Defense, and the Central Intelligence Agency (CIA). It was the mission of the bureaucracy, mused Arthur M. Schlesinger Jr., Special Assistant to the President, to turn the meatiest stew into the thinnest of purées. Its ingredients, he said, were cliché, repetition, "self-serving rhetoric," and the passive voice. ("The active voice assigns responsibility and was therefore hazardous," he scoffed.) Schlesinger, the house historian and *amanuensis emeritus*, dismissed the cautious pinstriped diplomats. "I suppose that, from the viewpoint of orderly administration, this was a bad way to prepare a major statement on foreign policy," he wrote in his diary on June 16. "But the State Department could never in a thousand years have produced this speech. The President is fortunately ready to assert control over the policy of his administration, however deeply it may offend the bureaucracy."

This time, no ideas had been solicited from the bureaucracy and no draft had been circulated. Indeed, the secretaries of state and defense would not see the full speech until less than twenty-four hours before it was given. "The president knew that the unprecedented message of the speech would set off alarm bells in more bellicose quarters in Washington, possibly producing leaks and political attacks in advance of his talk," Sorensen wrote in 2009. Moreover, in refusing to consult the usual suspects, Kennedy had another purpose: he wanted to break with conventional wisdom. As Sorensen said in 1965, Kennedy did not want the speech "diluted with the usual threats of destruction, boasts of nuclear stockpiles and lectures on Soviet treachery," which had been a staple of Cold War presidential rhetoric. So, while Kennedy ignored the bureaucrats, Sorensen freely solicited thoughts from trusted counselors outside government. One was Joseph Kraft, a columnist who had been a speechwriter for JFK in 1960. Another was Max Freedman, a Canadian who was the Washington correspondent of the *Winnipeg Free Press* and the *Manchester Guardian*. He was also a confidant of JFK: "I remember Ted calling me and saying that the President wanted to make a speech at American University and this was a chance to break new ground. I said, 'What's the speech on?' Ted said: 'Peace.' And I laughed and said, 'Tell the President I'm in favor of it.' And Ted said: 'Now look, this is no joking matter. There are no orders for this speech. We can say whatever we wish, and the State Department is staying out of it. They don't want us to make this speech.'"

A small group worked on the address. In addition to Sorensen, the draftsman, they were Schlesinger; McGeorge Bundy, the national security advisor; Bundy's deputies, Carl Kaysen and Adrian S. Fisher; and Tom Sorensen, Ted's younger brother, who was deputy head of the United States Information Agency. Convened by the president, the group had been discussing this speech, in general terms, for four to six weeks. Everyone had something to say. "Like many of the president's speeches, since it was a good speech, it's got more authors than you can shake a stick at," recalled Fisher, a legal advisor to the government. "Everyone had a finger in it. A lot of us now say, 'We wrote a paragraph – maybe two paragraphs – the part dealing with disarmament, and dealing with the test ban. And the statement that we would postpone atmospheric tests.'" Kennedy had wanted to say something different about the Cold War since the Cuban Missile Crisis. It had shaken him and Khrushchev, who had come "to the realization that there had to be better ways of resolving conflicts and disagreements between East and West," said Sorensen, reflecting, as he usually did, JFK's thinking.

Arms, nuclear and conventional, had been top-of-mind for Kennedy over the previous few days. The purpose of his tour through the western states was visiting military installations, where he had inspected troops and watched demonstrations of the latest weaponry. On June 5, he was in Colorado Springs, addressing the graduating class of the U.S. Air Force Academy and visiting the operational center of the North American Air Defense Agreement (as NORAD was known then), deep inside Cheyenne Mountain. There, Kennedy sat hunched forward in a glass control booth, in the chair the NORAD commander would occupy to direct defense in the event of a nuclear attack. He watched an eighteen-minute simulation of a Soviet strike. "The bombers were stopped, but the intercontinental missiles came on and erupted in white ovals as they struck American cities," wrote Hugh Sidey, *Time*'s White House correspondent. "Muttered one Air Force officer: 'We have no way to stop them.' The President emerged from the demonstration in a remarkably solemn mood."

Later, JFK flew to the White Sands Missile Range in New Mexico, where he saw a demonstration of seven missiles launched in two hours. One was the fabled Honest John rocket, hitting a target in a burst of phosphorescence, seventy miles away. Kennedy viewed the exercise in sunglasses, looking like a matinee idol, removing them occasionally to peer at the sky through thick binoculars. He politely declined a formal briefing by a captain who admitted, when the president asked, that he'd rehearsed it ninety-three times preparing for his big moment. Apologizing for running late, Kennedy suggested the two of them have a chat instead, a disarming request that put the nervous captain at ease.

On June 6, Kennedy was aboard the 80,000-ton USS *Kitty Hawk*, an attack carrier, steaming off the coast of California at the center of an eighteen-vessel flotilla. The president sat in a leather-padded rocker on the bridge, watching a spectacular display of armed might. One demonstration followed another. "Admiral, I'm afraid I can take no more," he groaned, his back pain forcing him to excuse himself. The next day, Kennedy visited China Lake, California, a test station covering 1,200 square miles of desert, 150 miles northeast of Los Angeles. It was, reported the Associated Press, "where scientists conceive, build, and test the weapons of tomorrow." He watched a demonstration of the HIPEG, an aircraft-strafing gun that could demolish enemy outposts, and was shown a bomb designed to clear jungle areas "conceived with places such as Vietnam in mind," and one that released bomblets the size of ping-pong balls, throwing up a dense smoke screen. What Kennedy, a decorated naval officer who had fought in the Second World War, thought of this display of modern firepower we do not know. If he was cynical, he would not let on; in public, the commander in chief can never be other than a booster of the military, and Kennedy was, out of necessity more than affection.

✳

All that was about making war. On *Air Force One*, the president was talking about making peace. After the Berlin Wall and the dark threats from Khrushchev at their somber meeting in Vienna in 1961, JFK had ordered the largest military buildup in peacetime history. He increased defense spending by 15 percent in his first year in office. The planned number of Polaris submarines (each with sixteen nuclear missiles) rose from twenty-nine to forty-one, and 207,000 soldiers were recruited by the Army in 1961 and 1962. Special forces doubled in size. Between 1960 and 1963, the United States increased its nuclear warheads from 20,000 to 29,000 (while the Soviet arsenal went from 1,600 to 4,200). Since the Cuban Missile Crisis in 1962, Kennedy and Khrushchev had been discussing halting nuclear tests. That winter and spring, however, they had been unable to agree on terms. Talks had stalled.

Kennedy wanted to break the impasse with an ambitious appeal to Moscow. Timing was key. Khrushchev was meeting the Central Committee that month in Moscow. Having withdrawn his missiles from Cuba, which was widely seen as a humiliation, Khrushchev was under new pressure from hard-liners in the Kremlin to affirm his leadership and denounce the United States or to show the benefits of peaceful coexistence. According to Norman Cousins, the eminent editor of the *Saturday Review* who had shuttled between Moscow and Washington carrying messages of peace, the Soviet Union was ready to parley. William C. Foster, the director of the U.S. Arms Control and Disarmament Agency, recalled that Kennedy put it this way to him and others: "Let us take another crack at this thing, because this is too important to let nature take its course."

As Carl Kaysen, the deputy special assistant for national security affairs, recalled, Sorensen sent around a memo in late April or early May to "the usual people saying: 'The President wants to make a speech on peace. Do you have any ideas?'" Sorensen collected the responses and wrote "a very rough first draft," which was then reviewed by Bundy, Kaysen, Schlesinger, and Fisher. It went back to Sorensen on Thursday, June 6, and he completed a new draft "overnight." The next day, he again met with the inner circle, who offered more suggestions. ("We got the bugs out unusually quickly with very little friction," recalled Bundy.) Sorensen planned to take the speech with him to Hawaii on Saturday, June 8. In the meantime, he gave the existing draft to Kaysen on Friday for "the necessary clearances."

Kaysen, who was acting in place of an absent Bundy that weekend, then spoke by telephone to the president. JFK's instructions were explicit: check the speech with the secretary of defense (Robert McNamara), the deputy secretary of defense (Roswell Gilpatric), and the secretary of state (Dean Rusk). Run it by Llewellyn Thompson, the U.S. ambassador to the Soviet Union. (This was hard because the speech was still being redrafted on the weekend. McNamara was in Williamstown, Massachusetts, giving a commencement address. Thompson was in San Francisco rather than in Moscow.) Kennedy issued other instructions: Kaysen was "to inform" the chairman of the Atomic Energy Commission, Glenn Seaborg, of the speech, "not get his views." He was also told to approach General Maxwell Taylor, chairman of the Joint Chiefs of Staff, "to seek" his views on the speech. Taylor's response was telling. Personally, he thought the speech was political and, as such, he should withhold comment. Yet he thought that it would be "unnecessary and perhaps unwise" to show the draft to the rest of the brass. "Their comments were predictable and he felt no purpose would be served," Kaysen said. The generals were neither informed nor consulted.

So, by the evening of Sunday, June 9, Kaysen had Taylor's views and those of the others. Significantly, though, the president had not consulted the State Department (known as Foggy Bottom) or the CIA. Nor Vice President Lyndon B. Johnson. Or the congressional leadership. If Kennedy did not seek their barnacled opinions on the Cold War and these grave questions of war and peace that bedeviled the world in 1963, it was because he knew what they would say. Too many of them had been hawks during the Cuban Missile Crisis. Johnson, the generals, and Senators Richard Russell and J. William Fulbright had wanted to invade Cuba rather than blockade it, the cautious approach that JFK ultimately chose over their opposition. Their belligerence alarmed him. They lost his confidence. He was not interested in what they thought though he was worried what they might say, publicly, before he spoke. In that case, better to keep them in the dark and let them read the speech in tomorrow's newspapers.

But managing the critics wasn't Sorensen's problem on *Air Force One* Sunday evening, as he reviewed the speech with the president after leaving Honolulu. Kennedy was seeing it for the first time. He suggested some changes but fundamentally liked it. The laconic Mansfield agreed. "He called me down from Montana to Los Angeles," he recalled. "He talked this matter over with me on the plane coming back from Honolulu. I told him I thought the idea was good." So did Harriman, who was ambassador to Moscow and London in the 1940s. In 1961, having served one term as governor of New York, Harriman had joined the administration in a senior position in the State Department. At seventy-one – direct, imposing, and lantern-jawed – he would play a key role in the nuclear negotiations with the Russians in the following weeks. Learning that Harriman was returning from a trip to Asia through Hawaii that weekend, Kennedy had asked him along on the flight home. Sorensen was pleased to hear that Harriman approved of the speech, which would disincline the president to revise it.

However, news from Moscow in recent hours required a response. Khrushchev, who the week before had signaled a new interest in opening talks to establish a test ban, had now made the offer more specific. It was conveyed in a cabled message that Kaysen believed was received at the State Department Friday evening after everyone had gone home. Khrushchev wanted to set a date and asked the Americans to name a negotiator. The speech had to be adjusted. Sorensen called Kaysen in Washington from *Air Force One*, which at that hour was flying over the West Coast. It was 3:00 a.m. Monday in Washington – midnight in California, 9:00 p.m. in Hawaii – when Kaysen answered his bedside telephone. Sorensen wanted the speech to reflect, among other things, the overture from Khrushchev. In that spirit, the president decided to make a substantive proposal, Sorensen said, "as a concrete demonstration of the speech's noble principles." This meant more discussion and more changes. That may be why Foster, who was not among the drafters of the speech but says he attended the meeting on Friday, called it "one of the most rapidly prepared speeches in history." It wasn't, but the hours on *Air Force One* were busy. Foster says the group in Washington had another meeting before the speech (a meeting none of the officials mention) and thinks that "the final pages of his speech may have been sent to the President as he was actually delivering it at the university." They were not.

After the new draft of the speech was completed overnight, it was sent out to the parties by Teletype. The president called Bundy and asked him to show it to Rusk and McNamara. (According to

Kaysen, they had already seen an earlier draft.) For Sorensen, the consummate professional, working diligently to get things just right was a routine occupational hazard. That's what it took for his words to sing, and they almost always did.

*

In his last hour or more on board *Air Force One*, Kennedy would have read the latest draft of the speech. He would have had breakfast and conferred with Sorensen. After landing at Andrews Air Force Base at 8:50 a.m., he would helicopter immediately to the White House. There, within one hundred minutes of hitting the tarmac, after that all-night, trans-Pacific, cross-continental flight, he would deliver his speech. This was the velocity of Kennedy's presidency. It demanded stamina. It did not normally recognize jet lag, mental fatigue, or physical pain. It did not acknowledge that the president had been away since the previous Tuesday, hopping around the other side of the country in what Hugh Sidey called "another of those busy, busy weeks." That morning, when he stepped off *Air Force One*, Kennedy had spent nine hours in the air and slept perhaps four or five of them. When he arrived it was 2:50 a.m. in Honolulu, the middle of the night. In Washington, it was the middle of the morning. Time to get moving.

Monday, June 10, 1963

CHAPTER 2

Midmorning

THE PRESIDENT ARRIVED at the White House on
Marine One, the olive-green-and-white presidential helicopter. It was 9:07 a.m., seventeen minutes after landing at
Andrews Air Force Base and seven minutes after leaving it. With a
crisp salute and a word of thanks ("He was always a gentleman,"
recalled Tom Miller, the pilot of *Marine One*) Kennedy descended
the four-step ramp, walked briskly across the South Lawn, and
went directly upstairs to the residence. Assuming his usual regimen, he eased into a hot bath, read the morning newspapers,
shaved in the tub (had he not done so on the plane), and changed
his clothes, the first of several times that day. Jacqueline and the
children were at Camp David, the presidential retreat in Maryland's
Catoctin Mountain Park, on a long weekend. They would not
return until Tuesday afternoon.

Kennedy was upstairs for forty minutes. At 9:49 a.m. he came
down to the Oval Office. There he would learn that Bobby – known
as "A.G." (for Attorney General) on the White House telephone

memorandum, a lined, handwritten record of the president's incoming calls – had called him at 9:12 a.m. In his twenty-one minutes spent in the Oval Office, the president returned his brother's call.

"Good speech in Hawaii," said Bobby from his office at the Department of Justice. He asked his brother when he was speaking at American University. When Jack told him 10:30 a.m., Bobby said that he had a meeting at 10:00 a.m. on Capitol Hill – the first of several with legislators on civil rights – but he could come to the White House after that. The reason for their meeting was Alabama. This was the president's first call of the day; he spoke to Bobby before he spoke to his wife. It would be the first of many discussions, over the telephone and in person, that the brothers would have Monday. At the heart of their fraternity was their unending, elliptical conversation.

Kennedy might have placed other calls, too. He would also have reviewed the final draft of the speech he was to make in less than an hour. It was ready. Had there been a problem, Ted Sorensen would have been working on it, but he wasn't around. Unwashed and unshaven, Sorensen drove the nineteen or so miles directly from Andrews Air Force Base to American University, where he took a seat at the back of the dais and awaited the president.

Now it was show time. Kennedy left the Oval Office, walked to the rear door of the White House, and slipped into the back seat of a black Cadillac. This was not *the* presidential limousine; his premier automobile, the blue Lincoln Continental convertible, was returning by transport plane later that day from Hawaii, having ferried the president through the teeming streets of Honolulu the day before. Like *Air Force One* and *Marine One*, the Lincoln had received unusual attention from Kennedy. He had all but retired the heavy, lugubrious hearses of his predecessors. At twenty-one-and-a-half feet long and weighing four tons, the Lincoln was clean, sleek, and thoroughly modern. Among other refinements, it had a Plexiglas roof, which could be snapped into place. With a phalanx of motorcycle escorts and police cars, and with Secret Service agents standing on its hydraulic steps, the Lincoln carried the president around Washington and the world like a pharaoh on a golden litter borne by an army of attendants. Five months and twelve days later, it would carry him through the streets of Dallas.

The president left the Southwest Gate at 10:12 a.m. He was driving to northwestern Washington. The direct route was around Dupont Circle, passing Riggs National Bank and the Sulgrave Club, where the Georgetown set used to dance in the 1950s, and the Jockey Club in the Fairfax Hotel, where Jackie liked to lunch. Up Massachusetts Avenue, that long tree-shaded boulevard studded with monuments, past the Phillips Collection, which opened in 1921 as the first permanent museum of modern art in the country, and Anderson House, the home of the Society of the Cincinnati, and around Sheridan Circle, a small park dominated by a statue of General Philip H. Sheridan, commander of the Union Army of the Shenandoah. And then, on both sides of the gently rising road, the foreign missions, as observed by E.J. Applewhite: the Turkish Embassy, resembling "a villa overlooking the Bosphorus"; the Japanese Embassy, a neo-Georgian mansion with "swept eaves roof"; and on Kennedy's left, the British Embassy, both residence and chancery, evoking "a Queen Anne" country house. The British had not yet raised a statue to Winston Churchill, whom the president had declared an honorary citizen of the United States on April 9. Then farther up the hill, the U.S. Naval Observatory, where the home of the chief of naval operations would become the official residence of the vice president in 1974.

Nearing American University, Kennedy entered residential Washington. The spacious homes and shaded gardens of the upper Northwest had attracted Lyndon Johnson, Richard M. Nixon, and others who shunned effete, close-quartered Georgetown. Before air-conditioning, Silver Spring, Woodley Park, Cleveland Park, and other neighborhoods here were desirable because they were higher and cooler than downtown. Not that the modest elevation of American University made any difference that morning. It was already more than ninety degrees Fahrenheit. The president arrived on campus at 10:25 a.m. It had taken thirteen minutes to drive from 1600 Pennsylvania Avenue to 4400 Massachusetts Avenue NW.

The date at American University had been fixed for some time. When arranging the president's calendar, matching speeches to venues, Ted Sorensen had wanted to find the right time and place for a major address on peace. As it happened, this week in June was the only opening in a spring and summer full of commitments. The White House solicited an invitation for this particular day from the university. Like all presidents, Kennedy was in demand to attend commencement exercises. As president, he addressed graduating classes at Harvard, Yale, Amherst, Rice, University of Colorado, and West Point, among others, on topics ranging from the arts to the moon.

American University had a past with presidents. Woodrow Wilson opened it in 1914. Two presidents had previously spoken at commencement exercises at what JFK called this "young and growing university." Three had received honorary degrees. Founded by the Methodist Church, it was less than a half century old in 1963. When his plans to give a major speech became known, some wondered why Kennedy did not choose a more prestigious platform. Adrian Fisher was among those surprised that Kennedy had chosen this forum for an "earthshaking" announcement. Ultimately the place did not matter. What did was that the president had decided to attend the forty-ninth commencement of American University and had chosen to say something important there. He called his speech "A Strategy of Peace." Eventually, it became known as the "American University Speech," or the "Peace Speech."

To accommodate the traveling president, the university had moved its convocation from the night before, a change that upset some graduates and alumni. "From a public-relations standpoint," university president Hurst R. Anderson concluded ten days later, "we feel this is one of the finest things that has happened at American University." It was. The speech was a stunning publicity coup, tying the institution to an historic declaration. In the years ahead, as the Peace Speech became a subject of seminars and search engines, the university never forgot that day. It marked the spot Kennedy spoke on campus with a stone monument, celebrated the silver and golden anniversaries of his address with colloquies and lectures, and continued to cherish – if not exploit – this accidental but happy association.

*

Commencement took place on a playing field under a troublesome sun amid wilting ruffles and fading flourishes. The United States Marine Band had been playing since 9:45 a.m., its overdressed musicians fused by the heat to metal folding chairs at the right of the platform. Behind them, official cars lined the side of a circular road. As the faculty and students took their seats on the field before the president's arrival, the band serenaded them with *Homage March* by Wagner, *Chorale and Fugue* by Bach, *American Overture for Band* by Jenkins, *Fanfare and Allegro* by Williams, and *The Universal Judgment* by De Nardis. Among the 991 graduates, 606 receiving their bachelors of arts, 242 their masters of arts, and 37 their doctorates. This was the university's largest graduating class to date. Higher education was soaring in the early 1960s – new programs, bigger campuses, more faculty and students. It made the Class of 1963, as *Life* magazine reported that week, "probably the best prepared, stablest and most promising college class in U.S. history."

The official party was waiting when the presidential limousine drove down University Avenue and approached the John M. Reeves Athletic Center. On the east side of the platform were Anderson;

33

Jack H. Yocum, the university marshal; and Robert C. Stone, president of the University Student Association. Stone carried a convocation gown and cap for the president. For a recipient of an honorary degree, the academic costume was *de rigueur*, however suffocating on a day like today. Stone helped the president slip the heavy black gown, with regal purple velvet borders, over his shoulders. Kennedy rejected the mortarboard.

It was irrepressibly hot. The university had planned for clouds but not for sun. "The Secret Service coordinators have stressed that the President does not mind a little rain," said an internal memo circulated the week before. "If the President can stand it, we will." Rain was not the problem. By midmorning the temperature had climbed to ninety-six degrees.

The "red-coated marine band took the full sun," read one account, "along with the commencement officials, trustees, and faculty, but many spectators moved up under the trees." Some of the ten thousand in attendance used the convocation programs to shield themselves from the sun; others huddled under bright umbrellas. "I received my MA that very hot June day," recalled Michael J. Durkin a half century later. "Since the Master's garb had no sleeves, we had to wear a suit underneath. My tie melted to my white shirt!"

There was an intermittent breeze that morning, filling the flags and rustling the leaves, but its effect was obviously limited. Two people fainted from exposure and were rushed by ambulance to nearby Sibley Memorial Hospital. At a first aid station on the edge of the field, a stern nurse practiced triage, warning that the watercooler was reserved for those ready "to pass out." Anyone else looking for a cool drink from her, the *Washington Post* reported, got a cool reception.

It was 10:30 a.m. The audience stood as the president was escorted to the rostrum. Behind his lectern bearing the seal of the presidency and a battery of microphones to broadcast the speech live on radio and television, Kennedy could gaze across the sultry field into a stand of thick trees across the road. Anderson introduced the president to the chairman of the board of trustees, Dr. John M. Reeves, for whom the field was named. On either side were an eclectic mix of deans, judges, bishops, and senators. At 10:32 a.m., Anderson introduced the Reverend Charles R. Smyth, headmaster of the Pennington School in New Jersey and the father of Sandra Smyth, Class of 1963. At 10:33 a.m., he gave the invocation. At 10:34 a.m., Anderson introduced Kennedy. A minute later, the president rose from his chair and approached the lectern.

✳

"I have . . . chosen this time and this place to discuss a topic on which ignorance too often abounds and the truth is too rarely perceived – yet it is the most important topic on earth: world peace." No cloying anecdotes, no charming witticisms, no college reminiscences. In a world that had been at risk of incinerating itself eight months earlier, there was nothing more pressing than a discussion of world peace, and that was why he was there.

"What kind of peace do I mean?" Kennedy asked. "What kind of peace do we seek? Not a Pax Americana enforced on the world by American weapons of war. Not the peace of the grave or the security of the slave. I am talking about genuine peace, the kind of peace that makes life on earth worth living, the kind that enables men and nations to grow and to hope and to build a better life for their children – not merely peace for Americans but peace for all men and women [he penciled in *women* on the typescript] – not merely peace in our time but peace for all time."

His address was not going to be another diatribe, polemic, or rant about Communism and the Iron Curtain – dark and doctrinaire. He had done that running in 1960 as a Cold Warrior. Today he would not discuss the missile gap or the Fulda Gap. Indeed, it was precisely because he did not want to give that kind of speech that he had not solicited the views of the diplomats, the politicians, or the Joint Chiefs. He knew what they thought: the Soviet Union was "the evil empire," a term Ronald Reagan immortalized as president two decades later. Kennedy had no illusions about the Soviet Union, but attacking it was not his purpose here; that, he knew, had been done often enough from this and other pulpits over the last eighteen years. Rather, here was an opportunity for him, as leader of the world's most powerful country, to talk about peace in a different way. It was a way that did not declare the triumph of America, the defeat of Russia, and the inevitable titanic struggle between good (us) and evil (them). Peace, he said, could not be just for us. It had to be for all; *we* had to find an accomodation acceptable to both sides.

The pragmatist, the self-described "idealist without illusions," Kennedy was petitioning for peace on practical grounds. "I speak of peace because of the new face of war," he said. "Total war makes no sense" in the nuclear age, he observed, when one atomic warhead had almost ten times the explosive force of all the bombs dropped by the Allies in the Second World War. Or, when nuclear fallout could contaminate the air, soil, and water for generations to come. The nuclear arsenal cost billions of dollars every year to expand and maintain, he lamented, simply in the hope that its threat of mutual assured destruction meant that it would never be used. Hardly an efficient way of assuring peace, he said. Then he appealed, again, for peace as a goal, which he thought was thoroughly reasonable. Kennedy thought reasonable people could always find common ground. He had not found it when he met Khrushchev in Vienna in 1961, but he had – they both had – in their confrontation over Cuba in 1962.

"I speak of peace, therefore, as the necessary rational end of rational men," he said. "I realize that the pursuit of peace is not as dramatic as the pursuit of war – and frequently the words of the pursuer fall on deaf ears. But we have no more urgent task." Kennedy took his argument further when he said, ". . . some say that it is useless to speak of world peace or world law or world dis-armament . . . until the leaders of the Soviet Union adopt a more enlightened attitude." Kennedy hoped that the Soviets would see things his way and hoped America could help them do that. "But I also believe," he said, "that we must reexamine our own attitude – as individuals and as a Nation – for our attitude is as essential as theirs." Every American should begin "by examining his own atti-tude toward the possibilities of peace, toward the Soviet Union, toward the course of the Cold War and toward freedom and peace here at home."

This was an unconventional – even radical – idea in 1963, when many thought it better to be dead than Red. It was part of the Cold War catechism. But here was the president saying: Don't think peace is just about winning them over to our point of view, conve-nient as that would be. Peace is about us, too. It's about reassessing the Cold War, the Soviets, and how we conduct ourselves at home. In raising freedom and peace at home, Kennedy made his only ref-erence to the struggle for civil rights, which was unfolding every day that spring, often violently. His address was about peace but it was also about rights, and as the two issues became entwined in the Oval Office over these two days, they also came together in his address that day and the next.

But Kennedy did not want to challenge Americans to rethink old verities on peace, the Soviet Union, and the Cold War, as if these were empty, rhetorical questions for ethicists or theologians. He told them why they should reexamine these three attitudes and addressed each of them, in turn.

First, he said, no one should think peace is "impossible" or "unreal," which he called "a dangerous, defeatist belief" that leads to the conclusion that war is inevitable. He did not use the term *deter-minism*, but he raged against it, or any suggestion that humanity was in the grip of forces that it could not control. That sense of help-lessness was common in postwar America, caught as it was in the 'maw of modernity.' As machines, systems, and the cult of efficiency became entrenched, as modern life became complicated, this lament for modern man was a theme of American culture, especially in art, literature, and theater. For Kennedy, who had ended his Inaugural Address by declaring that "on Earth God's work must truly be our own," this kind of fatalism, this feeling of powerlessness, was self-destructive. It was another way to think, as too many did on world peace, that we are all passengers on a ship of doom, that we cannot change the destination or chart a different course.

"We need not accept that view," Kennedy said. "Our problems are man-made – therefore, they can be solved by man. And man can be as big as he wants. No problem of human destiny is beyond human beings. Man's reason and spirit have often solved the seemingly unsolvable – and we believe they can do it again." This was the Kennedy canon. Don't accept an unacceptable fate. Wasn't the president telling Americans they could go to the moon? Hadn't he established the Peace Corps? Why, then, should a society that had settled the wilderness, created fabulous wealth, and invented the airplane and the light bulb think, for a moment, that it should give up on peace? On the face of it, he said, that notion was foolish.

Defining his peace, Kennedy dismissed "the absolute, infinite concept of universal peace and good will of which some fantasies and fanatics dream." He never had time for wooly or wishful thinking, which is why he distrusted liberals in the 1950s (while surrounding himself with them as president). Perhaps here he was thinking disparagingly of the philosopher's dreamy notion of the perfectibility of man, or the world federalist's squishy notion of universal harmony. Instead, again the hard-headed pragmatist, he proposed "a more practical, more attainable peace – based not on a sudden revolution in human nature but on a gradual evolution in human institutions – on a series of concrete actions and effective agreements which are in the interest of all concerned." In other words, peace was not about reforming or creating a new man, full of love, respect, and empathy. That wasn't happening. Don't count on some human reformation. Don't expect the Messiah. What was possible, though, in this reexamination of the meaning of peace, was establishing a process, a way of solving problems. But let's not be naive about it, he implied. "With such a peace, there will still be quarrels and conflicting interests, as there are within families and nations. World peace, like community peace, does not require that each man love his neighbor – it requires only that they live together in mutual tolerance, submitting their disputes to a just and peaceful settlement."

Again, as a student of the past, Kennedy knew nothing was permanent; enemies became friends, friends became enemies, alliances failed, alliances formed. Hatred between nations didn't last forever; in 1963, West Germany and Japan were two of America's staunchest allies. In two weeks, Kennedy would stand in Berlin as its stout defender. Things change. "So let us persevere," he said. "Peace need not be impracticable, and war need not be inevitable. By defining our goal more clearly, by making it seem more manageable and less remote, we can help all peoples to see it, to draw hope from it, and to move irresistibly toward it."

Second, he implored Americans to revisit their attitude toward the Soviet Union. Here, for a moment, his tone changed. Amid generosity, there was a flash of anger. It's discouraging, he said, that the Soviet leaders believe what their propagandists write: that Americans are fat, swaggering, cartoonish warmongers bent on unleashing preventive war, enslaving Europe, and ruling the world. To make his point, he drew on *Military Strategy*, which he called an authoritative Soviet text. He said this kind of caricature illustrated the gulf between the two peoples, serving as a warning not to descend into acrimony and delusion, and not to see communication as an exchange of threats and insults. It is here, in one of the seminal passages of the address, that he rejected that, and praised the Soviet Union.

"No government or social system is so evil that its people must be considered as lacking in virtue," he said. "As Americans, we find Communism profoundly repugnant as a negation of personal freedom and dignity. But we can still hail the Russian people for their many achievements – in science and space, in economic and industrial growth, in culture and in acts of courage." Among the traits shared by Americans and Russians, he noted, was "our mutual abhorrence of war." The two peoples had never fought each other, uncommon in the history of major powers. Nothing is more central to the Russians than the devastation they endured under the Nazis: the loss of 20 million lives, millions of homes and farms, a third of their territory, and two-thirds of their industry. "No nation in the history of battle ever suffered more than the Soviet Union suffered in the course of the Second World War," he declared.

This was startling from an American president. All nations were quick to trumpet their contributions to the war, and to note their losses, too. But how many were prepared to recognize the sacrifices of their adversaries, even if your adversary had been your ally? Like other members of his generation, Kennedy had fought in the Second World War, though not in Europe. He knew the well-traveled argument that, had it not been for the flow of American matériel (arms, food, uniforms) the Russians, whatever their heroism, might have fallen to the Nazis. Prudently, though, he avoided that here. He knew that that would qualify the praise and respect he wanted to convey to the Soviets now, with all the force of his office, in a way that his predecessors had not.

Kennedy was not naive about the Russians. He knew well their treachery, their brutality, their gulags, and their prisoners. It had made him the apostle of the missile gap, the master of military spending, the builder of bomb shelters. But he also knew, in the shadow of the Cuban Missile Crisis, that it was now time to try a new approach to peace. The way to do that was not to demonize the Russians – the code of the Cold War – but to humanize them. This he did, clearly and eloquently, in the most memorable passage of this most memorable speech:

"So, let us not be blind to our differences – but let us also direct attention to our common interests and to the means by which those differences can be resolved. And if we cannot end now our differences, at least we can help make the world safe for diversity. *For, in the final analysis, our most basic common link is that we all inhabit this small planet. We all breathe the same air. We all cherish our children's future. And we are all mortal.*"

Not to make the world safe for democracy, the Wilsonian promise of the Great War. Not to make it safe for capitalism, though capitalism was America. Not a peace for the United States – but a peace for all states. Here Kennedy was embracing a sense of universalism. He rejected the image of the Russians, whatever their differences with Americans, as bears, beasts, and subhuman forms of life. Ultimately, they were people who had been tempered by that hard and bitter war. (He didn't mention the decades of violence and privation, from Lenin's revolution to Stalin's collectivization, famine, and political purges to Khrushchev's gulags.) Let's try to see the Russians with fresh eyes, implored Kennedy. That they, like us, are human beings. That they are mothers and fathers. That they have sons and daughters. That they have the same fears, anxieties, dreams, and hopes. And they, like Americans, will not live forever.

His words hanging in the torpid air, Kennedy turned to the third of his appeals. He had already asked Americans to rethink peace and reassess the Soviet Union. Now he invited them to reexamine their attitude toward the Cold War itself. This wasn't about scoring debating points or pointing fingers. It wasn't about humbling an enemy or giving it a choice between humiliating retreat or nuclear war. It was about facing reality. "We must deal with the world as it is, and not as it might have been had the history of the last eighteen years been different," he said. The goal should be relaxing tensions without relaxing one's guard. We don't need to jam foreign broadcasts or impose our system on any unwilling people – a jab at the Soviets – but "we are willing and able to engage in peaceful competition with any people on earth."

In the meantime, Kennedy proposed strengthening the United Nations, solving its financial problems, and making it a more effective instrument of peace. He urged keeping peace within the non-Communist world, where disunity invited Communist intervention. He reiterated the importance of America's allies and the country's commitment to defend Western Europe and West Berlin. "The United States will make no deal with the Soviet Union at the expense of other nations and other peoples, not merely because they are our partners, but also because their interests and ours converge."

The convergence wasn't just about defense, he said, but about peace. He hoped to convince the Soviet Union that it, too, should let every nation choose its future, and repeated another criticism of the Soviet Union: "The Communist drive to impose their political and economic system on others is the primary cause of world tension today." If all nations respected self-determination, he said, the world would have a better, more durable peace. Still, Kennedy praised the proposed direct telephone line between Moscow and Washington "to avoid on each side the dangerous delays, misunderstandings, and misreadings of the other's actions which might occur at a time of crisis." The "hotline" had been discussed shortly after the Cuban Missile Crisis and was established that summer.

Kennedy was now about two-thirds of the way through his speech of twenty-two double-spaced pages. He had been speaking for twenty minutes. If he had stopped here, he would have already done something startling, if not unique: he had asked Americans to rethink peace and the Cold War. He had humanized the Russians, speaking of them in language no president had used – or dared to use – since Roosevelt in 1945. Kennedy was not Pollyannaish, though; at times he had punctuated his remarks with criticism of the Soviet Union, as if to show his critics that he had not gone soft. That would not go unnoticed in Moscow. But in saying what he had, Kennedy had broken with conventional thinking, including his own. Next, he would make a proposal.

*

From the back of the uncovered dais, Sorensen listened. As the wordsmith, as well as the advisor, his fingerprints were all over the president's remarks. Like any speechwriter, Sorensen could mouth many of the 3,449 words as Kennedy spoke them that morning, so carefully had he arranged them. Tellingly, for all the eleventh-hour trans-Pacific consultations the previous night, there were few real changes between his first draft on Friday and the speech delivered Monday morning. Indeed, McGeorge Bundy noted early on that "this marvelous draft appeared – a very remarkable speech. It was changed less than almost any major foreign policy speech in terms of editorial suggestion and comment." As always, Sorensen was proud to work for Kennedy, "again thrilled by the president of the United States stating principles so fully consistent with my own. . . ."

Defining those principles – and turning them into policy – had been the story of their partnership. Never was this more true than in this second week of June. Sorensen wrote the speech on civil rights that the president had given in Honolulu. He would write *another* speech on civil rights, with little warning, that the president would give the next day. And still there would be no respite. On June 26, in Berlin, Kennedy would give his third big speech ("Ich bin ein Berliner") in just over two weeks. Sorensen wrote all of them, as well as most of the three dozen public statements, toasts, speeches, and remarks that the president delivered in England, Ireland, Italy, and the rest of Germany. The demands on Sorensen (or those he placed on himself) that spring were crushing. Still, forty-six years later, Sorensen recalled them all cheerfully. He paraphrased Wordsworth to evoke the intensity – and the joy – of that busy month: "Bliss was it in that dawn to be alive, but to be young, and in the service of that President, was very heaven!"

It had not always been that way. When Sorensen arrived in Washington in 1951, he found work at the Federal Security Agency, dealing with social security. It was less blissful. He supported his young wife, Camilla, and his son, Eric, on $3,285 a year. In early 1953, just as Dwight Eisenhower was taking office, Sorensen was looking for work again. He interviewed with two newly elected senators, Henry "Scoop" Jackson of Washington and John F. Kennedy of Massachusetts. Both were comers. Jackson was thought to be smarter and more serious than Kennedy, and a friend advised Sorensen to choose him. A skeptical Sorensen had the audacity to request another interview with both senators so that he could size them up. Kennedy offered him the better job – second legislative assistant with a one-year trial – and he accepted. Sorensen often wondered why JFK, a moderate educated at Harvard, chose "an unknown liberal from an unranked college with no serious political experience or connections . . ." None of that mattered to Senator Kennedy. He wanted intellect and loyalty. Sorensen had both. He moved into a tiny dark corner of Room 362 of the Old Senate Office Building.

And so began one of the longest, closest, and most productive relationships of American politics. In Kennedy's eight years in the Senate, it was Sorensen who did much of the research, wrote many of the reports, crafted most of the speeches. Later, as Kennedy was establishing himself less as a thrusting Boston politico and more as a cerebral statesman, it was Sorensen who turned out the columns, essays, and book reviews that gave him gravitas. The two worked well together; Kennedy knew history, collected quotations, gathered literary anecdotes, and appreciated words. Sorensen had brains and ideas and could sew them together beautifully. By the time they reached the White House, their collaboration was seamless.

Sorensen's title, special counsel to the president, belies how special his counsel was. At the same time, to call Sorensen a "speechwriter" or "chief speechwriter" was a misnomer. Although speechwriters traditionally remain anonymous, Sorensen was widely recognized as the principal figure in Kennedy's inner circle. In May 1961, journalist Stan Opotowsky declared Sorensen "the second most powerful man in Washington" in *The Kennedy Government*, a primer on the new administration. Sorensen made no claim to a greater influence than Attorney General Robert Kennedy, who after JFK's difficult first year in office emerged as his brother's unchallenged confidant. "I wanted to be his most trusted advisor," Sorensen wrote years later. "I felt lucky to have that role. Ultimately, only his brother Robert had more access and was consulted more often." Sorensen protected that role, which made him (even to colleagues who liked him) intense, jealous, and possessive. Then again, perhaps that was predictable for someone who had worked so hard to get where he was – and to put John F. Kennedy where he was.

※

Theodore Chaikin Sorensen was born in Lincoln, Nebraska, on May 8, 1928. His mother, Annis Chaikin Sorensen, was a Jew of Ukrainian parents, a feminist, and a pacifist. She had studied classics at the University of Nebraska, earning degrees in Greek and Latin, and later studied social work in New York City. She returned to Nebraska to teach and write. His father, Christian Abraham (C.A.) Sorensen, was a Unitarian of Scandinavian descent, and a Republican. As a crusading lawyer, he took on progressive causes, such as opposition to capital punishment. He served as attorney general of Nebraska and ran unsuccessfully for higher office three times. Attracted by a mutual passion for social justice and committed to women's rights, world peace, and the abolition of child labor, Annis and Christian married in 1921. They were principled liberal intellectuals with "a delightful disregard for convention," as a friend put it. Theirs was a mixed marriage, rare in Nebraska in the 1920s.

Ted once referred to himself as a "Danish Russian Jewish Unitarian." Born a Jew, he was not raised as one nor did he see himself as one. It didn't seem to matter one way or another to him. He was the third of five children; he had two older brothers and a younger brother and sister. Early on, he used his position in the family to curry favor with his parents, claiming he was "the smallest of the biggest" and "the biggest of the smallest." Looking back as an octogenarian, Sorensen said he felt lucky to be born and raised in Lincoln, in a free country, to parents who were healthy, educated, and liberal, and who wanted the same for their children.

But his mother wasn't well. When Ted was sixteen, Annis developed a form of mental illness that would be diagnosed today as bipolar or manic-depressive disorder. It changed her and the family, plunging all into "a prolonged nightmare." She became withdrawn, sullen, and moody, with periods of lethargy. It was devastating for the children and particularly his father, whom Ted called "a saint." The nadir came one evening when his mother became hysterical and Christian called an ambulance. Ted remembers his mother fighting the attendants, his little sister and brother sobbing as she was carried away.

Sorensen did not reveal his mother's illness until the end of his life. The pain of the memory was too great, he allowed, as was the stigma of mental illness; he thought it was a betrayal of his mother even to speak of it. Her illness had an impact on him. He saw the world darkly and he matured quickly, learning to handle life's hardships on his own. Misfortune he knew: a beautiful girlfriend in Texas committed suicide shortly after he visited her ("an early horrifying lesson in life"), and he nearly drowned in a flood at Camp Strader ("my first brush with death"). He and his siblings worked hard, studied hard, and married young. As an adult, he was not without confidence or ego. Sorensen was serious, guarded, awkward, reserved, ascetic, and brittle.

What was most useful from his childhood, Sorensen recalled, was learning the elements of critical thinking, clear writing, and clear speaking, the last honed in vigorous debate around the family dinner table. All his brothers and sisters were debaters. It helped, in the future, that young Ted was a big reader, a star public speaker, and, at his mother's insistence, a student of Latin. At seventeen, he was high school valedictorian. He entered the University of Nebraska as a freshman in 1945. (Smart as he was, he didn't seriously consider studying out of state.) He entered a special six-year program that allowed him to take two years of undergraduate liberal arts and four years of law school. Curiously, given his future as a political advisor and speechwriter, he studied little economics, history, or literature, and took no classical rhetoric or English composition at all.

Two causes as a student influenced him in later life. The first was a persistent skepticism of war. He inherited this from his parents, particularly his father, who had opposed America's participation in the First World War. In the summer of 1945, as Ted left high school and prepared to enter college, he wrote his father that, given the threat that fascism presented to democracy, he intended to enlist in the Navy. That changed when the war ended with Japan's surrender. Still, given that the draft remained in effect and he had to decide on a course of action when he turned eighteen in May 1946, he chose to serve as a noncombatant, perhaps in the medical corps. He later declared himself a conscientious objector. In his five-page "statement of position" to the local board of authorities, he invoked his Unitarian faith and the Quaker faith of his new wife, Camilla, whom he married in 1949. He quoted philosophers,

eastern and western. He explained his deep-seated religious principles. The board accepted his argument.

The other, more compelling issue of Sorensen's youth was civil
rights. While not many blacks lived in Lincoln, there were incidents of racism and prejudice. Sorensen championed responses,
such as a State Fair Employment Practices Act. The bill died in
Nebraska in 1947, but one that eventually passed in 1965 looked
much like the one he had promoted and drafted as a young activist.
His religious convictions and his belief in racial equality flowed
from the "liberal idealism . . . imparted to me as part of my genetic
composition." When he wasn't fighting racism, he was organizing a
branch of Americans for Democratic Action (ADA), which, he
recalls, "was like organizing the Anti-Defamation League in Cairo."
His family was thought to be left, even pinko, which he denied. His
father was a progressive Republican, like Theodore Roosevelt, and
his mother was a New Deal Democrat, like Franklin Roosevelt.
Ted was a liberal, much more so than JFK.

Skeptical of war, devoted to social justice and racial equality,
steeped in Midwestern reformism, young Sorensen prepared to go
into the world. It was 1951 and Republican senator Joe McCarthy's
anti-Communist crusade was at full flood. Sorensen graduated
that spring from law school, where he had edited the law review
and tied for first in his class. Most of his classmates stayed in
Lincoln. He did not. "I always sensed that I had a larger purpose,"
he said. "I aspired to something I knew I would not find in Lincoln."
He also knew he would disappoint his father, who wanted him to
join his practice. This was not for Ted, though: "I wanted to make
a difference."

On July 1, 1951, degree in hand, he boarded a train for the one
place he thought he could do that: Washington, D.C. He knew no
one in the capital, his father knew no one of importance, and he
did not even have a license to practice law there. Frankly, he had no
real prospects at all. He was twenty-three years old. He had never

left the Midwest. But Mr. Sorensen was determined to go to Washington. So, here he was that postwar summer, a little anxious, carrying his father's battered suitcase, contemplating this "head-strong, impulsive decision" and "the immense gamble I was taking." He had little money, certainly none for any hostelry fancier than the YMCA in downtown Washington, where he found a small room with a narrow bed that barely accommodated his raw-boned, six-foot, one-inch frame. "I had never drunk a cup of coffee, set foot in a bar, written a check, or owned a car," he said.

When he reached Union Station the evening of July 3 and had to find his way to the "Y," he had never even been in a taxi; in Lincoln, only the wealthy or the inebriated took cabs. In his hasty departure, he had forgotten that the day after his arrival was July 4. Offices were closed. That night, dazzled by the fireworks on the National Mall, which was filled with more people than lived in all of Lincoln, he recalled: "I felt totally alone."

A decade later, this idealistic, liberal Unitarian – who was nei-ther a war hero nor an Irish aristocrat, who didn't go to Choate or Harvard – would become the second (or third) most powerful man in Washington. On that steamy day in July 1951, he would embark upon the adventure of his life. On this steamy day in June 1963, it would place him next to the most powerful man on earth, address-ing the greatest issue on earth, and he could honestly say that he had had something to do with both.

✳

At 10:57 a.m. Kennedy had been speaking for twenty-one minutes. He read from a text, not a teleprompter, and he had penciled in small changes. The last six minutes of this seminal speech tilted to the future. Kennedy had challenged a country weaned on a dark view of the Soviets and the Cold War to revisit old prejudices. He had appealed to the Russians to reexamine their views, too. Now, to make real, concrete progress, Kennedy would have to take another significant step. He had to send Khrushchev a signal that the United States was serious about establishing a new spirit of peace, and, more substantively, that it was serious about negotiating a treaty banning nuclear testing.

If this speech had been discussed privately for months, a nuclear test ban treaty had been discussed publicly for years. In August 1958, Eisenhower proposed such a treaty and promised that the United States would not test for a year. Negotiations stalled. They continued fitfully for five years. By the winter of 1963, though, events were in play.

Much had to do with Norman Cousins, the humanitarian who had edited *Saturday Review*, the popular weekly magazine, since 1940. His diplomacy had played a pivotal role. In November 1962, in the aftermath of the Cuban Missile Crisis, he informed the White House that he would be visiting Moscow as an envoy of Pope John XXIII. He hoped to explore the prospects of peace. Kennedy invited him to Washington for a chat. The intermediary was Ralph Dungan, special assistant to the president, who had been assigned the file; Cousins found him, like the other New Frontiersmen, "vigorous, highly intellectual, devoted to his chief."

Meeting in the Oval Office, the president told Cousins: "[Khrushchev] will probably say something about his desire to reduce tensions, but will make it appear there's no reciprocal interest by the United States. It is important that he be corrected on this score. I'm not sure Khrushchev knows this, but I don't think there's any man in American politics who's more eager than I am to put Cold War animosities behind us and get down to the hard business of building friendly relations."

When Cousins met Khrushchev in Moscow in December, the chairman had a message of his own: "One thing the President and I should do right away," he said, "is to conclude a treaty outlawing testing of nuclear weapons, and then start to work on the problem of keeping these weapons from spreading all over the world." Then Cousins passed on JFK's message: No one was more committed to peace and creating new relations than he. If that were so, replied Khrushchev, the president "would not find me running second in racing to that goal." He sent Cousins away with personal greetings for the president.

There was more personal diplomacy that spring. Cousins returned to the Soviet Union to meet Khrushchev at his retreat on the Black Sea on April 12. Cousins, a Unitarian like Sorensen, had gone there after meeting the Pope at the Vatican. His purpose was to advance the cause of religious freedom in the Soviet Union. But there was another reason: he wanted to press the idea of a new peace. During their conversation, Cousins recalled, Khrushchev told him that after the Cuban Missile Crisis "there was a real chance for both the Soviet Union and the United States . . . to advance the peace by easing tensions." An agreement on nuclear testing would help do that. Khrushchev told his Council of Ministers there could be an agreement with the U.S., if the Soviets would agree to three on-site inspections to verify that they were not cheating. Kennedy had said that that more were needed for the treaty to win approval in the Senate, where ratification required a two-thirds vote. But Khrushchev was miffed when the Americans then came back with a demand for eight inspections. "And so once again, I was made to look foolish," he complained to Cousins. "But I can tell you this: it won't happen again."

Cousins, who recounted his shuttle diplomacy in *The Improbable Triumvirate* in 1972, told Khrushchev the dispute over inspections was a misunderstanding. Khrushchev accepted that. He said the Soviet Union wanted a treaty to outlaw nuclear testing underground, above ground, in water, and in space. He said the next move was Kennedy's. Ten days later, more shuttle diplomacy. At the White House, Cousins reported Khrushchev's response, and Kennedy spoke to the challenges of pushing through a treaty, especially given the forces lined up against it in both countries. During the Cuban Missile Crisis, the two leaders had had to face down their own hardliners. Not much had changed. Kennedy mused that he and Khrushchev held the same political positions inside their respective governments. "He would like to prevent a nuclear war but is under severe pressure from his hard-line crowd, which interprets every move in that direction as appeasement," observed Kennedy. "I've got similar problems. Meanwhile, the lack of progress in reaching agreements between our two countries gives strength to the hard-line boys in both, with the result that the hard-liners in the Soviet Union and the United States feed on one another, each using the actions of the other to justify its own position."

Listening to Cousins, Kennedy thought that Khrushchev's position in Moscow was weaker than some thought. Cousins warned there was evidence to suggest a political crisis was developing in the Soviet Union and the test ban might be pivotal. The premier had to produce a treaty now to show that his openness toward the United States could yield something tangible. For their part, the Chinese wanted the treaty to fail. Said Cousins: "In any event, the test ban treaty has become something of a watershed inside the Communist world. The failure to achieve it would be hailed by the Chinese and their supporters as proof of the unrealistic nature of Khrushchev's policy." The Chinese, he said, believed there would be no more negotiation, the treaty was stillborn, and this would bring a greater rapport between the Soviet Union and China. In fact, a delegation from Beijing was to visit Moscow in early June. China was not a small matter in this discussion. The United States worried about a closer relationship between Moscow and Beijing, and saw a test ban treaty as a way to preempt it.

Cousins advised the president that "what was needed was a breathtaking new approach toward the Russian people, calling for an end to the Cold War and a fresh start in American-Russian relationships." Such an approach might recognize that "the old animosities could become the fuse of a holocaust." Kennedy lit a thin cigar and asked Cousins to give him a memorandum on their meeting and his visit to Khrushchev. Cousins did. Two weeks later, in early May, Sorensen invited Cousins to meet him in his office. Cousins was impressed by Sorensen. ("The range and incisiveness of his intelligence were enormously impressive.") Sorensen told him Kennedy wanted to use Cousins' arguments and asked for some more notes.

Meanwhile, in the Senate, where Kennedy and his advisors feared trouble, Cousins saw encouraging signs. On May 27, Senators Hubert Humphrey of Minnesota and Thomas Dodd of Connecticut introduced a bipartisan resolution, signed by thirty-four senators, proposing a nuclear test ban treaty that would apply to tests in the atmosphere, but not those underground, underwater, or in space. This was the *partial* test ban treaty. The idea wasn't wholly new and it fell short of the comprehensive ban that the administration wanted. However, the resolution was signed by a third of the senators, including some who had previously opposed a ban of any kind. Cousins said that Kennedy now had "some momentum and thought his speech at American University could have a profound effect on the atmosphere. It could create a favorable context for the consideration of the treaty."

When Kennedy spoke on June 10, a Chinese delegation was already in Moscow. The Chinese believed that there would be no test ban treaty. They thought a limited treaty would not interest Khrushchev, that negotiations would fail, and that they and the Soviets would forge a new relationship. If Kennedy wanted to forestall that, he had to find new ground and offer a new beginning.

*

At American University, Kennedy referred to the negotiations on disarmament in Geneva, those interminable, unproductive talks that had been going on fitfully for years. He confessed that the prospects for a breakthrough were "dim." But he said that the one ray of hope – and "a fresh start is badly needed" – was a treaty banning nuclear tests. He made the argument for such a treaty: it would "check the spiraling arms race in one of its most dangerous areas"; it would halt the spread of nuclear weapons; it would enhance security, by lessening the prospects of war. To pursue this opportunity, he announced that he and Khrushchev, as well as Macmillan, had agreed to resume their talks in the hope of "an early agreement" on a comprehensive test ban treaty (he was not embracing a limited test ban). "Our hopes must be tempered with the caution of history – but with our hopes go the hopes of all mankind," Kennedy said. As an expression of good faith, he said that the United States would not conduct nuclear tests in the atmosphere, as long as other states did not. "We will not be the first to resume," he promised. He allowed that such a treaty would not be a substitute for disarmament, but he hoped it would help achieve it. His proposal was greeted with applause.

Then, he did something entirely unexpected: he asked Americans to examine their "attitude toward peace and freedom here at home. The quality and spirit of our own society must justify and support our efforts abroad. . . . Wherever we are, we must all, in our daily lives, live up to the age-old faith that peace and freedom walk together. In too many of our cities today, the peace is not secure because the freedom is incomplete." In his two-and-a-half years in office, he had spent more than three-quarters of his time on foreign affairs, largely in response to one international crisis after another. But by the spring of 1963, the civil rights movement demanded its own response. The unrest in Birmingham, Alabama, in particular, had hit home. "My guess is that May–June 1963 will go down in history as the great turning point in the fight for Negro equality," Arthur Schlesinger wrote in his diary on June 16. "There has been nothing like it in the way of spontaneous mass democracy in this country since the surge of labor organization in the summer of 1937."

That day, and the next, Kennedy would move on racial equality, much as he had on world peace. He did not know on June 10 how things would play out in Alabama and Washington. Anticipating, however, that he might well ask Americans to apply the same introspection and generosity to advancing human rights as restricting nuclear arms, he made the association in his speech between peace at home and peace abroad, between .rights in Birmingham and rights in Belarus. A practicing Catholic, living in a more temporal age, he also enlisted the Bible in a righteous cause. "When a man's ways please the Lord," he quoted the Scriptures, "he maketh even his enemies to be at peace with him." With that, he asked, "And is not peace, in the last analysis, basically a matter of human rights – the right to live out our lives without fear of devastation – the right to breathe air as nature provided it – the right of future generations to a healthy existence?"

Finally, in his peroration, he made an eloquent appeal for a peace to end the Cold War. "The United States, as the world knows, will never start a war. We do not want a war. We do not now expect a war. This generation of Americans has already had enough – more than enough – of war and hate and oppression. We shall be prepared if others wish it. We shall be alert to try to stop it. But we shall also do our part to build a world of peace where the weak are safe and the strong are just. We are not helpless before that task or hopeless of its success. Confident and unafraid, we labor on – not toward a strategy of annihilation but toward a strategy of peace."

✷

The applause dissipated in the still air of the open field. In photographs, the scene looks hot, dry, and strangely empty – Kennedy at the podium, the official party behind him, the musicians beside him, the Class of 1963 before him (many of the guests having abandoned their chairs for the shade of nearby trees) – surrounded by outcroppings of spectators in a sea of green and brown. If this was the best speech of Kennedy's life, it was received politely but not with wild enthusiasm. Sorensen called the response over the next week "so-so." Yet many of the Class of 1963 thought it was special the moment they heard it. Faith Shrinsky, a drama major and a civil rights activist who was receiving her bachelor of arts degree that day, was tearful listening to Kennedy. "It was a radical position to take," she said almost fifty years later. "JFK went against what had been hammered into our heads: the Russians were horrible." Carl Cook, standing to the right of the stage, remembered "the extraordinary rippling of excitement . . . as President Kennedy delivered an address that electrified the crowd and circled the globe." Most had been on campus the previous autumn, during the Cuban Missile Crisis. It had left them scared and scarred. Nanci I. Moore, editor of the university's literary magazine, unsure that she would survive, recalls writing a poem to her lover called "October, 1962."

It was 11:02 a.m. The president had spoken for twenty-six minutes and fifty-six seconds. Now it was time for him to receive his honorary degree. But there were five other honorary degrees to confer that morning and he had to get in line. Although the ceremony took only a few minutes, Kennedy was restless under his heavy robes. Finally, the president was led down the stairs to the east side of the platform, where Dr. Reeves and Senator John Sparkman of Alabama waited. They awarded him an Honorary Degree, Doctor of Civil Law. "We are especially sensitive to the pressures under which you live and work, pressures not only of our own Nation's problems, but those of the entire world as well," said President Anderson. "This awareness makes us deeply grateful. It is a real privilege for the president of any university to award you, President Kennedy, an honorary degree."

The academic hood was then slipped over Kennedy's head and attached to the back of his robe. Anderson handed the diploma to the president and congratulated him. Just before Kennedy prepared to depart, he watched as Senator Robert Byrd of West Virginia – who entered the Senate in 1958 and would die in office in 2010 – received a bachelor of laws. His was a real degree. Earlier, in a lone light moment on a serious day, Kennedy had saluted "my old colleague, Bob Byrd, who has earned his degree through many years of attending night law school, while I am earning mine in the next 30 minutes."

It was 11:10 a.m. The audience was standing and applauding. Accompanied by Anderson, Kennedy walked to his limousine, idling on the east side of the field. Degree in hand, gown returned, speech delivered, he was done here. The overture was made and history was, too. He would not expect to hear anything imminently from Moscow, where it was early evening. In Washington, it was not yet noon; in Hawaii, it was not yet dawn. If Kennedy was flagging in the heat, he did not show it. Although he had been in the sun for almost an hour, he was not perspiring. He waved a last time to the crowd, climbed into his Cadillac, and roared back to the White House.

Monday, June 10, 1963

CHAPTER 3

Noon

TWELVE MINUTES AFTER leaving American University, the president arrived at the Southwest Gate of the White House at 11:22 a.m. Again, he went straight to the residence, arriving a minute later. He wanted to shower and change his shirt. Kennedy was fastidious about his appearance and hated feeling sweaty. He could change his shirt six times a day. His schedule gave him less than fifteen minutes upstairs, apparently too little time to return the calls from Jackie, who had telephoned from Camp David at 10:05 a.m. and again at 11:25 a.m. By 11:38 a.m., Kennedy was downstairs in the Oval Office.

Jack Kennedy was impatient. He would not wait for anything or anybody. He lived like he had no time to lose. Politically, his time was always now. He ran and won a seat in the House of Representatives in 1946 at twenty-nine. He ran and won a seat in the Senate in 1952 at thirty-five. He ran for the vice presidency in 1956 at thirty-nine – an impulsive, nearly successful gambit at the Democratic National Convention to become Adlai Stevenson's running mate.

He ran for the presidency in 1960 at forty-three. In 1960s America, when the average male lived to sixty-seven years old, in a time when age was a measure of worth, politicians were expected to wait their turn. Kennedy did not wait his turn. Only Theodore Roosevelt was younger when he took office in 1901, succeeding the assassinated William McKinley. Among world leaders, Kennedy was a stripling. When Kennedy took office on January 20, 1961, John Diefenbaker of Canada was sixty-five; Harold Macmillan and Nikita Khrushchev were both sixty-six; Mao Zedong of China was sixty-seven; Charles de Gaulle of France was seventy; Jawaharlal Nehru of India was seventy-one.

Richard Nixon, his opponent in 1960, was only four years older. Both had entered Congress in 1947. Having been vice president for eight years, though, Nixon presented himself as more seasoned. A president should have "a little gray around his ears," he said. There was no discernible gray in Kennedy's full mane in 1960, and he did not aspire to any. But gray conveyed experience. Nixon was intimating that Kennedy was not ready to be president. Others said the same; derisively, both LBJ and Eisenhower called him "the boy." That Kennedy, a war hero, had studied at Choate, Harvard, and briefly at the London School of Economics, had written two best-selling books (one awarded the Pulitzer Prize), had served fourteen years in Congress, had traveled widely – all that was less persuasive then. By the new century, major-league political experience was no longer a prerequisite. George W. Bush had been governor of Texas for six years when he was elected president in 2000. Barack Obama had been senator from Illinois for four years (and a state senator for eight) when he was elected in 2008. Obama's opponent in 2012, Mitt Romney, was governor of Massachusetts for four years. It did not disqualify any of them.

Impatience and ambition had brought Kennedy this far, this fast. His life was a steep trajectory. He did not see time extending over the horizon with the boundless confidence of someone in the flush of good health. Although he thought he would survive his presidency, he did not see a long life before him. His mood was sometimes morbid. By 1960, he had almost died from scarlet fever, Addison's, and other diseases. That made him see time differently. It is why Kennedy learned speed-reading. It is why his sexual liaisons were said to be fast and transactional. "God-damn it, you kept me waiting," he barked at a burlesque queen in 1955 as he sat fuming in his car. It is why he had no patience for idle chatter; although a lively conversationalist himself ("the world's greatest listener," he was called), he could not abide the sonorous and the long-winded. The moment he began twitching, shifting, or tapping the head of a pencil on his front teeth, he was bored. Seven seconds, declared Averell Harriman. That's how long you had to get his attention.

When Norman Cousins visited the White House in April, Kennedy mentioned that he would be speaking to visiting young musicians in a half hour. The subject was the arts. Cousins said that he had some new figures on the state of American culture, and Kennedy asked him for a few talking points. Cousins telephoned his office in New York immediately, got the statistics within six minutes, borrowed a typewriter, tapped out a few remarks, and gave them to JFK. "Now I've seen everything," Kenny O'Donnell told Cousins later that day. "The President had seven minutes before he was due to speak. He raced down to the White House pool, tore off his clothes, dove in, and swam with one hand. In the other hand he was studying the draft of the talk you gave him for the kids."

Kennedy welcomed work. "No one can dispute the fact that he was the hardest-working Chief of State we ever had," concluded Jim Bishop in 1966, after observing him in the White House for several days in the fall of 1963. Asked about his long hours, Kennedy said: "A man must have goals. There is not sufficient time, even in two terms, to achieve those goals. Almost all Presidents leave office feeling that their work is unfinished. I have a lot to do, and so little time to do it." But Kennedy was not a workaholic. His erratic health and bad back limited his hours in the office, and he was often absent in his first year in office. He did not reach his desk at dawn, he did not lunch there, and he did not stay past 7:00 or 8:00 p.m. He reserved time every day, in the middle of the day, for a swim, lunch, and a nap, and scheduled another swim at the end of the day. But when he was in, he was on. He listened intensely, absorbed information quickly, and asked discursive questions. On Monday, after his big speech, Kennedy faced the usual flow of presidential business – a bill-signing, meetings with advisors and appointments with visitors, press releases to approve, letters to sign and telegrams to review, telephone calls to make and return. That day there was all that, and a developing crisis, too.

*

When Kennedy reached the Oval Office at 11:38 a.m., some three dozen politicians, officials, and advocates, most of them women, had gathered there to watch him sign Bill S. 1409 into law. The bill was limited in scope, but was, like other important issues before the president that day, a precursor of the change coming to the United States in the 1960s. Signing a bill was a president's constitutional perogative and often, not always, a president's pleasure. Today, Kennedy welcomed the ritual.

Flanked by guests, Kennedy sat at his large mahogany desk. The bill he would sign sought to address the disparity in compensation between men and women, one of the glaring inequities in American life. "I am delighted today to approve the Equal Pay Act of 1963, which prohibits arbitrary discrimination against women in the payment of wages," he said. "This act represents many years of effort by labor, management, and several private organizations . . . to call attention to the unconscionable practice of paying female employees less wages than male employees for the same job. This measure adds to our laws another structure basic to democracy. It will add protection at the working place to the women . . . that they have enjoyed at the polling place."

In 1963, the average woman worker made 60 percent of the average wage for men. One in three workers in the United States was a woman, and women were underpaid. In 1960, a full-time woman worker earned $3,293 a year; a full-time male worker earned $5,147. Professional women made $4,384, professional men $6,848. There were 23 million working women (5 million more were projected by 1970). Their numbers were rising faster than the number of men in the workforce. Full equality of opportunity was still elusive, but Kennedy called the legislation "a significant step forward." At the same time, he also urged the creation of more "day-care centers," a new idea at the time. Because only 185,000 day-care spots existed nationwide, some 500,000 children under twelve of working parents were taking care of themselves, a situation that Kennedy called "a formula for disaster."

Like much of Kennedy's legislation, the equal pay bill had sat in Congress. It would have passed the year before but for one vote in the Senate. It was not contentious. After limited debate in the House, it had been approved overwhelmingly two weeks earlier by voice vote in the Senate. The new law amended the Fair Labor Standards Act of 1938, which regulated the wages and hours of the 27.5 million men and women who worked in industries engaged in interstate commerce. It would ensure – or try to ensure – that employers did not pay more to one sex than the other for "equal work on jobs, the performance of which requires equal skill, effort, and responsibility, and which are performed under similar working conditions." But the bill left out women working in hotels, motels, restaurants, and agriculture, as well as professional and administrative personnel. It covered only 6 to 7 million women, leaving out some 16 million others in the workforce. The law would be little help in urging employers to give women a greater role in supervisory or executive positions. No one was terribly excited about the act, and no one overstated its importance – certainly not the reliably skeptical *Wall Street Journal*, which cautioned that the act "was no sweeping declaration of economic emancipation." Still, it was a first step. To a man – and to a woman – the politicians, unionists, and activists in the Oval Office that day were pleased to be there.

"[It] is only one bite out of the cherry. It is a little too little and of course too late, but it is the best we can do now," said Representative Katharine St. George of New York, a veteran crusader for women's rights. Frances Perkins, the country's first woman to serve in cabinet (appointed by FDR), said the law was an "important occasion, because it gives expression to the worth of the work of women, which has been so much a part of the progress of the last half century." Andrew Biemiller, a burly, influential lobbyist for organized labor, remembered "a good bill" which he had worked hard to pass. "I've got a lovely picture of it," he recalled of the signing. "There are only three men in that picture. Everybody else is a woman. The President, the Vice-President and me . . . He had himself surrounded by all the dames he could find."

Slowly, deliberately, Kennedy scratched out his signature with eighteen different pens. When he was done he distributed the pens, much coveted as keepsakes. Among the men there that morning were Senators Jennings Randolph of West Virginia, Winston L. Prouty of Vermont, and Wayne Morse of Oregon, all supporters of the bill. Among the women was Maurine Neuberger, one of the two women in the Senate in 1963. (The other woman senator was Margaret Chase Smith of Maine, who was absent.) Neuberger, known quaintly as a champion of "the consumer and the housewife," had joined her husband, Richard L. Neuberger, then a state senator, in the Oregon House of Representatives in 1951. They were the first husband-and-wife team to serve simultaneously in both chambers of a state legislature. She left the statehouse in 1955 to join Richard in Washington after he was elected senator, working as his unpaid assistant. When he died suddenly in 1960, she succeeded him. She was known for her directness, warmth, and "freedom from affectation." When critics questioned "her dignity" in modeling a bathing suit at a charity show in the 1950s, she snapped: "What do you think a senator's wife wears when she goes swimming?"

The news photographs of the Oval Office ceremony catch the ambience. The women wear pastel suits or bright patterned dresses, some adorned with a string of pearls. A few wear flamboyant hats. All wear white gloves. Several congresswomen are present: Edith Green of Oregon, Martha Griffiths of Michigan, Catherine May and Julia Hansen of Washington, Elizabeth Kee of West Virginia, Edna Kelly of New York, Leonor Sullivan of Missouri, Florence Dwyer of New Jersey. The most prominent among them was Esther Peterson, assistant secretary of labor for labor standards, who was the most senior woman in the administration.

Being an assistant secretary was an achievement for a woman in 1963. Peterson, a Mormon from Utah, graduated from Brigham Young University in 1927 with a bachelor's degree in physical education and earned a master's from teacher's college at Columbia University in 1930. She had been in the labor movement since becoming an organizer for the American Federation of Teachers in 1938. She met Kennedy in 1948 and supported him for the presidency. In 1961, he appointed her head of the Women's Bureau in the Department of Labor. She did not like deferential men. "I'd often be the only woman in the room, and the men would stand up," she recalled in 1988. "And I'd say, 'Please don't do that. I'm not going to stand up for you. Don't stand up for me.' It was not easy. So many men are not comfortable working with women. I had a lot of trouble with that. But I never had any trouble working with Kennedy or any of his people."

There were no prominent women in the administration, a point made in a strong memorandum to the president from Clayton Fritchey of the United States Mission to the United Nations. "Today there are really no famous women serving the Government," he wrote on July 22, 1963. "But, perhaps even more important, there are few positions that would tend to make them famous." There was no Madame Justice and no Madame Secretary. The best known in government was Peterson, who had encouraged Kennedy to establish the President's Commission on the Status of Women. It had been chaired by the saintly Eleanor Roosevelt, FDR's widow, who had been cool to Kennedy when he ran for president. A supporter of Adlai Stevenson, she distrusted Kennedy; she doubted that he was a liberal and pointedly urged him to "show less profile and more courage." By the time she died in 1962, though, she had changed her mind. The commission she chaired laid the groundwork for change. It encouraged Peterson too, who acknowledged that for the White House "equal pay was never top priority. They helped me at certain times, but I carried that bill up."

Women's rights – much like racial equality, the environment, poverty, urban sprawl, and consumer awareness – were beginning to gestate in the public consciousness in 1963. Peterson was a pioneer. In the administration, the only other high-ranking woman was Katie Louchheim, deputy assistant secretary for public affairs at the Department of State. Like Peterson, she had worked for Kennedy in 1960. This was a man's world, re-created a half century later in the dark television drama *Mad Men*. As Simone de Beauvoir, the French writer, put it in 1949, women were "the second sex." (In the vernacular, *sex* had not yet yielded to *gender*.) While there were millions of women in the workforce, the majority were homemakers and mothers. Only 38 percent of college students were female and only 11 percent of doctorates were awarded to women. In the professions, 78 percent of college professors, 95 percent of doctors, and 97 percent of lawyers were men. Women newspaper columnists often did not have bylines.

Kennedy was pleased to sign the equal pay bill, even if its impact would be minimal until it was strengthened by court challenges in the 1970s. However, women's issues were not particularly important to him. His view of women was traditional in a traditional time. If *feminism* was not in the lexicon in 1963, nor was *sexism*. Kennedy was a sexist, as were most men around him. Yet he admired Esther Peterson, Katie Louchheim, and Eleanor Roosevelt, and said so. His own wife was a sensation – a tastemaker and a trendsetter. But Jacqueline was content to be known more for her style than her thoughts. "'Where do you get your opinions?'" she recalled being asked once. "And I said, 'I get all my opinions from my husband.' Which is true. How could I have any political opinions, you know? His were going to be the best. And I could never conceive of not voting for whomever my husband was for. Anyone who I'd be married to."

Jackie's fey, artless frankness offended some women (including her own granddaughters) when her oral history, recorded with Arthur Schlesinger in 1964, was released in 2011. But her self-deprecation was misleading. While JFK may not have discussed affairs of state often with her, she was no ingenue. She had attended Vassar College in New York, studying history, art, literature, and language (she spoke French and Spanish). She brought a sense of the past and grace to the restoration of the White House in 1961 and 1962. Later, as an editor with Viking Press and as a senior editor with Doubleday in New York, she showed range and depth. Authors praised her eye and ear, her editorial judgment, and her European sensibility. In her oral history, which is sometimes catty, her assessments of people and events are always illuminating. She can turn a phrase. JFK knew his wife's mind and admired it. When things went badly awry between the British and the Americans in late 1962 over the failure of the Skybolt missile program, he gave her a copy of a report he had commissioned from a Harvard professor to examine the reasons for the misunderstanding. He wanted her views. She took it with her to Dallas.

If women were subservient, patronized, idealized, underpaid, and underappreciated in 1963, that was about to change. The week

Kennedy signed the Equal Pay Act, *The Feminine Mystique* was on the *New York Times* bestseller list. The author was Betty Friedan, a suburban mother of three, living on the Hudson River, married to an advertising executive. Friedan held a *summa cum laude* degree in psychology from Smith College and was a successful freelance magazine writer. Although she was not typical of the women she described, Friedan was troubled by a world in which women could never do as well as men. In *The Feminine Mystique*, she challenged American women to address the myth of domestic fulfillment. Women had to affirm themselves and assert themselves to be more than appendages, she argued. Friedan identified a problem and struck a nerve. By her death in 2006, *The Feminine Mystique* had sold more than three million copies.

Ultimately, the law, and the sentiment it reflected in *The Feminine Mystique*, would make women's liberation one of the great social movements of the 1960s and 1970s. It would be led by Betty Friedan and journalist Gloria Steinem, who, as it happened, was beginning to see Ted Sorensen that spring. Beyond women's rights, other emerging social issues were explored in influential books in these years. As Louis Menand of *The New Yorker* wrote decades later: "In the early nineteen-sixties, books, for some reason, were bombs." In 1961, Jane Jacobs published *The Death and Life of Great American Cities* (urbanization). In 1962, Rachel Carson published *Silent Spring* (environment) and Michael Harrington published *The Other America* (poverty). In 1963, James Baldwin published *The Fire Next Time* (racism), and Jessica Mitford published *The American Way of Death* (dying). These were read and discussed in Kennedy's Washington, where books mattered to the president and his talented circle. Max Freedman, the journalist, autodidact, and prolific reader, recalls traveling with Kennedy and having to bring five or six books "to make sure he had something to read every night. He read the great books as if they'd been written specially for him." In some cases, books influenced policy. In a time of ferment, JFK was both catalyst and beneficiary.

*

The ceremony was over in thirteen minutes. The words spoken, the pens distributed, and the photographs taken, the visitors filed out of the Oval Office by 11:58 a.m. Since touching down from Hawaii earlier that morning, Kennedy had delivered a speech and signed a bill. Now it was noon. Strictly speaking, his official schedule was open for the next four hours; his next appointment was not until shortly before 4:30 p.m. That did not mean he was "sitting around with his socks off," as a saucy young Caroline once described her father at work. Now was the time for telephone calls; Kennedy might place or receive fifty a day. It was also time for meeting advisors, reviewing documents, and dictating memos. He would nap and swim later that afternoon. Now though, Alabama was on his mind.

Inevitably, it had come to this. Ever since Ross Barnett, the governor of Mississippi, had tried and failed to stop the integration of Ole Miss in Oxford in the fall of 1962, the administration had been expecting another challenge from another southern university. Eight months later, it had one. This time it was the governor of Alabama and the University of Alabama at Tuscaloosa. George Wallace had taken office in January vowing to uphold segregation from here until celebrity. He had served notice that he would stand in the doorway of the university, personally, to prevent two black students, Vivian Malone and James Hood, from enrolling. His position defied the order of the court integrating the university. Once again, it left the administration no choice but to enforce the law.

Its resolve had not gone down well at Oxford. On Sunday, September 30, 1962, the Ku Klux Klan arrived with its traveling carnival of thugs and mischief-makers brandishing clubs and hunting rifles. They turned the University of Mississippi into a battleground. Two people, one a French journalist, were killed and hundreds injured. By October 1, twenty thousand soldiers had descended on the campus. The riot raged for fifteen hours. The soldiers restored order and stayed for eight months, resented among Mississippians as an occupying army. As it happened, the last of the troops were leaving Oxford that day. The challenge for the president and Robert Kennedy, who was coordinating the government's response in Alabama, was to find a way to register the students and integrate the university, peacefully. The last thing they wanted was to send in troops again to keep order. This time they hoped to use the power of the federal government sparingly, even surgically.

The confrontation had been building for two months. In 1963, there was simply no avoiding the pathologies of George Corley Wallace. He was a former boxer and staff sergeant in the Second World War. Trained as a lawyer, he had been a judge and an assemblyman. In 1958, running for governor in the Democrat primary, he lost the race because he was seen as too moderate. Claiming privately he had been "outniggered" (in public, he said "out-segged") by his opponent, he vowed to become as racist as he had to be. He affirmed his belief in racial separation in his inaugural address in Montgomery on January 14, 1963. There, on the stone steps of the State Capitol, where Jefferson Davis had been sworn in as president of the Confederacy, Wallace proclaimed: "In the name of the greatest people that have ever trod this Earth, I draw the line in the dust and toss the gauntlet before the feet of tyranny, and I say, segregation now, segregation tomorrow, segregation forever." The speech was written by Asa Earl Carter, a Klansman with a literary touch. Had Wallace said "integration," rather than "segregation," he would have been a visionary.

Moderation for Wallace was a vice. His weakness was that he had no emotional or intellectual thermostat; on race, the Governor had no governor. He was out to provoke the federal government. To

69

be sure, he claimed a legal basis for his position, but it was nothing more than the discredited nineteenth-century doctrine of interposition, said to give the state the right to assert its sovereignty between that of the federal government and the people. He knew the power of image, Wallace did, and he knew that even if he lost, he would win.

From the beginning, then, the stand in the schoolhouse door was a show. This was theater – kabuki, experimental, absurd, political. Each side understood the other's need for a stage. What unfolded between Monday afternoon and Tuesday afternoon in Washington and Tuscaloosa was scripted in as much as the two parties would stand up and deliver their lines. Before the soliloquies, there would be a flurry of press releases, interviews, and public statements between the antagonists; an exchange of telegrams; gubernatorial and presidential proclamations; and two executive orders. There would be lines – white lines on asphalt, red lines in rhetoric. There would be a borrowed wooden podium and a forest of microphones. There would be a crush of politicians, policemen, lawyers, administrators, and soldiers parading before hundreds of journalists and a battery of cameras. The public would be largely absent.

*

For all the choreography, though, no one knew how this peculiar spectacle would end. Sure, Wallace and the Kennedys believed the university would be integrated. Of course it would be integrated, just like the University of Mississippi and every other state institution in the old Confederacy. But would Wallace step aside? Would he be dragged off in handcuffs and charged with contempt of court? Would he incite a riot?

The administration could make all kinds of preparations – lacing the campus with telephone lines, mapping its roads and buildings with military aerial reconnaissance, securing the keys to the dormitory rooms of the black students to circumvent Wallace. They could even moor a boat, manned by marshals, on the far side of the Black Warrior River, bordering the campus, should the students have to flee a lynch mob. The federal marshals could practice how to seize Wallace. They could play war games, anticipating every scenario. But they did not know what to expect from the wiry, mercurial Wallace, the little man with the dimpled chin and the big complaint.

"We were reasonably confident that Wallace did not want violence," recalled Deputy Attorney General Nicholas Katzenbach, who represented the Department of Justice in Tuscaloosa. "The only question was whether or not he could keep order in such an explosive environment. The question remained until the end as to how he would yield. Would he get out of the 'schoolhouse door'? Would he work with or against the [national] guard in maintaining order? Would he resist in such an adamant fashion that we would be compelled to arrest him for contempt?" Wallace had to be handled gingerly. The administration feared making a martyr of him and inflaming the South. Because the court had ordered the students admitted by June 11, because the Justice Department had to enforce that order, because Wallace vowed to defy the order and bar their entry, there had been too much time to ponder this showdown and too little will to avoid it.

On Friday, June 7, *Life* covered the latest chapter of the civil rights story with a three-page profile on Frank Rose, president of the University of Alabama. "Nation's Crisis Crowds In on One Man," read the headline. "Says Alabama U. President: We won't be sacrificed to violence." There, in a full-page black-and-white photograph, is Rose, seated on a white wrought-iron bench encircling a tall, shady tree. He leans forward in the broad shadows, in business suit, white shirt and tie, wrists dangling. Rose assures Americans: there will be no violence. It is as if the editors of *Life*, having served up months of graphic photography of sit-ins, marches, and demonstrations ("The pictures on these 11 pages are frightening," it explained over a montage from bloody Birmingham in its issue of May 14) decided they wanted to give their readers a break.

By June 10, 1963, pitched battles in the streets of southern cities had become commonplace. It was no longer just Birmingham, where the police had turned their high-pressure hoses on the protesters, but bigger and smaller centers, too. Tuscaloosa was the latest dateline from the race war. That month, there were 162 racial incidents reported across the country. If pleasant Tuscaloosa, population 62,370, erupted in violence, why would it be any different than Birmingham? Even Washington itself, which was 54 percent black, was mired in poverty beyond its colonnaded temples and banks of azaleas and dogwood. Black unemployment was three times that of white, and discrimination was rampant in housing and employment. "This city is not far from an explosion," warned *Look* magazine. Robert MacNeil, the broadcaster, arrived in the capital that spring. After a riot in 1962 at a high school city championship football game, in which a mob of black fans attacked white fans over the ejection of one of their team's players from the game, he agreed: "The city was seething."

The Kennedys hoped that Wallace would not let the situation get out of hand in Alabama. "Our view was that he would give up and get out of there," said Burke Marshall, the assistant attorney general who ran the civil rights division of the Department of Justice, the leading edge of the government's civil rights response. "And our view was that he would do it in a way that did not lead to rioting, that he would preserve order, but we weren't sure." No, they weren't. In a state choking with resentment, where 1,500 white-robed, hooded white supremacists had gathered in a field near Tuscaloosa on Saturday night to burn a cross at a Ku Klux Klan rally, anything was possible. Even if Wallace wanted to keep this under control, could he? Ole Miss had turned into what *Time* had called "the greatest conflict between the state and federal authorities since the Civil War." Inspired by the Battle of Oxford, a legion of keening malcontents was fixin' for the Battle of Tuscaloosa.

✳

After a morning courting Khrushchev, the president was facing an afternoon divining Wallace. Even if he wanted to focus on the Soviets and nuclear arms that afternoon, Kennedy was forced to concentrate on business at home. For a president who had barely mentioned domestic issues in his inaugural address, this was new. His agenda was now dominated by nuclear arms *and* racial equality, twin forces he could no longer ignore. His adversary today and tomorrow was in Montgomery, not Moscow. Kennedy respected Khrushchev but dismissed Wallace. Why would it be otherwise? It was not just that they were from different worlds – Kennedy the detached, debonair northern patrician, Wallace the flinty, flamboyant southern pugilist. It was that Wallace was impossible. He was exasperating. He was a jumped-up, preening opportunist, a bantam boxer punching below the belt. He represented a dying South which was not dying fast enough for the Kennedys.

Bobby suggested that when the time came, Katzenbach sneer at the governor. "Well, he's really a second-rate figure to you," said Bobby. "He's wasting your time. He's wasting the students' time. And let's not make a big deal of it. I don't want to put the students through that indignity. I don't want that man to stand there and say things to them. They've had a hard enough life." Poor George wasn't even a worthy adversary. Marshall, who would join Bobby, Sorensen, and others in the Oval Office early that afternoon, recalled that "the main concern was to get that over with in a way that was dignified, and dignified for the country, dignified for the President, and was the least injurious to the country."

The meeting between Kennedy and his advisors on Tuscaloosa does not appear on the president's schedule. Kennedy had not been part of the maneuvering in court or the careful planning at the Justice Department over the past two weeks. But he sensed an opportunity here. To let Wallace know where he stood, and to ensure that the governor did not underestimate his determination, Kennedy sent him a strongly worded telegram that afternoon. It was a reply to the telegram that had arrived from Wallace on Saturday night, informing the president that "out of an abundance of caution," the governor was calling up 500 Alabama national guardsmen. Kennedy was unimpressed.

"I am gratified by the dedication to law and order expressed in your telegram informing me of your use of National Guardsmen at the University of Alabama," Kennedy replied. "The only announced threat to orderly compliance with the law, however, is your plan to bar physically the admission of Negro students in defiance of the order of the Alabama Federal District Court, and in violation of accepted standards of public conduct." Kennedy was wary of this kind of caution; he knew Wallace was the problem, not the students. Kennedy continued: "State, city and University officials have reported that, if you were to stay away from the campus, thus fulfilling your legal duty, there is little danger of any disorder being incited which the local town and campus authorities could not adequately handle. This would make unnecessary the outside intervention of any troops, either State or Federal. I therefore urgently ask you to consider the consequences to your State and its fine University if you persist in setting an example of defiant conduct, and urge you instead to leave these matters in the courts of law where they belong." In other words, without the self-aggrandizing governor, there would be no grandstanding and no Guard. The danger was Wallace himself.

Kennedy could see where events were leading. He was rushing to catch up. His critics, including Martin Luther King Jr. that very morning, were complaining that he was dawdling on civil rights.

He was following rather than leading, the liberals said. His reply was that the country wasn't ready for a civil rights bill and Congress would not pass it anyway. Two years earlier, his reaction to the Freedom Riders (those young civil rights activists riding interstate buses in the South to challenge the legality of segregation on inter-city routes and in bus stations) was that they were embarrassing the nation. How could he argue the superiority of democracy during the Cold War if America was seen as a racist culture? Now things were different. In Hawaii, he had said that every American should share the American dream. He also said, "The time for token moves and talk is past." In his speech at American University, he had associated peace and freedom. The two were converging. As he was asking Americans to reassess their views of the Russians, he was asking them to do the same with 'Negroes.' Morality was in the air. In bidding Katzenbach good luck in Alabama, the attorney general had said, mockingly, "Don't worry . . . if you get shot . . . 'cause the President needs a moral issue."

Kennedy understood opportunity. He saw one here. He knew how quickly events can turn to your advantage, how calamity begets opportunity. Later that month, when King and other black leaders were at the White House attacking "Bull" Connor, the swaggering commissioner of public safety in Birmingham, Alabama, who had turned fire hoses and police dogs on peaceful demonstrators, Kennedy irreverently silenced the room. "You may be too hard on Bull Connor," he said to a collective gasp. "After all, Bull has proba-bly done more for civil rights than anyone else." Without those police wielding clubs and streams of water, without hundreds of soaking children filling the jails, there would be no revulsion at home and condemnation abroad. For all their contempt, the Kennedys owed George Wallace a lot that day. He might have been a poseur and a demagogue and a bumpkin, but he was now the leading protagonist in the useful melodrama playing out over the next thirty-six hours. Now, by George, they had a crisis – and a film crew to record it.

Early Afternoon

IN THE SPRING of 1960, Robert Drew was a filmmaker and editor of *Life* with a novel idea: he would make a documentary film on the presidential primary in Wisconsin, where Jack Kennedy and Hubert Humphrey were contesting the leadership of the Democratic Party. He promised both that he would take no sides and make no judgments in the filming and editing. All he asked was to follow them for five days from dawn to midnight. You'll just have to trust me, Drew told them. Kennedy was skeptical. "He gave me a long look and said, 'If I don't call you tomorrow, we're on,'" recalled Drew. "And he didn't call, and we were on." Humphrey agreed, too. Drew recruited Richard Leacock, another filmmaker, to join him in Wisconsin to follow Kennedy's campaign. A second team was assigned to Humphrey. Later, they were joined by D.A. Pennebaker, an engineer and filmmaker.

Drew was pioneering – some said refining – a revolutionary genre of filmmaking. In the documentary, the candidates would speak for themselves and not through others. There would be minimal narration. There would be no interviews, no title cards, no music, no cameras on tripods, no lighting. Nothing would be scripted or rehearsed. Everything would be spontaneous. To be more mobile and less obtrusive, the film crews carried small, light cameras, powered by a battery and linked to a tape recorder. Free of heavy equipment and cables, working with crews of two rather than eight, they could be nimble, almost invisible. The technology was so new that Drew had to improvise. True to the film crew's promise, the crews filmed everything and said nothing.

In Wisconsin, Kennedy was captivating and telegenic. So was Jackie. They were made for the camera. Humphrey was a fiery, folksy liberal who had neither the money nor the organization to compete with the Kennedys. What he did have, though, was an authentic populism and the familiarity of a native son of Minnesota, the state next door. He understood farmers and farming, which mattered in Wisconsin. For Jackie, courting the Badger State was a horror. "In Wisconsin, those people would stare at you like sort of animals," she recalled in 1964. "Because the people are alone all winter long, and cold, and just with animals, and they're so suspicious." For both sides, the campaign was exhausting and ultimately inconclusive. "Senator Humphrey and Senator Kennedy took us at our word, admitted us into their cars and buses, flogged themselves, and therefore us, to exhaustion every day," said Drew. He called it "a spiritual experience, based on something close to torture." Kennedy won, barely. To establish himself as the clear front-runner in the race, which would end that July at the Democratic National Convention in Los Angeles, he had to face Humphrey in another primary, this time in poor, Protestant West Virginia. He worried that his Catholicism would hurt him in Appalachia.

By then, though, Drew had his footage – twenty-six hours and 40,000 feet of it – and his film. *Primary*, a fifty-three minute documentary, was released later in 1960. The film is spare, honest, and revealing. Kennedy presses the flesh and bedazzles a young woman;

Humphrey grimaces on a televised call-in show when no one calls in. This is politics in still life, except that it isn't still. It's moving at its own pace, without embroidery. That's just what Drew wanted. He called it "candid" cinema, or "direct cinema," meaning no director or direction. In Europe, *Primary* became known as American *cinéma vérité*. "It was received as kind of a documentary second coming," Drew says. In 1990, *Primary* was listed on the National Film Registry of the Library of Congress. In 1960, no American network would broadcast it. "You've got some nice footage, there, Bob," they told Drew, but the film was too unorthodox for television. Still, *Life* asked Drew to keep making films.

After the election, Drew screened the film for JFK at the Kennedy family's winter home in Palm Beach, Florida. Kennedy liked it and invited his father, Joseph P. Kennedy Sr. (who had been a Hollywood mogul in the 1930s), to watch it. In *Primary*, Kennedy "saw himself day after day in different situations. There had never been a film like that on a president." Following the screening, Kennedy asked Drew what he wanted to do next. "I told him I wanted to make a film about a president having to make a decision with his back to the wall." He had read *Profiles in Courage*. "At the time I was proposing that we make a new kind of history of the presidency," recalls Drew, "that we would see and feel all the things that bore on the presidency at a given time – the expressions on their faces, the mood of the country, the tensions in the room, so that a future president could look back at this and see and learn. And I thought Kennedy, who had written a history book, might agree that history should be recorded in a different way." Kennedy was intrigued. "What if I could see what went on in the White House during the 24 hours before FDR declared war on Japan?" he wondered.

If recording history in the making was a persuasive argument, so was politics. Kennedy understood the impact of television. He may well have owed his narrow margin of victory in 1960 to winning the first-ever televised presidential debate, against Richard Nixon. Nixon sweated and squirmed; Kennedy was cool and still. Kennedy agonized over how he looked in photographs and on television. Was his hair in place? Had he put on weight? He wanted to come across as both a stylish and serious president. In front of Drew's cameras, he could appear to be just that. Kennedy invited Drew to the White House to do some tests; he wanted to see if he could forget the camera while Drew was filming. When Kennedy raised the idea of Drew's film with Jackie, in the director's presence, she was frosty: "Nobody moves into the White House with me." In the winter of 1961, Drew and two colleagues filmed Kennedy in the Oval Office while he was dealing with poverty in West Virginia and military maneuvers off Cuba. They were supposed to be there two days but stayed nearly eight. During one meeting with the Joint Chiefs of Staff, Drew recalls, one of the generals reminded the president that the camera was running. Kennedy smiled at Drew, Drew smiled back, and quietly left the meeting. In the end, forgetting the camera was easy for Kennedy; he was reliably unselfconscious, the kind of guy who could consult a prudish middle-aged nurse about his father's health while soaking nonchalantly in the bathtub. He was also, as Drew says, "the most astonishing package of confidence I've ever met." Drew's film became *Adventures on the New Frontier*. It was broadcast as a news special on ABC. Although it was the first time a sitting president had been filmed in this way, the film lacked tension. It had no impact.

For two years, Drew looked for a crisis. From time to time he would telephone Pierre Salinger and pitch an idea. Drew saw a tantalizing opportunity in the Bay of Pigs in 1961 and the Missile Crisis in 1962. The press secretary would always say no, claiming national security. Drew realized that it would have to be a domestic crisis. Then, in May 1963, Greg Shuker, who had worked for *Life* and was now researching for Drew, saw a newspaper story about Wallace's refusal to integrate the University of Alabama. "This is the crisis," Drew told Salinger. "This is it." This time, the cooperation of Robert Kennedy and the Justice Department was critical. Originally, the film was going to be shot in the office of the attorney general, in Alabama with Wallace, and, only if necessary, in the White House. In return for doing Salinger a minor favor, Drew asked Salinger for access to the Oval Office during the negotiations and got it. Drew made the same appeal to Wallace. Hearing the Kennedys had agreed, he agreed, too. So did the two students.

On the afternoon of June 10, film crews were in place in Montgomery, Birmingham, Washington, and Tuscaloosa. Robert Drew was overseeing the production from New York, where he would gather and edit the film. In Tuscaloosa, Richard Leacock was following Nicholas Katzenbach and his deputies. In Washington, D.A. Pennebaker and Greg Shuker were following the Kennedys. The film would be called *Crisis: Behind a Presidential Commitment*.

✳

Alabama laid claim to much of Kennedy's open afternoon. The attorney general, the assistant attorney general (Burke Marshall), special counsel (Ted Sorensen), appointments secretary (Kenneth O'Donnell), and special assistant (Lawrence O'Brien) do not appear on his agenda. Not that they ever would. But they flowed in and out of his office to discuss strategy. They were asking the same questions they had been asking one another for weeks. Should authorities remove Wallace physically if he did not step aside? Should they jail him? Should the students accompany the federal officials to the door? Should the president go on television that evening? Should he announce the civil rights bill? What would be in it?

It was 12:30 p.m. The bill-signing had ended a half hour earlier. In one of the early scenes of *Crisis*, the camera follows Robert Kennedy and Marshall as they ride in the back of a black-and-chrome, fin-tailed Cadillac from the Justice Department to the

White House. A meeting with the president, which had been scheduled for 5:30 p.m., had been rescheduled for now. Bobby, who talked to his brother from his office just after JFK had arrived at the White House, would spend much of his day on Capitol Hill selling civil rights. The camera alights on his neat typewritten schedule of meetings, which Mike Manatos, an assistant to the president, had arranged the week before. Bobby had taken his charm offensive to Capitol Hill to generate support for the bill. At 10:00 a.m., he would meet southern senators; at 2:30 p.m., liberal and other Democratic senators; at 4:00 p.m., the Democratic Study Group of the House of Representatives (a loose organization of liberals); at 5:30 p.m., border state and southern representatives (whom Manatos calls "doubtful but possible"). Bobby was there to explain the bill, though its precise contents were undecided on Monday.

The scene opens with the monstrous Cadillac approaching the wrought-iron gates of the White House. An anxious guard rushes to open one of the heavy gates, then the other, and scurries back to the first as it closes again. The car sweeps up the long, winding driveway to the south entrance. Bobby spills out before it comes to a stop, bounding up the manicured knoll to the columned portico outside the Oval Office. Inside, Bobby doesn't ask permission to enter from Mrs. Lincoln or Kenny O'Donnell, the two gatekeepers. It isn't necessary. He is the attorney general and the president's brother and holds just about every other extravagant title the contemporary press can confer: "the power behind the throne," "the second most powerful man in the government," "assistant president." To Jack, Bobby is indispensable – and never more so than on this day.

That is how the visit begins in the televised version of *Crisis*, the fifty-two-minute documentary broadcast on ABC that October. The two brothers confer quietly by the window. They haven't seen each other since the previous week. Soon everyone is seated in the Oval Office. JFK is in his padded rocking chair between two soft cream-colored couches. His brother and Marshall are to his left; Sorensen, O'Brien, and O'Donnell are on the right. They are discussing when to send the civil rights legislation to Congress. Someone proposes Thursday, then Friday. "There has to be a reason for putting this off," says the president, a challenge to those advising delay. O'Brien reports that the congressional leaders have asked the administration not to send it up before Wednesday. In fact, it will not reach the Hill until June 18, eight days from now.

Sorensen is chairing the meeting. He enjoys the responsibility and runs through the agenda briskly: "The next question is whether you'll make a nationwide TV address in connection with sending up the message."

JFK: "I didn't think so. It just really depends on whether we have something – trouble up on the University – then I would. Otherwise, I don't think that we would, at this point."

RFK: "I think it would be helpful. I think there's a reason to do it. I think you can talk about the legislation then talk about education, unemployment. To do it for fifteen minutes, I think would alleviate a lot of problems."

JFK: "I don't want to do it for a half hour."

RFK: "Fifteen minutes. Even if there isn't trouble in Alabama, it's a step forward. You would give a real explanation of the situation. That these problems are going to be with us for many years."

JFK listens, chin resting in his hand.

"We would come across as reasonable, understanding –," says Bobby. He's interrupted by a skeptic who says, "You're gonna make a speech and nothing is going to happen."

His brother remains silent. RFK insists that the speech would affirm that the federal government "is making an effort and, although there will be problems, we'd hope the Negroes would understand their responsibilities [to be lawful]. . . ."

However, Larry O'Brien, the stocky special assistant, flatly opposes the speech. At 52, he counts votes in Congress and he knows they aren't there. "I don't see any advantage" in having the speech now, he says. "This thing carries itself."

Bobby interrupts with a larger point: "You're going to have a lot of people saying: 'Why doesn't the president speak on this?'" O'Brien thinks the speech should come later, when it can be most effective. "I think you get to the nut-cutting on the Hill . . . that's when you want to do this . . . [give the speech]."

"But that won't be until September, October, or November," counters Bobby. "I don't think you can get by now without . . . having an address on television, at least during that period of time, giving some direction and having it in the hands of the president."

O'Brien lights a cigarette. Once or twice, when JFK begins speaking, Bobby pre-empts him, and he winces and relents with a hint of exasperation. JFK says, "We're gonna get something ready anyway cause we may need that tomorrow." He defers to his brother.

"We have a draft," says Bobby. "Now it doesn't fit all the points, but it is something to work with. And there are some pretty good sentences and paragraphs."

"All right," says JFK. "It will help us get ready, because we may want to do it tomorrow."

Now we know that Kennedy is considering an address on civil rights on Tuesday, June 11. The conversation leaves the impression that such a speech is a strong possibility and will be written. The narrator certainly thinks so. "The president is still undecided, but the speech will be prepared," he intones. In fact, nothing is decided and no instructions are issued. Kennedy, who will make the speech, leaves the meeting apparently thinking that a speech will be written, just in case. Sorensen, who will write the speech, leaves the meeting apparently thinking that a speech will not be written, because it is unnecessary. Their divergent interpretations will collide the next afternoon.

※

As the president and his advisors talked in Washington, things were taking shape in Tuscaloosa. Despite confident claims, then and now, there was no script for this spectacle. How could there be if no one knew what Wallace would say and how the federal government would respond? There was an amphitheater, a cast, props, and stage directions. There were stagehands, ushers, dressers, and a circle of critics in the caravan of journalists rolling into town. When students began arriving at the University of Alabama for the first day of summer registration, they found entrances blocked and state troopers manning checkpoints. "Many of the troopers bowed to the charms of the coeds trying to move their clothing past the tight campus barricades," reported UPI. "Some, with sheepish grins, left their positions to carry electric fans, armfuls of clothing and luggage for the girls returning for the summer session."

Wallace left Montgomery in a red-and-beige, single-engine Cessna at 1:33 p.m. on Monday and landed in Tuscaloosa at 2:18 p.m. (4:18 p.m. in Washington). Motorcycles escorted him to the Hotel Stafford, where he set up headquarters. Later, at dinner, he met the university trustees. They obediently issued a unanimous statement maintaining that the "presence of Governor Wallace is necessary to preserve peace and order." Of course, as Kennedy had told Wallace in his wire earlier that day, Governor, posture all you want, but you're the provocation, not the students. The trustees, cowed by Wallace, gave him the empty endorsement he wanted.

The federal officials from Washington, led by Nicholas Katzenbach, were also assembling that afternoon. Katzenbach, at forty-one years old, was the administration's point man – clever, quick, lanky, funny, and tough. As a navigator in the Second World War, he was shot down over the Mediterranean Sea and sent to prisoner-of-war camps in Germany and Italy. He tried twice to escape. With time on his hands, he read 400 books. A graduate of Princeton and Yale Law School, he was a star goalie in college hockey. He also spent two years at Oxford as a Rhodes Scholar.

After teaching law at Yale and the University of Chicago in the 1950s, he was recruited as one of Bobby Kennedy's hotshot lawyers. He was named assistant attorney general in 1961 and the next year deputy attorney general, the second-highest position in the Department of Justice.

Katzenbach spent Monday afternoon reviewing the meticulous arrangements for Tuesday's confrontation. At the government's headquarters on campus, he was pleased to see a spidery antenna on the back of the building; remembering the breakdown in communications at Ole Miss the previous fall, the Army Signal Corps had installed a sophisticated radio system. There was even a direct line to Berlin and NATO (no one knew why); Katzenbach said he would be satisfied with a dependable connection to the White House. He studied the route to the campus that he would take the next day and went over the plans "for the nth time." Importantly, he had decided that Malone and Hood would not accompany him to the door. They would stay in the car. He and Bobby didn't want them exposed to insult from the governor or the pain of rejection. And then, what? Katzenbach worried that leaving the campus would look like "a retreat." So he shrewdly collected the keys to their dormitories from Frank Rose. He would take the students directly to their rooms if Wallace refused to yield.

Maybe, Katzenbach wondered that afternoon, he might not have to confront Wallace at all. Legally, the students were already enrolled; technically, the university had accepted them. Couldn't they just register and pay their fees for the summer term? It seemed reasonable enough. But when Katzenbach talked to Bobby on the telephone and suggested bypassing Wallace, Kennedy disagreed. "Bobby said, I think rightly, that if we denied Wallace his show, the danger of violence would increase." Then again, if Wallace had his show and refused to move, that was another danger. "If they arrest Governor Wallace, all hell will break loose," a "high university official" told the New York Times on June 9. If all hell did break loose, though, this time the government would be ready. More than three thousand soldiers were in the state ready to be deployed. Major General Creighton Abrams, deputy chief of staff for operations at the Pentagon, was in charge in Tuscaloosa. As arranged with Bobby, he dressed in civilian clothes to play down his rank, purpose, and authority.

In the meantime, Wallace was assembling a large supporting cast of his own and preparing himself for the next day. Under the direction of Colonel Albert J. Lingo, Alabama's much-reviled director of public safety, he had turned Tuscaloosa into a garrison. Lingo had raised a constabulary of 825 law enforcement officers made up of 425 state troopers and 400 revenue agents, game wardens, and others deputized as officers. In addition to sealing the campus entrances with yellow barricades ("No Trespassing" read the signs), the university had agreed to order students to stay in their dormitories between 10:00 p.m. and 6:00 a.m.

*

A second unscheduled meeting of JFK and his advisors took place on Monday, probably later in the afternoon. Its purpose was to review strategy for the next day. As with much of Drew's film, whether outtakes or the documentary, it is hard to know exactly what happened when. Scenes appear out of sequence. In the raw film, there are sometimes pictures with no sound, sometimes sound with no pictures. When the president orders, "Let's cut this now," the filmmakers shut off the cameras immediately. They understand they may be asked to leave the Oval Office at any time.

In the meeting, Kennedy is enthroned in his rocking chair, where he always sits. By now his dark oak rocker, with its low rattan seat and broad armrests and pale cushions, has become an image of his presidency. It is ironic that it should come to represent a man of action, but for Kennedy it does; for a man in pain, the rocker was relief. Actually, there was more than one rocker. There were rockers in the Oval Office, Mrs. Lincoln's office, the Yellow Oval Room, and JFK's bedroom. There were also rockers at Camp David, Hyannis Port, and Palm Beach. After Jackie left the White House, she took them with her. Two were sold in an auction of Jackie's estate in 1996 for $442,500 and $453,500. Another went to Anthony Radziwill, the son of Lee Radziwill, Jackie's younger sister. Aunt Jackie sent it to Anthony with a note when he moved to his cramped bachelor pad on 78th Street in New York City: "I thought you might like to have this. It belonged to Jack." Radziwill refused his live-in girlfriend's entreaties to return the cumbersome rocker, which had practical as well as sentimental value. "Where would I dry my gym clothes?" he asked.

In his office, the film shows JFK rising from his rocker and resting his hands on its back. Then he walks to the center of the room, his hands in his pockets. He and his advisors are now discussing the wording of a warning to Wallace on the prospect of sending in federal troops, which he expects he will have to order tomorrow if Wallace doesn't step aside. "Your defiance of the law may compel others to do the same," Kennedy says, trying out language. "Therefore I am compelled to call up the National Guard. . . ."

JFK moves behind his desk. It was built from the mahogany timbers of HMS *Resolute*, a nineteenth-century British exploratory vessel, which was abandoned in the Arctic, found by the U.S. Navy, refurbished, and returned as a gift to Queen Victoria. When *Resolute* was broken up, a grateful Victoria had the desk made for President Rutherford B. Hayes in 1880. Jackie discovered the desk in the basement of the White House and had it restored for her husband. On its gilded leather top sits a black alligator leather blotter with brass trim. Nearby is a plaque with a line from one of JFK's favorite nautical poems: "O God, thy sea is so great and my boat is so small."

Kennedy looks tired, his eyes sunken, his expression somber. Yet his whole body is in motion. There is a jumpiness about him.

This was not peculiar to that afternoon; it was his nature. (William Manchester mentioned this hyperactivity after he had observed the president closely two years earlier.) Kennedy taps the desk. He slips his hand in his jacket pocket – everyone wears suit jackets in the Oval Office – as if he isn't sure where to put it. RFK walks to the side of the desk and picks up the receiver from the large, green, multiline telephone console. He is trying to reach Cyrus Vance, secretary of the army. While Bobby is on the phone to his left, the president leans back in his chair, one foot on the desk, gyrating, slapping his knee, rhythmically. He cannot sit still.

With a note of impatience in his voice, JFK discusses, with Sorensen, the wording of the warning to Wallace. They test other words and phrases. Bobby consults Sorensen, too, then leaves through the French doors the way he came in.

✳

It was now 1:56 p.m. Kennedy had been conferring with his advisors for almost two hours. It was time for his midday recess. Usually, he would have had a swim before going upstairs, but he skipped it that day. If he was following his usual route, he left the Oval Office through the Colonnade that leads past the Rose Garden, through the red-carpeted hall, and up the elevator to the family quarters on the second floor.

In June 1963, the White House looked far different – inside, outside, upstairs, and downstairs – than it had in January 1961. Jackie had found it as dowdy as a budget motel. "Everything looked like it came from B. Altman [a defunct New York department store]," she sighed. Walking through the state rooms on February 18, 1961, economist John Kenneth Galbraith lamented that the paintings "have deteriorated in quality with the later presidents." Repelled by mediocre art, imitation antiques, worn carpets, and wooden floors pockmarked by Ike's golf shoes, Jackie decided to restore the residence. "I want to make the White House the first house in the land," she declared.

Jackie enlisted "Sister" Parish, the leading interior decorator of the time, and Stéphane Boudin, the Parisian designer who had advised on the restoration of the Palace of Versailles. Then she appealed to wealthy benefactors to fund the project. Without public financing, she needed them. It wasn't easy. "You'd have ninety-nine cups of tea with some old lady and she'd give you fifty dollars," she sniffed. To raise money, she created the White House Historical Association. It published *The White House*, a 143-page, richly illustrated guide to the history, architecture, and decor of the mansion. It sold 500,000 copies in six months.

Ten months later, the White House glowed. Jackie hosted a one-hour televised tour on February 14, 1962. Broadcast on CBS, the program was called *A Tour of the White House with Mrs. John F. Kennedy*. She chatted with correspondent Charles Collingwood as she took viewers through the newly restored rooms. She described the silverware, china, paintings, and furniture, confidently throwing off the names of artisans and painters, as well as the donors, their gifts, and the dates of acquisition. It was, in its way, a history lesson. Later, she was joined by her husband. Fifty-six million Americans watched. They saw and heard a poised, articulate Jackie, with a voice so breathy, soft, and small that her friends doubted it was hers at all. She felt that she had done badly, and critics found the broadcast poorly edited and directed. But viewers applauded and visits to the White House surged.

The first couple's interest in the aesthetic extended beyond the Executive Mansion. They were aghast to hear of plans to tear down some of the nineteenth-century townhouses on the edge of Lafayette Square across from the White House. They helped stop the demolition. The Kennedys were alarmed as well with the deterioration of Pennsylvania Avenue, the ceremonial thoroughfare running from Georgetown, past the White House, to Capitol Hill. It had interested Kennedy for years. On the afternoon he returned from his Inauguration, he was struck anew by its tawdriness, a blight that was infecting the city's core. He created a committee, advised by the esteemed sociologist Daniel Patrick Moynihan, a future senator, to address the problem. Kennedy followed the committee's progress closely.

＊

Kennedy was changing the image of the presidency in 1963. Roosevelt, Truman, and Eisenhower had not cared how things looked. Now, in a new decade, beauty, vitality, and gaiety mattered. It's "Jack's Town," declared Hugh Sidey in *Time* on June 7. "Just 29 months into his presidency, Kennedy sets the style, tastes, and temper of Washington more surely than Franklin Roosevelt did in twelve years, Dwight Eisenhower in eight, Harry Truman in seven. A politician's politician in a city that loves and lives politics, Kennedy is slavishly followed – and more than slightly feared." Sidey contemplated the phenomenon of the New Frontiersman – the young and brainy strivers "who like to talk of their travels, always by jet and generally to some far-off land." "When they talk," he said, "it is as if they had invented the town."

Or, reinvented. Cigar sales were up. Dark, well-cut, two-button suits were in (JFK wore them); button-down shirts were out (JFK disliked them). PT-boat tie clasps – a replica of the flimsy speedboat that JFK skippered (and lost) in the South Pacific in the Second World War – were fashionable. The new distaste for hats was blamed on the president, who refused to wear one, though hat sales had been falling since the 1920s. Yet such was JFK's influence that "a hatless Jack" was a killer of hats. In 1963, American hatmakers were apoplectic. They sent Kennedy hats and pleaded with him to wear them.

The president's sphere of influence surpassed style. In 1963 came a mania for self-improvement. Runners crowded the towpath along the Chesapeake and Ohio (C&O) Canal, and the Royal Canadian Air Force exercise manual was in demand. Touch football was popular. At a pool party at Lyndon Johnson's home in northwest Washington in 1962, an entertainer parodied the fitness craze, mimicking Kennedy's Bostonian accent:

> Walk to work, folks, it ain't hard,
> Pak your cah in the Hahvard yard;
> Never mind the tax cut, never mind Goa –
> One and a two and a three and a foah.

Politicians were collecting historical quotations on cards to use in speeches, as JFK did. Speed-reading gained a following on Capitol Hill. Le Bistro and The Jockey Club, restaurants serving the light Continental dishes that Jackie favoured, were flourishing while The Colony, beloved by the Eisenhower administration, had closed. Even Jackie's pregnancy was noteworthy. "Now she is pregnant," wrote Sidey, "and a favorite greeting among the capital's menfolk is: 'Is your wife pregnant? Mine is.'"

✳

Unlike her sister-in-law, Ethel, and her mother-in-law, Rose, both mothers of large broods, Jackie had only two children: Caroline Bouvier Kennedy, born November 27, 1957, and John Fitzgerald Kennedy Jr., born November 25, 1960. She had had a miscarriage and, on August 23, 1956, a stillborn baby girl the couple named Arabella. In the second week of June 1963, Jackie was two months away from giving birth again. She was already limiting her official commitments. When JFK returned to the family quarters at this hour, Jackie would normally lunch with him. On June 10 and the morning of June 11, though, she and the children were at Camp David.

On his way to the residence, Kennedy passed through, or near, the newly restored Blue Room, Red Room, Green Room, East Room, and Main Hall. The president was accompanied by a Secret Service agent, and his movements were clocked. The staff always knew when to expect him. "The President has left for the mansion," was the signal. The family quarters awaiting him had also been redecorated. If the downstairs was history, the upstairs was domesticity. If downstairs was public like a museum and purposeful like an office, upstairs was intimate like a home. The tone was subdued and tasteful. It was also a touch aristocratic, like its tenants. Unlike the middle-brow Eisenhowers, the Kennedys did not listen to the "champagne music" of bandleader Lawrence Welk or eat supper on metal trays watching television. Their rarefied tastes in color, art, and furnishings reflected their privileged lives in Newport, Hyannis Port, Palm Beach, and Georgetown.

The day after the Inauguration, a brigade of tradesmen laid siege to the seven rooms of the mansion. Jackie saw horrors everywhere, recalled J.B. West, chief usher of the White House. Mamie Eisenhower's bedroom curtains were "seasick green," and their fringe "a tired Christmas tree." Jackie gleefully cast aside "Mamie pink," the "Grand Rapids furniture," and the "hideous" Victorian mirrors. She rearranged and reorganized. When the color of a wall was not exactly the tone she wanted, she had it repainted until it was. Jackie didn't want her own bedroom to be "severe enough for a man to share," because "it is mainly my room and I do not want it *too* severe." She chose a light blue chintz, accented with leopard-skin throws. West called it "soft, relaxed, and elegant."

The family quarters were not ideal. One visitor found the living space "makeshift, a potpourri of rooms which do not relate to the whole." William Manchester recalled that the hidden elevator that JFK rode up and down every day opened "into a small vestibule which debouches into a huge hall. This passage runs east and west, bisecting the entire floor like a concourse and creating something of a traffic problem." Manchester felt "the effect could easily be that of a refurbished New York elevator flat. It's not, because the great, barnlike corridor has been toned down by an ingenious use of color, *objets d'art*, and graceful furniture. Slipcovered French chairs are grouped invitingly on off-white rugs. Lovely chandeliers sparkle overhead. American paintings by . . . Maurice Prendergast, Winslow Homer, and John Singer Sargent hang on tinted walls, and below them are handsomely mounted vases and sculptures, a Louis Quinze desk, and a spinet." Manchester also took note of the bookcases filled to overflowing with first editions and old favorites. Prints and paintings were everywhere: in the bedrooms, in the public rooms, in the nursery, in Caroline's room, where Jackie hung a primitive oil painting by Grandma Moses she had found in West's office.

The Kennedys devoured books. Jack and Jackie were literary animals. Both wrote and appreciated writing. Whatever the strains in their ten years of marriage, they would always meet, metaphorically, in the library in the way other couples, notably Harold Nicholson and Vita Sackville-West were said to meet in the garden. The volumes rose in endless tiers: art, history, biography, Churchill's memoirs, Harper Lee's *To Kill a Mockingbird*. There was a battered copy of JFK's *Profiles in Courage*, which Manchester thought "a shabby orphan here, because everything else is tidy and quietly expensive." Lest the bedazzled visitor forget where he or she was, embossed matchbooks announced, in gold: *The President's House.*

*

Kennedy never ate at his desk as president, though he often did as a senator, tucking into the hampers that Jackie sent over from Georgetown with the president's valet, George Thomas. Occasionally he had a business lunch in the Family Dining Room downstairs, but he tried to avoid them. "They were really heavy," said

Jackie. "They were hard for him. You're always awfully tired at the end of one of those White House mornings in your office, and your nerves are on edge." That day, as usual, he had put some files under his arm before heading upstairs. Lunch was often a grilled-cheese sandwich, or slices of cold beef on their own, or a hamburger, perhaps with a cup of consommé. There was sometimes tea at lunch, or a glass of milk. He drank coffee only in the morning.

Divided between office and home, Kennedy's average work day was around fourteen hours. He had come to realize the value of a rest after lunch. Sleep was also his way of separating things. For Kennedy, it was like friends, lovers, associates, pleasures, ideas – just another of life's compartments. "He never took a nap before, but in the White House, I think he made up his mind he would because it would be so good for his health," said Jackie. He knew that Churchill had napped and, like Churchill, Kennedy found it restorative, particularly when he was very busy. At this hour, the second floor was always still. "The Kennedys' early afternoons, while the children were napping, were spent in absolute privacy," recalled J.B. West. "Quite often, music was heard floating out into the hall. . . ." The president repaired to his deep-blue bedroom, usually with official papers; a four-poster, canopied bed had migrated from another room to Kennedy's. For his back, he slept on a custom-made horsehair mattress, the same kind he had on *Air Force One*. Jackie had put one on his side of their two-mattress bed in her room as well.

In October 1963, Jim Bishop spent a few days in the White House watching the Kennedys. *A Day in the Life of President Kennedy* was published shortly after JFK's death. Bishop noted the ritual of the nap, how typically at this time of the afternoon, around 3:00 p.m., the president undressed and slipped into bed. Jackie marveled that he changed into his pajamas. "I used to think, for a forty-five-minute nap, why would you bother to take off all your clothes? It would take me forty-five minutes to just snuggle down and start to doze off." George Thomas would ritually draw the drapes. "Mr. President, what time do you want me to call you?" he would ask. "Three-thirty, George," was the usual reply. It didn't take Kennedy long to fall asleep. "After a few minutes the papers are tossed on a chair, the light is snapped off, and the President stretches out on the bed, his eyes closed," wrote Bishop, as if he were tucking him in.

But Bishop doubted that Kennedy slept much at naptime: ". . . his mind is alert to the problems of his office, and whether he wills it or not, they ride the mental carousel as they do with other mortals. Still, there is a relaxation, a midday lassitude which permeates the second floor." On the afternoon of June 10, 1963, Kennedy's carousel was crowded. He had returned to Washington after an absence that would create work in the most efficient office. He had flown overnight for nine hours through six time zones. He had given a seminal speech under an unforgiving sun and was now awaiting a response. Then after attending a signing ceremony, he had spent two hours conferring with his advisors on a racial crisis. It was only midafternoon.

Monday, June 10, 1963
CHAPTER 5

Late Afternoon

ON DECEMBER 26, 1960, an unusual essay appeared under an unlikely byline in *Sports Illustrated*. The topic was physical fitness. The author was John F. Kennedy. The newly established magazine – not yet profitable and not yet publishing its risqué annual swimsuit edition – had given the president-elect a platform three-and-a-half weeks before taking office. Instead of a light reflection on football, swimming, or golf – the kind of breezy, personal testimonial you might expect from a new president – he chose, more gravely, to sound the alarm over America's declining physical fitness. Physical fitness would become a minor theme of his presidency, a forerunner of the next generation's obsession with exercise and diet. Here, in Kennedy's two thousand well-chosen words, was an early manifesto on the benefits of physical *and* intellectual health. He called it, a little sternly, "The Soft American."

Invoking the ancient Greeks, Kennedy tied the physical well-being of the individual to the well-being of the nation. The United States was missing that lesson, he warned, with disturbing consequences in the Cold War. The physical strength and ability of Americans had been in decline since the Korean War, he observed; the Selective Service was rejecting one of every two young men as mentally, morally, or physically unfit. He was particularly disturbed by the findings of a fifteen-year comparative study of the physical fitness of European and American children by Dr. Hans Kraus (a physiatrist in New York City who would later treat his ailing back) and Dr. Sonja Weber. They found almost 60 percent of American children had failed one or more of six tests of muscular strength and flexibility; only some 9 percent of the Europeans had. On five strength tests, 35 percent of American children had failed; only 1 percent of Europeans had. Furthermore, he said, things were getting worse. In 1950, 51 percent of freshmen at Yale had passed physical fitness tests; in 1960, only 38 percent had.

"The harsh fact of the matter is that there is . . . an increasingly large number of young Americans who are neglecting their bodies – whose physical fitness is not what it should be – who are getting soft," Kennedy wrote. "And such softness on the part of individual citizens can help to strip and destroy the vitality of a nation." JFK thought one way to get the country "moving again" was to get fit again. There was something else here, too. Bemoaning the missile gap and Soviet advances in space in the 1960 campaign had made him a reliable rhetorician of the Cold War. On January 20, 1961, he would deliver an Inaugural Address asking Americans to "pay any price . . . oppose any foe . . . to assure the survival and the success of liberty," harsher than his appeal of "making the world safe for diversity" that he had made that morning at American University.

In *Sports Illustrated*, Kennedy linked physical fitness and national security. Young Americans had won wars because they were fit. Their stamina had not come from a few weeks of basic training; it came from a lifetime of physical activity. "Our struggles against aggressors throughout our history have been won on the playgrounds and corner lots and fields of America," he said. "Thus, in a very real and immediate sense, our growing softness, our increasing lack of physical fitness, is a menace to our security." In the Cold War, physical fitness was fundamental. "To meet the challenge of this enemy will require determination and will and effort on the part of all Americans," Kennedy wrote. "Only if our citizens are physically fit will they be fully capable of such an effort." If the language sounded jingoistic, its intent was not to turn America into Sparta. Kennedy wanted strong bodies to build strong minds, not to wage war. Physical fitness was the basis of intellect, creativity, imagination; it was about fulfilling human promise. "If our bodies grow soft and inactive, if we fail to encourage physical development and prowess," he warned, "we will undermine our capacity for thought, for work and for the use of those skills vital to an expanding and complex America."

In this struggle the enemy was abundance and leisure. Too much time, too many conveniences. Labor was being "engineered" out of working life by clever industrial devices and machines. Parking lots in high schools were full because students were driving rather than walking to class. All those frivolous distractions – movies, television – were as fattening as a Duncan Hines chocolate cake for dessert and Coca-Cola for breakfast. Long before DVD players, remote controls, video games, and laptop computers, Kennedy warned of the armchair culture. In 1963 Americans smoked heavily, drank heartily, ate badly, exercised rarely, and died early.

Kennedy himself led an active life. As these two days show, he was restless by nature. He was always in motion, so much so that he would not sit still for an artist painting his portrait or a national security briefing. While he may have been called "an outdoorsman" – a *de facto* constitutional requirement of every president – he was not in any conventional sense. He did not fish like Herbert Hoover or hunt like Teddy Roosevelt. At Harvard, Kennedy had been a competitive swimmer, making the varsity squad, and a dogged football player, making the junior varsity team. As adults, the Kennedy brothers played touch football boisterously on their broad lawn at Hyannis Port. Jack played golf (he sent Arnold Palmer a film of his swing, asking the 'King's' advice). Mostly, sailing was his thing. This was the iconic Kennedy pictured on the cover of that *Sports Illustrated*, with his essay inside. In cuffed khakis, polo shirt, tortoiseshell sunglasses, hair tousled in the salty breeze, always at the tiller.

Vain to a fault, Kennedy fussed about his weight which he checked every day, even when he was travelling, bringing his scales with him. He drank Metrecal, a diet drink introduced in 1959 with a name generated by a computer (a combination of *metre* and *calories*). Two hundred and twenty-five calories of milkshake in a can, it was filling and tasty. In 1963 it was flying off supermarket shelves along with the new diet drinks, Diet Rite Cola and Tab. Kennedy had never been heavy – in fact, as a young congressman he was scrawny – but cortisone injections for his back left his face puffy. He worried about developing both a paunch and "the Fitzgerald breasts" inherited from the men on his mother's side of the family. Few things interested him more than a discussion of his own weight, recalled Ben Bradlee, the journalist, who often dined with his wife, Antoinette ("Tony"), at the White House.

On the evening of March 12, 1963, Kennedy invited the Bradlees into his bedroom to show off the ceramic jewelry box that Tony had made him for Christmas. As their host disrobed unselfconsciously for bed, Bradlee observed that he had put on weight. "Isn't it fantastic?" JFK sighed. "Friday I weighed 171 and everyone told me I was looking great. Four days later, I weigh 177 and I had two helpings of that dessert tonight." The dessert had been meringues with whipped cream and chocolate sauce. Bradlee thought that he weighed more than 177. Kennedy rushed to the scales and reported that he was exactly 177 pounds, not acceptable to this Narcissus. "But I weighed 175 after swimming," he moaned.

If good health was an obsession for Kennedy, it was because he had known so little of it. On some days, when his back was in revolt, he was almost an invalid, far from the public image of him as a member of the *jeunesse dorée*. He was bound by his corset and back brace, a medieval harness of straps and clasps and buckles; he often needed help to get it on and off. For much of his presidency, he could not bend down or pick up his children. Beyond his bad back, which some suggested would have put him in a wheelchair by the end of his forties, Kennedy was taking medication for other problems. Forty years would pass before his many illnesses and ailments (influenza, malaria, jaundice, arthritis, osteoporosis, adrenal insufficiency, colitis, Addison's disease, Crohn's disease, duodenal ulcer) became known.

On these two days in June, Kennedy was not free of pain, although that summer he said he felt better than he had in years. In fact, his back was bothering him this week as it had last week. Like Woodrow Wilson and Franklin Roosevelt, he found ways to hide weakness. In 1963, Americans knew little of Kennedy's infirmity other than that he had undergone back operations, which had kept him absent from the Senate in the mid-1950s. Occasionally they saw him on crutches. He kept quiet because he worried the truth would undo him. Perhaps it might have, but his quiet forbearance might also have ennobled him. The reality was that he dissembled and prevaricated about his health before and during his presidency, all the while projecting great vitality. If living with pain was the art of being John F. Kennedy, denying it was the artifice. He was superb at both.

As a candidate, Kennedy called sports participation and physical fitness "a basic and continuing policy of the United States." While the president could issue no order, Congress could pass no law, and the Supreme Court could deliver no judgment creating a fitter America, he used his soapbox to trumpet it. That's why on the afternoon of Monday, June 10 – having lunched, napped, changed his clothes (again), and returned to the office at 3:52 p.m. – he turned his attention to the nation's health. Over the next two hours and twenty-seven minutes, he would see more than a dozen visitors in five meetings on different issues. At 4:28 p.m., it was time to discuss "the soft American" with Bud Wilkinson, his envoy of exercise.

*

In 1963, Wilkinson was perhaps the leading college football coach in the United States. (His rival was "Bear" Bryant of the University of Alabama.) As coach of the University of Oklahoma Sooners, the team finished first in the "Big Seven" from 1948 to 1959; their forty-seven straight victories from 1953 to 1957 was a National Collegiate Athletic Association record. In a country mad for college football, Wilkinson's style was legendary. "Never at any time did Coach Wilkinson raise his voice at a player other than to offer encouragement," said a former player. "Never did I hear Coach Wilkinson make an alibi when we lost. Never did I hear him boast or put down the other team when we won." At six feet two inches and 190 pounds, forty-seven years old and strikingly handsome, "Bud Wilkinson could probably charm the mittens off a polar bear."

Within a month of taking office in 1961, Kennedy had established an annual National Youth Fitness Congress, attended by all the governors, to assess progress every year. He placed responsibility for physical fitness within the Department of Health, Education and Welfare and reorganized the President's Council on Physical Fitness, which he asked Wilkinson to lead. Unwilling to leave football, Wilkinson agreed to take on the position as an unpaid consultant for six months of the year. That was enough to make him the face of physical fitness. Wilkinson was Kennedy's kind of guy – a Navy man, a fine athlete, a winning coach with a master's in English and a talent for music. He married the toughness of the gridiron with the refinement of the academy. It made chats like today's one of those pleasant diversions of office.

Coach Wilkinson worried that one of four Americans was overweight and one of two died of diseases of the heart and circulatory system. He worried that 'chore' was no longer a household word and that teenagers were spending fifteen to thirty hours a week watching television. Americans needed to exercise more. Over the past two years, Wilkinson had developed the basic concepts of a physical fitness program, which was now in use in more than half the country's schools. He also urged the general public to adopt an exercise regimen, including knee bends and knee lifts, of fifteen to twenty minutes a day. So keen was the White House to champion physical fitness that it launched an ambitious national publicity campaign in schools and the press. It even enlisted Superman, the comic book hero. DC Comics collaborated with the administration on a special issue encouraging young Americans to lead healthier lives. It was called "Superman's Mission for President Kennedy."

But nothing in 1963 "generated more public enthusiasm than the hiking craze that burst forth in mid-winter," Wilkinson reported. It began when Kennedy read a letter Theodore Roosevelt had written to the commandant of the U.S. Marine Corps in 1908 proposing that marines walk fifty miles in twenty hours. Kennedy wrote General David M. Shoup, the current commandant, suggesting that his marines undertake the hike to show they were as fit as their predecessors. Shoup accepted the challenge and ordered his marines to set out from Camp Lejeune in North Carolina the next week on a fifty-mile hike. Kennedy thought someone from the White House should join them. "Looking at my waistline as he spoke," Pierre Salinger recalled, the president asked him to go. His press secretary was not a physical specimen. Despite a reputation as a womanizer – Katie Louchheim speculated about the infidelity of the much-married Salinger in her diary – he was twenty pounds overweight.

"Why not Ken O'Donnell?" countered Salinger, volunteering Kennedy's humorless special assistant, who had captained Harvard's football team. "No," Kennedy replied. "It should be somebody who needs the exercise — somebody who would be an inspiration to millions of other out-of-shape Americans." Salinger pressed the point, suggesting Kennedy shouldn't take TR too literally. Hadn't he taken San Juan Hill on a horse? The president insisted: "There is no escape, Pierre, I intend to follow Teddy's letter to the letter."

Salinger was thirty-seven years old, five feet nine, 185 pounds, and in terrible shape. True, he had been a cross-country runner at San Francisco College, where he had twice finished tenth when the eleventh runner dropped out. Once a boxer, he claimed that he had knocked himself out with an uppercut that deflected off the paunch of his opponent and hit him in the chin. He was no longer running or boxing. "I was never without a cigar, a thirst, or an appetite," he admitted. "I was clearly *not* a fit representative of the New Frontier." He tried manfully to extricate himself, but the president was too amused to let it go. Kennedy relished this kind of joke and sometimes took it too far, even with his resident Falstaff.

Salinger heard that General Godfrey McHugh, the president's Air Force aide, had said that he would walk. Seizing upon this, Salinger offered McHugh and issued a press release saying the president wanted the aide to go. McHugh refused. So Salinger concocted a challenge from General Chester Clifton, the president's ranking military advisor, arguing that McHugh, an airman, should not usurp the role of the foot soldier. Later, after a day of dueling press releases, the White House announced that Salinger, McHugh, and Clifton *all* would walk. They would set out at 7:00 a.m. on February 15, 1963, along the C & O Canal towpath, chosen, Salinger cracked, because it was accessible to ambulances. Actually, he was feeling cocky; he had slyly begun training the week before, walking five miles.

Before February 15, though, Bobby Kennedy took a fifty-mile hike of his own. With characteristic bravura he persuaded four colleagues, all athletes and war veterans, to accompany him. They planned to walk from Washington to Camp David. The attorney general wore less-than-sensible leather oxford shoes. Eventually everyone but him dropped out. Bobby made it, through slush and snow, his feet blistered and bleeding. It took him seventeen hours. But as Bobby walked, so did the nation. The White House received letters about "the 50-mile hike" and a deluge of recommendations for routes, records, and awards. It became a national craze through February and March. "The sight of Boy Scout troops, college students, housewives and middle-aged husbands and fathers marching along the nation's highways and backroads was commonplace," Wilkinson wrote. "Relatively few lasted the distance but most of them set out to walk 50 miles."

Salinger was not among them. Despite his new confidence, he warned Kennedy, "You are backing a loser." The president agreed. He relieved Salinger but asked him to find a creative excuse for withdrawing. Salinger called Dick Snider, the administrator of the Council on Physical Fitness. "The fifty-mile hike craze is getting out of hand," he told him. "Don't you agree there's a danger that people with bad hearts or other infirmities might do permanent harm to themselves by attempting hikes that are clearly beyond their capability?" The council then issued a warning. Subsequently, in a facetious exchange with reporters, Salinger mentioned the warning, noted that Robert Kennedy had walked on behalf of the administration, and announced his withdrawal. "I may be plucky but I am not stupid," he told reporters.

Of course, no one was asking the president to walk. He had no interest in hiking. He knew how to ride, but his sports were not canoeing, mountaineering, hiking, skiing, or skating (all of which his brothers Bobby and Teddy did). As much as he enjoyed the sea, he had no passion for the wilderness of Teddy Roosevelt, a rancher, horseman, hunter, ornithologist, botanist, and explorer, or FDR, who collected and stuffed birds as a boy. Arthur Schlesinger thought

Kennedy was "too eastern in his background" to be interested in the outdoors. Ben Bradlee called JFK "the most urbane person" he had ever met. Kennedy did establish the Cape Cod National Seashore and propose a Wilderness Act. Personally, though, the natural world held little appeal for him. Stewart Udall, a refined Arizonan who was secretary of the interior under Kennedy and Johnson, regretted Kennedy's indifference. Udall hoped that Kennedy would "make a record as a conservationist which will compare favorably with that of Theodore Roosevelt." When Kennedy visited Grand Teton in Wyoming in September 1963, Udall innocently asked O'Donnell to schedule a half-hour walk to show Kennedy some of the park's wonders. O'Donnell declined. "The fact that I couldn't even get the President to take a little walk bothered me," Udall recalled. "[They] laughed behind my back when I even suggested it."

✻

It was now 4:40 p.m. On this busy afternoon, Kennedy's attention moved from the nation's physical fitness to its fiscal fitness. As Bud Wilkinson left the Oval Office, the president's circle of economic advisors filed in. The most senior was Douglas Dillon, secretary of the treasury, accompanied by his two top deputies, Henry Fowler, undersecretary of the treasury, and Robert Roosa, undersecretary of the treasury for monetary affairs. The others were Elmer Staats and Charles Schultze of the Bureau of the Budget; William McChesney Martin, chairman of the Federal Reserve Board; Walter Heller, chairman of the President's Council of Economic Advisers, and his colleagues on the council, Gardner Ackley and John Lewis.

All were following the progress of Kennedy's most ambitious domestic initiative: the largest tax bill in the country's history. That Martin – the venerable custodian of the nation's money supply as chair of the Federal Reserve since 1949 – was present that afternoon suggested they might also be talking about interest rates, the dollar, or the balance of payments. Not necessarily, though. Kennedy had integrated Martin into his economic circle with more authority than the chairman had had under Eisenhower or Truman. Until civil rights emerged as a priority that spring – inspiring the landmark law that Kennedy was discussing today and would announce tomorrow – persuading Congress to embrace tax reform, by way of a tax cut, was the administration's biggest legislative challenge.

The tax cut was innovative and unorthodox. Theodore White, the admiring chronicler of Kennedy's rise to power in his ground-breaking *The Making of the President 1960*, called Kennedy's original revenue bill "a revolution in thinking" because it used a tax measure as an instrument to encourage both investment and consumption. It "was a marvelous and still fragrant compost of conservative and liberal thinking on taxes," he wrote. Fundamentally, Kennedy was proposing to cut taxes for everybody, including the wealthiest, who were paying rates as high as 91 percent. But he faced critics who worried about the loss of revenue in a fragile economy that had weathered a mild recession in 1961 and who feared another recession in 1963.

On the whole, they had little to criticize. The United States was flourishing in 1963. Most of its 189 million citizens were enjoying unprecedented prosperity. The gross national product, personal income, civilian employment, corporate profits, average weekly earnings in manufacturing – even plant and equipment outlays – reached record highs. In June 1963, the weekly pay of the average industrial worker passed $100 for a forty-hour week, four times what the same job had paid in the Great Depression. Some ninety thousand Americans were millionaires, rising from twenty-seven thousand in the early 1950s. The value of the New York Stock Exchange had grown from $46 billion after the war to $411 billion. This was a big – staggeringly big – economy, the greatest industrial state the world had ever seen with companies like Kodak,

Pepsi-Cola, General Motors, and Bell Telephone – all advertising prominently in magazines and newspapers that week.

It was true that at the beginning of the year the economy seemed stalled. While 70 million Americans were working, unemployment exceeded 6 percent in January and February. Politically, that kind of trend was dangerous for the administration. Kennedy believed that the recession of 1960 had "ruined" Nixon in the major industrial states; a recession in 1964 could cost him the election. "I hate to get myself as vulnerable as that, at the mercy of bankers who I know would probably like to screw us anyway," he told Dillon in September 1963.

Like most of his predecessors, Kennedy had no expertise in business or economics. At Harvard he had studied mainly history and foreign policy. Afterward, on his father's advice, he had attended the London School of Economics in 1935, planning to study under one of the leading leftist intellectuals, Harold Laski; he got sick and withdrew early. Kennedy was never in business (he was briefly enrolled at the Stanford Graduate School of Business), but he was a quick study and, as president, recruited the best financial minds around. One was John Kenneth Galbraith, the dry economist who had counseled Kennedy in his fourteen years in Congress, where he witnessed "his emerging competence and mastery" in economics. When Galbraith served as ambassador to India during the first two years of the administration, he corresponded regularly with Kennedy. Galbraith still offered occasional advice. As for the other economic advisors, they were now seated on the pale couches of the Oval Office – so low and cushy they seemed to swallow visitors – flanking the president in his rocker.

Kennedy surprised Washington when he appointed Douglas Dillon. He was a Republican. Kennedy thought it wise, given his tiny plurality in 1960, to bring Republicans (Robert McNamara, McGeorge Bundy, and Henry Cabot Lodge Jr. were others) into his administration. They could give him political cover in the event of foreign or domestic failures. Dillon, a wealthy investment banker and an able public servant, had served as Eisenhower's ambassador to France and his undersecretary of state. He was said to have "an orderly, logical mind, not hobbled by an unruly imagination." Bobby said Jack "thought he was a brilliant man . . . a very substantive, valuable figure," particularly in matters of foreign policy. Jackie said JFK "loved" Dillon. Theirs was a warm relationship, which extended to their wives. Bobby also thought Walter Heller "was very good . . . [but] always talked to the press too much. It used to irritate the President." Jackie was blunter: "Walter Heller was a sort of a jerk. . . . I never could believe he was such a brilliant economist."

If Kennedy liked the company of his economists, he generally disliked businessmen and industrialists. They didn't like him, either, particularly after his showdown with the executives of U.S. Steel in 1962 when he forced them to roll back price increases. Arthur Schlesinger recalled a cool meeting at the White House. When Kennedy, Bobby, and LBJ came in, "not a single one among the waiting businessmen stood up," Schlesinger said. "This really shows what sons of bitches they are. Not only did they fail to stand when the President entered the room, but most did not have the courtesy to stand when they asked the President questions. . . . The complacent stupidity of the American business community would be outrageous if it were not so comic."

Recession, the tax cut, the gold supply, monetary policy – all may have been subjects of discussion over the next fifty minutes, a long meeting among the others of that afternoon. Another topic may have been the Federal Reserve's proposal to raise the discount rate on loans to its member banks to 3.5 percent from 3 percent, which it did in July. Quite possibly, though, the advisors were discussing the tax cut, the administration's marquee proposal. Joseph P. Hutnyan, the chief financial writer with UPI, called JFK's tax cut "one of the most fascinating issues ever to come before Congress." What made it audacious was the nation's $12-billion budgetary deficit. "The situation was rather like an unsuccessful business-man, who is spending more money than he is making, suddenly deciding to attack the problem by cutting even more." Kennedy had proposed the tax cut in his State of the Union Message in January. He thought the economy was tepid, largely because of high taxes. Lowering rates would stimulate spending, increase incomes, generate larger revenues, and help balance the budget. In his address, he foresaw greater purchasing power, the creation of two million jobs, and more investment, production, and industrial capacity.

Kennedy proposed reducing taxes by $13.5 billion over three years, beginning in 1963. It would be the biggest cut in American history. At the same time, the bill would eliminate a suite of deductions (interest on mortgages, charitable contributions, state and local taxes) which would generate $3.5 billion, offsetting the loss of revenue from the lower rates. Supporters said it was sensible to cut taxes to stimulate spending. Critics said it was dangerous to reduce revenue when running a deficit. Hutnyan, writing in 1964, said the bill was "a political phenomenon," because it was not a "clear-cut [case of] conservative-versus-liberal or labor-versus-management conflict." For the first few months of 1963, when a recession threatened, the bill had absorbed much of the administration's attention. That changed when the threat receded and civil rights legislation became more urgent.

Fifty-one years later, it is striking that there was no public clamor in 1963 for lower taxes. After years living with high taxes, a remnant of the Second World War, Americans were used to it. The hue and cry over taxes, which would animate the 1980s and 1990s and spill into the 21st century, was unheard in the 1960s. Americans seemed unconcerned.

On June 10, the administration knew the bill did not have strong public support and would have trouble passing. With that in mind, Kennedy and his advisors might have discussed the changes that were eventually implemented. The new, proposed bill, approved by the House in September, would reduce individual income taxes by an average of 20 percent over two years, beginning in 1964. The new individual tax rate would fall from the current 20 percent to 90 percent to 14 percent to 70 percent (originally Kennedy's highest bracket was 65 percent). The corporate rate would fall from 30 percent to 23 percent on company incomes under $25,000, and from 52 percent to 47 percent on higher earnings. These amendments – preserving those hallowed personal deductions – meant that the bill would raise $600 million, less than a quarter of what was anticipated. Kennedy had retreated but it was still not enough to get his bill through Congress in 1963.

*

At 5:45 p.m. Kennedy had a few minutes with William T. Gossett between his meeting with his economic advisors and his next appointment. For the president, this was a personnel matter. Gossett was resigning as deputy special representative for trade negotiations. Losing a senior official was troublesome but typical of the staffing changes that presidents have to manage all the time. At this point in his presidency, Kennedy had lost more senior people than Gossett – Arthur Goldberg (secretary of labor), Abraham Ribicoff (secretary of health, education and welfare), George McGovern (director of the Food for Peace program), and John Kenneth Galbraith (ambassador to India). The administration would survive the loss of Gossett. Seeing him this afternoon was presidential politesse.

A native of Texas, Gossett joined the Ford Motor Company as counsel and vice president in 1947. On the advice of Robert McNamara, who had been president of Ford, Kennedy named Gossett trade envoy in 1962. As the administration embraced liberalized trade in international negotiations, Gossett had played "a major part in the difficult tasks of getting a new and complex enterprise started in a job which concerns the widest interests of the American economy, involves the responsibilities of many executive departments, and requires negotiations with fifty foreign nations," Kennedy wrote the departing Gossett with heraldry. "The importance of your contribution will become increasingly apparent as the negotiations develop."

Despite that contribution, Gossett was resigning after less than a year. Why? The job was killing him. In his letter of that day, Gossett told Kennedy that he was leaving the post because "unfortunately, the experience of the past few months has shown me that my state of health will not permit me to provide the great energy and around-the-clock concentrated effort required for the proper performance of the duties of this demanding position. And I would not want to give it any less, for to do so might jeopardize the success of the current trade negotiations that are of such transcendent importance, not only to the nation, but to the entire free world."

Gossett said he hoped to resume his full-time duty "after a period of rest and attention." In the end, he returned to private practice in Detroit and never came back to Washington. Gossett was fifty-eight in 1963, which was old in the New Frontier. It was no place for faint hearts and weak flesh. Marriages failed and so did health. The unending work made it hard to get away. "When you leave the hospital, take a long vacation," Sorensen wrote an ailing colleague who was recuperating that week. "It's a sneaky way to get one – but the only way around here." When Kennedy saw Gossett that day – it was a five-minute courtesy call – he knew that Gossett did not want to end up divorced or dead. Gossett endured. After a distinguished career in law and philanthropy, he died at ninety-three.

*

Focused on physical fitness, the tax cut, and his departing trade envoy, Kennedy had not talked about civil rights since his return to the office that afternoon. He would now, for the next twenty minutes, directly and uncomfortably, with one of its staunchest advocates. At 5:55 p.m., five minutes after Gossett left, Kennedy sat down with Andrew J. Biemiller, political director of the American Federation of Labor and Congress of Industrial Organizations (AFL-CIO). That title was misleading; years later, the *Washington Post* called Biemiller "perhaps the single most influential lobbyist in town." For a generation Biemiller was the voice of organized labor on a number of issues – foreign aid, health care, manpower retraining, industrial safety, and now, in the spring of 1963, civil rights.

Biemiller wore a clipped mustache and rumpled suits. He was aggressively gregarious and charmingly blunt. Physically, he was a big man; he looked like a stevedore and moved like a locomotive. Roaming the halls of Congress, he often wore a flower in his lapel. A native of Sandusky, Ohio, an attractive industrial town on the shores of Lake Erie, Biemiller was a union organizer in Wisconsin during the Depression and served five years in the state legislature. In his disjointed career in the House of Representatives, he was elected in 1944, defeated in 1946, re-elected in 1948, and defeated in 1950 and 1952. It was in the House that he met Jack Kennedy, who was in his second term when Biemiller returned in 1949. The two sat on the House Labor Committee and collaborated on legislation. Their relationship deepened when Kennedy entered the Senate in 1953. Kennedy joined the Labor Committee while Biemiller joined the newly created AFL-CIO, the country's most powerful union. As its legislative director, he led an office of a half-dozen lobbyists. In Kennedy, organized labor "had a real champion in the Senate," recalled Biemiller. "Bill after bill would come up in which Jack Kennedy played a very important role."

By 1961, organized labor was delighted to have a friend in the White House. Kennedy consulted labor leaders on legislation and appointments of interest to them. They were happy with Arthur Goldberg, the labor lawyer, as secretary of labor. But when labor pushed JFK to appoint Willard Wirtz as head of the National Labor Board, Kennedy balked. "I can't have two Jews in leading labor spots in my administration," he told Biemiller, who explained that Wirtz was German, not Jewish. (Kennedy named Wirtz undersecretary of labor and appointed two Jews to cabinet: Goldberg and Ribicoff.) Labor's influence in the White House was notable given its ebbing importance. Union membership had fallen to less than 22 percent of the workforce, losing half a million workers between 1960 and 1962. There were now four million fewer blue-collar workers and ten million more white-collar workers than in 1945. It was harder to organize white-collar workers. The middle class of managers, salesmen, and professionals was growing. The country was richer. Even wages for industrial workers were rising; 40 percent of American families earned more than $7,000 a year.

The relationship between Kennedy and George Meany, the plainspoken president of the AFL-CIO, "was close, warm, almost ardent," noted Arnold Beichman of the *Christian Science Monitor* in 1963. When Meany had reservations, he offered them in private. Labor opposed the administration's proposal in 1961 to increase the hourly minimum wage to $1.25 over three years; labor wanted the increase sooner, but lost. It wanted a shorter workweek, which JFK opposed. On most matters, though, it won. Kennedy was popular among the autoworkers and pipefitters and rank and file; a week before his death, the AFL-CIO gave him a thunderous ovation at its convention in New York City. It was said that Kennedy knew more labor leaders of high and low rank than any president, including Franklin Roosevelt. For labor, access and influence were intertwined. "We lived in the White House," said Biemiller. It certainly seemed so on Monday; this was Biemiller's second visit to the Oval Office that day. He had been one of the men among "the dames" watching the president sign the Equal Pay Act. While he was there, he left Kenny O'Donnell a memo on civil rights he had written for Senator Hubert Humphrey, at Humphrey's request. "Kenny, I think your boss might be interested in this," Biemiller said nonchalantly, dropping it on O'Donnell's desk like a grocery flyer.

The memo explained labor's commitment to a Fair Employment Practices Commission (FEPC) in the proposed civil rights bill. The purpose of the entrenched FEPC was to end job discrimination in all public and private places of employment, rather than solely in government institutions. Meany had first proposed it in a speech in January 1963, on the hundredth anniversary of the Emancipation Proclamation. Since then, Meany and Biemiller had been lobbying the administration and Congress hard. It was vitally important to Meany – "He was hot as hell on it," recalled Biemiller – who believed that the unions needed that kind of power to end racial discrimination. But the administration resisted and by the spring, as consultations between the Justice Department, Congress, and labor intensified, it had become what Biemiller called "a very nasty fight."

Midafternoon on June 10, Biemiller took a call from Meany, who was in Italy. "What kind of memo did you leave with Jack Kennedy today?" he asked. "He's had me on the phone here. He's all hot and bothered. Said we're going to ruin his bill. What did you do?" When Meany heard the memo was about the FEPC, he reassured Biemiller that he was "absolutely right. That's our position." Meany told him to call the White House: "The President wants to talk to you." At 4:25 p.m., Biemiller called Evelyn Lincoln, who confirmed that "our bosses have been talking for a long time." Meany had returned Kennedy's call at 1:30 p.m. when the president was discussing civil rights with his advisors. Mrs. Lincoln promised Biemiller she would put Kennedy on the phone shortly; knowing this kind of delicate matter was better handled in person, he asked to see the president. Such was his familiarity – and Kennedy's informality – that they could meet on short notice. A few minutes later, Mrs. Lincoln instructed Biemiller: "Come over. Come through the back door. We don't want any publicity on this."

Sixteen years later, this battle-scarred unionist called it "one of the most painful meetings I've ever been in in my life." Kennedy was annoyed. He worried that too many moderates in Congress – particularly the Republicans he desperately needed – would oppose the FEPC. "Jack Kennedy insisted we were going to kill the bill," Biemiller said. "That would be the end of this bill, and he wanted a civil rights bill. And he kept insisting you didn't really need the FEPC at this stage." Kennedy wasn't opposed in principle to an expanded, legislated FEPC (which FDR had created by executive order in 1941), and he would not mind it as a separate piece of legislation. "But I don't see it is as important as these other things [voting rights and equal access to public accommodations] are," he told Biemiller. "And I can't go with you on this."

Although Biemiller anticipated "a real head-on confrontation" between labor and the administration, he refused to back down. "We're sorry, but we're going to stick it out," he insisted. Biemiller heard the frustration in Kennedy's "voice tones." Here he was, after two-and-a-half years of pressure from black and labor leaders, ready to cross the Rubicon of race. Whether he would announce his civil rights bill tomorrow or the next week, he wanted to know that he could reach the far bank and establish a beachhead. There would be resistance, sure, but he had to survive the crossing. Understand, he told Biemiller, he was committed to civil rights. He fully expected opposition from southern Democrats, the implacable conservatives, but now from northern Democrats, the impractical liberals? What was too much for some was too little for others. This was why the day's conversations with Meany and Biemiller were so unsettling to him: he saw the fire he would now draw from both camps. He was miffed that he could not get his friends to go along with him.

Kennedy was cautious on the FEPC, as he was generally on civil rights. While he was prepared to risk introducing the legislation now, opposed by almost all his advisors, he worried this kind of clause would sink it. In the end, it didn't. The Civil Rights Act of 1964 included fair employment language. On this day, though, he thought that it was he who was prudent and Meany and Biemiller who were not. It was as if Kennedy were saying: *Jesus Christ, your goddamn self-righteousness will kill the whole thing!* "He thought we were doing him in," recalled Biemiller.

✴

Kennedy's heated conversation with Biemiller ended at 6:15 p.m. He had fifteen minutes before his last scheduled appointment of the day. A stack of telephone messages awaited him. Jackie tried to reach him from Camp David at 5:20 p.m. and 5:34 p.m., as she had three times that morning. His brother, Ted (who had been elected to the Senate from Massachusetts in November 1962), called at 5:37 p.m. His mother-in-law, Janet Lee Auchincloss, called at 4:45 p.m. Willard Wirtz, who had succeeded Goldberg as secretary of labor, called at 5:42 p.m., presumably to discuss the FEPC.

As George Wallace hunkered down in Tuscaloosa and Nikita Khrushchev mulled over the Peace Speech, Kennedy sat down with James C. Hagerty, vice president and director of news operations for ABC. Hagerty arrived at 6:30 p.m. It was Kennedy's third off-the-record meeting of the afternoon. There was no obvious reason for Kennedy to see Hagerty that day, though it is possible that given the two big issues he was facing over these forty-eight hours – civil rights and nuclear arms – he wanted Hagerty's advice. Everyone in Washington liked Hagerty who wore heavy glasses and had a straight-edge part through his slicked-back hair. For eight years he had been a highly visible and much-trusted press secretary to Eisenhower. A former correspondent with the *New York Times*, like his father, Jim Hagerty was respected for his candor. He was the soothing voice and comforting face of his frail commander in chief, no more so than in September 1955, when Ike had had a heart attack and disappeared from public view for several days. It was Hagerty whose daily briefings reassured an anxious nation, while in private he helped run the government.

Hagerty lacked the partisanship of his fellow Republicans. He had been generous to Pierre Salinger, his successor as press secretary, in the two-and-a-half-month transition between administrations. Kennedy remembered that and had asked his advice on several matters. During the Cuban Missile Crisis in October 1962, Salinger approached Hagerty about the prospect of establishing an office of wartime censorship. "I told Hagerty I needed someone of unquestioned honesty and integrity. . . . The only man, in the President's view and mine, who fitted the necessities of the time was Hagerty himself." Hagerty didn't want the job, but he agreed to take it if the president asked. Kennedy remembered that, too.

The meeting with Hagerty might have been about his former boss. Although Kennedy was not enamored of Eisenhower, he had courted him since becoming president, even consulted him during the Cuban Missile Crisis. When Eisenhower asked Kennedy to restore his rank as a five-star general, which he'd lost when he became president in 1953, Kennedy obliged. JFK liked to call him "General" rather than "Mr. President," and the old soldier liked to hear it. Given their differences of party, intellect, personality, and age (Ike was seventy-two that June), theirs was not the avuncular relationship Kennedy had with Harold Macmillan. Of course, given the inevitable rivalry between sitting and former presidents (especially those who follow one another), it could never be. "I don't think he thought much of him," Jackie said of Jack's view of Ike. In May 1963, Arthur Schlesinger recalled drafting remarks for JFK in which he had "written two sentences praising Eisenhower's contributions to friendship among the English-speaking peoples. Kennedy read it and said: 'I think you have gone too far,' took his pen, and crossed one of the sentences out."

Eisenhower had no use for Kennedy, either. He thought he had mismanaged the Bay of Pigs and was bullied by Khrushchev at Vienna. "That statement that he'd be his own secretary of state and do everything himself – shows his complete unawareness of the job," he told Hagerty in the summer of 1961. He resented the talk of youth, vigor, and action, in implicit contrast to the somnolence of his administration. But the presidency, with its own code of conduct and army of expectations, has a way of overcoming the natural friction among those who have served. Ike and JFK exchanged cheery letters in 1962 affirming their mutual, if false, respect for each other. Eisenhower said his political views, different than Kennedy's, "contain nothing of personal animus on my part. Any allegation to the contrary that may come to your ears . . . is either untrue or highly exaggerated. . . ." He condemned individuals who "distort or falsify in striving for a feeling of self-importance in the limelight that plays about the Presidency." Kennedy retaliated with equal insincerity, insisting that "I have been a great admirer of yours," since a meeting between the two in Frankfurt in 1945 when JFK was accompanying Secretary of Defense, James Forrestal, on a trip to Europe. Kennedy was closer to the truth when he said that, although they would inevitably disagree, he would try mightily "to prevent any misunderstandings of thought, actions or motive from eroding our association."

In the spring of 1963, Kennedy needed Eisenhower. It didn't matter if he felt that Ike had done nothing for America or the English-speaking peoples. Kennedy was repositioning himself that day and the next on the two biggest issues of his presidency. If there was to be a nuclear test ban treaty, Kennedy wanted the endorsement of the country's highest-ranking soldier, the victor of the Second World War. If there was to be a civil rights act, he wanted the endorsement of the president who had sent troops into Little Rock, Arkansas, in 1957, even though that was as badly handled as Kennedy's sending troops into Mississippi in 1962. While it was only a few hours after the Peace Speech, race was now more on his mind than war. Sometime on June 10, Kennedy had written Eisenhower a letter to solicit his support on civil rights. On the afternoon of June 12, he and Johnson would spend an hour with the former president at the White House discussing the proposed bill. Following the letter and the conversation, Eisenhower would offer his support. "I think this matter has become one that involves the conscience of the individual and the nation, and indeed, our moral standards," he wrote on June 14. "As to the details of the legislation that might be needed, I am not able to give a definitive opinion . . . but I do believe that we must strive in every useful way to assure equality of economic and political rights for all citizens."

Publicly, though, Eisenhower was withering in his criticism. The day after meeting Kennedy, he addressed leaders of the Republican Party in Hershey, Pennsylvania. *U.S. News & World Report* noted that "his words were stronger than any he has used in a political speech since leaving the White House." It was as if Ike, having offered the president assurances in private, was now free to excoriate him in public – and did. He accused the administration of "a sorry record that stands naked to behold when the cunningly manipulated veneer of imagery is peeled off. The roll-call – a long record of glowing promises and anemic deliveries – would include such campaigning catch phrases as 'missile gap,' 'stroke of the pen,' 'strong presidency' and 'get the country moving again.'" Eisenhower lamented "the headlong retreat on matters of national survival and domestic well-being on which they [Democrats and independents, in particular] were promised firm, unequivocal decision and action." The general's barrage didn't bother Kennedy. That was politics. On the two issues that mattered to him Monday, he had – or would have – Eisenhower where he wanted him.

✳

Hagerty's quarter-hour with the president was over by 6:45 p.m. In the office, more telephone messages awaited. Kennedy's callers included friends, family, assistants, journalists, legislators, and petitioners. His brother Ted called again at 7:17 p.m. and 8:05 p.m. Senator Warren Magnuson of Washington called at 5:50 p.m. Congressman Torbert Macdonald, one of Kennedy's best friends, called at 7:19 p.m. John McCone, director of the CIA, called at 6:23 p.m. Senator John Sparkman of Alabama phoned at 6:35 p.m. He was the only caller put through to Kennedy, who was meeting with Hagerty. As they talked, Wallace was meeting his advisors on the campus of the University of Alabama. The two students were settling secretly into private homes in Birmingham for the evening. Not even their parents knew where they were.

Kennedy liked the telephone and used it liberally to conduct business, gather information, and keep in touch. Just as he was willing to see people of value to him, he was open to taking their calls. That day, for example, Emmet John Hughes, a columnist with *Newsweek*, called the White House at 11:35 a.m., 3:55 p.m., and 4:22 p.m. Hughes brought out JFK's cunning. In 1961, two days after Inauguration Day, Hughes wrote the president a note of praise that Kennedy would have found extravagant. In it, Hughes describes his feeling toward Kennedy "as a vast amount of personal respect, reasoned admiration, a binding sense of kindred concern and understanding. This kind of applause comes, not merely from the hands, but from the heart." Hughes coyly suggests in the note that if Kennedy wants testimony to this, "proof by deed, not mere word," he need only ask. It sounded like Hughes was after something – work, access, information. To the letter he appends *three* post-scripts, as if he just couldn't stop. In the second he asks: "After another fortnight, when I hope to [be] back in Washington, I may ask of your secretary a chance for 10 – repeat 10 – minutes quietly with you, to offer a notion or two."

It may be that Hughes got his ten minutes with the president but not out of any well of affection on Kennedy's part. JFK loathed sycophants. "Of course, we all know and love Emmet," he said to Ben Bradlee, referring to Hughes in November 1962. "He's a son of a bitch." That year Hughes published *The Ordeal of Power,* a scathing memoir of serving Eisenhower as a speechwriter. It was "kiss-and-tell journalism," which JFK nonetheless called "a terrific book." Why, though, was Hughes calling on Monday? Was he seeking presidential illumination for a column? That he telephoned three times suggests that Evelyn Lincoln led him to believe, in the morning and again in late afternoon, that he might have a word with Kennedy that day. Perhaps JFK, for his part, wanted to discuss the the memorable speech on peace Hughes wrote for Eisenhower in April 1953. Fundamentally, a conversation with "Eminent John," as JFK called Hughes, was another way to manage the news and burnish his image. Each was using the other.

Charlotte Eldridge called at 10:22 a.m. and at 4:20 p.m. She was an assistant to Representative Frank Thompson Jr. of New Jersey, a progressive Democrat and advocate of public education during his twenty-five years in Congress. In 1963, he was spearheading the administration's effort to create a national service corps, a domestic counterpart to the Peace Corps, which was entering its third year putting young Americans to work in the developing world. Then, of course, there were the usual calls that afternoon and evening from members of the staff – Larry O'Brien, Kenny O'Donnell, and Pamela Turnure, Jackie's press secretary, who called Kennedy three times, twice in the last hour.

✳

At 7:08 p.m., Kennedy left the Oval Office for the White House Swimming Pool. He usually swam at 1:15 p.m., before lunch, and again at 7:00 p.m., before dinner. On June 10, absorbed by the civil rights crisis well into early afternoon, he had missed his midday swim. The indoor pool lay between the mansion and the Oval Office. Kennedy left his office through the French doors and walked under the Colonnade, bordered by the Rose Garden, to the pool entrance on the west terrace.

The room was sixty feet long and twenty-five feet wide; the pool itself was slightly smaller, at fifty feet by fifteen feet. Built in 1933, it was originally a clinical white with terra-cotta brick walls. Light streamed in through half-moon windows cut under the ceiling. The pool had cost $22,316.34 which was raised by the *New York Daily News* and forty-three other newspapers. It was a gift to the White House for the benefit of the newly elected Franklin Roosevelt, who was paralyzed from the waist down by polio. As he struggled to adjust to the loss of the use of his legs, swimming was therapy for him. Harry Truman used the pool regularly. Eisenhower did not. For Kennedy, swimming was as much a part of his regimen as napping in the afternoon and reading at night.

In 1961 the swimming pool had been as uninviting as "a school for the deaf," Jackie's all-purpose epithet for the aesthetic atrocities of institutional Washington. The pool's only embellishments were white-braided life buoys from naval vessels such as the USS *Oriskany* and USS *Joseph P. Kennedy, Jr.* Like the president's plane, car, house, and helicopter (the Kennedys had changed *Marine One*'s color scheme), the pool did not escape the First Lady's critical eye. She could not leave it untouched. In 1962, she commissioned Bernard Lamotte, a French artist, to create tropical-themed murals on three walls; the fourth was mirrored. The murals had been proposed and paid for by Joe Kennedy, who had been inspired by a similar scene in Le Pavillon, his favorite restaurant in New York. Before they were completed, the patriarch suffered a stroke in December 1961 and was condemned, speechless, to a wheelchair for the last eight years of his life. Jackie pursued the project as a gift in his name.

Lamotte took to the job with Gallic flourish. Brush in hand, he perched on elaborate scaffolding that had been erected over the pool, which was left full of water to allow the president his swims. He wore a blue peaked cap (alas, no beret), and one day was "so engrossed in painting a seascape . . . that he lost his balance and fell into the pool . . . paints, pants and all . . . ," reported UPI. The pool had to be drained and cleaned before "the Boss," as Lamotte called Kennedy, returned from Palm Beach. At lunch Lamotte liked to repair to the flower room (beside the gymnasium, which was next to the pool) for a standard lunch of wine and cheese. He was often joined by his compatriot, René Verdon, the White House chef, and Pamela Turnure, the three of them sharing food and conversation in French among the potted plants. The day Lamotte finished the floor-to-ceiling murals, a grateful Jackie invited him for "a sumptuous lunch" in the State Dining Room.

The pool now resembled the harbor at St. Croix and its surroundings in the Virgin Islands. What had been somber, sterile, and stark was now breezy, sunny, and romantic. For the swimmer, gazing up from the water, it was a transporting panorama: mountains kissed by clouds, palm trees edging the water, tall-masted sloops and low-lying smacks, their sails luffing, rigging distended. The colors were bold and varied, the sky in shades of turquoise and royal blue. An ingenious lighting system gave it a touch of theater, the mood changing with the time of day. "When the President swam at noon, the waterfront and landscape beyond were lit with bright sunlight," Pierre Salinger recalled. "When he swam after dark, there were lights twinkling around the harbor and a moon and stars in the sky." A sound system piped in music. The new ambience delighted Ralph Paiewonksy, governor of the Virgin Islands. "We have read . . . of your father's gift to you of murals for the White House Swimming Pool," he wired Kennedy on July 21, 1962. "Naturally, we are highly pleased. And if we cannot say that the White House has come to the Virgin Islands, at least we can say the Virgin Islands have come to the White House." The temperature of the water in the swimming pool was always between eighty-seven and ninety degrees Fahrenheit, "as warm as a bath-tub," reported one frequent guest.

So it was here, in his Tropic of Cancer, that Kennedy came for relief and distraction twice a day. The pool was a sanctuary, even if a red telephone sat on a pillow at the edge of the water, which meant, author Jim Bishop intoned, "the president of the United States is never more than a few feet from the telephone . . . in a position at all times to make instantaneous decisions – even if that involves nuclear war." Kennedy changed in an adjoining dressing room ("wrinkled swim trunks hang on pegs") and emerged a moment later. Usually he wore nothing at all. Kennedy would swim laps for twenty minutes to a half hour. Often he was accompanied by Dave Powers, who could draw on a fund of jokes and political folklore. "The New England tones of the men ricochet off the walls of the room, and the President appears to draw as much good from the recollections of Dave Powers as he does from the swim," wrote Bishop. If there was a pressing matter, aides came to the pool and raised it with Kennedy while he was swimming. Sometimes he was joined by Jackie, sometimes by Caroline and John Jr.

Kennedy's aquatic children drew offers from a solicitous country. One came from Johnny Karrant of Fort Smith, Arkansas, a life-guard at sixteen years old, who wrote JFK in July 1961 that he knew "your [sic] an expert swimmer" and asked for "the privilege of teaching your daughter to swim when she becomes five or six years of age, or any time you may suggest." On behalf of the president, Larry O'Brien replied: "He appreciates your offer. . . . However, at this time, it is impossible to make arrangements for you to perform this service."

Kennedy had an affinity for water, perhaps because he had spent so much of his life in it or on it. No man of the mountains or the plains, he was always a son of the sea. As a boy, he had raced his sailboat, *Victura*, off Cape Cod; his name appears among the victorious sailors of regattas past emblazoned on the wall of the small wooden clubhouse at Hyannis Port. As a student at Harvard, he left the infirmary, where he was recovering from one of his illnesses, to try out for the swim team. As the captain of *PT-109* in the Solomon Islands in August 1943, his patrol boat sunk by a Japanese destroyer, he towed a badly burned sailor through the waters of the South Pacific to an island three miles away. From there, on subsequent nights, he swam into the channel with a lantern to hail a friendly vessel and to save his crew. As president, he took several baths a day to soothe his back and sometimes conducted business while in the tub.

Kennedy did not like to swim alone. Besides Powers, he invited others spontaneously to join him. One was Hugh Sidey. "Let's go swim," he suggested in the Oval Office on July 25, 1961. Sidey said he did not have a bathing suit. "That's OK," Kennedy said. "In this pool you don't need one. It's a little hot, but I need it for my back." Sidey recalled the dark blue-green water, perfectly still, as a "stiff-backed" Kennedy slowly lowered himself down the chrome ladder. At the far end, one of Caroline's blue plastic boats bobbed near the diving board. Kennedy was a strong swimmer. "He backstroked down the pool, showing some of the old Harvard style that had put him on the swimming team. He clung to the side and kicked gently, tread water and then just walked about in the warmth." Kennedy was also a strong talker; that day, he kept up a steady commentary on his generals, Laos, Berlin, Cuba.

Sometimes he was joined by women. One was Mimi Beardsley (later Alford), who had joined the press office at nineteen as an intern in the summer of 1962. On her fourth day on the job, Powers telephoned her before noon and invited her to the pool. Powers, she noted, was not at all "discomfited by the circumstances – a private swim in the middle of the day with a younger woman he didn't know." He reassured her there would be bathing suits to wear and that others would accompany them. Two members of the staff, Priscilla Wear and Jill Cowan, soon appeared. Wear worked for

Evelyn Lincoln, Cowan was an assistant in the press office. They were known as Fiddle and Faddle, so spirited and enthusiastic ("Triffic!" they'd trill) that they were profiled in a four-page, ten-picture spread in a special issue of *Look* on the administration's first anniversary in January 1962. "Though no classic beauties, they have such youthful dash and vigor that everyone in Washington seems to know Fiddle and Faddle," said *Look*.

That first time, Beardsley remembered slipping into an imperfect suit, which still showed off her coltish figure. "The space felt vast, and you were completely enclosed by the faux warmth and sun." She soon joined Fiddle and Faddle in the pool, thinking to herself that this midday exercise was not unusual for them. Beardsley noticed a tray of sandwiches and drinks. Then, to Beardsley's surprise, the president entered. "Mind if I join you?" he asked. "Our pleasure, Mr. President," said Fiddle. He introduced himself to Beardsley, inquired about her job, and swam away. Beardsley thought him remarkably fit – flat stomach, toned arms.

For Beardsley, it would be the first of many swims with Powers and the president. Some said that the swimming pool was about assignation as well as exercise; decades later, Secret Service agents (who sat behind closed doors outside the pool while the president entertained guests) described the pool parties to journalist Seymour Hersh and others. To preserve his privacy, Kennedy had the glass on the windows of the doors frosted. While Beardsley found Kennedy a "sweet and thoughtful and generous man," she recalled "a callous and unforgivable episode" in the White House pool involving him, her, and Powers, for which, she added, "a chastened President Kennedy apologized to us both." As for Fiddle and Faddle's aquatic (or terrestrial) relations with the president, Beardsley doesn't speculate and the pair never told.

Often the swims were just that – swims. Beardsley recalls inviting two of her former classmates from Miss Porter's School in Farmington, Connecticut, to take a dip with her in the pool in the summer of 1963. She was pleased that they were excited and surprised when the president walked in for a swim. After introductions were made, he ordered a box of animal pelts brought to the pool. He was going to give Jackie (who had also attended Miss Porter's) a fur stole for Christmas, he explained, and he wanted the refined Farmington girls to tell him which one was the softest.

On Monday evening, Kennedy probably swam alone. He might have had a massage or done back exercises in the small gym off the dressing room, a carefully prescribed regimen coordinated with swimming. The exercises – push-ups, knee-bends, lifting his leg while lying on his back, standing and touching the floor with his hands – were designed by Dr. Kraus and supervised by two navy physiotherapists assigned to the White House Dispensary. After his swim and exercises, Kennedy usually changed in less than ten minutes. A newly constructed glassed corridor allowed him to put on a bathrobe in the dressing room, walk through the exercise room and the flower room, and go up an elevator and into the residence on the second floor. It was the responsibility of George Thomas to ensure there was always a fresh bathrobe for the president at the pool. Kennedy was so oblivious to nudity that J.B. West, the chief usher, reported that the White House servants had "bets" on what the president would do if there was no bathrobe there after his swim. "Would he dress, again, in the clothes he took off, or would he stride through the flower room and up the elevator, stark naked?"

On this particular day, it is uncertain how long he was at the pool after he arrived there at 7:08 p.m. But he did not linger. After a day that had begun languidly at dawn, accelerated through a morning and noon of public events and private talks, paused in mid-afternoon for a nap, and surged again in late afternoon with more appointments, it was time to relax. But not alone, not upstairs. He was due for dinner in Georgetown at eight.

Monday, June 10, 1963
CHAPTER 6

Evening

JACK KENNEDY CRAVED company. He had many friends,
in many places and in many stations, who engaged him,
entertained him, informed him, indulged him, served him, loved
him. Kennedy was no loner brooding at Camp David or on any other
mountaintop; he sought companionship as president as he had all
his life. He had a gift for making and keeping friends. His social
circles encompassed friends from Palm Beach and Hyannis Port;
friends from the Choate School and Harvard College; friends from
Boston, London, and Washington; friends from the Navy; friends
from Congress. Professionally, they were authors, journalists, diplomats, politicians, executives, and artists; socially, they rarely
included Ted Sorensen, Bobby Kennedy, or staff. Kennedy liked the
mix of tastes and talents. He and Jackie entertained often – dances,
state dinners, concerts. Upstairs, on the second floor, they favored
impromptu private dinners, often pulled together at 6:00 p.m. for
8:00 p.m. The usual guests were Ben Bradlee, the *Newsweek* correspondent and former Georgetown neighbor, and his wife, Tony;

David Ormsby-Gore, the British ambassador and friend of twenty-five years, and his wife, Sissie; and Charles Bartlett, the columnist, and his wife, Martha, who had introduced Jack and Jackie in 1951. From them the president would hear news from the symbiotic worlds of diplomacy and journalism. He needed stimulation. Arthur Schlesinger recalled an early evening in the autumn of 1963 when he was conferring with JFK in the Oval Office: "As I was leaving, he called after me, almost a little wistfully, 'What are you doing tonight?' I told him that we were going to a dance. . . . The President gossiped for a moment or two. I hate to repeat the cliché about the loneliness of the job, but it *is* a lonely job."

Now it was 7:50 p.m. on Monday. Having taken his statutory swim, showered, and dressed in a brisk forty-two minutes, the president left the White House for the home of Joseph Alsop in Georgetown. An evening out was not unusual. In nearly two-and-a-half years in office, Kennedy dined with friends when he could, though that pattern was irregular. "It's certainly true that I'm more isolated socially," he told William Manchester in 1962. "In the beginning I tried to carry on the life I had led, going out, seeing people; but I soon realized that was impossible. Apart from state dinners I suppose I see only three or four people socially. But I have no feeling of withdrawing. After all, everyone's life is circumscribed. And in many ways I see and hear more than anyone else."

Tonight was an opportunity to see and hear. Alsop and his wife, Susan Mary, were entertaining the Ormsby-Gores; David Bruce, ambassador to the Court of St. James's; William Attwood, ambassador to Guinea, a former journalist and boarding school chum; Sir Maurice Bowra, the Oxford classicist; Sir Hugh Fraser, a junior minister in the British cabinet, and his wife, Antonia; Robert McNamara, and his wife, Margaret; Marion "Oatsie" Leiter, a Washington socialite; Alice Roosevelt Longworth, the city's grande dame and outspoken daughter of Theodore Roosevelt; and Mary Meyer, a school friend, painter and libertine.

Here, in private, the president was in search of diverting conversation. Generally speaking, he did not reprise his day at the office in the evening. Politics would be discussed, yes, but the *sujet du jour* could also be journalism, history, theater, movies, or books. Or people, who always fascinated Kennedy. Windbags and poseurs bored him; he liked his interlocutors witty and crisp. On this particular evening, the topic of conversation would be unusual in light of the day's events. Ten hours earlier, he had made the most important speech of his presidency, so intellectually unorthodox, some thought it subversive. It raised questions. *How would Khrushchev respond to his view of Russia? Would his overture fail, like others had? If the Soviets said yes, would they agree to a treaty? Would the Senate kill it? What would Americans think?*

That afternoon, Kennedy was preparing for George Wallace the next morning. He sensed that the confrontation would create an opportunity for him to give another signal address the following evening on civil rights. His advisors, he also knew, opposed that. More questions, then. *Would Wallace resist tomorrow? Would Alabama explode as Mississippi had last September? Should he make the speech and send up the bill? Would it kill his program in Congress, hurt his popularity in the South, and risk his re-election?*

If Monday, June 10, 1963, was typical of this administration, Kennedy made some thirty decisions. He had scores of telephone calls and received hundreds of letters. It was multitasking before there was a word for it. As William Manchester observed, eventually everything happening in the world became the president's problem, demanding an answer, a position, a judgment. Now, awaiting Khrushchev and anticipating Wallace, events were piling upon events. Beyond these complex matters, there would be a nasty surprise for him from overseas in the morning. It would require a decision, too.

This was what it was like to be president of the United States in 1963. This was what it was like to be Jack Kennedy. The pace was slower and the latitude greater for him than it would become in the next century, when advancing technology, a more intrusive media, and increasingly polarized politics accelerated decision-making and intensified public scrutiny. But a president had to be able to do more than one thing at a time, and there were challenges aplenty at home and abroad facing this president. In Saigon, Buddhists were continuing to demonstrate against the regime's religious strictures. In Berlin, the city remained divided by a wall, contemplating the president's visit. In Washington, the House Ways and Means Committee was rewriting the tax bill. Across the nation, a rail shutdown threatened.

＊

At the Alsops' Kennedy looked forward to setting aside Moscow, Montgomery, and all the rest. He wasn't going to dinner for advice on Wallace or applause for his speech; truth be told, he was more intrigued in learning about a scandal that had broken in London two-and-a-half months earlier. For weeks, Kennedy had been obsessively reading the raw cables from the U.S. Embassy in London to the State Department. Given his lively libido and appetite for gossip, he *had* to know more – and this evening he would. And so, as the sun began to set over the capital, bringing a mild respite from the heat, Kennedy was not thinking about race or the bomb. He was thinking about the Profumo Affair.

Then again, who wasn't? Who wasn't following the saga of a leggy young prostitute, a promiscuous senior British cabinet minister, and a phlegmatic Russian naval attaché? A broadening cast of roués and their titillating revelations had shaken London since March. Now it was threatening to bring down the tired government of Harold Macmillan, America's closest ally and a pillar of the Atlantic Alliance. More than any other leader, he had pressed JFK to seek the ban on nuclear testing that he had proposed earlier that day. As *Life* declared on its cover (featuring a sultry Shirley MacLaine in emerald lingerie playing a French prostitute in *Irma la Douce*), this was the "scandal that has the whole world buzzing."

Arthur Schlesinger, having spent three days in London earlier that spring, raised the affair with the president in an illuminating, eight-page memo on the state of British politics dated March 25. JFK told Bradlee it was the best memo – "bar none" – he had ever received. Bradlee, who kept a diary of his tête-à-têtes at the White House, noted the president's ravenous interest. "Kennedy had devoured every word written about the Profumo case; it combined so many of the things that interested him: low doings in high places, the British nobility, sex and spying," he wrote. "Someone in the State Department had apparently sent him an early cable from David Bruce. . . . Kennedy had been so fascinated by that cable that he ordered all further cables from Bruce on that subject sent to him immediately. 'His cables are just fantastic,' the president reported. 'He writes so damn well, full of insights about our British friends.'"

David K.E. Bruce, who would join Kennedy at the Alsops' that evening, was one of the illustrious diplomats of his generation. When Kennedy appointed him to London in 1961, he had been ambassador to Paris (1949-1952) and Bonn (1957-1959), the only American to serve in all three countries as ambassador. Bruce, sixty-five in 1963, had been a leading candidate to be secretary of state but was thought too old for the New Frontier. To Arthur Schlesinger, it was more that he was too "conventional" and "unimaginative." (Later, Bruce noted that he and the president were separated by twenty years, "an entire generation. Yet, when with him, I never felt conscious of this disparity, for his interests were dateless. Physically and actually, he was young; psychologically, he was without age.")

Bruce, an aristocrat from Virginia, went to Princeton and served in the Great War. Before becoming serious about diplomacy in the 1940s, he was a landowner, farmer, traveler, writer, and connoisseur of art. In 1959, when Bruce and his ethereal wife, Evangeline, returned home from Bonn and moved to 34th Street in Georgetown, "they instantly ranked among the best-known and best-connected denizens of the nation's premier political village." A Democrat, Bruce had backed Adlai Stevenson in 1960, but he still became one of the administration's leading men. Bruce revered Kennedy. "His mind is acute, quick, and comprehensive," Bruce wrote in December 1962. "He reads papers swiftly, but seems to catch every slip or specious argument. He expresses his thoughts easily, and with polish. He is unusually courteous and hospitable. I find nothing in him unpraiseworthy."

Now Bruce was sending racy dispatches from Babylon-on-the-Thames. In March 1963, John D. Profumo, the secretary of state for war in Harold Macmillan's cabinet, was said to be sleeping with Christine Keeler, with hair the color of fallen leaves, a high-priced call girl. At the same time, Keeler was sleeping with Captain Yevgeny M. Ivanov, a deputy naval attaché with the Soviet Embassy in London. As a Russian, Ivanov was suspected of being a spy; as a minister, Profumo was accused of divulging secrets; as an intimate of both, Keeler was accused of passing secrets between them. In the Cold War, allegations of espionage were common, though not at this level. The story became an international sensation. Not since Wallis Simpson had forced King Edward VIII to abdicate in 1936, *Life* cooed, had "a woman set in motion such an upheaval."

It had begun on a summer night in 1961, when Keeler, nineteen, emerged semi-naked from a swimming pool at Cliveden, Lord Astor's fabled estate outside London. (JFK's father, Joseph P. Kennedy Sr., had been a frequent visitor when he was ambassador.) Keeler was the guest of Stephen Ward, an artist and society osteopath who was renting a cottage on the estate. Profumo, visiting that evening, was of Italian descent. He was tall, upright and stately. In 1940, at age twenty-five, he was the youngest candidate elected to Parliament; in 1960, he was appointed minister of war. He was married to Valerie Hobson, a raven-haired actress, with whom he had three sons. Years later, the youngest of them, David, described the devastating revelations "as a veritable shitstorm." He was staggered by the interest in 1963. "Considering this was essentially a British political convulsion," he wrote, "the extent of the global response was virtually unprecedented."

The low, slow undoing of Profumo began when he rose in Parliament on March 22 to defend himself against claims of a security breach; there was "no impropriety whatsoever" with Christine Keeler. When Keeler talked, Profumo's denial collapsed. On June 5, amid mounting pressure, he resigned from cabinet and the Commons. It was a stunning reversal of fortune. "But more than that, it will entail his disgrace," Ambassador Bruce wrote from London, "since the telling of such falsehood in the House is considered even more serious than cheating at cards in a gentleman's club." The scandal would not end with Profumo's resignation. There would be questions about Macmillan's handling of the affair – he had accepted Profumo's word and defended him in the Commons – and who else might be involved, as well as what secrets might have been leaked.

On June 8, Bruce flew to Washington for the visit to the United States of Iain Macleod, leader of the House of Commons and chairman of the Conservative Party. Coincidentally, Secretary of State for Air Hugh Fraser and his wife, Antonia, were on a ten-day tour of American air bases, stopping in Washington. When Bruce dined at the British Embassy on June 9 with the Ormsby-Gores, the Frasers, and Macleod, the topic was again Profumo. Bruce noted that Stephen Ward had been charged in London the previous day for procuring Keeler. "Macmillan is accused of collusion with Profumo in the foisting of a lie on the House of Commons, or else of extreme naïveté," he wrote. "I do not believe the former, it would be out of character; but he does appear to have displayed a remarkably credulous lack of sophistication. He will be bitterly attacked for negligence in Security matters, in which respect his record is already vulnerable."

Earlier Monday, Bruce had had a meeting at the State Department. There, too, he faced questions about Profumo. Everyone, including Averell Harriman, wanted news. "As was natural, great interest was manifested over Miss Christine Keeler and the men involved with her," Bruce wrote. "It is one of the juiciest scandals in modern political history. How the French papers must be embroidering on what is not a simple tale." Over lunch, Bruce and McGeorge Bundy discussed British Guiana, disarmament, the test ban, and "call girls." Later, Dean Rusk was also "disturbed over the British political mess, and its potential consequences for American policy."

Their anxiety was well founded. Macmillan and Kennedy were unusual confidants; Bruce observed that "the frequency and frankness of their interchanges had few parallels in modern diplomatic discourse." The two were so close that after Kennedy's death, Macmillan could barely discuss him without crying. "That was a very rare and touching relationship between those two men," Jackie recalled in 1964. "They really loved each other." In the long-running discussion about managing the Soviets, Macmillan was reliable, creative, and prudent. There had to be an overture to our adversary, he insisted. Make it, he advised, and the details will fall into place. It made Macmillan an architect of the Limited Nuclear Test Ban Treaty.

If Profumo was on Bruce's mind on Monday, so was the weather. "I roast outdoors in my lightest suit," he complained, "and am chilled by the air conditioning indoors and in automobiles." When he reached the Alsop house that evening, the air was heavy but the conversation light. "The President . . . was in a gay mood," Bruce recalled, "and there was a good deal of persiflage about the Profumo case, Dr. Ward and sensations still to be revealed." Bruce had joined, as Joe Alsop put it, "a jolly party."

⁂

All jolly parties in Kennedy's Washington were in Georgetown, the capital's most fashionable quarter. It sat in studied isolation a couple of miles west of the whitewashed governmental precinct. In 1963, it still had the air of a nineteenth-century village in its familiar, if overpriced, establishments on or around the hilly Wisconsin Avenue. The Kennedys patronized them all: Martin's Tavern, Doc's Pharmacy, Neam's Market, the Savile Bookshop, Little Caledonia. Toward the Key Bridge, one resident remembered "a faceless loft building said to host the secret goings-on of a CIA safe house." In the 1940s and 1950s, Georgetown became a byword for power. Politicians, journalists, diplomats, mandarins, and spies lived there. They worked together and played together. In a town with little entertainment (no concert hall and few theaters) and few good restaurants (no haute cuisine), they made their own fun (dance clubs) and their own food (dinner parties, especially on Sunday). Affairs of state competed with affairs of the heart. Compact and composed, Georgetown had an enduring elegance. Its sturdy, red-brick homes, often uncomfortably narrow, dated from the Federal Period. Its languid streets and lanes, shaded by towering oak and chestnut trees, accommodated both "cave dwellers" (the old families) and arrivistes alike in the postwar world. Among them had been Senator Kennedy and his young bride.

As a bachelor, JFK had moved into the neighborhood in 1947, shortly after his election to Congress. He rented a row house for $300 a month at 1528 31st Street, which he shared with his sister, Eunice. Later, he lived at 3260 N Street from 1951 until he was elected to the Senate in 1952. He and Jackie lived at 2808 P Street for less than a year, in 1957, after returning to Georgetown from Hickory Hill, the estate in Virginia they sold to Bobby. (The property was too far from Washington and held too many memories of their stillborn daughter, Arabella.) Next, they moved to 3307 N Street, three weeks after Caroline was born in November 1957. It was from this three-story Georgian house, with fanlight and shuttered windows, that Kennedy led his transition team as president-elect between November 1960 and January 1961. It was there that he announced the members of his cabinet. And it was from that house that he set off in full dress on the morning of his Inauguration, waving to the staff at the windows.

On the evening of June 10, the small motorcade ferrying the president to dinner from the White House pulled up at 2720 Dumbarton Avenue. The president knew the house well. He was there the first night of his presidency, after the Inaugural Night balls and leaving an exhausted Jackie at the White House. At 1:50 a.m. that festive morning, an astonished Alsop opened his front door to find the beaming, snow-flecked, tuxedoed president, standing on the floodlit stoop high above the street. To Alsop, Kennedy was a cinematic dream, in life and in art. "Kennedy's Veuve Clicquot, and a starlet on each arm," Joe tells his brother, Stewart, in *The Columnist*, David Auburn's Broadway play. "And each of them has a degree from the Sorbonne." That night of the Inauguration, Auburn's Alsop enthuses: "He's our man. A tough man and a thoughtful one, too, the kind we've been dreaming of and waiting for. He's like Stevenson with balls. Brains and balls, finally, in one package!"

Kennedy returned often to Dumbarton Avenue. Alsop said Kennedy visited every six weeks or so while he was in the White House; even if it was a quarter that often, Jack was there frequently with and without Jackie. Alsop savored every visit. "I long to see you both, and I was greatly flattered when the President said, the other day, that you two would enjoy coming to dine quietly on Dumbarton Avenue," he wrote Jackie on April 23, 1963. "I know how difficult it must always be to go anywhere, but if you would like to come, it will give us more pleasure than I can say."

Like Kennedy, Alsop was a sensualist. After politics, his great passion was food. "The mere thought of fresh foie gras on a bed of purée truffles makes me pale with combined liver fear and greed," he enthused. He liked good books, fine furniture, rare antiques, and the ways of the classical world, on which he was an authority. An aesthete, he was concerned as much with the cut of his Savile Row suits as the contour of his sentences. He wore distinctive round horn-rimmed glasses and expensive polka-dot bow ties. He padded about at breakfast in a silk kimono carrying a large porcelain Chinese teacup. A graduate of Groton and Harvard, Alsop was descended from one of the country's old New England families. He and his wife, Susan Mary, also a blueblood, hosted the capital's most prestigious salon. They had formal dinner parties for sixteen every two weeks or so as well as small lunches and breakfasts with administration officials. Alsop planned the menus with his chef and arranged the seating.

At the table, Alsop directed the conversation, which often became rancorous. Part treacle and part tartness, Alsop was given to Vesuvian eruptions. On Alsop's fiftieth birthday, in October, 1960, Philip Graham, publisher of the *Washington Post*, noted "how free of any taint of tentativeness were his opinions and how overwhelming was his omniscience. He is a rasping geyser of bad temper, and he is a gentle fountain of friendship." Occasionally a guest would explode at Alsop and stomp off into the night. Still, the nation's luminaries gathered at Dumbarton Avenue. If there were a lord mayor of Georgetown, an arbiter of taste and class, it was Joseph Wright Alsop V.

Alsop's day job provided his salon's habitués. He was among the most powerful journalists in the United States. After the war – he had spent a year in a prisoner-of-war camp in Hong Kong – he entered journalism, writing a column called *Matter of Fact* with his brother, Stewart, until 1958. Their intelligence and courage (particularly in opposing Joe McCarthy in the 1950s) made them widely syndicated and highly influential. In 1960, Alsop had publicly supported JFK early for the nomination and then the election. When his man won, Alsop reveled in his access to the president and his circle.

In a career of forty years, Kennedy's Washington was Alsop's zenith. "His column now penetrated even deeper than before into inner councils of government; it was indispensable for anyone who wanted to know what the Kennedys were doing or planning," says his biographer, Robert Merry. His writing brimmed with sharp asides and confident conclusions. Like Ben Bradlee and Charlie Bartlett, his stature was enhanced – if his objectivity compromised – by his friendship with the president. In 1963, the rules were different, and both politician and journalist benefited.

※

At 7:56 p.m. Kennedy climbed the familiar spiral stairs leading to Joe Alsop's dark green front door. He stepped through a small vestibule with black-and-white checkered floor into the dining room. On the right was the kitchen. On the left, behind bifolds, the living room, lined with floor-to-ceiling bookshelves, its fireplace flanked by two dark brown Japanese silk screens. There was a large Louis XIV desk and the *pièce de résistance* – large windows framed by tapered drapes coiled on the floor. The furniture was French, the fabrics olive and brown, and blue-and-white stripes. There was much chinoiserie. Kennedy made his way to the back, where the living room's windows looked out on the loggia, connecting the two wings of the house. Between them was the garden, a little fountain on a patch of lawn surrounded by box bushes. There, the guests were gathering before dinner.

Kennedy was not even on the list until that afternoon. He had called Alsop and solicited an invitation only to change his mind and then change it again. In between, David Bruce was asked in his stead. "Actually, he filled the place for the President, who had said he would like to come at the next-to-last moment, and then at the last moment, after a female had been procured for him, had a bit of bother with his back, caused by his taxing weekend trip to Hawaii,"

139

Alsop wrote Evangeline Bruce in London. "I must say, we are getting rather grand . . . Ambassadors to fill President's places, indeed!" His oblique reference suggests that as much as Kennedy had come that evening to hear about Profumo from the visiting Londoners, he was also interested in something – or someone – else. His thickly forested interior life was coming into the light in the way it often did. Kennedy had his secrets. He was in good company. Others that evening had theirs, too.

The (nominal) guest of honor was Sir Maurice Bowra, who was visiting America that month to receive an honorary degree at Harvard. Alsop was finishing an eclectic book on ancient Greece (*From the Silent Earth: A Report on the Greek Bronze Age*) for which Bowra provided a glowing introduction. Bowra was one of the world's foremost Hellenists – a translator, poet, and historian, author of more than a dozen books on Greek poetry. Knighted in 1951, he had been president of the British Academy since 1958. He was warden of Wadham College for thirty-two years. A cosmopolitan who ranged far and wide, his stage remained Oxford. His look was squat, like a concrete pillbox; his voice, stentorian. The philosopher Isaiah Berlin, a colleague at Oxford, called him "the greatest English wit of his day" and a peerless talker: "The words came in short, sharp bursts of precisely aimed, concentrated fire, as image, pun, metaphor, parody, seemed spontaneously to generate one another in a succession of marvelously imaginative patterns, sometimes rising to high, wildly comical fantasy."

Kennedy was interested in the ancient Greek view of life and believed, as Bowra said of the Greeks, "that each individual had his own world to make." Jackie much admired *The Greek Way*, the popular exploration of the ancient soul by classicist Edith Hamilton, who had died in Washington at 95 a fortnight before. While Bowra had never met JFK until that evening, he was known to McGeorge Bundy, the president's national security advisor. In February Bundy had impulsively asked Bowra to write a character study of Harold

Wilson. It came to nothing when everyone realized, especially Bowra, that contemporary politics was not his field and he would have nothing to say.

That evening in June, Kennedy shared pleasantries with Bowra but dismissed him in thirty seconds. Bowra dismissed Kennedy, too. In a letter to Felix Frankfurter recalling his visit to Harvard, he belittles the college president ("I made no contact and suspect there is none to make") and makes no mention of meeting the American president at all. The next year, having met a widowed Jackie, he found the Kennedys more appealing. "It is like 18th century England, rich and powerful, but not uncultivated and with a few nice people," he wrote.

The other Britons at the dinner were all Kennedy intimates. David Ormsby-Gore was one of Kennedy's closest friends. "Jack used to say that he was the brightest man he'd ever met," recalled Jackie. There was no one JFK liked better and respected more. Ormsby-Gore was the gentle skeptic who warned that the Bay of Pigs invasion would fail because the Cubans would not overthrow Castro. He was the careful conciliator who helped put things back together after the misunderstanding over the Skybolt missile threatened to rupture Anglo-American relations in 1962. He was the cautionary voice during the Cuban Missile Crisis, suggesting the United States delay intercepting Soviet ships carrying missiles to Cuba to give Khrushchev more time to respond, while urging JFK to release the aerial photographs of the Soviet missiles to discredit those who said the Americans had invented them. Ormsby-Gore and Kennedy met in 1938 when Kennedy was taking time from Harvard to help his father at the American Embassy in London. They became distant relatives when Kennedy's sister, Kathleen ("Kick"), married Billy Hartington, Ormsby-Gore's cousin. Kennedy's season in London was the beginning of his lifelong affection for English literature, history, heroes, rogues, and gentry. In taste and ideas, some said JFK was more British than American.

Ormsby-Gore fondly recalled their "25-year conversation" about the world.

Ormsby-Gore was the son of a baron and a descendant of Lord Salisbury, the nineteenth-century British prime minister. His pedigree made him "one of the diminishing bands of landed aristocrats in our time." He had the credentials: Eton, Oxford, soldier (major in the Second World War), gentleman farmer (managed two dairy farms), parliamentarian (elected as a Conservative in 1950), parliamentary secretary and cabinet minister (minister of state for foreign affairs). Although he held a junior cabinet position, Ormsby-Gore impressed everyone with his skill as a negotiator in disarmament talks and his effectiveness as a spokesman. In 1961, Kennedy asked Macmillan to send his friend to Washington. He did. Ormsby-Gore resigned his seat, gathered his willowy wife, Sissie, and three of their five children and arrived on October 24, 1961. Two days before, the Queen had knighted him. In June 1963, he was forty-five. Tall, thin, stylish, and scholarly, Sir David was polite, mild-mannered, and typically underspoken, which hid a diamond-hard intelligence. "He can knock down the other fellow's debating points with just the proper mixture of sympathy and contempt," wrote A.M. Rosenthal of the *New York Times*.

※

"Get me the British Ambassador," JFK would instruct Mrs. Lincoln, and Ormsby-Gore would marvel at the places he was "ferreted out to talk to Jack." Beyond the White House, the two couples spent weekends in Hyannis Port, Palm Beach, and Camp David. The Kennedys would have seen them every week had their friend not been ambassador, Jackie said. She stopped inviting them at the last minute because she felt guilty that the accommodating Ormsby-Gore (who could say no to the president?) was having to ignore his official obligations to join them. Bruce noted that "the

President's confidence in David Gore was fully justified by the transcendent qualities and unimpeachable character of the British Ambassador." It may be that no ambassador and no president had ever enjoyed this kind of association, and it rankled other diplomats in Washington.

An evening like this one in Georgetown – though it was not the president's house or his invitation – was the social hierarchy at work. Diplomats, like journalists, did business over drinks and dinner. They knew well who was in favor with the White House and who was not. This scorekeeping was obsessive among the well-tailored accountants of envy who expected attention by virtue of the size of their country. Generally speaking, Kennedy thought little of diplomats. As James Reston, the columnist, told one of the city's social lepers in 1962: "The President has not much use for professional diplomats and thinks them a lesser breed of men who are useful if they produce facts or memoranda but do not take risks or face the decisions of politics. He says that this attitude dates back to the days when the President's father was Ambassador in London, and to the contemptuous view that old Kennedy took of his diplomatic staff." In a capital of ins and outs, this created its own Society of the Aggrieved. Among the diplomats, its recording secretary was Hervé Alphand, ambassador of France.

Alphand was funny, erudite, and cultured with a high sense of self-regard. He and his wife, Nicole, had been fixtures in town since 1957; she was a classic beauty and one of the best-dressed women around. Alphand and Kennedy had met when Kennedy was a senator who, unusually, supported independence for Algeria. For the first two years of Kennedy's presidency, they had a cordial relationship. Alphand proudly told his diary that he and his wife had dined with the president the night of his Inauguration, "the only foreigners among his American friends." A few days later, JFK invited Alphand to the White House, assuring him that he wanted to meet him at once because he wanted "to entertain the best possible relations with our country." In 1961, after the Kennedys' glittering visit to Paris, Alphand says that Kennedy wanted to see him as much as possible and invited him to call "even at midnight, if need be." In Palm Beach, in 1962, Alphand mused about an upcoming conversation with the president: "What to discuss this evening? Europe? Without a doubt! What is going on in the Kremlin? Of course! China? Of course!" He found Kennedy "never pretentious nor pompous" and marveled at "his casual simplicity, [which] is part of the tradition of the President of this country."

Alphand's albatross was Charles de Gaulle. As much as the French-speaking Jackie and her handsome husband had charmed the French during their 1961 visit, relations had soured between the French and Americans in 1963. De Gaulle had vetoed Britain's entry to the European Common Market, worried that the organization would come "under American domination and direction," and he had been obstinate on disarmament. Both annoyed Washington. Although de Gaulle "never spoke to Hervé," according to Jackie, his sins were visited upon Alphand. The ambassador became less useful. As his stature fell, Ormsby-Gore's rose. Once Alphand went to see the president in Palm Beach with a message from de Gaulle. As he entered one room of the seaside villa, he saw Ormsby-Gore coming out the other. By the spring of 1963, Alphand felt that he was getting "the cold shoulder" from the Kennedys; Ormsby-Gore reported to Macmillan that the French were "in the doghouse" in Washington. Jackie noted Alphand's "desperation about Ormsby-Gore," and recalled how JFK "always tried to be so nice to Hervé and sometimes he'd say, 'We should ask him to dinner because he's about to explode again.'" Still, Hervé and Nicole remained a preeminent couple in Washington, a stature recognized when Nicole graced the cover of *Time*. The date was November 22, 1963.

*

Alphand wasn't the only outcast. West Germany resented its insignificance in Washington. (Ormsby-Gore observed that its exile was largely due to two successive ambassadors who were "both extremely bad.") Canada, America's neighbor, historic ally, and largest trading partner, was also seething on the sidelines. In 1963, its ambassador was Charles Stewart Almon Ritchie, a hawk-nosed, dapper blue blood from Nova Scotia, with a mid-Atlantic accent, a sharp ear, and a gifted pen. In 1938, having read history and literature at Oxford, he joined Canada's fledgling foreign service, which, in 1959, Senator Kennedy deemed "probably unequalled by any other nation." Ritchie served in Ottawa, London, Bonn, and New York. He was the personification of "the golden age of Canadian diplomacy," when Canada, by virtue of its disproportionate military and financial contribution to the Second World War, had some influence in the postwar world. Ritchie was one of a constellation of stars who helped Canada play a role in the making of the new international architecture, including the establishment of the World Bank, the International Monetary Fund, the United Nations, the General Agreement on Tariffs and Trade, and particularly the North Atlantic Treaty Organization. The best of them was Lester B. Pearson, ambassador, foreign minister, Nobel Laureate, and future prime minister.

Like others in this story, Ritchie was an aesthete and a Casanova. He had an affair of some thirty years with Elizabeth Bowen, the Anglo-Irish novelist, which continued after he was married. His secret life informs the diary he kept (with some gaps) from 1922 until his death in 1995. In retirement, he published four volumes, the first of which won Canada's most prestigious literary award. His diaries are diverting but less revealing than his more voluminous unpublished journals and letters, which were not opened until 2011.

Ritchie was even more isolated in Washington than Alphand and for the same reason: the administration's antagonism toward his government. It tormented Ritchie, and he complained bitterly about it. Yet from his perch at Canada's official residence on Rock

Creek Drive, or at the Embassy of Canada in Embassy Row on Massachusetts Avenue, Ritchie watched – and recorded – the social parade and political drama of the capital. Bored with his official duties, he scribbled away, putting diplomacy in the service of his diary. As a confidant of many in Kennedy's court – though not the King himself – Ritchie offered a skeptical, sometimes trenchant, view of the New Frontier and its cast of acolytes, toadies, and retainers. From earlier diplomatic posts he knew almost everyone in the Establishment, beginning with that evening's host, Joe Alsop, whom Ritchie called "the most thoroughly hated man in Washington."

After a dinner party in 1962, Ritchie moaned that Alsop ignored or dismissed everything he said, "but it's hard to tell whether this was personal, for he seems to live in a perpetual angry argument with events and people, like the cartoon character Donald Duck but not like him because Jo [sic] has teeth and can bite." Later he puzzled over the "great cult for him in his circle in Washington." Ritchie was unpersuaded, much as he liked Susan Mary, an old friend. "The other day someone said to me, 'You must come on Thursday. Jo [sic] is coming and is in a very good mood.' I felt inclined to answer, 'I'd love to come if I am in a good mood.'"

Of the other guests that evening who had come under Ritchie's steady gaze, Oatsie Leiter stands out as "that generous-natured beauty who brings a breeze of high spirits into this town." Alice Longworth, though, "looked like a witch, in her big shovel hat. She is amusing in a gossipy, bitchy way, but not, I find, very funny or congenial." Etchingly honest and painfully self-deprecating, Ritchie's observations do not appear in the chronicles of Camelot. But from the moment Ritchie arrived in Washington on April 28, 1962, he looked up and down the New Frontier and offered an uncharitable view.

Ritchie had the misfortune to represent a country led by John George Diefenbaker. The relationship between the Conservative prime minister and the Democratic president (historically a mis-match) had started badly when the Kennedys visited Ottawa in March 1961 and never recovered. Diefenbaker thought Kennedy elitist, imperious, and too enamored of Lester Pearson's Liberals; Kennedy thought Diefenbaker ornery, pompous, and bloviating, reminding him of swaggering prairie populists. Both Jackie and Bobby later maintained that JFK "hated" Diefenbaker, who nursed a spirited anti-Americanism. When Ritchie presented his creden-tials to Kennedy in the Oval Office on May 26, 1962, he found Kennedy "civil" but "distinctly cool," and "deliberately creating a distance," which Ritchie thought reflected his antipathy for the prime minister. Their conversation was strained – banalities punc-tuated by long pauses – which was unnatural for two natural con-versationalists. "No, it was not 'a click' with the President," an embarrassed Ritchie wrote in his unpublished diary. "I felt ineffec-tive . . . and nervous. That's what occasions are for – to rise to them. This was one I didn't rise to."

For the next year or so, Ritchie was shunned. He felt the administration distrusted Canada's "self-righteousness and self-centredness." They "think we are a small-time bunch who don't belong in the big league." It did not help that a suspicious Diefenbaker had been slow to support the United States during the Cuban Missile Crisis, prompting Bobby's cutting wisecrack: "Canada offers all aid short of help." Sure, Ritchie was able to see McGeorge Bundy, whom he liked but did not understand, and Dean Rusk, who looked like "Buddha" or "a Chinaman – a short one." But if Ormsby-Gore was a high priest and Alphand was an outcast, Ritchie was an untouchable. In February 1963, Ritchie acknowledged his isolation: "Having virtually given up on the Kennedys, I have now . . . resigned myself to having a housemaid's keyhole view of them. But even if I boast, as I now do of being OUT, I still find it tiresome to be treated from that moment as if I am not only OUT but non-existent."

That began to change – if not personally, at least politically – when Pearson became prime minister on April 22, 1963. Kennedy knew and liked "Mike" Pearson, whom he had welcomed to the White House with other Nobel Laureates in 1962, and whose published collection of speeches he had reviewed admiringly in 1959. Kennedy immediately invited Pearson to Hyannis Port. Ritchie tagged along and found the meeting "an ordeal," because he worried about putting a foot wrong with Kennedy.

On June 10, Ritchie was preparing to leave for a holiday in England, his refuge, where he would see Elizabeth Bowen. Given his discomfort in the hub of the universe, he confessed surprisingly that he was leaving with mixed feelings because "the Washington Game has me in thrall." Like everyone else, particularly those with unconventional sex lives, he was following the Profumo Affair. From Oxford, he wrote that Profumo was engaging big minds at High Table as well as prurient ones in the Common Room. "I have been seeing something of Isaiah [Berlin] and other philosophers with a taste for scandal," he wrote, staying up until 1:00 a.m. with them "drinking on and on and talking of Profumo." He noted the admonition of a fellow diplomat, who was agog at this secret, sex-charged world of 1963: "There but for the grace of God go so many of us."

✳

In Georgetown, the guests were in the garden, chatting over drinks. Keen to know more about Profumo, Kennedy approached Antonia Fraser. They sat down – he in the ubiquitous rocking chair which she assumed was "a semi-permanent fixture" in the house, graciously provided by the Alsops for their frequent guest – and fell into "a quite long conversation." It would occupy most of Kennedy's evening. "He picked me out," Fraser recalled fifty years later. "The reason he wanted to talk to me was because I was the wife of an

MP and he thought that I could fill him in on what was going on in London: the drugs, the this-and-that. He wanted to hear about it. It [the conversation] was fairly light-hearted. He wanted to get the picture." He knew "the elements," yes, but wasn't there color and tone that those diverting cables and titillating newspaper stories had missed?

Antonia Fraser would know. She would transmit the welter of anecdote, innuendo, and rumor in London that an observant wife of an even lesser cabinet minister than Profumo would hear and that a future biographer of kings and queens would parse. And she was young, smart, irreverent, and stunning. In drawing out information, Kennedy was prosecutorial. His curiosity was relentless; when he fixed on a subject, he fired questions until either his powder was gone or his interlocutor's well was dry. Then, with nothing left to learn, he would move on to someone else. As Hugh Fraser remembered: "I think he was always a great questioner. He was very interested in things. For every one question one asked him he asked two, I think, at least. Why? He always wanted to know why things were and how things worked."

In this inquisitive mind, gossip had a corner. As Alsop said after JFK's death: "He adored gossip. There is a grave shortage of gossip in Washington because, as I always say, real estate replaces sex in this city. . . . We'd get back from London and he'd ask: 'What's the news?' He had a very human fondness for gossip and all that." What he liked about Susan Mary was that she could tell a good story. Slender and soigné, she had lived in Paris and London, where she had had an affair with Duff Cooper, the British statesman and author. Moving among the grandees of Britain, France, and America, she always knew what was happening on both sides of the Atlantic and learned early that, as Joe put it, "the only feminine conversation that [Kennedy] really enjoyed was straight-out gossip." Once, Alsop admonished his wife after one of their soirées: "You were very good this evening. But stop talking only about serious matters and David Cecil's books. Tell him who's sleeping with whom, he loves that."

On Monday evening Kennedy was not interested in Susan Mary or his old friend, Hugh Fraser, whom he had seen the week before out west. Fraser and Kennedy went back to 1938, when Kennedy met Ormsby-Gore and those other young gentry destined to go to war and into politics. Hugh dated Jack's sister, Eunice, and socialized with his other sister, Kathleen, and his brother, Joe Jr. Although Hugh and JFK were contemporaries and friends, Kennedy was never as close to Fraser as he was to Ormsby-Gore. Fraser preceded Ormsby-Gore into Parliament, winning a seat in 1945. He then joined the cabinet as junior minister in the War Office (1958-1960), followed by the Colonial Office (1960-1962), and ending up as secretary of state for air (1962-1964). Jackie was scornful of these "sad lives" of unfulfilled aristocrats. "Hugh Fraser was a sort of friend," she told Arthur Schlesinger in 1964, "but not very bright, and you'd always wonder if Hugh would get a job in some government and he never did, or, it was a pathetic one." As she saw it, her husband was president and Fraser was a junior minister, and they had both entered politics around the same time.

In 1945, Fraser was running for Parliament as a Conservative and Kennedy, then a correspondent with Hearst Newspapers, came to his constituency in Staffordshire. JFK wanted to see what he could learn before launching his own career in Boston the next year. The night of the nomination, he marveled at how well Fraser spoke. On their visit to the United States eighteen years later, the Frasers had accompanied JFK on *Air Force One* to Colorado Springs, one of the stops on the president's five-state western tour ending in Hawaii on June 9. Fraser was surprised to hear Kennedy recall his tumultuous nomination, particularly the role of the chairman, "imitating accent, mannerisms, and voice of that long-forgotten declaration as to how lucky the audience were to have me,

Hugh Fraser, as their candidate. 'You see,' he [JFK] ended, 'what you British can't understand, no one in this country ever thinks they're lucky to have anyone as a candidate, even less as a President. That's the difference between our systems.' It was total and managed recall, funny, and a homily from a proper democrat."

For the president, this evening was more about Antonia than Hugh. She had attracted the attention of the American press, which she seemed to relish; her newspaper clippings, her black-and-white photographs, and her handwritten entries in fountain pen from her two visits to the New World, in 1961 and 1963, fill two leather-bound albums, which have rested for a half century on the top of a dusty bookshelf in a corner of her drawing room. The Frasers had visited Kennedy at the White House in 1961, when they had joined him for a swim. Hugh paddled about talking about the crisis in British Guiana with the president, who was uninterested, and changed the subject. Antonia snapped a picture of the two of them splashing around. Then she joined them in "the boiling pool." "I managed to squeeze into one of Jackie's bathing suits," she recalls, "hoping to catch the Presidential eye."

Catching any man's eye was easy for the sensational Lady Fraser. That June she was thirty years old, daughter of the eccentric Earl of Longford, who was an author, scholar, and leader of the Labour Party in the House of Lords. She was a graduate of Oxford, a mother, and author of her first book, *Dolls*. She had been married since 1956 and had become "an enthusiastic Conservative." The Frasers and their brood lived in a rambling pile at 52 Campden Hill Square, near Notting Hill. (She would later occupy the house with her second husband, playwright Harold Pinter, whom she married after a highly publicized affair. When he won the Nobel Prize for Literature and she became a best-selling historian and novelist, it was called London's leading literary address.) In 1963 she was described as a winsome Julie Christie, the young British movie actress starring in *Billy Liar* that summer. On her visits to the

United States, Antonia Fraser's exoticism and taste for adventure had made an impression on the colonials.

Ever the accommodating wife, she took up flying when Hugh Fraser became air minister. As she and her husband toured the air bases with General Curtis LeMay, the blustering, cigar-chomping, trigger-happy chief of staff of the Air Force, she was invited to fly the plane carrying the dignitaries between the bases. "You don't meet someone every day like Curt LeMay," Lady Fraser says today. "He asked me to fly the plane. I did. The British politicians on board were horrified." (A family boating accident, though, ended her career as an aviatrix. "My mother said, 'you have children.' She said, 'Please stop.'" She did.) At the headquarters of Strategic Air Command, she was invited to use the special telephone that could reach anywhere in the world. She called Campden Hill Square, to the nursery, to speak to the children. "Gave them a total shock!" she exclaims.

The local newspapers swooned at the "statuesque" visitor who had dropped into their midst "refuting all the clichés about the typical English woman. She was extremely easy to approach and converse with," they reported. The newspapers enthused about her exquisite, off-white, two-piece shift, bought ready-made in a dress shop. They noted that she thought wigs (then the rage) were practical and that she had a greenhouse and was an avid gardener. "She was the picture of coolness and elegance in the Florida heat," said one report, on her visit to Cape Canaveral to see the space installation there. "Except for her English accent, she projects the image of a woman anywhere in the world."

Attending the parties, the lunches, and the receptions that filled the itinerary of any visiting minister, Antonia Fraser remembers the heat. When she emerged from a hairdresser in Georgetown with a fashionable beehive, it wilted within minutes. "It was intensely hot," she writes in her diary, "and that seemed to accentuate the heat coming from Profumo." On June 5, while the Frasers were on tour, Pierre Salinger relayed the bombshell from London that Profumo had resigned. The visiting Britons joked among themselves that it was Sir Alec Douglas-Home who had resigned. They found that riotously funny because the homely Sir Alec was an unlikely candidate for sex or scandal.

At the dinner party, Antonia and Jack chatted in the small garden tended by Rachel "Bunny" Mellon, the horticulturalist whom the Kennedys had asked to remake the White House gardens. The president fired his predictable volley of questions, most of which she could answer even though she had been away from home for several days. "I was telling him all I knew," she recalls. "I knew him, I wasn't a courtier." The subtext, she noted, was sex. "Here in Washington, we raise a cheer if anyone can do it at all," Kennedy coyly told her. It was an authentic sentiment, even if his choice of word sounds strange. Fraser took it in and wanted to respond. Were he not president, she says, she might have said, "'Well, I don't think you have a problem in that regard.' Or, 'Well, Jack, I think you're in the minority who could do it all the time.'" Of course, she would not have called him "Jack" (it would have been "Mr. President," she says) and that kind of reflexive observation would have been too impolitic or impertinent. But knowing JFK and his proclivities, as she did, the conversation made perfect sense. If Kennedy was falsely lamenting that no one was having much sex in Washington – which he knew was not true, at least in personal terms – her instinct was to challenge him. She knew that he was toying with her and she wanted to do the same. Kennedy had no more romantic interest that evening in Antonia Fraser – at least not one she saw – than he had in Susan Mary (who maintained, to her disappointment, that he never made a pass at her). No doubt he found Fraser's audacity attractive. Three years later, visiting the United States on a book tour, Fraser told the *New York Times* playfully that she would like to see her picture hanging in the National Portrait Gallery in London, "with a little plaque like there is under one marvelous man, saying, 'Wit, Raconteur, Author, Dandy, and Balloonist.' I would like it to say, 'Beauty,' too."

Kennedy spent about forty-five minutes in the garden with Fraser, the entire time he was there. It may have been thirty minutes, as David Bruce recalled. "Actually, it was extremely cozy," concluded Joe Alsop. "The President did come for a drink and stayed so long (talking to Antonia Fraser and looking rather like a small boy, wondering whether to plunge his spoon into a fresh dish of peach ice cream) that he might almost as well [have] stayed to dinner anyway." In any event, they did not talk about his speech at American University that morning (Fraser was unaware of the speech then) or the president's date with the governor the next morning. Scandal was more interesting and gossip, for him, as Fraser says, was "light relief from all that he had to do." She assured Kennedy that whatever Profumo said in the months before he rose in the House in June and admitted that he had lied, no one had believed him. Except, perhaps, the forlorn Harold Macmillan, who had been cuckolded by his wife, Dorothy. "Jack Profumo was a charming man," Fraser told JFK. "What did they think they [he and Keeler] did? Discuss the constitution?" Kennedy was amused. "I thought he was having a good time, listening to [the details] of what was a hot affair."

In 1963, Fraser had not yet established herself as a serious historian who would turn out, over the decades, a clutch of fine biographies of European monarchs. When she wrote *King Charles II* in 1979, she saw a parallel in Kennedy and Charles. Both drew divisions between their Catholicism and their office, and their characters were similar. "They both had a dry, witty sense of humor, not exactly cynicism but close," she said in 1979. "Their sense of fun was marked." Indeed, both Kennedy and "the Merry Monarch," as he was called, shared a lively libido.

There was no talk of the monarch in the garden. Only Profumo. His curiosity quenched, Kennedy was ready to move on. If he had been going to stay for dinner, he had changed his mind, as he had about even coming in the first place. Why? Perhaps there was "a little bother with his back," as Alsop reported that he had told him that afternoon. Perhaps he had something else to do that evening. Before going, though, he chatted with the other woman of interest there. Seeing her again, after several days away, may have been the reason he had come that evening. Her name was Mary Pinchot Meyer.

✳

Mary Meyer, Mary Meyer. What to say about Mary Pinchot Meyer, the blonde enchantress, the society adventuress, the "Lady Ottoline of Camelot"? What to say about the president's most serious lover, with the most persistent claim on his affections and the most plausible influence on his thoughts, especially those questions of war and peace that he had raised that very day? How to explain her mysterious end? No one has.

On June 10, 1963, Meyer was forty-two years old. She was a divorcée, living in a garden house on N Street in Georgetown, behind the home of her sister and brother-in-law, Tony and Ben Bradlee. Meyer was called "a socialite," but she wasn't wealthy and was less interested in money and station than art, ideas, and influence. She was the free-thinker in the Court of King Jack. She had been raised in the 1930s in Milford, Pennsylvania, where she was exposed through her parents to Louis Brandeis, Harold L. Ickes, and other liberals. Her father was Amos Pinchot, a prominent Progressive, and her uncle was Gifford Pinchot, a leading conservationist whom Theodore Roosevelt appointed as the first chief of the reconstituted U.S. Forest Service. She went to Vassar College, wrote for *Mademoiselle* and the *Atlantic Monthly*, and later became a painter. Her politics were confidently left-of-center. She met and fell in love with Cord Meyer Jr., a handsome marine who was a champion of world federalism. So was she. They married in 1945, had three boys, and lived in postwar, suburban Washington. Like other men of high education and pedigree, Cord worked for the Central Intelligence Agency.

Mary was quirky and rebellious. Peter Janney, then a nine-year-old classmate of Michael, one of Mary's sons, recalls chasing a baseball into the Meyers' back garden in McLean, Virginia, and finding her reading on a blanket, "completely naked, her backside in the sun. I was breathless." He was startled but she was not. A year later, he remembers seeing her looking out from her studio, and thinking "there was something unique about Michael's mother, beyond her glistening, radiant beauty. She was so unlike any other adult in my world at that time. Calm and still, at peace with herself, she had a presence and a demeanor that struck me." In 1956, Michael was hit by a car as he was crossing a busy road and killed. He was nine years old. Mary's marriage to Cord, which was already in trouble, dissolved two years later. Affairs followed, one with an Italian nobleman, another with the abstract painter Ken Noland. Of all of them, the most publicized, the most dangerous, and the most consequential, was with Jack Kennedy.

Kennedy and Meyer had known each other since he was at Choate and she was at Brearley, the prestigious girls' school in New York City's Upper East Side that taught the daughters of the Establishment, including, in the future, Caroline Kennedy. They met in 1935, in Kennedy's senior year. She had been escorted to a school dance by William Attwood, one of his classmates. Over the years, Jack and Mary encountered each other at college, as journalists (they were both at the founding of the United Nations), and in Washington. On that evening in June, Kennedy found himself sitting in Joe Alsop's garden between his two school friends, Attwood and Meyer. One was his ambassador, the other his lover. Attwood, a paratrooper in the Second World War, had been a correspondent in Paris for the *New York Herald Tribune* before writing speeches for Adlai Stevenson and then Kennedy in 1960. Kennedy sent him as envoy to Guinea, where he contracted polio, which gave him a permanent limp. He returned home after two busy years. Attwood was in Washington awaiting a highly secret new assignment to Cuba; Kennedy didn't know he was in town until he ran into him at the dinner party and asked Attwood why he hadn't dropped by to see him. Attwood said he'd requested an appointment but none had been arranged. Characteristically, Kennedy asked Attwood to stop by the White House for a chat, which he did two days later. That night, when they were not discussing the scandal in London, the three revisited the past. "I remember that we sat in the garden talking about the Profumo case and reminiscing about our school days," Attwood recalled in 1967. "Mary Meyer, a Washington artist who'd been my date at a prom twenty-eight years before, was between us, and Kennedy happily recalled having cut in on her on the dance floor. It was hard, at times like that, to realize he was President of the United States." Attwood, like others, remembered Meyer as "the best," and the best always attracted JFK.

One unwitting observer of Meyer's elegant deception was Marian Schlesinger, the wife of Arthur Schlesinger. In an unpublished manuscript among her former husband's papers at the New York Public Library, she describes a glamorous dinner dance at the White House. "I do recall an amusing exchange with the artist Mary Meyer and her sister, Toni [sic], as we retired to the powder room and mutually complained about being wall flowers in the face of youthful beauties from New York. Years later, when it was revealed that Mary Meyer had a passionate affair with the President, I was amused to reflect that I had [been] genially bamboozled by the attractive woman. I reflected that in Mary Meyer, the president had shown excellent taste, for she was a person of talent, beauty, and class."

Mary Meyer was also adventurous, dabbling in psychoanalysis, mysticism, and drugs. In the spring of 1962, she turned up unannounced in the Department of Psychology at Harvard College. She was looking for Timothy Leary, who was leading experiments into

LSD, an emerging hallucinogen (legal until 1963). The drug was becoming popular among those hoping to expand their consciousness and creativity. "I looked up to see a woman leaning against the door post, hip tilted provocatively, studying me with a bold stare," Leary recalled in his memoir. "Good looking. Flamboyant eyebrows, piercing green-blue eyes, fine-boned face. Amused, arrogant, aristocratic. 'Dr. Leary,' she said cooly. 'I've got to talk to you.'" Meyer asked Leary how to run an LSD clinic. She apparently told him she had used the drug and wanted to learn to use it with "this friend who's a very important man." Mary visited Leary some seven times over the next eighteen months, when she was also seeing JFK.

It is preposterous to suggest that Kennedy would have taken LSD as president; the poison of choice for his generation was alcohol, and he rarely drank more than a daiquiri or a Bloody Mary. But the story hints at Mary Meyer's relationship with JFK. She had access to the president that few others did. That she was a frequent visitor to the White House, often when Jackie was away, and that she was seen by aides and others upstairs with JFK in the residence has been well documented in a host of chronicles of Kennedy's private world. Said Myer "Mike" Feldman, who worked for Ted Sorensen as deputy special counsel to the president: "I'd walk in and out of the office all the time and I would see her in the Oval Office or over in the residence. Around eight-thirty, when the day was over, often I'd walk over to the residence and she'd be sitting there. There wasn't any attempt to hide her the way there was with some of the other women."

Ben Bradlee says that he did not know about the affair between the president and his sister-in-law until a year after JFK's death. Dave Powers, who knew all the secrets and took them to his grave, insisted that theirs was not a romantic relationship, though he allowed that "Jack loved to talk to her and he talked to her about just about anything. He trusted her and didn't feel he had to restrict himself around her." Powers dissembled about the relationship, as would other Kennedy loyalists in the decades to come. In fact, Meyer herself talked and wrote about her affair. Friends saw it. More important, though, it may have been more than an affair; in Kennedy's heart, which seemed closed to romantic love, Kennedy may have truly loved Meyer. She kept a diary that wasn't found until after her early, awful death. Before it was destroyed, Ben Bradlee saw it. In handwritten notes on the manuscript of Bradlee's memoir, he writes: "I remember only one phrase: 'He says I am the only woman he kissed while making love,' or words to that effect." On this day, what mattered was whether Meyer shaped Kennedy's late-life thinking on peace and reconciliation, which was the point of his appeal to the Russians earlier that day.

Did she? It's unlikely that she was at American University that day. Or that she knew about his speech before he gave it. Or, even that she said anything to him that night about it. Whatever his reason, Kennedy had wanted to see her that night; she was surely the "female [who] had been procured for him," as Alsop had put it. Meyer would see him two nights later, at the White House, and many nights after that, as the test ban treaty was negotiated, debated, and ratified.

✳

If Washington was a society of secrets in 1963, Georgetown was its seat. The elite wrote its own rules and discretion was cardinal. Although many people knew of illicit assignations, what is truly remarkable is how few talked. Before Facebook, Instagram, and Twitter, restraint ruled. "Sharing" wasn't a religion. Those who did speak of their lives on the other side of Camelot did not speak until years later, if at all.

On June 10, the affair between Mary and Jack was *the* secret of the dinner party, though the Alsops seemed to know. Other guests had secrets that evening. Maurice Bowra was gay, which wasn't unusual among Oxford dons, but he could not come out for fear of ending his academic career. Joe Alsop was also a closet homosexual. He was nearly outed in 1957 when he was photographed in a hotel room in Moscow with a man and threatened with blackmail. Refusing to be cowed, Alsop appealed to the U.S. ambassador, and was spirited out of the country. The liaison never came to light. Years later, incriminating photographs surfaced in Washington. Alsop told Isaiah Berlin of his sexual orientation and others suspected it, but it never mattered. In *The Columnist*, his character is defiant when he meets the former lover who tried to entrap him and blackmail him with photographs. He told him he had gone to the State Department and the FBI. "I said, 'Here's what I am. If my career's to end, I want *you* to end it, not those depraved blackmailing psychopaths over there.' And they *didn't* end it. And *that* is the difference between my country and yours."

In 1960, when Alsop proposed to Susan Mary, who was the widow of his best friend, Bill Patten, he revealed his homosexuality. She married him in what Antonia Fraser calls "a marriage of convenience." It made them the reigning couple of Washington. The arrangement gave each what they wanted: for Susan Mary, stature and influence; for Joe, at fifty, two children, to whom he became a committed stepfather. In the 1940s, while living in Paris, Susan Mary's affair with Duff Cooper produced a son, Billy. He was raised thinking his father was Bill Patten. Late in her life, she disclosed that Cooper was his father. It shattered her son, who tells his story in an anguished account called *My three Fathers*.

Secrets, secrets, secrets. That spring was suffused with sex, in London and in Washington. Arthur Schlesinger had returned from Britain in March struck by the spreading immorality. "It is hard to overstate the atmosphere of political squalor in London today," he wrote Kennedy. Surveying the scandals – among them, the indiscreet letters between a junior admiralty minister and a homosexual clerk who was a Soviet spy – he found "the cumulative effect . . .

has been to reinforce the impression that the Government is frivolous and decadent, and that everything is unraveling at the seams." In Washington, too, men and women were straying and marriages were dissolving.

While Charles Ritchie was on the wrong side of the New Frontier, he recognized the sexual undercurrent of Kennedy's Washington. It was a part of his own life, too, turning up starkly in his diary. Beyond his affair with Elizabeth Bowen, Ritchie spent days and nights thinking about sex, or sex as a motif, when he wasn't whiling away afternoons reading novels. Contemplating his dreary official obligations in steamy Washington, he laments: "I can see that I must abandon thoughts of frivolity, amusement, sex, snobbism, and intimate 'Personal Relations,' and give myself to such subjects as lumber exports, interest rates, and levels of North American rivers." On JFK, he knows nothing of the women the commander in chief is reviewing but observes: "He [Kennedy] is a power symbol, and it is hard to think of him apart from the power he now exercises, as it has been to think of Elizabeth Taylor apart from the sex she symbolizes." During the capital's obsession with the Profumo Affair, he notes that a friend tells him that "she envied Christine and Mandy [Rice-Davies, one of Stephen Ward's courtesans] because she had so little or no sex in her youth. 'It was a waste and I hate waste,' she lamented." One languid summer afternoon that year, a bored Ritchie postulates, "What about sex in the afternoon, or would it be too humid?"

Those who knew Kennedy well, like Antonia Fraser, knew of his philandering, which was why she thought as she did that evening, even if she checked her impulse to counter Kennedy's assertion of the sexual ennui of Washington. "He shared a flat with my husband in Shropshire," she recalls, when he had visited Hugh in his constituency in 1945, "and it was sex all the time." When Hugh Fraser was politely asked about Kennedy as "a playboy" in 1966, he was delightfully arch. (JFK was only with him a couple of days, he said.) "I think he liked a good time," Hugh allowed. "He liked girls. Very healthy attitude toward life." Lady Fraser, who knew Jackie better after Jack's death and contemplated writing her biography in the 1970s, suggests today that their marriage worked because "she must have done some deal with herself – some emotional deal that would allow her to put up with it."

Hervé Alphand was also aware of Kennedy's private life. "He . . . likes the pleasure of women," he told his diary. "His desires are difficult to satisfy without fearing a scandal and its use by political adversaries. This may happen one day, as he does not take sufficient precautions in this puritan country." Pleasure? No one could say that Jack Kennedy didn't seek it and savor it. "He enjoyed pleasure, you know," mused Joe Alsop. "It was one of his attractive traits. I think it's very unattractive not to enjoy pleasure."

On the evening of June 10, Kennedy enjoyed a particular pleasure. He was teasing, jesting, joshing, pretending. He was irony itself. While bemoaning the prudish capital, he lived like a Regency rake, exercising almost a *droit du seigneur*. The White House was no monastery and he was no monk. He pursued sex – brisk, varied, easy, and often. He did what he wanted and went where he wanted, as he would later that evening. Whatever impression he left with Antonia Fraser, he knew well there was no absence of sex in Washington – at least not for him and his promiscuous friends. But it amused him to talk about it and tempt her to reply in kind. In the same way, he would ask Tony Bradlee: "How's your sister?" He asked so frequently that Tony asked her husband, "Why doesn't he ask about *me*?" (She revealed later that when Kennedy did make a pass, she politely declined.) When Kennedy sat between Attwood and the bewitching Meyer in the garden, he knew that his old classmate had no inkling of their affair. Or, if he did, Kennedy didn't care. After all these years, Jack was still dancing with Mary, and no one was cutting in.

*

The unanswered question is why Kennedy was obsessed with Profumo. Was it the scandal itself that fascinated him? Or, was it because he worried that it was coming close to him? Some have explored the association between Stephen Ward, his callgirls, and others, like Suzy Chang, who are said to have slept with JFK before he was president. Christine Keeler, for her part, is said to have had a fling with Kennedy in New York City on a weekend in 1962. There is no evidence of that either, let alone a passing of secrets. Kennedy was linked more strongly with Ellen Rometsch, an East German émigré living in Washington. The press was on to her story and their liaison nearly exploded in the fall of 1963. She was quietly deported from the United States by Robert Kennedy, and a Senate commit-tee was persuaded not to pursue an investigation into "high-level administration officials" thought to be involved with her. Quite plausibly, Kennedy worried that his philandering would be exposed and it would undo him as it had undone, in a different way, Harold Macmillan. He was about the same age as Profumo, went by the same name (Jack), and had the same recklessness around women.

When Kennedy referred to Profumo in these months – as he referred to others accused of sexual misconduct – he was always sympathetic. Charles Spalding, an old friend who called JFK on June 11, reliably offers the most telling insights into Kennedy's char-acter. He remembered somebody making "some obvious remark, some critical remark. But he [JFK] was so quick to see, to defend him, and to say how easy he thought it might have been for a fellow under Profumo's circumstances, as he understood him, to make that kind of mistake, and how unjustified, in a sense, that extreme criticism was. He was very tolerant that way." At the end of his interview for an oral history, Spalding was asked if "there is any-thing about his [JFK's] attitude toward sex in American life that stands out in your mind?" "No," he replied.

Kennedy was also sympathetic later when he heard, through his brother, that Martin Luther King Jr. had been entertaining women in his room (some called it an "orgy") the night of the March on Washington on August 28, 1963. "Jack would never judge anyone in any sort of way," Jackie said. "He never really said anything against Martin Luther King." However, Kennedy would say something to Reverend King – a warning, really – which arose from the drama unfolding in Britain. For Kennedy, the threat of the Profumo Affair was now obvious. When Arthur Schlesinger had raised it with him in a short telephone conversation on March 22, the day Profumo issued his denial in the House of Commons, Schlesinger reported that the Conservatives "are in very bad shape and the party is falling apart . . . the most accident-prone party you have ever seen." He piqued Kennedy's interest when he mentioned a connection between Christine Keeler and Lord Astor – "Oh, was she?" Kennedy asked. It was early days, and he didn't press Schlesinger. His tone had none of his later curiosity. In March, though, the Profumo Affair was an accusation, bringing a denial from a minister; in June, it was a resignation threatening to bring down a prime minister and his government.

As details of the scandal emerged, there was a sense of *fin du régime* in London. Kennedy saw the lessons and the dangers more clearly by June. On June 22, he would pass them on to King in a conversation in the Rose Garden, where he escorted his guest out of worry that the Oval Office might be bugged. "You've read about Profumo in the papers?" he asked King. "Macmillan is likely to lose his government, because he has been loyal to a friend. That was an example of friendship and loyalty carried too far. You must be careful not to lose your cause for the same reason." Kennedy had been urging King to get rid of Stanley Levison, one of his prominent supporters, and Jack O'Dell. Both were Communists, or had been Communists, and King's enemies would use them to discredit the movement. King didn't believe Kennedy, demanded proof, and resisted severing relations. The warning had come from the attorney general through J. Edgar Hoover, the paranoid director of the FBI, which had Levison and O'Dell under investigation.

Jack Kennedy was a Cold Warrior, now evolving, but he wasn't a red-baiter (even if, when he arrived in the Senate, he had been less critical of Joe McCarthy than others had been). Decoding the Profumo Affair, Kennedy knew that it wasn't about spying anymore but about class, propriety, and hypocrisy. Having publicly committed himself and his presidency to civil rights, Kennedy was worried about allegations that might taint his government. "If they shoot *you* down, they'll shoot *us* down, too. So we're asking you to be careful," he warned King. Within a week, Levison and O'Dell were gone from King's circle.

Profumo never left Kennedy's mind. That fall, when scandal swirled around Bobby Baker, who had worked for Lyndon Johnson when he was Senate majority leader, Kennedy told Schlesinger that "this might be the Profumo Affair of the administration." Schlesinger said there was no sex involved, just money. "The President looked quizzical and remarked, that, when a newspaper man rang the doorbell at Bobby's townhouse, supposedly occupied by a couple of his secretaries, a girl in a negligee opened the door." Schlesinger told his unpublished diary that a well-placed friend told him "that Bobby had been running a kind of high-class whorehouse for the Senate," and that his friend feared "that a number of our friends – i.e. liberal Democrats – might be involved." As senator three years earlier, Kennedy knew Baker, his favors, and his secrets. As president, he knew what could happen if they came to light.

*

At the Alsops', it was now twilight. The sun had set at 8:33 p.m., bringing a merciful respite from the heat. It was not yet dark. Washington was approaching the solstice, the longest day of the year and the beginning of summer. It remained warm at this hour. As Joe Alsop noted, it was a jolly party, typical of the kind of salon that he and Susan Mary hosted.

Despite Alsop's entreaties, the president didn't stay for the meal. He would miss the soft-shell crabs, which David Bruce called "delicious, as is all the Alsop food." Bruce and the others stayed until "all hours;" Kennedy stayed fifty-three minutes. More likely than not, he had gotten what he wanted. He had learned more about Profumo from Antonia Fraser and had made a date with Mary Meyer, whom he would see the day after next. At 8:49 p.m., he climbed into his purring limousine and sped away.

Monday, June 10, 1963

CHAPTER 7

Night

LIKE THE EVENING LIGHT, Kennedy should have been fading by now. He had been on the go for the past fourteen hours, which was taxing for a man with a bad back, even with that restorative nap in midafternoon. He had slept less than usual on the nine-hour flight from Hawaii to Washington the previous night; before turning in on *Air Force One*, he had had dinner in his stateroom and joined Ted Sorensen, who was working on the Peace Speech. If His Restlessness had left the Alsops' early that evening, declining dinner and conversation for an early night, it would have been understandable. So when the president departed at 8:50 p.m. and arrived at the White House at 8:58 p.m., as the White House diary shows, his busy day appears to be over. A little night reading, perhaps a little television, then bed.

But Kennedy did not go straight home. Not if we believe the Secret Service, which kept the most reliable record of his movements. According to its logs, Kennedy left Dumbarton Road at 8:49 p.m. and did not arrive at the Southwest Gate until 9:56 p.m., reaching the residence a minute later. The drive to the White House from Georgetown takes less than ten minutes. That evening it took one hour and seven minutes. Where had he gone?

Perhaps Kennedy had plans to rejoin his brother Ted, who had not accompanied him to dinner (though the diary said he did). Perhaps they were slipping unannounced into a theater to catch part of a movie, as he, Jackie, and the Bradlees had done as they awaited the results of the West Virginia primary in 1960. That Monday night, in Washington, they might have seen *Hud*, an edgy drama starring Paul Newman and Patricia Neal, or *Dr. No*, starring Sean Connery, the latest in the James Bond movies that Kennedy loved. They might have belatedly joined Sorensen and his brother Tom for the 8:30 p.m. screening of *Irma la Douce* at the United States Information Agency. Then again, he never socialized with Sorensen.

Perhaps the president had gone to see someone. This was not out of the question. Decades later, former Secret Service agents reported that Kennedy would occasionally go unannounced to Mary Meyer's house or meet her at the Alsops' when the couple were away. But she was at the Alsops' that evening. It's unlikely she would have slipped out with Kennedy before dinner. Maybe she followed a few minutes later.

Or did JFK meet someone else? One possibility was Pamela Turnure, Jackie's press secretary, described as "a small fine-boned brunette with palest complexion and blue-green eyes which gazed unswervingly when she spoke." She was discreet and "totally unflappable." In the late 1950s she and Kennedy had had an affair. Turnure's disapproving landlady sent a less than incriminating picture, allegedly of Kennedy leaving her home, to a newspaper. Nothing was published and the landlady was dismissed as a crank, though she began a long, noisy campaign to show Kennedy morally unfit for the White House even after he moved in. In 1958 Turnure left that apartment and stayed, at Kennedy's request, with the recently divorced Mary Meyer at her home on 34th Street in Georgetown. Some intimates, such as Senator George Smathers, say their affair continued, episodically, in the White House. So do some members of the Secret Service. Others doubt it. We don't know. On Monday, though, Jackie was away and Turnure had called him three times that afternoon and evening – at 12:02 p.m. and again at 6:56 p.m. and 6:58 p.m.

On nights JFK was alone that summer, Mimi Beardsley says she often joined him. She had been a furtive but steady presence the previous summer and occasionally during the course of the year; she had returned to Wheaton College but made occasional visits to Washington or other places to see Kennedy. Most notably, she was upstairs in the residence on Friday, October 26, 1962, when the Cuban Missile Crisis was at its most dangerous. On a day the president had many things on his mind, she was among them. "Come to Washington," urged Powers, calling her at Wheaton that morning to relay the presidential invitation, as he often did. "Mrs. Kennedy is going to Glen Ora [the family's leased country home in Virginia]. I will send a car." Beardsley hastily caught a train but observed later that she didn't know what she – a twenty-one-year-old undergraduate – was doing with the president. It was "surreal," she later said. When Bobby Kennedy came upstairs that evening to confer with his brother, she hid in JFK's bedroom. "God knows I didn't belong there," she wrote. "But it was intoxicating."

Now, in early June, after finishing her sophomore year at Wheaton, she had returned to the White House press office for another summer. She arrived shortly after her fiancé's graduation from Williams College in early June. Her job that summer was to accompany press photographers around the White House. She says that she saw Kennedy every day, both in public and in private, though she didn't "stay over at the residence" as often as she had the previous summer.

Whatever the reason, the president disappeared for sixty-seven minutes beginning at 8:49 p.m. on June 10, like an airplane vanishing from a radar screen. Historically, for that hour or so, Kennedy is a missing person; we do not know where he was. In 1963, a president could still have a secret life, and this one enjoyed his.

❊

Kennedy's daily routine was less mysterious. William Manchester, Jim Bishop, Hugh Sidey, and other contemporary chroniclers followed him around as president and wrote about his day. Evenings, like mornings and afternoons, had a rhythm of their own. When Jackie and the children were away, as they were this evening, he usually called on Dave Powers. A friend and fixer, quick with a gag and deadly to cross, Powers arranged all things, high and low, for Kennedy. In 1963, he was fifty-one years old, a loyal retainer since 1946.

In *Johnny, We Hardly Knew Ye*, a memoir co-written in 1970 with Kenny O'Donnell, Powers calls himself "Jack's other wife." Jackie didn't mind the competition. She spoke affectionately of Jack's circle – the friends, relations, advisors, courtiers – whom he managed to keep separate from one another so that no one knew "the whole man," as Sorensen deftly put it. Among them, Powers was unique. "No one ever thought Jack had a favorite," Jackie recalled, "unless it was Dave Powers, who was a favorite for what everyone hoped he would have a favorite for – someone to relax him, you know."

Powers was used to being summoned for "night duty" at the White House when Jackie was away, which she often was in the spring and summer of 1963, when she was pregnant. "The President hated to be alone in the evening," Powers and O'Donnell recalled. "It was understood that Dave would be available to keep him company in the mansion. . . ." In the summer, they noted, Jack faced "solitary confinement" in Washington on Monday through Thursday evenings, before flying to Cape Cod on Friday for the weekend. A steward would leave a dinner of broiled chicken or lamb chops for reheating on a hot plate. One long-time butler at the White House was struck by "how Kennedy liked to take care of himself" more than any other president he had served. "He'd tell me, 'Those butlers don't need to hang around waiting for me. I'll get my own dinner.'" Powers and the president would have a swim, eat dinner, and talk. Kennedy might smoke a cigar on the Truman Balcony while Dave sipped a Heineken or two.

Their relationship was easy and enduring. "Dave's official title was special assistant to the President; unofficially, he was known as the First Friend," recalled Mimi Beardsley. "He placed his mischievous charm at the President's disposal. No one was more loyal to the President or more in his thrall. . . . Above all, Dave Powers' job was to make the President happy." That he did, with laughter and irreverence and a propensity to call everyone "Pal," including Kennedy. "He was one of the most entertaining men I've ever met, and he was nobody's fool," Beardsley said in 2012. "He deftly blended his jovial personality with a serious, win-at-all-costs commitment to President Kennedy."

If the president did not return to the residence until shortly before 10:00 p.m., Powers probably had the evening off to spend with his wife and children at his home in McLean, Virginia. Once at the White House, Kennedy might have been content to watch television or read a book. *Monday Night at the Movies* on NBC was showing Robert Mitchum and Deborah Kerr in *Heaven Knows, Mr. Allison*. *David Brinkley's Journal* was reporting on "Nevada's marriage mills." The program was broadcast "in color" in a world moving from black-and-white-television to a more vivid new frontier of its own. Had Kennedy wanted to read a current bestseller, he might have turned to *Seven Days in May*, a thriller about a military coup in the United States. (JFK did read it and mused that under the right circumstances a coup was possible.) Or, since he preferred history and biography, Kennedy might have chosen from other favorites such as John Steinbeck's *Travels with Charley*. Perhaps he would welcome the distraction.

Then again, Kennedy might have done some work. He liked sprawling on the couch in the West Sitting Hall framed by a large lunette window on the west wall. The couch was familiar; it and some of the other furniture in the room had come from Jack and Jackie's home in Georgetown. Typically, he would lie amid a stream of papers spilling from his black alligator briefcase. There might be correspondence and documents to sign, a briefing note from Arthur Schlesinger, a memorandum from the interior secretary, a report from the Defense Department. Or more of those diverting diplomatic cables. Or, perhaps, a speech draft from Sorensen to review. He may have written something on the yellow, ruled legal pads he favored. Kennedy liked to scribble notes throughout the day. During meetings, he often doodled.

Then, of course, there was the telephone. People were always trying to reach him through Mrs. Lincoln or the White House switchboard. That evening brought calls from his assistants – Larry O'Brien at 7:34 p.m. and Kenny O'Donnell at 7:36 p.m. Charles Bartlett, his old friend, telephoned twice at 7:23 p.m. and 7:44 p.m. Perhaps Bartlett, a syndicated columnist, wanted to check a story before he went to press with his column. Bobby had called at 8:50 p.m., presumably to discuss preparations for the next day. Lastly, Jackie had called at 9:30 p.m. from Camp David. He had missed all their calls because he was not there to take them. One thing we do know: he telephoned Bobby at 9:00 p.m. From where is unknown, though he might have placed the call from the presidential limousine, which had returned from Hawaii. It had a two-way radio-telephone in the rear passenger compartment. Wherever the call originated, it was consistent with their intimate pattern of communication. As Bobby's was Jack's first call of the day, at 9:12 that morning, his brother was most likely Jack's last call of the day that evening.

✳

Kennedy would not have expected to hear a response to the Peace Speech from Moscow before retiring. Moscow was eight time zones away, and substantial reports of the speech would not have reached there until early Monday evening. It would take awhile for the Russians to digest it. By one account, though, news reached the White House around midnight that *Izvestia*, the Soviet daily newspaper, intended to publish the whole text, and the government would not jam a Voice of America broadcast of the speech in Russian. That was an unprecedented and encouraging early signal from Khrushchev.

At home there had been little encouragement from the Republicans. That afternoon word leaked that the White House would announce that Averell Harriman would lead the American delegation to Moscow to negotiate the test ban treaty. Senator Barry Goldwater of Arizona, who was most likely to face President Kennedy in the election of 1964, called him "dead wrong" for agreeing to a conference with Khrushchev and halting nuclear tests. He said it was "naïve" and "foolish" to seek compromise with the Russian bear. "We are walking on dangerous grounds," he warned, urging the president to keep on testing until the reliability of the nuclear arsenal could be determined. Senator Everett Dirksen of Illinois had similar reservations. "Is there anything more than a speculative hope as he [JFK] contemplates a high-level conference in Moscow?" he asked. "Will it be another case of concession and more concession to Khrushchev to achieve some kind of a test ban treaty?"

Around 11:00 p.m., Kennedy would usually slip into his Brooks Brothers nightshirt, which he preferred to pajamas. Powers and O'Donnell recalled the ritual in their memoir. "Dave would watch him kneel beside his bed and say his prayers. Then he would get into bed, and say to Dave: 'Good night, Pal, will you please put out the light?' Dave would put out the light, leave the apartment, say good night again to the Secret Service agent on duty in the downstairs hall, and drive home . . ."

That night, the moon rose at 11:27 p.m. over a cloudy capital. In the silent White House, Secret Service agents sat downstairs. In the basement, teletypes clattered in the Situation Room. On the top floor, George Thomas, the butler, slept in Room 324, close enough to assist the president if he were needed. Having said his nightly prayers, observed Bishop, it was as if Kennedy were "reserving the final minutes of consciousness for God."

Tuesday, June 11, 1963

CHAPTER 8

Early Morning

ON JUNE 11, 1963, as on most of the 870 mornings of Jack Kennedy's presidency, George Thomas padded down the corridor of the second floor of the White House and knocked gently on the door of his bedroom. "Mr. President," he'd say. "It's close to 7:30." If the president was in Jackie's bedroom, Thomas would rouse him gently there, trying not to wake the first lady, who liked to lie in past 9:00 a.m. Although Thomas was responsible for waking the president, Pierre Salinger noted that "his lack of reliability in this department was legendary." Once, in Minnesota, he awoke Kennedy an hour early when he forgot to adjust his watch to Central Standard Time. The president was not amused. Still, Salinger found Thomas "a Negro of unfailing humor," who had served JFK faithfully since 1947. Thomas had worked for Arthur Krock, a prominent columnist with the *New York Times*, who had recommended him to Kennedy, a family friend. Thomas was fifty-five in 1963. He had several duties in the White House. None was terribly onerous. He attended to Kennedy's wardrobe – fifteen to eighteen suits (most two-button rather than three), his ties, and his shirts. Beyond laying out his clothes, Thomas drew his bath and helped Kennedy, who could scarcely bend over because of his back, in and out of his corset.

Kennedy knew few black Americans beyond Thomas and Preston Bruce, the White House doorman and usher. (They included Andrew Hatcher, the assistant press secretary, and Louis Martin, an advisor, but he was not close to either.) That the lives of the black underclass were unknown to him was not unusual for someone of his background. Kennedy was raised in a wealthy Irish-Catholic family in Brookline, Massachusetts, and Bronxville, New York, in the 1920s. After attending Choate and Harvard in the 1930s, he served in a segregated Navy and a nearly all-white Congress in the 1940s and 1950s. (The Senate did not seat its first black senator since Reconstruction – from Massachusetts – until 1967.) What *was* unusual about JFK – particularly on this day, when he would address race in America as no president had before – was that he was different in one respect from his predecessors and some of his successors. Kennedy had no discernible racial or religious prejudice, unlike his older brother, Joe Jr., who had inherited some of his father's distrust of Jews. It had much to do with the suspicion that he had faced as a Catholic running for president in 1960. Unlike Harry Truman of Missouri or Lyndon Johnson of Texas, Kennedy did not use the crude vernacular of the former slave states. He found it unseemly. "I can't get used to Harry Truman talking all the time about 'the niggers,'" he told Daniel Patrick Moynihan. Johnson would also pepper his conversations with references to "nigras," particularly when chewing the fat with a southern good ol' boy. While Truman integrated the armed forces and Johnson championed civil rights, neither could overcome his personal history and the inexorable geography of race. Kennedy arrived in the White House with a black valet but without the baggage of bigotry.

Given where he was for as long as he was, Thomas would have

observed much about the thirty-fifth president of the United States. Yet if he was the man who saw Kennedy most, even more than Dave Powers, Thomas is the man we know least. In this story, he appears as a plodding, portly, dutiful manservant who has served Kennedy so long that "he has no other permanent interests." Whatever this butler saw – and he saw everything – he made no judgment. "Mr. Thomas always greeted me kindly but was too discreet and loyal ever to hint – through a word or a knowing glance – that he disapproved of my presence," recalls Mimi Beardsley. He was heard to complain that other butlers at the White House made $4,000 a year, which was more than he did. The explanation was that he had a room upstairs and they did not, even if he did not want the room. Whatever his reservations, Thomas never talked. Unlike others serving the Kennedys – Maud Shaw, the nanny; Janet Travell, the doctor; Evelyn Lincoln and Mary Gallagher, the secretaries; O'Brien, O'Donnell, Sorensen, Schlesinger, and Salinger, the advisors – Thomas never wrote a book about upstairs (or downstairs) at the Kennedy White House. He never gave a published interview, either – at least not after Jim Bishop asked him about the president's wardrobe. When Kennedy heard that Thomas had volunteered that his boss had twenty-five pairs of shoes, he was annoyed. "How many pairs of shoes do you own, George?" JFK asked. "One," Thomas replied. "Well, don't you see how most of the people who own only one pair of shoes might resent my having twenty-five . . . even if it were true?" Kennedy told him. Actually, Kennedy had never counted his shoes. He was just worried about being seen as a rich man with too many. In fact, Bishop reported, the president owned eight pairs.

Thomas amused the president and the first lady. "He leads in the guy who brings breakfast," said Jack. "He'd open the door so that some other slave could carry in Jack's breakfast tray," added Jackie. "The only thing he did was pull open the curtains and then turn on the bath, and then he'd go up and all the little White House

Mess-boys were shining his shoes and everything." Underlings in the residence watched in amazement as Thomas happily delegated authority, down to the shoeshine boys. As Preston Bruce recalled, Thomas "wasn't a bit possessive about his boss. He was glad for any help he could get." Once, shortly after Thomas began at the White House, he was going out for lunch and asked Bruce (who was known by his last name) to get the president up after his nap and draw his bath. Bruce worried that Kennedy would not appreciate finding an unfamiliar face in his bedroom. "Oh, just tickle his toes, Bruce!" Thomas advised. Bruce did. "He [JFK] jumped out quickly, like a jackrabbit, took his bath, and dressed. In less than five minutes, he was ready for the Oval Office," Bruce recalled.

✳

In the mornings, the pace was slower. Whoever delivered it, the president's breakfast was always the same – a large glass of orange juice, two four-and-a-half-minute eggs, toast and jelly, a piece of broiled bacon, coffee with cream and sugar. He ate in his bedroom even when he had working breakfasts downstairs. Wearing a shirt and underpants, he would eat on a tray in bed, or sitting in a chair, wreathed in briefing books, his typewritten daily agenda, and a sheaf of miscellaneous papers. If the children were around, they would rush into the bedroom and turn on the television "absolutely full blast," said Jackie. Kennedy would exercise with them on the pale carpet, getting them to touch their toes, imitating the popular morning television exercise man, Jack LaLanne. "He loved those children tumbling around him in this sort of – sensual is the only way I can think of it," said Jackie. Later, he might have a bath with them. In the bathtub, he and the children played with a raft of rubber ducks, a resplendent yellow, which were stationed neatly along the rim when they were not in service.

With the children and Jackie away, Kennedy bathed alone that

Tuesday morning in what a regular visitor described as an elegant bathroom, "with thick white towels, luxurious soaps, and fluffy robes with the presidential seal." Baths were a balm for his back. They were also a few moments to shave and to read, papers arrayed on a board across the bathtub, Kennedy sometimes returning annotated, sodden memoranda to his assistants. As a politician on his way up, he would soak in the tub while practicing his speeches and training his voice, barking like a seal.

The centerpiece of the president's early morning ritual was reading the newspapers. As columnist James Reston said, Kennedy had "printer's ink for breakfast." Each day the papers included the *New York Times*, the *Washington Post*, the *St. Louis Post-Dispatch*, the *Wall Street Journal*, and perhaps the *Baltimore Sun*. William Manchester says he read every inch of the *Times*, less so the others. He liked the columns, particularly if they agreed with him. Barbs and bouquets alike were noted. Whatever the newspaper, he devoured it. "Few persons can read with the speed and absorption of this man," remarked Bishop. "As his hazel eyes traverse staggering mountains of eight-point type, it seems as though he is reading vertically, rather than from left to right. Within fifteen minutes he can read four newspapers, and be prepared to discuss every story of consequence in any of them."

Kennedy's appetite for news was the habit of a lifetime. He liked journalism and journalists; he much enjoyed a sojourn as a roving correspondent for Hearst Newspapers in 1945. Other than politics, that was his only profession. He talked of becoming the publisher of a big city newspaper after the White House. Many of his friends – Charles Bartlett, Ben Bradlee, Joe Alsop, Max Freedman, William Attwood, Joseph Kraft – were journalists. They did not include Merriman Smith, the Senior UPI correspondent, whom Jackie called "a bitter old man." Newspapers were recreation for JFK; as Bradlee noted, Kennedy "was one of the great news junkies that ever lived." Every day newspapers brought a harvest of news and opinion – generating ideas, raising questions, flagging issues. Pierre Salinger found that Kennedy would usually get through the morning newspapers before he did. The phone calls from the president would start coming before Salinger reached his office in the West Wing. Once, Manchester said, Kennedy called to note a newspaper's opposition to the administration's plans to increase the number of regular army divisions. "They said just the opposite in another editorial six months ago," he said. "Find it." Salinger couldn't. Then the phone rang again, and the president told Salinger when the previous editorial had run, even citing the exact page and figures. That was not unusual for Kennedy.

That day, on the front page of the *New York Times*, usually his first read, was the report on his speech at American University. The speech had prominent positioning but no banner headline, suggesting editors found it important but not monumental. Of greater interest was the crisis in Alabama; there was a story on Kennedy's appeal to Wallace to avoid the campus as well as one on a statement from forty-six lawyers in Philadelphia urging Wallace to obey the law. Other news for the president's eye: the administration's effort to delay the railway labor shutdown; the rejection by the House Ways and Means Committee of a repeal of special tax allowances on income; and, from Saigon, the attempts by the United States to mend the rift between the South Vietnamese government and the Buddhists.

On the front of the *Washington Post*, Kennedy saw two stories on the Peace Speech ("Big 3 A-Ban Talks Set for July in Moscow; U.S. Halts Air Tests") and a well-placed news analysis by commentator Chalmers Roberts ("To Bridge Gulf of Suspicion: Hope, Fear Timing Pace A-Brake Effort"). He would have seen the latest on Tuscaloosa ("Stay Away, JFK Urges Governor"). And then, just above the fold, another report of black protests in Virginia. The night before, police had turned fire hoses on 150 anti-segregation demonstrators in Danville, a textile and tobacco city near the North

Carolina state line. The mayor, Julian Stinson, had issued the same threats heard in Birmingham, Alabama. "Our patience is just about at an end," he warned, blaming the trouble on "hoodlums" from out-of-state. "We will hose down the demonstrators and fill every available stockade." The *Post* also reported on tensions in Cambridge, Maryland, a small city on the eastern shore of Chesapeake Bay. It had been simmering all spring, too, and that day would ignite again, bringing two hundred national guardsmen and twenty-five nights of near martial law. As the president contemplated Wallace's intransigence and the broader question of civil rights, he knew this cancerous civil unrest demanded an answer beyond the orders of the courts and the protection of the authorities.

On most mornings, Kennedy would go to the Oval Office around 9:00 a.m. Caroline or John would sometimes join him. On the morning of June 11, 1963, his first appointment was at 8:45 a.m. It was the Legislative Leaders Breakfast, a meeting of senior congressional Democrats, the vice president, the president, and his legislative advisors. Before that, the president talked to Bobby, who had called around 8:00 a.m. to brief him on the situation in Alabama, which would climax in about five hours. This was the first of a dozen or so calls RFK would place to his brother that long, eventful day. At this early hour, Bobby was calling from Hickory Hill, just before leaving for the Department of Justice.

Robert Drew's documentary cameras find Bobby amid the domestic chaos of five children seated around a circular table in the kitchen, teasing, taunting, shouting, roughhousing. A uniformed black maid tries to serve them breakfast. In the absence of his wife Ethel, eight and a half months pregnant with their eighth child, Bobby is in charge. Once his call goes through, he leaves the kitchen to talk to Jack from a room off the hallway. The two revisit the question of whether to send the National Guard to Tuscaloosa. Then, in the course of their conversation, with no warning, the president exclaims: "Jesus Christ!"

✳

Blame the newspapers. While Kennedy was talking to Bobby, he was scanning the front pages of his unread newspapers. He turned one over on his lap and stopped cold. It wasn't a story in the *New York Times*. It was a photograph in the (Washington) *Evening Star*. For a squeamish Kennedy – who was once so disgusted by a dead bird that Caroline had brought in the house that he made her take it away – the image was arresting. The photograph before him would take on a life of its own, helping to unseat a regime and recast American policy in Indochina. Before IMAX, digital photography, wafer-thin laptops, and big-screen televisions, a black-and-white photograph on the front of a morning newspaper could do that. It could shock. This one did.

Above the picture, the headline: "Protest in Vietnam: Monk Sacrifices Self in Flames." Below the picture, the caption: "As thousands watch, a Buddhist monk burns himself to death in Saigon, to protest Viet Nam government policies." The picture: a man on fire, in agony. Who was the monk and why had he killed himself?

Thich Quang Duc was sixty-six years old. He was a Buddhist from the Linh Mu Pagoda in Hue, the old imperial capital four hundred miles north of Saigon. For months he and other bonzes in the monasteries across South Vietnam had resented the restrictions of President Ngo Dinh Diem and his eccentric and venomous sister-in-law, Madame Ngo Dinh Nhu. Under her influence, Diem had created a culture of favoritism, if not discrimination, in public institutions. He had promoted Catholics over Buddhists in the army and civil service. A devout Catholic, Madame Nhu had banned adultery, abortion, divorce, contraception, polygamy, and concubines. This kind of moral prohibition was jarring in a society of relaxed social mores, in which Buddhists made up about 60 percent of the population of 15 million. Diem claimed he was fair to the Buddhists, and it may have been that their mistreatment was due less to state policy than to the zeal of local officials.

On May 8, there was a clash in Hue, the see of Diem's brother, Archbishop Ngo Dinh Thuc. While Catholics were allowed to fly Vatican flags honoring the archbishop, Buddhists were not allowed to fly their flags celebrating the birthday of Buddha. Protests followed, government troops fired, nine people were killed. Buddhists blamed Diem. It set off riots across the country. In one of those coincidences of history, the Buddhists were protesting in Hue at the same time blacks were protesting in Birmingham. Both looked to the government of the United States for help. The worry in Washington was that a Buddhist uprising would benefit the Viet Cong. While many Americans had doubts about Diem, U.S. Ambassador Frederick Nolting had personally supported him. Something had to give.

Although self-immolation to protest injustice was not unknown to Buddhists in Indochina, it was new to this cause. That it was shocking gave it moral influence. That it was public – disseminated in word and image through the reach of the modern media – gave it political influence. The monks knew that when they arranged for their spokesman, who spoke fluent English, to telephone a half dozen American reporters in Saigon on June 10, urging them to appear at Xa Loi Pagoda the next day at 7:00 a.m. He said vaguely there would be a meeting and "something important may happen." It was easy for reporters to ignore the invitation and they did; there had been daily anti-Diem protests for weeks and these calls came all the time.

But Malcolm W. Browne, the self-described "overworked, thirty-two-year-old" bureau chief of the Associated Press in Saigon, suspected something was up. Solitary, independent, and eccentric, Browne wore red socks and zigged where others zagged. Raised in Greenwich Village, he had attended Swarthmore College, studied chemistry, and entered journalism after writing for Pacific *Stars and Stripes* while he was in the U.S. Army in Korea. In 1961, after lesser assignments in the United States, he landed in South Vietnam, where 16,500 American military "advisors" were helping the South in its war against the communist North. "There was an intensity about Mal, a blaze in his eyes, a directness that contrasted with the easygoing attitude of the American journalists I met up to that time," said Peter Arnett, who worked under Browne in the AP bureau. Browne's reading of events that month – not necessarily shared by his competitors – led him to believe "that the Buddhist revolt would become a national revolution." It was more than a hunch. He had come to know the monks, shared their food, and observed their faith. He went early that day to the pagoda off Phan Dinh Phung, a broad thoroughfare a few blocks from the residence of the U.S. ambassador. He wasn't a professional photographer – that job in Saigon belonged to the formidable Horst Faas, one of the greats of his generation – but he took along a cheap Petri camera. Arriving at that place, at that moment, with that camera, changed Browne's life – and many others, too.

Although he was not alone, Browne said he was "the sole foreign journalist to witness the fiery suicide that would shock the world." In 1963, before smartphones could take clear images and disseminate them anywhere instantaneously, he could make that undisputed claim. Shortly after arriving at 7:45 a.m., Browne was served tea in the pagoda by a woman smiling weakly through her tears. He was told, emphatically, not to leave the pagoda until events ran their course. The chanting began at 8:00 a.m. – the most hypnotic Browne had ever heard, rising in volume and numbing in its repetition. Joss sticks burned. The crowd swelled. The funereal chorus continued for one hour, growing in intensity. At 9:00 a.m., it abruptly stopped. Then hundreds of saffron-robed monks and nuns dressed in customary gray began moving slowly from the pagoda down a narrow alleyway and on to Phan Dinh Phung. They unfurled banners in Vietnamese and English, appealing to the government to answer their demands. At the head of the procession was a gray, four-door sedan with four monks inside. Odd, Browne thought, *monks always walked.* Then it struck him – he was watching street theatre.

The procession stopped at the intersection of Le Van Duyet, one of the busiest boulevards in the city. The monks had chosen this stage for "their horror show" for maximum effect. Sweating, Browne cocked his camera. At 9:20 a.m., the sedan stopped in the intersection, as the monks, six or eight deep, formed a tight circle, thirty feet in diameter. One opened the trunk of the car and produced a five-gallon canister. It was a customized mixture of pink gasoline and jet fuel perfected by the fastidious monks after some experimentation to burn longer and hotter than conventional gasoline. Three monks walked to the center of the intersection and laid a cushion on the road. One sat down on it, cross-legged, in the lotus position. It was Thich Quang Duc. The three monks exchanged words, then one doused Quang Duc with the gasoline, soaking his bald head and shoulders. They stepped away. At 9:25 a.m., the monk took a match and struck it. Immediately, he was an inferno, a ghoulish tableau of fire, flesh, and smoke.

David Halberstam of the *New York Times* slept late that morning. He received a panicked call from a colleague and raced the six blocks from his villa to the intersection. When he got there he thought it was just another demonstration and cursed the false alarm. Damn! Then he saw the monks encircling the burning monk. "I was to see that sight again, but once was enough," he wrote. "Flames were coming from a human being; his body was slowly withering and shriveling up, his head blackening and charring. In the air was the smell of burning flesh; human beings burn surprisingly quickly. Behind me I could hear the sobbing of the Vietnamese who were now gathering. I was too shocked to cry, too confused to take notes or ask questions, too bewildered even to think." From the burning monk, not a sound.

Thomas Delworth, a young Canadian diplomat seconded to the International Control Commission in Saigon, reached the steaming pavement twenty minutes later. He was stupefied that the Buddhists were so angry with their government that they would resort to this kind of sacrifice, even if there were rumors in Saigon that the elderly monk was dying of terminal cancer. "It was so bizarre, so uncommon to our experience," he said in 2012. "No one processed it." To John Mecklin, the press attaché at the U.S. Embassy: "Saigon was like a mental institution. Neither the Vietnamese nor the Americans understood what was happening, nor what to do about it, nor even what to say." It was incomprehensible. Diem was not just a Catholic, he was "a personalist," which Delworth called "a funny French frippery." For Madame Nhu, "it was the heart and soul of her dogma. The sacraments were like spiritual vitamins to her."

Fighting his revulsion, Browne pointed the camera and took pictures. "Numb with shock, I shot roll after roll of film, focusing and adjusting exposures mechanically and unconsciously, almost as an athlete chews gum to relieve stress," he recalled. "Trying hard not to perceive what I was witnessing, I found myself thinking: 'The sun is bright and the subject is self-illuminated, so f/16 at 125th of a second should be right.' But I couldn't close out the smell." He shot six or eight rolls of 35-mm film. Forty years later he observed: "As shock photography goes, it was hard to beat. It's not something I am particularly proud of. If one wants to be gruesome about it, it was a very easy sequence of pictures to take. Work is a great panacea for the horrors of that sort of situation. . . ."

Now Browne had to send his pictures to the world. It was impossible for him to file them through the new wirephoto system that AP had recently developed to transmit black-and-white photos through an international telephone line. In Saigon, the regime's censors would not allow that. They would have to go by "pigeon," which meant asking a passenger on a commercial flight to carry the undeveloped film to Manila. From there Browne's colleagues could send the pictures electronically to San Francisco. In that offhand manner that foreign correspondents everywhere recognize when dealing with head office, the Associated Press never notified Browne that the film had arrived in Manila and that the pictures had been flashed around the world. He learned this only later when he was flooded with congratulations. The *New York Times* did not publish the picture ("too grisly . . . for a breakfast paper," recalled Browne), and Halberstam's report from Saigon on June 11 played down the suicide. In fact, it was less graphic than his account in *The Making of a Quagmire*, his book on Vietnam published in 1965. On June 11, though, he reported that "a full-scale protest" had begun.

The Buddhists had ensured this public suicide would have maximum exposure. This was a human tragedy with a political purpose. "Before closing my eyes to Buddha," Quang Duc wrote in a last testament released after his death, "I have the honor of presenting my words to President Diem, asking him to be kind and tolerant toward his people and to enforce a policy of religious equality." When the flames had died, the monks arrived with a wooden coffin to remove the body. The limbs, splayed and rigid, would not fit. Quang Duc's charred heart survived, which the bonzes thought significant. Later, they put it on display in a glass bottle.

At the presidential palace, Madame Nhu was unmoved; she mocked the suicide as "a barbeque" and accused Browne of bribing the monk to kill himself. This was the first of seven self-immolations over the next few months. None would have the impact of the first. Almost a year later, Bobby Kennedy observed that "of course no one writes about them anymore and . . . I don't know *what* they prove now." At the time, though, Browne's photograph "had a shock effect of incalculable value to the Buddhist cause, becoming a symbol of the state of things in Vietnam that a thousand rosy, statistics-laden speeches could never undo," recalled Mecklin. China distributed millions of copies throughout Asia. Newspapers everywhere carried the picture. It was chosen World Press Photo of the Year for 1963.

"The [South Vietnamese] government handled the Buddhist crisis fairly badly and allowed it to grow," said William Colby, chief of the CIA's Far East Division. "But I really don't think there was much they could have done about it, once the bonze burned himself." Roger Hilsman, assistant secretary of state for Far Eastern Affairs, said that suicide made perception the reality, whatever the reality. "Self-immolation is an emphatically persuasive argument that one believes in his cause," he wrote in 1967. "The facts of whether or not there had been religious persecution in Vietnam instantly became irrelevant – the world believed that there must have been."

In Washington, JFK believed there was. His reaction went beyond his eight o'clock imprecation. Henry Cabot Lodge Jr., whom Kennedy had chosen (but not announced) that week as his new ambassador to Vietnam, reported that the president felt "that no news picture in recent history had generated so much emotion around the world as that one had." When Kennedy saw Lodge in the Oval Office the next morning, June 12, the picture smoldered on his desk as if the newspaper itself were going to burst into flames. "We're going to have to do something about that regime," said Kennedy to Lodge. "And that was the beginning of the end of American support for the Diem regime," wrote Browne.

In a wrenching Washington moment, Kennedy had learned that he had a bigger problem than he thought. "I just cannot have a religious war out there," he told Michael Forrestal, one of his Asia hands on the National Security Council. "It isn't just that I am a Catholic myself and therefore in an immensely difficult situation. It's just that to add to all our difficulties in Vietnam, the prospects of a religious conflict will make the problem completely unmanageable. I know about religious conflicts. I know how strongly people feel." But there was something else that morning as he faced the racial crisis in the South. There was a frightening parallel between the two situations. In Vietnam, the marchers were Buddhists, not blacks. The danger was fire, not water. The cause was religion, not race. But the story was discrimination. And although Vietnam was a poor, steamy, backward dominion, like Alabama, it was now *his* poor, steamy, backward dominion. As the leader of the free world, he had promised "to ensure the survival and the success of liberty." That's why America had sent "advisors" to Vietnam. The war was tolerable as long as it was small, asked little blood and treasure, and did not invite too many questions from those pushy correspondents in Saigon who were not "on the team," as one of his generals groused. Now the war was demanding his attention.

As long as the monks were protesting and the United States was backing the regime in Saigon, Kennedy knew he was on the wrong side. President Ngo Dinh Diem was his man, even if he hadn't chosen him. In the ashes of a monk's self-inflicted auto-da-fé, Diem might as well have been George Wallace. On the day Kennedy was embracing civil rights, this appalled him.

It was another thing to ponder that morning as Bobby pressed him on the telephone for a decision on sending soldiers to Tuscaloosa, the Democrats waited downstairs at breakfast to push him on the civil rights bill, and the secretary of state was on his way over to tell him that his foreign aid bill was in trouble in Congress.

This was how things now looked to the president at 8:30 a.m. Tuesday, June 11.

Jesus Christ.

✳

At 8:45 a.m., Kennedy went downstairs to the Legislative Leaders Breakfast. They used to meet upstairs every week in the Family Dining Room. But Caroline or John Jr. would sometimes wander in or Jackie would emerge "in my dressing gown and all those men would come out in clouds of smoke." One morning one of the antique chairs in the room shattered, sending a politician crashing to the floor. Now they met downstairs in the Private Dining Room.

Only Democrats attended these breakfasts because the Democrats controlled both houses, as they had since 1954. From the Senate came Majority Leader Mike Mansfield, the plain-spoken progressive from Montana. Kennedy had so wanted him as majority leader during his presidency that it was another reason to name the obstreperous Lyndon B. Johnson, then majority leader, as his running mate in 1960. There was also Assistant Majority Leader, or whip, Hubert Humphrey of Minnesota, the bouncy liberal who had lost to Kennedy in the primaries in Wisconsin and West Virginia in 1960. And there was Senator George Smathers of Florida, an intimate of Kennedy and a conservative responsible for the southern wing of the party. From the House came Speaker John McCormack of Massachusetts, who was cool to Kennedy because they were rivals from the same state, as well as Majority Leader Carl Albert of Oklahoma, and the whip, Hale Boggs of Louisiana. There was also Johnson, now shrunken and dispirited after two-and-a-half years in Kennedy's White House. From the president's staff came Kenny O'Donnell and Larry O'Brien, his legislative assistants, as well as Ted Sorensen and Andy Hatcher.

In the ways of Washington, where seeking advantage or favor was common, these sessions had their own peculiarities. Jackie recalled O'Brien, who "couldn't stand" Sorensen, telling her that Sorensen would prepare "an agenda for the breakfasts and just before they were about to start, Ted would ask to see it and take it. And he'd just change one or two sentences and then initial it 'TCS' and pass it all around that way. . . . You know, he wanted his imprint on so many things." Among the politicians there was a clubbiness. As the first senator to be elected president since Warren Harding in 1920 (and the last until Barack Obama in 2008), Kennedy knew Congress. He wasn't a moralizing governor riding into town vowing to clean up the Augean Stables; he had been in Washington, in both houses, for fourteen years. Everyone knew everyone else, perhaps too well. Humphrey and Kennedy were friends again, their presidential rivalry behind them. So were Kennedy and Smathers, though Smathers had so annoyed Kennedy in resisting his program that Schlesinger wondered how "he survived in the West Wing." Still, Kennedy remained loyal to his friend, whose philandering, Jackie suspected, reinforced the same in her husband.

Despite its obstinacy, Kennedy did not resent Congress. He made congressional relations a priority and entrusted them to O'Brien, a shrewd, tough politico from Springfield, Massachusetts, and O'Donnell, his rasping, terse appointments secretary from Worcester, Massachusetts, with a face cut from alabaster. Jackie thought the breakfasts were "rather fun" for Kennedy. By 1963, though, dealing with Congress wasn't fun. His program was stalled. O'Brien argued that Kennedy's legislative record was excellent in his first two years, and good in his last year, but the contemporary view was that he could not get much passed. That his party controlled both houses comfortably was no help because conservative southern Democrats dominated. In the Eighty-eighth Congress, there were sixty-seven Democrats and thirty-three Republicans in the Senate, but the decisive split was between liberals and conservatives. Those thirty-three Republicans could form a coalition with the twenty-two southern Democrats and carry the day, fifty-five to thirty-five. In the House, there were 258 Democrats and 176 Republicans. The trouble for Kennedy was that Southerners also controlled the most important committees in both houses where legislation was shaped.

Kennedy had not arrived with a strong electoral mandate; he was a minority president (49.8 percent of the popular vote) with a remarkably thin national margin of 118,000 votes. Some members of Congress felt they had more moral authority than the president. This was why Kennedy had been wary of sending a civil rights bill to Capitol Hill. He felt it would never pass; worse, it would so antagonize the Southerners that they would kill his legislative program, particularly his innovative tax cut. Since 1961 he had chosen to court southern moderates by trying to pass legislation such as a youth employment bill, which would create jobs for whites and blacks. Birmingham had changed things, though, pushing Kennedy to present legislation even if it was unlikely to pass.

On the morning of June 11, the *Washington Post* published a sobering assessment of the chances of the administration's anticipated civil rights bill by Rowland Evans and Robert Novak, two of the country's most astute political commentators. They reported that Kennedy's advisors had told the president that an easing of the racial crisis would come less from legislating equality for blacks than creating jobs for them. "What good is the legal right to sit in a fancy restaurant if you can't afford to eat there?" asked one. If he did go ahead, Evans and Novak warned that finding twenty-five Republican senators to join forty-two Democrats in order to reach the sixty-seven votes needed to cut off a filibuster on a civil rights bill "may well turn out to be the greatest discovery since 1492." They reported "that the prospect that the new bill may not pass at all, however, is already being explored in detail, both within the Administration and the Senate." Whatever the merits of the legislation, they thought that "the odds are no more than 50-50, and probably a good deal less, that a really meaningful bill can pass."

Every week, O'Brien compiled a report on bills coming before Congress. His report of June 10 reviewed legislation ranging from the Military Construction Authorization Bill, which was not important, to the Foreign Aid Bill, which was. That bill was under fire; to win over skeptics, the administration had enlisted John Kenneth Galbraith, who had returned home from India. He offered "inspiration and encouragement to our friends and shrewd inside information to the not-so-friendly, including meaty reasons why they should think twice about any anti-aid thoughts they might harbor . . . especially to India." O'Brien's report also dealt with the tax bill, which was being amended in the Ways and Means Committee, controlled by the powerful Congressman Wilbur Mills of Arkansas. This frustrated Kennedy.

Foreign aid and the tax cut were not on the menu at this morning's breakfast. Instead, Kennedy began talking about Moscow and Vietnam. The legislators listened politely but they were more interested in discussing Alabama and civil rights. Whatever Evans and Novak were predicting, Mansfield wasn't buying; he urged Kennedy to present a civil rights bill soon. If he didn't, Mansfield implied, he would lose control of the situation. "We're still talking about that," replied Kennedy. He told the congressional leaders that he wanted a bill that would be "the minimum we can ask for and the maximum we can stand behind." Kennedy seemed to give no hint to the group that morning that he planned to announce the bill that evening. Then again, with things in play in Tuscaloosa, he hadn't decided yet.

✳

The breakfast meeting lasted forty minutes. At 9:24 a.m., Kennedy arrived in the Oval Office. He had twenty minutes to review and return phone calls, among other matters. Bobby had called at 8:50 a.m. and 8:57 a.m., and would call again at 9:44 a.m. Charles Bartlett, the journalist, had called the president at 8:57 a.m. He would be in touch with Kennedy several times that day, as he had the day before. The telephone was one of the ways Kennedy stayed informed. The eighteen-button green telephone console on his desk, or the broad range of radiophones in his cars or planes, was one of the ways he could "see and hear more than anyone else," as he told William Manchester.

To Bartlett, Kennedy was always a friend first. It was that relationship that mattered most to him. The White House files are full of his letters, messages, notes, and memoranda to the president. From his table at the Metropolitan Club (before he resigned over its restrictive membership) or his office in the National Press

Building came a torrent of warnings, suggestions, hints, tips, and plaudits. The president's news conference? "Charlie Bartlett called," reads one handwritten memo. "Wanted you to know that he thought you did a terrific job this morning. You had all the answers." Appointments? "It occurred to me that Ruth Golden might be good for the Federal Council on the Arts," Bartlett writes. Cigars? "These are those small Upmann cigars," he says. "I think they are pretty good and will be interested in your reaction." Fashion? "You're setting the style for everyone else," he says, enclosing a newspaper clipping that reports "this fall . . . there's a move to the single-breasted, two-button suit, with a snugger fit, trimmer lines and a little more tailoring." The Rose Garden? Get rid of the "tired yews" and "worn-out American box" and plant some color, he advises. Entertaining? "I would like to register one vote against the 'Twist' at your White House dance," he wrote. "The crowd has been getting on for years on champagne and the Fox Trot and they won't need the Twist to get them stirred up. It's bound to get out and it doesn't seem worth the price however small." Diet? "Get the National Institute of Health to send over a specialist in the chemistry of the body and let him look at a list of your menus for a week."

If Bartlett's avocation was JFK, his vocation was journalism. As Washington correspondent for the *Chattanooga Times,* he won the Pulitzer Prize for National Reporting in 1956. By 1963, he was no longer bureau chief and was writing a syndicated column. Bartlett was careful about what he wrote about Kennedy and his caution hurt him professionally. Pierre Salinger felt that his "copy became particularly dull during the Kennedy administration, because he did not want to give the outside world the appearance he was trading on his friendship with the President." On June 2, Bartlett produced a flattering portrait of JFK on his forty-sixth birthday (on May 29), which appeared in the *Pittsburgh Press.* He talks about "Kennedy's deep fascination and concern, a sense of opportunity and his native urge to succeed." He says one of Kennedy's "great gifts is an instinct for reducing complexity to practical terms in which they can be met by practical responses."

Unlike Alsop and Bradlee, Bartlett, who turned ninety-three in 2014, has never written a memoir touching on his relationship with Kennedy. But careful as he was then, he is not afraid to be critical of him now, particularly in regard to his marital infidelity. Nor is Bradlee, who got more professionally out of his association with JFK than Bartlett, which isn't to say that Kennedy didn't profit, either. "Did he [JFK] use me?" Bradlee asked in 1975. "Of course he used me. Did I use him? Of course I used him."

On that Tuesday, perhaps Bartlett wanted something from the president – or the president wanted something from him. Later that month, Bartlett wrote columns on the new pope and the strange strategy of the southern Democrats. Perhaps he discussed Khrushchev and Castro with Kennedy that day, the subject of his column on June 12. More likely, though, he called simply to offer more advice and applause to "Mr. President" from "Charley."

✳

At 9:45 a.m., it was time for Kennedy to see Dean Rusk, the secretary of state. The two had a distant, if respectful, relationship. Until late in his presidency, Kennedy called Rusk "Mr. Secretary," the only member of his cabinet whom he addressed that formally. Kennedy was aware of the opposition to Rusk when he chose him in 1960; in a memo to Kennedy a week after his election, Schlesinger called Rusk "essentially the perfect chief-of-staff" and doubted "whether he would have the inner confidence and security to make a fully effective Secretary." JFK appointed him anyway, probably because he wanted to be his own secretary of state. Charles Ritchie observed something of "the sphinx" about Rusk, whom he called "Buddha." By 1963, Rusk, fifty-four, had acquired a noisy chorus of detractors. That spring their salons were buzzing and their talons were flying. The loudest was Joe Alsop, the grand panjandrum, who appealed personally to Kennedy to fire Rusk, whom he felt was slow and dull. As *Time* reported in March 1963, the paunchy, moonfaced Rusk didn't "look or act like a New Frontiersman." He had critics in Foggy Bottom, as well, and in Congress. Rusk was a somnolent, inscrutable Georgian. He resented the rumors and snarled when he felt undermined by the White House.

In fact, there had been another dustup that week so serious that Schlesinger mused that Rusk was "on the skids, though the final execution may be delayed until after the election. He has become more sensitive about his position than before, more bristling, and more intent on asserting his prerogatives on small matters, while continuing not to assert them on major ones." The *casus belli* here was that the secretary had wanted Kennedy to appoint Henry Cabot Lodge Jr. to Saigon. He had sold the idea to JFK, "who had a weakness for the Lodges." Both McGeorge Bundy and Michael Forrestal opposed Lodge's appointment. Rusk made an issue out of it and won. "As he left the President's office, he told someone . . . that this time he had beaten the White House," Schlesinger reported. Rusk was asserting himself in other ways, such as insisting that he should be personally in charge of emerging international aviation negotiations rather than sharing the responsibility. "If I'm not the Secretary of State that is wanted, maybe they had better get another," Rusk harrumphed.

Kennedy resisted the calls to replace Rusk with Bundy or Robert McNamara or David Bruce. He once asked Rusk a routine question on the Russians and waited weeks for an answer. That was unforgivable in the go-go New Frontier. Jack moaned to Jackie that "Bundy and I do more in the White House in one day than they do over there [in the State Department] in six months." As *Time* also said, "There can be no doubt that Bundy, in the White House, runs a foreign policy operation that is closer to the President, both spatially and personally, than the State Department." To the professionals, dealing with matters in phone calls meant doing them twice. "I wish they would move them over to this building, just to get them off the phone," *Time* quoted one bureaucrat. "Then we would all be one big, unhappy family." Whatever his frustrations, the president would not fire Rusk. "He didn't want to hurt the man," explained Jackie. Shortly after Rusk had returned from India and the Far East that May, Kennedy wrote: "Dear Mr. Secretary: I would hope that you would take a few days off. You and Secretary McNamara work much too hard and it gives me a guilty feeling. . . . It seems to me that after a long trip like you have had, that it really would be wise for you to take three or four days in the sun. I would be delighted if you would use Camp David."

This was one of the five hundred or so times Kennedy would consult Rusk during his presidency – the most of any cabinet officer – and there was a lot of ground to cover on Tuesday. First, the reaction to the Peace Speech. The early signs were encouraging. A cable had arrived at 6:14 a.m. from Foy Kohler, the U.S. ambassador to Moscow, reporting that the Soviets had not only allowed Voice of America to broadcast the president's speech, but the Russian translation of the speech had also come through on three frequencies. This was unprecedented. The Soviets had jammed broadcasts from the West since 1948 through a costly network of 3,000 transmitters. The previous night, the transmitters had been turned off. "Jammers were obviously deliberately ordered silenced in the Moscow area in spite of frank language of speech and Russian listeners had unusual chance to hear major U.S. policy statement on US-SOV relations," wired Kohler. As the director of Voice of America before JFK sent him to Moscow in August 1962, Kohler, perhaps more than anyone, understood the importance of what the Soviets had done. Moreover, *Izvestia*, the state newspaper, planned to publish the Peace Speech in full on June 12. *Pravda*, the Communist Party newspaper, would also devote thirteen column inches to the report on the speech by TASS, the government news

197

agency. "This is the most extensive Soviet press coverage of remarks by a U.S. official in many months," Kohler cabled, which was surely an understatement.

Another encouraging signal had come from the U.S. Mission to the United Nations. The Americans there reported that their Soviet counterparts were "favorably surprised by the tenor of the speech," because it reflected "a broad, progressive approach" to long-standing issues. "The atmosphere created by this speech is now such that the possibilities of agreeing on a test ban treaty are very good. No chief of state would make such a speech unless he were completely convinced that an agreement was probable." The problem had always been credibility; if the Soviets were now confident that the United States was serious, the old obstacles (the number of inspections, for example) could be overcome. "President Kennedy's speech has gone a long way toward assuaging Soviet doubts of United States sincerity," the mission reported. But much as they liked the speech, the dispatch noted, the Soviets "definitely disliked the fact that President Kennedy mentioned communists as being sources of world tension" and equally disliked his comments on West Berlin.

The mission made two other useful observations. The Soviets in New York thought the speech would not heighten tensions between the Soviets and the Chinese when they met in Moscow. It also asked why Kennedy planned to go to the Berlin Wall in two weeks, which they thought provocative. On June 11, though, the mood was optimistic. "The Soviets feel the speech has created an excellent atmosphere. . . . and believe that Premier Khrushchev will make a gesture in response to this speech." His gesture was allowing the speech to be read and heard.

In the international press, the speech was generally greeted warmly. In France, *L'Aurore* enthused that "never had a U.S. President used such cordial language to the Russians in the past . . ." In Holland, *de Volkskrant* said: "This new initiative may be the first historical step toward easing international tensions." In Switzerland,

Gazette de Lausanne declared: "It is now possible to speak of an American peace offensive." In Germany, *Die Welt* called it one of "the President's most important foreign policy speeches," while *Westfälische Rundschau* said: "The President had availed himself of every opportunity to bring about détente; he has mobilized the full strength of the West against potential aggression." But the greatest bouquet came from the *Manchester Guardian*, which declared that Kennedy's tacit warning to Americans "not to fall into the same trap as the USSR and see only 'a distorted, disparate view of the other side' should rank Monday's speech among the great state papers in American history." It added: "What is far more important, it may also help to generate strong public backing for a conciliatory policy toward the East."

At home, the *Washington Post* was effusive: "President Kennedy's speech at American University was much more than an appeal for a ban on nuclear testing. It was, indeed, another bid for an end to the Cold War." Walter Lippmann, perhaps the preeminent columnist of the time, called it "a wise and shrewd action, which is intended primarily to improve the climate of East-West relations." David Lawrence, another influential voice, said the president's purpose was "to show the Russian people that basically the American people are not hostile to them."

Unsurprisingly, critics saw Kennedy as naive, weak, and rash. The *Boston Herald* said the president's confidence in the Russians was misplaced; when the United States "diminishes its military power, it diminishes its opportunities to make peace a persuasive objective." The *Wall Street Journal* warned: "We have already conceded much in the test ban talks; if the Soviets . . . should agree to a treaty this summer it might not be a safe treaty for us, and the Soviet treaty record indicated they would evade it if it suited them." The *Chicago Tribune* said: "Mr. Kennedy expresses his willingness to turn the other cheek . . ." All of these newspapers had opposed Kennedy in 1960.

The public split along ideological lines. John P. Roche, national chairman of the Americans for Democratic Action, a liberal body founded by Schlesinger, J.K. Galbraith, and Eleanor Roosevelt, declared: "The President's speech at American University was nothing short of noble and may well mark the beginning of an upturn in the history of this fateful century. Great leadership always involves risks. In this world only fools search for fool-proof solutions to intricate problems, and it is perfectly clear that no path into the future is without great hazards. As we solemnly stood behind the President in the Cuban confrontation, let us now join him in equal dedication in the cause of peace and disarmament." Critics who contacted the White House were unpersuaded. "What's wrong with the United States of America?" wired Jane Bohannon of Powell, Ohio. "Haven't you looked at a map of the Communist world? If we continue to give the Communists all the breaks and all the countries of the world, as they are now acquiring them, you will have your peace – but no freedom. War is not so fearful as slavery." From J.A. Wheatley of Bartlesville, Oklahoma: "No treaty with Russia. You are selling U.S. for a mess of pottage." R.L. Price of Louisville, Kentucky, wrote: "Khrushchev himself might have dictated your peaceful co-existence speech."

In tone, most of the president's mail on the speech was favorable. In volume, the speech barely registered. In the week ending June 13, the White House received 527 letters and cards for the speech and 11 against. In the week ending June 20, it received 923 for and 27 against. And in the week ending June 27, it received 875 for and 5 against. If mail was any measure of public opinion – and Kennedy cited the meager response on this issue to remind Schlesinger that it never was – those who noticed the speech overwhelmingly liked it. Other matters, such as the rail freight bill, proved much more contentious; it brought 23,662 letters to the White House. Generally, the early public response to a speech called "among the great state papers" was guarded, if hopeful.

There were some more personal letters. Joseph Kraft, whom Sorensen had approached for ideas (as he did Max Freedman and others) but who offered none, wrote Sorensen that "the speech was one of the very best the President has made. Indeed, in my judgment, it was the best statement of its kind made by any American official since the Cold War set in." Another valentine came from Norman Cousins, who had travelled tirelessly between Moscow, Washington and the Vatican. From his office at *Saturday Review* in New York, he wrote a note of thanks to Pierre Salinger, who had telephoned him on June 10 at 10:45 a.m. to brief him on the address, while Kennedy was speaking. "It met the demands of the situation brilliantly and inspiringly," Cousins said of the speech. "This is the stuff of which historical change is made."

Adrian Fisher, one of the small circle who crafted the speech, agreed. "I think that anyone who had anything to do with that speech will always look back on it as a red-letter day," he said. "It was a great speech." At the time, though, the praise was less extravagant. "I don't think any of us thought that it was as a great speech as it turned out (to be) in terms of history," said McGeorge Bundy, speaking in 1964. "That's one of the things that happen. In fact, I once heard the President laugh about that (the speech) afterwards, and (say) how 'one of the most important things Sorensen isn't going to tell the papers is where my great peace speech came from.'"

✻

Before the burning monk, there had been no reason to discuss Vietnam with Rusk that morning. Although the Buddhists had been protesting there for weeks, Kennedy had not thought the situation was grave. Neither had the State Department. Kennedy asked Michael Forrestal: "How could this have happened? Who are these people? Why didn't we know about them before?" What he'd seen that morning was disorienting, not just because the images themselves were shocking, but because it revived persistent doubts in Washington about Diem as an ally. Kennedy was acutely aware of the relationship between the civil rights movement at home and the fight for freedom abroad. He had made that association pointedly in his speech at American University. "But wherever we are, we must all, in our daily lives, live up to the age-old faith that peace and freedom walk together," he had said. "In too many of our cities today, the peace is not secure, because the freedom is incomplete." He had long known that segregation at home undermined his appeal for freedom abroad. Realistically, how could he denounce Communism in Albania when the United States tolerated racism in Alabama? Now he had to explain, or rationalize, his ally's repression in Vietnam. In fighting Communism in Southeast Asia, the United States accepted that it was in league with an authoritarian regime. As Thomas Delworth observed, Vietnam was not a "New England town-hall democracy." But a system so odious that it drove monks to set themselves ablaze?

"The situation [in Vietnam] is deteriorating," Rusk warned Kennedy. The immediate question: given the Buddhist Crisis, as it came to be known that spring, how long could the United States tolerate Diem? A cable on June 11 from the State Department to the U.S. Embassy in Saigon was unsparing: "In our judgment, the Buddhist situation is dangerously near the breaking point. Accordingly, you authorized to tell Diem that in the United States' view it is essential for the GVN [Government of Vietnam] promptly to take dramatic action to regain confidence of Buddhists, and that the GVN must fully and unequivocally meet Buddhist demands. . . ." This must be done, it said, in "a public and dramatic fashion" to be effective. "You further authorized to tell Diem that unless the GVN is willing to take effective action . . . the US will find it necessary publicly to state that it cannot associate itself with the GVN's unwillingness to meet the reasonable demands of the Vietnamese Buddhist leaders."

The cable warned that "the international repercussions of the Buddhist troubles cannot help but affect US world-wide responsibilities." To maintain support for the Vietnamese regime, the US needed the support of Congress and the American people. It might crumble amid a tableau of repugnant images from Saigon, in much the same way that public opinion was changing in the face of the brutal images of racial violence in the South. Kennedy was worried that maintaining popular consensus in support of a dictatorship would be untenable as he went to Berlin to criticize the Soviets for building a wall to keep in East Germans. The cable instructed the Vietnamese on what they had to do to retain US support, such as establishing a permanent National Religious Council representing all sects, churches, and denominations. Then, the ultimatum in boldface type: "If Diem does not take prompt and effective steps to re-establish Buddhist confidence in him we will have to reexamine our entire relationship with his regime." It was drafted by Roger Hilsman and signed by Rusk.

So here it was, then. Here was the strongest signal yet that the administration was alarmed by deteriorating events in Vietnam, and that it was reassessing its support for Diem and might fall in with those who could overthrow him. A little less than five months later, these two forces would meet. It would end badly for Diem. These slow, fateful events were set in train the morning of June 11 on that sad street corner in Saigon.

※

If there was time – the meeting with Rusk was scheduled for twelve minutes – Kennedy might also have discussed the foreign aid bill. Less urgent than events in Moscow and Saigon, the administration's annual request for $4.5 billion for foreign aid was in trouble in Congress. Later that day, Rusk would testify for three hours before the Senate Foreign Relations Committee. His statement was a plea for engagement in a dangerous world. "Surging change continues and the need, as well as the opportunity, to support a community of free nations persists," Rusk said. "The times do not call for us to leave the field, either in discouragement, boredom or complacency. Rather, we must continue our efforts and seize the initiative wherever we can."

As cabinet secretaries did, Rusk appeared before the committee to defend the aid program against critics, especially Senator J. William Fulbright of Arkansas, its venerable chairman. Kennedy greatly admired Fulbright, whom he had decided against as Secretary because of Fulbright's indifference to civil rights. Rusk was a Southerner too, but he was more sensitive to civil rights. He devoted a chapter to race in his memoir, *As I Saw It*, drawing the connection, in the soft distinctions of language, between civil rights at home and human rights abroad. Rusk was stung by the complaints of African diplomats in Washington, who could not have lunch and dinner in the best restaurants or hotels or clubs, such as the Metropolitan, who could not find office space or living accommodations, who could not swim on public beaches in Maryland and Virginia. One envoy asked Rusk where he could get a haircut; Rusk did not know, but offered him his barber, who worked in a little room next to his office. This prejudice appalled Rusk because it exposed his country's hypocrisy. "We were facing a crisis that went to the very heart of our society, in which our deeds fell far short of our ideals, and we had to eliminate this inconsistency," he wrote.

These musings, from the nation's chief diplomat from Georgia, had eerie resonance this Shakespearean morning as things played out in their peculiar way in Washington, Saigon, Moscow, and Tuscaloosa.

Tuesday, June 11, 1963
CHAPTER 9

Midmorning

THE PRESIDENT'S TALK with Dean Rusk ended at 9:57 a.m. His next appointment was at 10:05 a.m. with a large delegation from the American Committee on Italian Migration. Based in New York, the committee was founded in 1952 to help resettle Italians in the United States, as well as to lobby Congress for an end to national quotas on Italian immigrants. The committee was holding its Third National Symposium in Washington on June 10 and 11. Eight minutes was ample time for JFK to review his prepared remarks, presumably written, as usual, by Ted Sorensen. It is possible that Sorensen might have delegated them to one of his two associates, given the volume of presidential speeches, proclamations, and statements that week, the week before, the following week, and the one after that, when Kennedy would be in Europe. It is also possible because the remarks were less significant than others. But sharing was not usually his way. As Schlesinger observed, "Ted cannot abide any one else doing important speeches for the President."

Although today's remarks would be a short, *pro forma* statement to a national delegation of some 250 – which included Miss Ellen Cannata of Queens Village, New York; Mrs. John Jay Blesso of Hartford, Connecticut; and the Reverend Sylvan Bossi of Chicago – they served a purpose beyond welcoming visitors to the White House. Kennedy was seeing the Italian-Americans that morning to underscore the flaws in the country's immigration policy and to rally support for his new legislation. In the summer, Kennedy would send Congress comprehensive proposals to modernize the cumbersome, antiquated, and restrictive system. Surrounding himself with a crowd of Italian-Americans would generate publicity around the issue. For the next ten minutes, then, the president turned his attention from a big issue to a smaller one. Preoccupied as he was with George Wallace's posturing in Tuscaloosa, he would not cancel his meeting with Judge Juvenal Marchisio and his compatriots. A president had to do more than one thing at a time. If it's Tuesday, June 11 at 10:00 a.m., it must be time for immigration.

Immigration was one of the few issues that had truly interested Kennedy as a legislator. "I know of no cause which President Kennedy championed more warmly than the improvement of our immigration policies," Robert Kennedy wrote in 1964. Perhaps it was because JFK represented Massachusetts, which had the highest share of foreign nationalities of any state in the country. Or, because he was Irish and understood their hardships in the New World. Whatever the reason, Bobby maintained that every progressive step in immigration reform in the postwar era bore his brother's imprint. That included the Displaced Persons Act and the Refugee Relief Act, which Kennedy had sponsored, as well as a bill in 1957 to bring immigrant families together. Now, in June 1963, JFK was proposing sweeping immigration reform, imagining the multicultural society that would flower in the next generation. He approached immigration with a passion unusual for a dispassionate politician.

In 1958, Kennedy had written a slender book on immigration, *A Nation of Immigrants,* which, as RFK described it, "tells us what immigrants have done for America, and what America has done for immigrants." It groans with graphic accounts of discrimination, including drawings (a deck plan of a slave ship) and photographs (the Ku Klux Klan) illustrating American nativism and injustice to immigrants. You might mistake it for a radical pamphlet. Thurston Clarke, who has written three fine books on the Kennedys, calls it "possibly the most passionate, bitter, and controversial book ever written by a serious presidential candidate." For this, Kennedy had no regrets; that spring he and Sorensen were preparing a revised edition for 1964.

Three generations removed from Ireland, Kennedy cherished his origins. Later in June, after his electrifying visit to Berlin, he would make a sentimental trip to Ireland. Standing on the quay in the village of New Ross, on the same ground on which his great-grandfather, Patrick Kennedy, had stood as he embarked on his perilous voyage across "the bowl of tears," the president said: "When my great-grandfather left here to become a cooper in East Boston, he carried nothing with him except two things: a strong religious faith and a strong desire for liberty. . . . If he hadn't left, I would be working over at the Albatross Company . . ."

Now Kennedy was working in the White House and meeting a delegation of Italians in the Colonnade, the long, covered, cream-pillared corridor on the north side of the new Rose Garden. The garden had been Kennedy's inspiration. In his first few months in office, gazing out from his desk, he was dismayed at the unruly Rose Garden. It was a greensward 125 feet long and 60 feet wide created by Woodrow Wilson's wife, Ellen, in 1913. Eisenhower cut down the roses and put in a putting green. "Nothing but crabgrass," Kennedy grumbled to Bartlett in 1961. He asked Bunny Mellon, the heiress and self-taught horticulturist, to redesign it. As with other projects, he had his own ideas and carefully reviewed Mellon's plan to re-create an eighteenth-century American garden. Two years later, surveying the rectangular lawn bordered by boxwood hedges, crab apple trees, and rose bushes, he was delighted with the flourishing blooms.

The Colonnade ran from the Oval Office to the residence, providing an agreeable place to welcome visitors. Here, amid the pansies, daisies, geraniums, and magnolias, Kennedy announced legislation to correct "the inequities" of American immigration laws, which had allowed "a mal-distribution of quotas in Europe," creating "a nearly intolerable" situation. He thought it unconscionable that countries with populations one-twentieth or one-twenty-fifth that of Italy had much greater annual immigration quotas, which they were not fully using. Kennedy's ancestral Ireland, for example, had an annual quota of 17,757 immigrants, but only 6,054 Irish a year actually wanted to come to America. Meanwhile, the annual quota for Italy was 5,666, against 132,435 Italians who wanted to emigrate. Under the existing law, the Immigration Act of 1924 (also known as the Johnson-Reed Act), a system of national quotas governed immigration from each country. It allowed 156,700 immigrants to enter the United States each year. The system was based on the ethnic composition of the population as it had been in 1920.

In his message to Congress on July 23, Kennedy would argue that this system had no basis "in either logic or reason. It neither satisfies a national need nor accomplishes an international purpose. In an age of interdependence among nations [*globalization* had not yet entered the language] such a system is an anachronism, for it discriminates among applicants for admission into the United States on the basis of accident of birth." Indeed, as the Italian Americans visiting that day knew well, the system favored Northern Europe over Southern or Eastern Europe. It meant that an Irishman or a Briton could immigrate to America virtually at any time, but a Greek, Hungarian, Pole, Lithuanian, Estonian,

Latvian, or Italian – as well as an aspirant from Asia, Africa, or South America – could not.

The point was to recognize that all people make equally good citizens. The Italians had. Five million had come to the United States between 1820 and 1963, four million of them in the first two-thirds of the twentieth century. They were the country's largest nationality after the Germans. Yet the policy was frustrating their ambitions. In *A Nation of Immigrants*, Kennedy noted how America had twisted the soaring words of poet Emma Lazarus, which were engraved on the pedestal of the Statue of Liberty in New York Harbor: "Give me your tired, your poor, your huddled masses yearning to breathe free." That was true before 1921, Kennedy wrote bitingly. "Under present law it would be appropriate to add: 'as long as they come from Northern Europe, are not too tired or too poor or slightly ill, never stole a loaf of bread, never joined any questionable organization, and can document their activities for the last two years.'"

Kennedy imagined a system blind to race, origin, and ethnicity. Instead of choosing immigrants on the basis of where they were born or how they appeared, he wanted to make the decision more practical (assessing skills) and humanitarian (reuniting families). In this, like other secondary matters he addressed over these two days, he was ahead of his time. Immigration policy, he would tell Congress, should be "generous . . . fair . . . and flexible. With such a policy we can turn to the world, and to our own past, with clean hands and a clear conscience." His proposal would go to Congress the next month (not the next week, as he assured his audience). Before then, he had travel plans.

"I hope to go to Italy within the next two weeks," he said, "and have a chance to see where it is from whence you came and to say hello to those members of your families who are still waiting at the docks."

✳

The meeting over at 10:15 a.m., Kennedy returned to the Oval Office. At 10:35 a.m. he met John Moors Cabot, the U.S. ambassador to Poland, who was in town on other business. Kennedy liked to confer with his ambassadors. That morning he would also meet David Bruce, and the next morning Bill Attwood, both of whom he had seen socially at the Alsops' the night before. Cabot was a fellow Bostonian (one of the patrician Cabots) and a fellow alumnus of Harvard (he had studied history there and at Oxford). At sixty-one years old, he had spent some thirty-six years in the State Department, serving in Peru, The Hague, Guatemala, Argentina, Yugoslavia, and Shanghai. In the 1950s, Eisenhower had given him successive appointments as ambassador to Sweden, Colombia, and Brazil.

Cabot had worried that the new administration would see him as "a reactionary Republican," much as he had tried "to keep out of politics and do what I was told." But Kennedy had no such qualms. Cabot was one of the thirteen ambassadors he asked to stay on in 1961. Perhaps he remembered that Cabot had called on him as a senator in the mid-1950s; they had discussed sending aid to Yugoslavia and both felt that the United States should, despite broad opposition at the time. It also helped that Cabot agreed with Kennedy that the U.S. "should challenge the Communists in Latin America for leadership of social reform movements, rather than simply defending reactionary regimes in the area." That got Cabot into trouble in Brazil with President Jânio Quadros, a nationalist. Under pressure, Kennedy recalled Cabot in August 1961 (though Cabot maintains that he was returning home anyway). Soon after, Kennedy sent Cabot to Warsaw, a listening post in the Communist world and a clandestine venue for talks with the Chinese Communists over disarmament, Formosa, and Vietnam.

Today Kennedy wanted to discuss the Poles in Laos, a country that had been "neutralized" (aligned with neither the non-Communist nor the Communist bloc) for the previous two years. He also wanted to review Poland's role on the International Control Commission (ICC), which had been established to monitor the ceasefire of 1954 in Indochina as part of the Geneva Accords. With Canada and India, Poland was one of three members of the commission. Kennedy's questions were particularly pertinent this morning given the domestic unrest in Vietnam, and America's growing involvement there. "To the White House to see the President," Cabot wrote in his diary. "We had a cheerful fifteen minutes conversation. He wanted to know what the Poles were up to in Laos and why, which I explained as well as I could." Cabot reported that the Polish member of the ICC "was just a communist agent. That's all. And he was busily sabotaging every effort to have the ICC work."

Cabot had his own questions for Kennedy. He was "thoroughly mad" to learn that the State Department had increased the agricultural loans that the United States was making to Poland. It had been policy to sell surpluses to the Poles for years, and the latest loan was $60 million. Cabot fired off a note to Dean Rusk questioning the loan. It would burden the Poles and their fragile economy with too much debt, he said, and they might default on the loan "out of pure cussedness." He also didn't think the U.S. "should be so particularly friendly to Poland, when they weren't being particularly friendly to us." The State Department told him that the order came from "a very high source." When Cabot met Kennedy that morning, he wanted to know if the president had ordered the sales. If so, Cabot wanted Kennedy to know that it was a mistake. "So, I argued against the large sales," Cabot recalled in 1971. "I remember when the President said, 'I always thought it was a poor idea. Of course, they're never going to pay us.' And so I said — suddenly reversing my field completely — 'Mr. President, we don't want to cut it out altogether. We just want to cut it down, so as not to give them extra leverage.' And he didn't comment on that."

Later in the conversation, Cabot asked Kennedy about the Agricultural Trade Development and Assistance Act (Public Law

480), which authorized these sales, and Kennedy surprised him by implying that the United States should not give Poland anything at all. Cabot, now more advocate than ambassador, pointed out "that we stood to lose a good deal if we cut them off completely." He noted in his diary: "He [JFK] is obviously sore at the Poles about Laos, and obviously isn't the mysterious influence [who is] pressing for bigger PL-480 handouts in that argument."

Cabot's intervention that day seemed to pay off. He argued that the United States should give Poland help under PL-480 but under less favorable terms. The president agreed. For the ambassador, it was a fruitful fifteen minutes.

✳

The meeting with Cabot ended at 10:50 a.m. Ten minutes later, Kennedy met David Bruce. Bruce would find a half hour with the president between visiting the dentist at 9:00 a.m. to get his teeth cleaned, lunching at the 1925 F Street Club with his daughter, Sasha ("a wonderful companion"), and consulting the State Department on Kennedy's imminent visit to Britain. His meeting was "off the record," and Bruce says little about it in his diary. "He [JFK] is the most excellent company," Bruce reported. "We talked about UK affairs, especially the MLF [Multilateral Force]. He is seeing Iain Macleod [the leader of the House of Commons] later this morning, so I think our preliminary talks may have some utility." That's it. When you see a lot of the president – and Bruce saw more of him than any other American ambassador – you may not feel a need to record every word of every encounter. The discreet Ambassador Bruce remained tight-lipped after Kennedy's death, too. Refusing to record an oral history with the John F. Kennedy Presidential Library, as almost every other senior administration official did, he submitted a thin statement of two-and-a-quarter pages. He explained, somewhat weakly, that because he was abroad, he could not comment usefully on the administration. In the statement he notes how Kennedy made "intelligent use of his Ambassadors, but he gave them, in unusual degree, a sense of participation in the decisions affecting the Government to which they were accredited."

One of those questions for Bruce and Kennedy was the Multilateral Force, the centerpiece of the administration's "grand design" to revitalize the Atlantic Alliance. It proposed a seaborne force of ships, manned by crews from the nations of NATO, a strategy that would place nuclear weapons under joint control. Ideally, MLF would foster a more united Europe with its own armed capability shared by the French, the Germans, the Turks, and others. It had strong support within the administration from Walt Rostow, the president's deputy special assistant for national security affairs, whom Bruce called its "torch carrier," and from George Ball in the State Department, who believed fervently in European unity. But the MLF was ridiculed in Britain, which had its own independent nuclear force that it was reluctant to share with its continental neighbors, even if they were NATO brethren. In 1963, the debate became heated. One Conservative British MP, a supporter of the idea, noted that using multinational crews was not new. Why, he told Bruce, Admiral Nelson's flagship at Trafalgar carried twenty-two Americans and twelve Dutchmen, as well as Italians, Maltese, Portuguese, and Swiss! On the other hand, Bruce reported that some British wiseacres were calling it "the multilateral farce."

One melodious American agreed with that assessment. Tom Lehrer was a mathematics professor at the Massachusetts Institute of Technology (MIT) in Boston, who moonlighted as a popular balladeer and pianist. His satirical ditties, released on albums with names like *An Evening Wasted with Tom Lehrer,* had a cult following in the early 1960s. Thinking the MLF faintly ridiculous, he wrote this lullaby:

Sleep, baby, sleep, in peace may you slumber,
No danger lurks, your sleep to encumber,
We've got the missiles, peace to determine,
And one of the fingers on the button will be German.

Why shouldn't they have nuclear warheads?
England says no, but they are all soreheads.
I say a bygone should be a bygone,
Let's make peace the way we did in Stanleyville and Saigon.

Once all the Germans were warlike and mean
But that couldn't happen again.
We taught them a lesson in nineteen-eighteen
And they've hardly bothered us since then.

So sleep well, my darling, the sandman can linger,
We know our buddies won't give us the finger.
Heil – hail – the Wehrmacht, I mean the Bundeswehr,
Hail to our loyal ally!

MLF – will scare Brezhnev
I hope he is half as scared as I!

Kennedy planned to raise the MLF with the British prime
minister and asked Bruce what was on Macmillan's mind. Bruce
was said to have had almost as much access to Macmillan as David
Ormsby-Gore had to Kennedy. Bruce was ambivalent about the
MLF. According to historian David Nunnerley: "On the one hand,
he [Bruce] saw the MLF as a step toward achieving a united
Europe and interdependence in nuclear defense. Yet, at the same
time, he understood the desire of many Britons to retain 'great
power' status." Kennedy wanted the MLF to work. In the face of
stiff British opposition, though, it never happened.

＊

A lesser issue that day was what to do about Harold Wilson, the new leader of the Labour Party, who wanted to see Kennedy on his visit to England. In 1962, Arthur Schlesinger had found Wilson, then a private member of Parliament, "immensely clever, immensely self-satisfied, and skates on the edge of pomposity. He conveys no sense of principle whatever but a considerable sense of competence and intelligence." Now Wilson was Leader of Her Majesty's Most Loyal Opposition. After a few days' inquiry in London in March, Schlesinger praised Wilson's "intelligence, self-control, mastery of the House and cool political skill." He marveled at Wilson's personal popularity a month after winning the party leadership. Kennedy met him on April 2 in Washington, and they talked largely about Profumo beyond a scheduled forty-seven minutes. "I couldn't believe it," reported Wilson after the meeting. "The man talked and talked about the Profumo business. He really grilled me on what I knew." The president agreed with Ben Bradlee that Wilson was "a pretty cold fish." Jackie said JFK "couldn't stand him." Meeting Wilson in Washington, as his host, was one thing; meeting him in London, as his guest, was another.

The U.S. Embassy had received a request from the Labour Party asking the president to receive its leader to discuss Wilson's recent visit to Moscow. JFK was unenthusiastic. "I am rather fed up with Harold Wilson," he told Schlesinger. "Have you seen the record of his talk with Khrushchev? Too much ass-kissing, so far as I'm concerned." Bruce suggested they defer to the Foreign Office or 10 Downing Street, and Kennedy deferred to him. Kennedy didn't want to offend the beleaguered Macmillan by meeting his new rival, particularly after Kennedy had insisted that he and the prime minister meet in relative seclusion at Macmillan's country home, Birch Grove, rather than in scandal-plagued London. Politics was trumping friendship. Kennedy did not want to be seen too much with Macmillan, his old confidant, fast becoming a spent force. But even if Wilson were to become prime minister, Kennedy would not want to offend Macmillan. It was delicate.

Bruce did not say whether Profumo had come up in their conversation Tuesday morning. Given Kennedy's obsession, how could it not? He had been devouring Bruce's cables from London, and with him was the resident expert. To his dismay, Bruce had recently discovered that he had had a passing acquaintance with Stephen Ward, the artist and whoremaster. One morning in January 1962, Ward had come to the U.S. Embassy to paint Bruce's portrait for *London Illustrated*. Bruce had forgotten he had sat for Ward, of all people, and was horrified when he learned of their association, however brief. He told Washington, a little defensively, that Ward had also painted members of the royal family, which put Bruce in "goodly company."

After Bruce's return to London from Washington on June 14, he lunched with Fleur Cowles Meyer, the artist, author, and socialite, four times married. She and others, he reported, were "full of gossip . . . over Profumo, Ward, Keeler, and the rest of that unsavory crew. They think there are many unpleasant revelations still to come." Bruce spent most of the evening drafting a telegram on Profumo for Washington. He continued to report fallout from the scandal. A wounded Macmillan told Parliament that week that he had been "grossly deceived" by Profumo, and asked for sympathy and understanding. Bruce confirmed Schlesinger's sense of the new sexual license in London. "Fantastic stories are afloat," Bruce wrote. "It is open season for the irresponsible." Of the hanky-panky in high places, he said: "I've never witnessed such a mess; famous politicians are accused of having intimately intermingled with a squalid underworld." Bruce religiously passed along what he heard. His réportage, as always, was appreciated in the White House.

※

It was now 11:40 a.m. The senior class of the Capitol Page School was visiting the White House. The well-scrubbed pages had gathered in the New Flower Garden, where the president would spend ten minutes with them. It was time to celebrate public service. The school was established in the 1820s to train boys to work as pages in the House and Senate (there were no girls admitted until 1971). Having served in Congress, Kennedy knew and applauded the program, mentioning *serve* or *service* four times in his two-paragraph statement.

Kennedy had made public service his signature. He called politics "an honorable profession." In a time a higher percentage of Americans voted in presidential elections – the turnout of 62.7 percent in 1960 has been falling ever since – they believed him. He saluted the military (whatever his doubts about its leadership) and was proud to create the Peace Corps. Service was the totem of his world; between his father's embassy in London, the Navy, and his career in politics, he had spent almost half his forty-six years in the public realm. In his remarks to the students, he praised the program for giving the pages "almost a unique vantage point" in seeing how Congress worked and how laws were made. At the same time, he urged them to consider public service: "I hope all of you will make a determination to continue your interest in political life either as active participants on the national level, on the state level, or local level or working in the Executive Branch of government, and putting back into this free system of ours some of the values which you have derived from your service with us."

Every day Kennedy was reaching Americans through appearances and presentations like this one, as well as speeches, interviews, and press conferences, which he held, on average, every sixteen days. He was also reaching Americans by mail. Every week the White House received some seventeen thousand letters, cards, and telegrams on nuclear arms, civil rights, freight rates, and a host of other issues. Many letters sent blessings or sought endorsements from or appearances by the president. Kennedy's correspondence staff, led by Fred Holborn, a special assistant, monitored and managed the huge volume of daily mail. Sometimes they responded in their own name on behalf of the president, sometimes in his name. Both Sorensen and Schlesinger also received many letters and dutifully answered them – often with wit and erudition. Schlesinger was a particularly prolific epistolarian; over sixty years, his sons say he sent and received more than thirty-five thousand letters.

On June 10 and 11, 1963, Kennedy sent notes of gratitude, congratulation, and condolence. He also dispatched birthday greetings and anniversary wishes. Most are standard; some offer explanation, illustration, or anecdote. On Monday, June 10, for example, Kennedy wrote August Heckscher II ("Dear Augie"), his special consultant on the arts, who was resigning. Kennedy had appreciated his report on government and the arts. It had inspired him to create the President's Advisory Council on the Arts, which he would announce that week. In a letter Schlesinger drafted, Kennedy declared: "The quality of America's cultural life is an element of immense importance in the scales by which our worth will ultimately be weighed." He believed the government had a role to play "in helping establish the conditions under which art can flourish – in encouraging the arts as it encourages science and learning."

That same day, he thanked President Sarvepalli Radhakrishnan of India for his gifts (a tapestry rug and a carved wooden chest) presented on his recent visit to the White House. He thanked Sister Mary Clement of St. Louis for sending him birthday wishes, the commanding officer of the White House Communications Agency for the same, and Mercedes McCambridge, the actress, for supporting his tax program. He sent greetings to the Reverend Eugene Dinsmore Dolloff on the one hundred fiftieth anniversary of the founding of the First Baptist Church of New Bedford, Massachusetts. He sent birthday greetings to Representative William S. Mailliard, sympathies to the Honorable Joseph W. Barr, and congratulations to

the Reverend Felix Hummer on the fiftieth anniversary of his ordi-
nation to the priesthood.

On Tuesday, June 11, more letters arrive, more are sent. Warm
greetings to the Rotarians at their fifty-fourth annual convention in
St. Louis, Missouri. Best wishes to the employees of the *Daily
Journal* of Wheaton, Illinois, on the modernization of their production facilities. Great thanks to Sandra Ann Kozacka of Amesbury,
Massachusetts, for her biography of his life, with drawings, which
had earned her a good grade at primary school. Many happy returns
of the day to Admiral George Burkley, one of his doctors, and to
Virginia Senator Harry Byrd, a segregationist who had taken fifteen
electoral votes from him in the 1960 election. Bearer of thanks,
carrier of news, a letter from the White House in your mailbox,
typed on quality cream stationery adorned with presidential seal
and signature, was something to cherish and keep.

The power of the letter was greatest – and saddest – when the
president wrote to the families of soldiers who had died on active
duty. On Tuesday, Kennedy sent condolences to the parents of First
Lieutenant James N. Daniel, who died serving with the 7th Aviation
Company in Korea, praising "his outstanding leadership, professional skill, and devotion to duty." He sent condolences to the wife
of Captain James H. Brodt and the parents of Private First Class
Neil K. MacIver, both killed on combat patrol in Vietnam; to the
parents of Private First Class Frank D. Rodriguez, who died with
the 93rd Engineer Company in West Germany; to the wife of First
Lieutenant James L. Futrell, who died at the U.S. Army Aviation
School in Fort Rucker, Alabama; to the parents of Specialist
Norman L. Borden and the mother of Private First Class Terry M.
Stoddard, both of the California National Guard, who died serving
with the 2nd Mechanized Infantry Battalion, near Barstow,
California; and to the wife of Private Malcolm L. Myers, who died
serving with the 1st Airborne Battle Group, 501st Infantry, in Fort
Campbell, Kentucky.

For the most part, the letters are boilerplate. They open with an expression of deep regret and then declare: "While I realize there is little that can be said to lessen your grief . . ." They praise the courage, perseverance, or professionalism of a fallen son or husband, wherever he was or whatever he did. The United States was at peace in 1963, and strictly speaking, no combat troops died while Kennedy was president. But soldiers, sailors, and airmen did die on the job in training accidents at home. In Vietnam, they died "advising" the Vietnamese. Others died in Korea or Europe where the United States maintained large garrisons. "Mrs. Kennedy joins me in extending to you our deepest sympathies . . ." these letters would conclude. On Tuesday, Kennedy signed eight of them by hand, as always. He refused the facsimile signature machine.

Other letters were political in nature. The president wrote George E. Taylor of Seattle, Washington, appointing him with "great pleasure" to the Board of Foreign Scholarships. He wrote Secretary of the Army Cyrus Vance, congratulating him on "the inspiring demonstration of the Army's striking power" he saw at the White Sands Missile Range the previous week. He wrote William A. Riaski, executive director of the Izaak Walton League of America, honoring his "long and distinguished service in the cause of conservation" on the occasion of the league's forty-third annual conference. "Outdoor living for an urban society is a subject meriting earnest and immediate attention," Kennedy wrote. "Man's need to keep in touch with the earth and the sky, his need for more outdoor recreation, are clearly known and recognized." Now it may be that Kennedy was not delighted to appoint Taylor and he was not impressed with the Army's striking power and he did not give a damn about conservation. No matter. Kennedy may have owed Taylor a favor. He may have had to look interested at White Sands. He had sent a bill to Congress to create a Land and Water Conservation Fund, and he needed support.

This was the job. A president is many things: manager of prosperity, first diplomat, principal educator, master of the bully pulpit, commander in chief, official mourner and consoler. That day, to those bereaved parents in California and Alabama, to that schoolgirl in Amesbury, to that appointee in Seattle, to that minister in Massachusetts, and to that conservationist in Ohio, Kennedy was someone less exalted, though, to them, no less important. He was correspondent in chief.

Tuesday, June 11, 1963

CHAPTER 10

Noon

THE PRESIDENT HAD two more appointments on his
schedule. The first, at 12:03 p.m. was with the visiting Briton,
Iain Macleod, leader of the House of Commons and chairman of
the Conservative Party. He was accompanied by Ambassador
Ormsby-Gore. As Bruce suggested, another meeting with another
British politician had to include some discussion of Kennedy's
imminent visit to Britain, the state of the Macmillan government,
and, of course, Profumo. But was that why Macleod was in
Washington? In his memo to the president on March 26, Arthur
Schlesinger reported that Macleod had wanted to come to the
United States, in part, to meet RFK and Stephen Smith, Jack's
brother-in-law. The two had run the campaign in 1960 and were
preparing for 1964. Macleod wanted "to get some ideas for the
[Conservative] campaign [in Britain]" in the coming general election there. He was not alone in wanting to learn from the Kennedys.
Wilson was also preparing to borrow lines from Kennedy's play-
book, casting himself as a new leader for a new time and promising

to get Britain "moving again." He planned to run "a Kennedy-style campaign rather than an old-fashioned Socialist campaign," Schlesinger reported. Shrewdly, both Wilson and Macleod wanted to consult the architects of what became known as "the first modern campaign."

Whatever the subject, Macleod would be worth a few minutes of Kennedy's time, even if Schlesinger pronounced him "in eclipse" in the spring of 1963, "bright and likeable but not deeply impressive." His party's ailing fortunes notwithstanding, Macleod was a polymath who intrigued Kennedy, a committed anglophile. Macleod was a lover of poetry (like others of that generation, he often recited verse by heart), a student of the past (he read history at Oxford), and one of Britain's best bridge players (he won tournaments in the 1930s). He was also a playboy, recalled former foreign secretary Douglas Hurd, who said that Macleod "believed in pleasure" as if it were a sacrament. Not that he looked like a playboy; at forty-nine years old in 1963, he had a bald dome to rival the United States Capitol. As a soldier, Macleod took part in the D-Day landings at Normandy; he was run over by a tank and, like Kennedy, he entered middle age in pain. He won a seat in Parliament in 1950 and held a succession of cabinet positions in Conservative governments, including health, labour, and secretary of state for the colonies, in which he supported decolonization. He was a spellbinding orator. "He was the star," said Hurd, who, as a young Conservative in the 1960s, was awed by him at party conferences. "He had an extraordinary voice. It was not exactly bell-like, but it was sonorous. He talked with great emphasis and force. A lot was witty and funny and he got a laugh out of every speech." It wasn't just the joke; Macleod had "that feeling of commitment" that others did not.

Kennedy and Macleod obviously had much in common, personally and professionally. They discussed Profumo, of course, which JFK noted afterward. But had they never discussed Profumo, Skybolt, MLF, de Gaulle, or any other questions of the day, their conversation might have as easily touched upon the Second World War, contemporary politics, the power of oratory, women, even bridge. Whatever the topic, the president found thirty-seven minutes to spend with Macleod at the very moment George Wallace was preparing to make his stand in Alabama.

*

Five minutes after the two Britons departed, Kennedy was pulled back home. At 12:45 p.m., he greeted a quartet of influential congressional Republicans: Senator Everett Dirksen of Illinois, minority leader; Senator Thomas Kuchel of California, minority whip; Representative Charles Halleck of Indiana, house minority leader; and Representative Leslie Arends of Illinois, house minority whip. Lyndon Johnson, who knew Congress better than anyone in the administration, also attended. The purpose of this off-the-record meeting was to discuss the impending civil rights legislation – to learn what was acceptable to the group and what was not. Kennedy knew that he would need the support of northern progressive Republicans to make up for the loss of southern conservative Democrats. This was the art of gentle persuasion, and he was more likely to persuade them than those in his own party. Courting these folks was at the heart of the strategy to push the civil rights bill through Congress.

All four were venerable standard-bearers of the Grand Old Party. Arends had been in Congress since 1935 and been Republican whip since 1943, a position he would hold until his retirement in 1975. He had opposed most of Kennedy's legislation on labor, housing, and education. Halleck had also come to the House in 1935, and had been minority leader since 1959. Like Arends, Halleck was against most of Kennedy's program. In particular, he had led the opposition in 1961 and 1962 to federal assistance to schools and to creating a housing and urban development cabinet department.

Given their record, it was unlikely that Halleck and Arends would embrace a civil rights bill. Dirksen, on the other hand, was more amenable. In the Senate since 1951, he had been minority leader for the past four years. When Richard Nixon and the Republicans lost the White House in 1960, Dirksen emerged as his party's most influential national figure. While he had led the opposition to the urban affairs department, the farm bill, and school construction, he was bipartisan on foreign policy. He refused to attack Kennedy over the disastrous Bay of Pigs, endorsed the administration's policies on Laos, Berlin, and foreign aid, and had supported JFK during the Cuban Missile Crisis. He and Kennedy liked each other; the disheveled Dirksen was a natural ham, mellifluous of voice, opaque in speech, dramatic in gesture. Kennedy hoped Dirksen would help forge a bipartisan coalition in support of civil rights legislation. He needed Kuchel, too. Kuchel had been in the Senate since 1953 and Republican whip since 1959. He had arrived in Washington as a conservative who voted against the censure of the red-baiting Joe McCarthy. But evolving, he had supported Kennedy on federal aid to education, the United Nations, and mass transit.

Kennedy desperately needed them all. Given their roots – three were from the Midwest and one from the Far West – he believed he had a far better chance of bringing them to accept his proposals than winning over those ornery, messianic Southerners. In the end, these Republicans would surprise him; their efforts paid big dividends which Lyndon Johnson would bank later. In June, though, it was early days. There wasn't even a civil rights bill yet. The question this afternoon was what they would accept in it.

Kennedy told them that civil rights "is our major problem now." Things had changed dramatically since Birmingham, he said. "Where they [black Americans] were accepting a pace of progress before and rather seemed to be pleased with it, they are not accepting it now." He said that they needed "a judicial remedy." That's why he would be sending Congress a civil rights bill. "I am hopeful we can get it by," he said, with understatement. "It doesn't seem to be unreasonable." Specifically, Kennedy talked about three key elements: public accommodations, school integration, and voting rights. The big problem was integrating private enterprises. "When it comes to stores and shops that are privately owned, I think you are going to have some trouble," warned Dirksen. "Because, after all, you have got a concept of private property involved there." Kennedy mentioned a restaurant or lunch counter with fifteen seats or more as a target of the law. "You make them do a lot of things," he said of these businesses, such as paying their employees a minimum wage. The federal government could make them integrate their clientele, too. "I think it would be useful for us to do it" he said, again with some understatement.

There was no immediate commitment from the Republicans. "Both Dirksen and Halleck were skeptical," wrote Hugh Sidey. "They needed more time, more information." Ultimately, as the face of congressional Republicans, their endorsement in whole or in part would be fundamental. They couldn't guarantee that all Republicans would vote as they asked, but they would only need about half of them. If Dirksen and Halleck were seeking clarity, so was the administration. Within the White House and the Justice Department, the legislation had been discussed for weeks; however, it was only at the beginning of the month that the Kennedys had decided to proceed with it.

Louis Martin, a political advisor to JFK and one of the few senior black men in the administration, had been called to a meeting in the Cabinet Room at 11:30 a.m. on Saturday, June 1. There he was surprised to see the president, RFK, Johnson, and several cabinet secretaries. They were discussing how to cool racial tensions. Bobby, seated next to his brother, motioned Martin to sit beside him. "Louis, what's the mood of the country and what should we do about it?" the president asked. It was the first time Martin had been asked his view in a meeting of that stature. Martin warned that the unrest was no longer just in the South, in cities like Birmingham. It was spreading to Chicago, Detroit, Pittsburgh, and New York. A veteran journalist, Martin had joined Kennedy's campaign in 1960; he was one of those who persuaded JFK to make that influential telephone call to Coretta Scott King while her husband was in jail. The overture – widely reported, much discussed, and deeply appreciated among black Americans – may have been decisive in electing Kennedy. That day, Martin proposed a program of $1 billion for jobs and development. Legally, there would have to be provisions on the rights of blacks to eat, shop, and sleep anywhere. "That was the day, I believe, that the administration made up its mind that the time for delay was over," he recalled in 1983. "They had to move on civil rights legislation." After listening to Martin, LBJ said: "Louis is right." Martin emphasized one thing: the civil rights bill had to cover public accommodation or "we're going to have one hell of a war in this country."

Johnson was at the meeting with the Republicans on Tuesday, as he was at other meetings, although not those in the Oval Office on Monday afternoon. At fifty-four, he had become a forlorn presence in the administration, a diminished figure, no longer Master of the Senate or, even worse, of his own fate. He was derided by RFK and ignored, benignly, by JFK, who treated him with courtesy but distrusted him. The vice-presidency was an agony for Johnson. As Katie Louchheim observed, he was wan, almost gray, that spring. Arthur Schlesinger noted that "he really has faded astonishingly into the background and wanders unhappily around, a spectral and premature elder statesman." On civil rights, though, he came alive. He had fire. His commitment was more visceral than Kennedy's.

On June 3, eight days earlier, Johnson and Ted Sorensen discussed the bill over the telephone. In his memoir, Sorensen described a conversation that seemed to go for hours, and he wondered if Johnson's declamation was more for the historical record (Johnson tape-recorded the conversation) than the legislation. LBJ offered advice on tactics, strategy, content, language, amendments, and legislators. The words came in a deluge, unrelenting. It reduced the deferential Sorensen to sputtering, short interjections, as if Johnson were speaking a foreign language that Sorensen pretended to understand by grunting an occasional word or two.

Johnson worried that presenting a civil rights bill that month would touch off "a three- or four-month debate that will kill his program and inflame the country . . . It might cost us the South, but these sorts of states may be lost anyway. . . . But if he goes down there and looks them in the eye and states the moral issue and the Christian issue, and he does it face-to-face, these Southerners at least will respect his courage . . . I don't think the Negro's goals are going to be achieved through legislation . . . I think that he [JFK] will be cut to pieces with this, and I think he'll be a sacrificial lamb. His program will be hurt, if not killed . . . I don't think the bill's been thought through . . . I don't think you'll ever pass the bill as it is. . . . You haven't done your homework on public sentiment . . . I don't know who drafted it; I've never seen it. Hell, if the Vice-President doesn't know what's in it, how do you expect the others to know what's in it? . . . This crowd, they're experts at fighting this kind of thing, and we're not prepared for them. We got a little popgun, and I want to pull out the cannon. The President is the cannon. Let him be on all the TV networks, just speaking from his conscience. . . ."

Here was Johnson warning Sorensen to delay the bill – at least for now – because it could destroy the administration's agenda. His caution was shared by others, particularly Larry O'Brien and Kenny O'Donnell. Johnson was urging JFK to talk more about the issue, which he saw in moral terms. Kennedy had come to that realization himself – that civil rights was morally right – but it was also true that most of his advisors did not want him to speak about it at all. It is unlikely that Johnson shared his deep-seated views at the meeting that morning with the Republicans, or with JFK, who by 1963 had doubts about his vice president's judgment as well as his style.

It offended, amused, and alarmed him. "Oh, God, can you ever imagine what would happen to the country if Lyndon was president?" he asked Jackie. After Kennedy's death, she told Sorensen of her husband's "steadily diminishing opinion" of Johnson as vice president. "As his term progressed, he grew more and more concerned about what would happen if LBJ ever became president. He was truly frightened at the prospect," she said. Evelyn Lincoln maintained that Kennedy was considering dropping Johnson from the ticket in 1964. Bobby, who scorned LBJ and did not want him to succeed JFK in 1969, always denied that.

The president's meeting with Johnson and the Republicans ended around 1:15 p.m. Kennedy had heard their doubts on what was possible and who would support his bill. Kennedy continued to talk about a national effort, and a sustained one. "I would think most people would feel by the end of this summer that we've got to do something in this area," he said. "I have talked to some of the southerners, they don't like it but I think there is a realization that we have to do something about this."

While Kennedy sat with them, having addressed a brace of domestic and foreign issues throughout the morning spilling into the afternoon, the government of the United States was colliding publicly and unpredictably with the state of Alabama. After calling the president early, Bobby kept him informed of events throughout the morning. When the adversaries took up their positions in Tuscaloosa, Bobby interrupted his brother's meeting with the Republicans. Then JFK made the first of two or three critical decisions that day, none of them until necessary. He was fundamentally cautious, as he had been during the Cuban Missile Crisis. "I don't think I ever react emotionally to a problem, but that doesn't mean that I'm not emotional," Kennedy once said. "It simply means that I reason problems out and apply logic to them." Each time, he listened carefully to his brother. If Tuscaloosa was George's Cotillion, Bobby wasn't going as a debutante.

Tuesday, June 11, 1963

CHAPTER 11

RFK

ON SUNDAY, JUNE 2, 1963, Robert Kennedy gave the commencement address at Trinity College in Washington, D.C. Lush and leafy in late spring, Trinity was "one of the finest liberal arts colleges in America," educating affluent Catholic women since 1897. The attorney general had accepted the invitation because, he quipped, his brother had spoken at the college in 1957 and "I looked at his career and what happened to him." Bobby's mordant sense of humor played on his youth and inexperience. Humor humanized him, belying his reputation of ruthlessness as family consigliere. To the doe-eyed, fresh-faced ingénues seated before him in the chapel, RFK made light of the obstacles they faced on their big day – getting dressed in cap and gown, finding their way through the crowded hall to the rostrum to receive their degrees – and ventured that the rest of their lives would be comparatively easy. His little-known address speaks eloquently to the future. In those tumultuous weeks, the Kennedys had come to understand, painfully, the forces remaking the United States. The "crisis in civil rights" – a term the two brothers began using around this time – would gain presidential voice and official recognition on Tuesday, June 11, what some would call the single most important day in the civil rights movement.

Bobby saw it earlier and felt it more deeply. As the country's chief law-enforcement officer, he was more exposed to the frustration of black Americans than his brother and his circle. In one bruising encounter on May 24 in New York City, a gathering of eminent black entertainers, artists, and authors, including James Baldwin, Harry Belafonte, and Lena Horne, attacked the administration's lassitude on racism, blaming him personally. The session lasted three hours and left the attorney general silent and sullen. Kenneth Clark, the psychologist and social reformer, called it "the most intense, traumatic meeting in which I've ever taken part . . . *the* most dramatic experience I have ever had." That meeting, and the racial unrest in the country's cities, had made Bobby acutely aware of the urgency of the issue.

At Trinity College, beyond the civil rights crisis, Robert Kennedy touched on social challenges – persistent poverty, the suffering of the American Indian, attention for the mentally ill, and the shifting expectations of modern women. His impassioned message that day telegraphed his emergence as champion of the underclass in the last chapter of his life, which would end violently the first week of June exactly five years later. Robert Drew saw RFK's influence in 1963. For nine days, from his speech at Trinity to the showdown in Tuscaloosa, Drew's cameras followed Bobby from his home to his office to the White House, into his limousine, through television studios, into corridors, and on to the streets.

While the women of Trinity College might find that ending four years of study was touched with sadness, Bobby told them, they were beginning something new. They were joining the 9 percent of Americans who had degrees in higher education. The purpose of that education, he said, was "to *free* the mind – to free it from the darkness, the narrowness, the groundless fears and self-defeating passions of ignorance. And so perhaps it's not too much to say that what we are celebrating today is the liberation, the setting free of your minds."

They had now earned the right to do their own learning and to develop their own insights, he said, which meant seeking out reality and understanding that "reality is often a far more painful matter than the soft and comfortable illusions of the intellectually poor." For them, this would be a huge advantage. "In the light of a truly freed mind no prejudice can disguise itself as zeal, no bullying can masquerade as leadership, no pettiness can pose as importance. The freed mind will never confuse a sentimentality with a true emotion, an act of violence with an act of heroism, a slogan with a cause," he declared.

Kennedy was referring to the "bullying" Bull Connor in Birmingham, the swaggering police chief who had unleashed those snarling dogs and high-pressure water cannon on black protesters. He was referring to the "pettiness" of George Wallace in Montgomery, who would carry to Tuscaloosa his ancient grievance and misplaced sentimentality. Endowed with this freedom of mind, RFK challenged the graduates: "How are you going to use it? What are you – and I mean each of you, as individuals – what are you going to do with this hard-earned and priceless power?"

He saw three choices. They could keep it, savor it, and never use it, which he thought "a terrible waste." They could use a small part of it to advance their own status, showing no understanding of "the distinction between education and training." Or, they could use their minds "to the full, for the benefit of others as well as yourself – to take an active, creative part in the community, the nation and the world you live in." For Bobby, whose brother had asked Americans what they could do for their country, this was the only course worthy of them. Hunger, disease, discrimination, ignorance – all demanded their interest in the 1960s.

232

"The current crisis in civil rights, for example, is not something that can be solved by governmental edict," he said. "It is an intensely human problem, and its ultimate solution will rest in the ability of men and women everywhere to recognize and follow their own best instincts. They will need guidance in this quest for right as opposed to wrong – for vision as opposed to blindness, for reason as opposed to hysteria. Our answer to the extremists must be to move quickly in establishing those reforms which all of us know in our hearts, should have been made long ago."

Here RFK was admitting the country's (and his own) failure to address the black American's fight for equality. Not that it was his or the country's only failing in 1963. "Conditions among the American Indians, seldom publicized, are so poor that I could devote the rest of my talk to them alone," he said, noting their high infant mortality rate and low life expectancy. One of eight Americans was mentally ill or mentally handicapped, and facilities for their treatment were inadequate. He appealed to his audience, as young women, to embrace a life bigger than that of wife and mother, suggesting that that classic role "belongs to simpler times than ours – and to simpler minds than yours." The portrayal of that stereotype by advertisers was "a real and present danger: a growing concept of ideal family life as containment within an air-tight capsule of coziness and consumership, a bright plastic bastion from which all the range and clamor of the world is shut out – from which reality is forever held at bay. Don't . . . let this happen to you."

So, with the characteristic vigor of the New Frontier, he urged them to act (suggesting four voluntary organizations in Washington they could join). After all, he said, ". . . we live in a perilous, exciting, potentially disastrous and yet also potentially the best of times." This was no time for faint hearts. "My message here is simply that there can be no allowance for your complacency in the days and years ahead, and there will be every reason and every need for your intense, personal involvement. As people with free minds in a free society, we have literally everything to live for. And, as we use our faculties to the maximum, as we apply ourselves fully to do God's work we have nothing to be afraid of."

Moments after the address, Drew's cameras followed him into a small room near the chapel where he watched *Meet the Press*, the venerable Sunday morning public affairs interview program. The guest was George Wallace. That morning in New York City, escorted by nine detectives and with a phalanx of policemen ringing NBC Studios at Rockefeller Center, he had navigated hundreds of chanting protesters. Relishing his moment on national television, the governor was all bluster, bravura, and magnolia. He reiterated his refusal to negotiate with the administration, even to accept mediation. "I shall stand at the door as I stated in my campaign for Governor," he promised. "The confrontation will be handled peacefully and without violence." He would oppose unwarranted intrusion of "the centralized government" in the affairs of Alabama. He would resist the federal government because that was the duty of a son of Dixie. In Washington, Bobby stared grimly at the flickering screen.

✳

He had been shadowboxing with Wallace all spring. It did not help that the governor refused to take his telephone calls. On April 25, though, Wallace listened to the appeal of a trusted intermediary and granted the attorney general an audience. RFK, accompanied by Ed Guthman and Burke Marshall, flew down to Montgomery, the self-described "Cradle of the Confederacy." When a state trooper met them at Maxwell Air Force Base and informed them he was responsible for their security, Bobby politely extended his hand; the trooper crossed his arms across his chest and turned his back. The attorney general was then escorted into town by the state highway patrol as if he were "a foreign dignitary." RFK called Alabama "a foreign country." Demonstrators along the road held signs saying "Mississippi Murderer" and "Kosher Team – Kennedy/ Kastro/Khrushchev." Six hundred state troopers ringed the Capitol, an intimidating show of force. When Bobby entered the rotunda of the legislature and walked over to greet some young women, a beefy state trooper placed a billy club against his stomach and shoved it, playfully. It wasn't funny. "The point was to try to show that my life was in danger in coming to Alabama, because people hated me so much," RFK recalled. A few minutes later, in his office, Wallace welcomed his guest to "the courtesy capital of the country."

Bobby knew the meeting would be pointless when Wallace asked to record the conversation; he wanted to trip him up and release the audiotape. What followed was a dialogue of dismay. RFK told Wallace the federal government would have to enforce the law and integrate the university. Wallace said that he would never allow integration, asserting: "There is *no* time in my judgment when we will be ready for it – in my lifetime, at least." Bobby, almost pleading, hoped that this would end up in the courts rather than in the streets. "I don't want to have another Oxford, Mississippi," he said. "That's all I ask." Wallace agreed, but insisted that it was "you folks . . . who have control of the troops." Bobby hoped again that it would not come to that. Wallace kept pressing him for an assurance that Washington would not use force. Bobby insisted that there were no plans to use it; he expected the law would be obeyed. And so it went, for one hour and twenty-two minutes. Nothing changed. As Wallace recalled in 1967, "When we left, the attitude was, 'Well, we both felt the same as when we both came together.'" Bobby was "dumbfounded" by Wallace, recalled Guthman, his assistant, "the closest I ever saw him to . . . despair."

Three weeks later, the president met Wallace on a flying visit to Alabama. It was no more useful. Wallace maintained his position through May and early June with the same airiness he would display on *Meet the Press*. The difference now was that Judge Seybourn H. Lynne of the federal district court had ruled on May

21 that the university must enroll the students in the summer session beginning June 11. That meant the Kennedys would have to confront Wallace, which was unpalatable, or ignore the court order, which was unthinkable. The problem was that no one in Washington – or even in Alabama – knew what Wallace would do. That made it hard to plan. The word from Tuscaloosa, said Bobby, was that Wallace "was acting like a raving lunatic." Conveniently, reports surfaced that week that Wallace had a history of mental illness diagnosed when he was in the Air Force in 1943. While RFK was respectful toward Wallace in public, he thought the governor was unhinged. If the administration couldn't treat him as a rational being, how would it know how to respond? How to apply maximum pressure with minimum force? Bobby succinctly summarized the challenges facing the administration: not having to charge Wallace with contempt of court, not having to arrest him, not having to take him away, and not having to send in troops while enforcing the court order, allowing the students to register and attend the university.

In the days leading up to June 11, Drew captured the strategy sessions, hour after hour, in the attorney general's cavernous office in the Department of Justice. One well-travelled visitor called it the biggest office he'd ever seen, "more elaborate than his brother's." The decor was baroque. A stuffed tiger lay on the red carpet. A mounted, varnished sailfish hung over the fireplace. A white dented helmet, worn by a marshal at Oxford, sat on a table. Crayoned children's drawings floated on the walnut paneling. Telephones were everywhere, including an outsize console on RFK's desk with a direct line to the president, and four black telephones arranged on a narrow table behind the desk. In the film, when one of them rings, Bobby comically picks up three different receivers before finding the right one.

Preparations were feverish. Bobby used every public opportunity to insist that the administration was responding responsibly to unrest. On June 3, he appeared on *Press Conference USA*, a current affairs program broadcast abroad. The subject was civil rights, and RFK noted that the city of Atlanta, for example, had desegregated its bus and train terminals. He said the federal government had hired five hundred black citizens. "Lip service is not sufficient," he insisted. "Negroes want to see gains. But it won't be done by government edict." The panel of interviewers included Chinua Achebe, the acclaimed Nigerian novelist who had written the sublime *Things Fall Apart* in 1958. Afterward, RFK shook the hands of the three journalists in the studio before moving to the control room to greet each of the cameramen, soundmen, and producers. Politicians did that then.

In his office, the telephones never stopped ringing. On June 4, Bobby learned that Ted Sorensen had called, asking the Justice Department to review the proposed legislation with Lyndon Johnson; he was trying to draw attention to the vice president's indirect intervention with him the previous afternoon. LBJ sent a similar message through a Kennedy aide. Every day Bobby conferred with Nicholas Katzenbach and Burke Marshall on strategy. He was alarmed by an angry telegram from the National States' Rights Party, promising to mobilize Alabamans to march on the campus. "This is to notify you that [we] will be in Tuscaloosa . . . to back Governor Wallace, whether he wants our help or not, in keeping the Negro out of our university," wired Dr. Edward R. Fields, the party's spokesman. "We also urge every other white Alabaman . . . to come to the aid of our Governor if needed. Alabama will never surrender to your carpet-bag rule."

Bobby and his deputies speculate at length, on camera, on "the long list of crazy things" that Wallace could do. They worried about the hundreds of policemen that Wallace could muster and about a clash with federal troops if he stood his ground. They wondered how Wallace might be found "in contempt of court" by Judge Lynne. If the governor made a statement and quickly left, for example, that would not be contempt. But if he tried to block the students from entering, that would be contempt, for which he could get two years in jail. "Could he be pushed aside in a dignified way?" someone asked. That, though, would still be contempt, these lawyers agreed, because he would have thwarted the wishes of the court.

Removing Wallace gracefully – if that were possible – became a practical challenge. According to Ben Allen, an Alabama state detective attached to the governor, soldiers based in an abandoned school in the town of Vance, twenty miles from Tuscaloosa, were rehearsing a particular maneuver. "They had been practicin' at the school how to snatch Wallace up *and walk off* [italics in original] with him . . . grab him by the wrist with one hand and up under the armpits with another and forcibly walk him off." The worry in Washington was having to drag off Wallace, kickin', screamin', and cussin'. Now, how would that look on television and in the newspapers? Would it turn George Wallace into Sewell Avery, the white-haired president of Montgomery Ward and Company, who had defied wartime rules on strikes and lockouts in 1944? An angry Franklin Roosevelt ordered the Army National Guard to seize the plant and remove Avery. In the celebrated photograph, Avery, arms folded over his chest, is stiff and impassive as two soldiers carry him out of his office and on to the street. The Kennedys did not want another Avery.

As the government prepared, RFK conferred with John Doar, assistant attorney general for civil rights in the Justice Department. He was in Birmingham coaching the two black students. "I saw your daughter," Bobby teased him over the telephone. "She doesn't know what you are doing down there." In Drew's film, Bobby sits in his big leather chair, feet on his desk, sleeves rolled up, tie askew, playing with a gavel or tossing a ballpoint pen into the air. He tells Doar that he's entering "the hop, skip and jump" contest with Kathleen, his eldest daughter, at an upcoming field day. "John," RFK says, "while you are down there, look what I am doing up here." Then, deadly

serious, his tone low and anxious, he asks: "Is Wallace coming?"
Doar doesn't know.

More discussion of walkie-talkies and telephone communications. More talk of the geography of Tuscaloosa. Without recent maps,
which even the Forest Service lacks, they order a military plane to
photograph the campus. (When word leaked, the administration's
critics made comparisons with the American U-2 reconnaissance
flights over Cuba. Wallace gleefully exploited federal "spying" on
Alabama.) The cameras run silent in this extended sequence. Hour
after hour, men in short-sleeve white shirts, their ties in clasps,
chain-smoke in hazy rooms and discuss battlefield strategy.

"Every little thing counts in a crisis," said Nehru, and it did
here. Burke Marshall worried that the soldiers sent to Tuscaloosa
might come from Alabama's Marengo County, a racist stronghold.
They might refuse to enforce a federal directive they found personally repugnant. "The county is out of the nineteenth century,"
Marshall says on camera. No wonder RFK demanded daily intelligence reports from Alabama. He had come to rely on Frank Rose,
who was committed to integration as university president, as well
as on sympathetic university trustees, local businessmen, and moderate civic leaders who opposed Wallace. The disaster at Ole Miss
was top-of-mind. Above all, Vivian Malone and James Hood had to
be kept safe. "If this thing blows, we will need a means of escape,"
says one of the deputies at the Justice Department. The nation's
finest legal minds then ponder their options to rescue the students
should there be a riot. Katzenbach, the former POW who knew
something about planning escapes, suggests spiriting them away
in an ambulance. Or a postal truck. Maybe a helicopter? Better
yet, that boat piloted by marshals to ferry them across the Black
Warrior River bordering the campus.

Nothing must go wrong – especially if it does go wrong.

✳

Ultimately, Tuscaloosa was about two young Americans wanting to go to school. All the machinations of all the president's men – the plans, pronouncements, and proclamations leading to the knock on the schoolhouse door on June 11 – began with them. All the governor's threats, cries, and laments, his posing, strutting, and taunting, began with them. Every victory in the civil rights movement began with a man or a woman with a sense of outrage. It was Rosa Parks refusing to give up her seat on a bus in Montgomery in 1955, and Autherine Lucy enrolling at the University of Alabama in 1956 (expelled three days later when the university said it could not protect her from hostile classmates). It was John Lewis and the Freedom Riders challenging segregated bus stations in 1961, and James Meredith entering the all-white University of Mississippi in 1962. It started with someone. It did here, too. The end of Jim Crow's Alabama began with Vivian Malone and James Hood. They were the story, and Robert Drew knew it immediately. His cameras were following Robert Kennedy and the president in Washington, Nicholas Katzenbach and Ed Guthman in Tuscaloosa, and George Wallace in Montgomery. They were also following Malone and Hood to Birmingham, then to New York City, back to Birmingham, and on to Tuscaloosa. Fifty-one years later, an archive of raw footage presents an intimate, affecting portrait of two innocents in a maelstrom.

What is consistently arresting about Malone and Hood is their serenity. Here they were, thrust on the national stage, pressed by police, lawyers, politicians, journalists, and minders, caught between a clash of governments over race and rights. They had chosen to challenge an injustice and to do it in public. They were giving up their privacy, their safety, and, at times, their dignity. They were exposing themselves and their families to ridicule, fear, and injury. Even if they were to enroll on June 11 at the university, overcoming one barrier, they would face another, the next morning, in the cold stares of many of their classmates.

They did not come from money or celebrity. They were not students of philosophy or sociology at Columbia or Berkeley, schooled in Marx or Marcuse. Neither Malone nor Hood was a flower child or a seasoned protester – smoking pot, wearing faded blue jeans and tie-dyed shirts, carrying a long-stemmed flower for the barrel of a guardsman's rifle. Neither was a black radical, raising a clenched fist. That was the future of protest. In 1963, a somnolent America had not yet entered that decade of unrest as the next generation would come to perceive it. Malone wore a dress and Hood a tie, a suit, and a hat with a feather in it. They lived in a world of deference and decorum. They spoke softly and carried books. They did not want to overthrow the system. They wanted to join it.

"You are free to do what other students do," John Doar assures them on June 6, five days before registration. In front of the cameras, Doar is discussing student life at the University of Alabama, home of the Crimson Tide, its storied football team quarterbacked then by the rising Joe Namath. Taciturn, lanky and boyish, Doar is asking the students if they plan to spend weekends on campus; he wants them to know they are free to go home or stay in their dormitory. In 1973, Doar will be chief counsel to the House of Representatives Judiciary Committee during its hearings on Watergate; in 2012, following a career as a distinguished jurist on the frontline of several civil rights battles, he will receive the Presidential Medal of Freedom. Here, in 1963, a forty-one-year-old Midwesterner, he is a guidance counselor, reviewing summer courses with two eager students. Malone will study algebra and "Principles of American Government" from 8:00 a.m. to 9:30 a.m. Monday to Friday. Hood will study psychology. Given the circumstances, Hood's interest in human behavior is as ironic as Malone's interest in political institutions.

First, though, there will be a spectacle. For this, Doar promises to prepare them as he would "a witness at a trial." The university and the federal government, he tells them, have tried to ensure that there will be no trouble. "Your families will be relieved to know this," he says. Privately, like everyone else, he worries about a crimson tide of another kind. He briefs the students on what to say, what to wear, what to do: "The thing to remember is that there will be people watching you. The country will be watching you." Oh, it would be so much easier, sighs Katzenbach, if they could just seize the campus the way the Infantry took Omaha Beach on June 6, 1944, nineteen years before.

With a few days before registration, the students visit New York City. The cameras show them arriving wide-eyed at Newark Airport on June 7. They take a bus to the Westside Airline Terminal and a taxi to the headquarters of the National Association for the Advancement of Colored People (NAACP), which is organizing their challenge. The two seem to meet everyone in the sprawling offices, from secretaries to attorneys, patiently chatting with each. Off camera, they accept $350 raised by eighty sympathetic high school students from Great Neck, Long Island; Malone and Hood donate the money to the NAACP Legal and Defense Fund, which is underwriting their costs. Afterward, in a dark boardroom, they sit for long, revealing interviews with their sponsors to prepare them for the national spotlight. Unfazed by the cameras, they talk searchingly about themselves, their families, and their hopes.

In June 1963, Vivian Juanita Malone was twenty years old. She was from Mobile, Alabama, the gritty, industrial port on the Gulf Coast. The fourth of eight children, she went to Central High School, where she was a member of the National Honor Society. Later she attended the Alabama Agricultural and Mechanical College in Normal, Alabama, an all-black institution, where she majored in business education. She was close to graduating when she decided that what she really wanted to study was personnel management. Unable to afford to go out of state and knowing the School of Commerce and Business Administration at the University of Alabama offered a good program, she resolved to go there. The tuition was reasonable, and her grades were good. "I had scored in the ninety-ninth percentile, I had a 3.8 average," she said in 2003. "So why shouldn't I have gone? I just wasn't ready to back down, and I said, 'If George Wallace is going to stand there, I'm going to find some help.' And fortunately the NAACP found me . . ."

The local civil rights organizers learned of Malone's interest and encouraged her to apply. Her conviction would open her and her family in Mobile (who, with Malone, had been involved in local desegregation campaigns) to a world of hate. She persisted. "Here they were telling me, a citizen of Alabama, that the only reason that I couldn't attend was because I happened to be black," she recalled. "It was just absolutely ridiculous. . . . A person can get very emotional about a thing like that when you really sit down and think about it." Malone *never* got emotional. Not with John Doar. Not with her patrons at the NAACP. Not with her jeering classmates. In New York, the interviewer asks: "Do you expect anything untoward to happen?" Her reply: "I don't expect anything to happen." Later, she poses for a photographer, smiling on demand amid a fusillade of flashes. Her hair coiffed, she wears a triple string of pearls and a well-cut dress. She is poised, polite, and pretty. Next week she will appear on the cover of *Newsweek*.

James Alexander Hood was also twenty. He was from Gadsden, Alabama, northeast of Birmingham, the eldest of three boys and three girls. He was a fine athlete and a prominent student leader. While in his second year at Clark College in Atlanta, he read in the *Atlanta Journal-Constitution* that black students were "300 years underdeveloped mentally. And I was one of those students." He got angry and wrote the author of the study, W. C. George, who replied that "as a black boy you have no right to challenge an academic like myself." Hood could not let that stand. Unhappy with Clark College, he applied to the University of Alabama. More than Malone, he was deeply involved with the civil rights movement. He had helped organize a local affiliate of the Southern Christian Leadership Conference in Gadsden, and he attended meetings of other civil rights organizations. Julian Bond, a rising activist, encouraged him to apply to the University of Alabama. Hood wanted to study psychology because "I want to look at the behavior of people, why they act the way they do." He chose the University of Alabama because it was close to home, affordable, and well regarded. "Are you anxious?" the interviewer asks him. "No more anxious than entering college anywhere else," he replies. "I am thoroughly convinced that there will be no incidents."

Like Malone, Hood dresses conservatively and speaks quietly. Neither conveys a sense of moral crusade or personal passage. They don't talk like that. No one delivers homilies or makes threats. They are activists, yes, selected and tutored by professionals, or they wouldn't be here. But they are less flamethrowers than torchbearers. There is no anger, ego, or self-pity about them. Much later, Malone attributed her forbearance to her faith. "God was with me," she recalled. Her experience at the university, and her life, would be happier than Hood's; as a student, he "was rather high-strung and suffered bouts of anxiety, or what his mother called 'nervous spells.'" Malone was more self-possessed. As much as she wanted to make a point, she wanted an education more. "I went to the University because I thought I could get the best education as far as Alabama was concerned," she recalled in 1967. "I certainly didn't go for the publicity."

Publicity there was. This was all about publicity, at least for Governor Wallace. This was about jumping up and down and waving his arms and shouting and pointing. The governor had to do this and the Kennedys had to let him do it. On Saturday, June 8, the cameras follow RFK to his office, where he sits at his desk, puffing on a cigarillo. His ill-tempered black Labrador Retriever, Brumus, stretches out beside him. He, Katzenbach, Guthman, Marshall, and others are holding one last strategy session. A touch of morbid humor lightens the mood. Bobby muses about the prospect of "a high administration official killed [for] enrolling Negro students." It would be helpful to the cause if it put the administration in a good light. "Take all the pressure off," he says. Smiles and guffaws all around. An assistant shows Bobby the sophisticated communications system that will keep him in touch with Tuscaloosa; the last time, at Ole Miss, it had broken down. That cannot happen again. "Any last thoughts, anyone?" Bobby asks. The group breaks up and he prepares to leave.

And so, as the hour draws near, the players take their places. Katzenbach and Guthman, followed by Drew's cameras, arrive at Washington National Airport Saturday afternoon, June 8. They pick up their tickets at the counter and walk breezily to the gate. At 2:30 p.m., they board United Airlines Flight 353 for Birmingham. They will have meetings there, before driving the hour or so to Tuscaloosa. On Tuesday, June 11, Katzenbach will confront Wallace. Guthman will go with him. Earlier, from Birmingham, John Doar will escort the students to the campus, with Katzenbach, and remain with them. Bobby Kennedy and Burke Marshall will monitor events at the Department of Justice. The president will remain at the White House, in constant touch with his brother.

*

Just before RFK talked with the president from Hickory Hill around 8:00 a.m., Tuesday – their conversation interrupted by the burning monk – Bobby was on the telephone with Katzenbach in Tuscaloosa. It was 6:00 a.m. in Alabama. For all the intense deliberations that had taken place over the previous few days, no one in Washington knew any more about how Wallace would react when the students arrived on campus that morning. "If they arrest Governor Wallace, all hell will break loose," a "high university official" told the *New York Times*. Wallace knew of the estimated fifty thousand Klansmen who were ready to storm the campus on the governor's command. If all hell did break loose, though, this time the government would be ready. More than three thousand soldiers were in the state ready to be deployed. Major General Creighton Abrams (formally known as assistant chief of staff in the Office of the Deputy Chief of Staff for Operations) was in charge in Tuscaloosa. As arranged with Bobby, he dressed in civilian clothes to play down his rank, purpose, and authority, and he kept his staff to a minimum.

So, if you're the federal government, how are you going to handle this tinderbox? Guthman said there were two serious plans under consideration from the time he and Katzenbach arrived the weekend before registration. One was to let the students approach Foster Auditorium, where they would register, on their own and try to enter unaccompanied by federal officials. This would mean that Wallace would have to endure the disgust (in most of the country, though not in the South) of turning away a young black man and a young black woman trying to go to school. Wallace would still get his much-coveted confrontation with federal authority. The other plan was to have Katzenbach accompany the students. Wallace would stand in their way and Katzenbach would withdraw, arguing that, legally, it did not matter anyway, because they were considered enrolled by virtue of the court ruling. In a word, Wallace could deny admittance – but not admission – to the university. Still, Wallace's defiance would force the Kennedys to summon federal troops to the campus.

Now, having talked at 7:00 a.m. (in Washington) on Tuesday, Marshall and RFK were proposing another plan. Bobby told Katzenbach that the 31st Division of national guardsmen, from Tuscaloosa, would be federalized at 7:30 a.m. (in Alabama) that day. As Guthman remembered, the plan was to secure the campus and prevent Wallace from entering. But when they talked to Katzenbach, he balked. In his memoir, he says that there was no legal reason to move troops in earlier, or to take law enforcement away from the governor. Although he and his federal colleagues expected Wallace to bar the students, Wallace had not yet done so. "I was concerned that premature use of troops would in fact stir up resentment, be a cause of violence, and take away from the support and understanding that simple defiance of a court order promoted among most people." He wanted to bring the two students on campus without the troops. "Besides, I think we should let Wallace have his show," he told Bobby, who replied: "Well, Nick, we don't have much time. What do you propose?"

After a few more minutes of conversation, they decided that the students would drive on campus with Katzenbach and Doar. They would stay in the car while Katzenbach met Wallace. If, as expected, the governor barred their way, Katzenbach would return to the car and take the students directly to their dormitories. They would remain on campus. Then, if Wallace still blocked them, the president would federalize the Alabama National Guard. "All right," said Bobby. "That's it. Wallace will get to read his proclamation or whatever he is going to do, but he won't bar anyone. Be sure you make that clear."

Katzenbach believed that taking the students to their dormitories was sound. He did not want to leave the campus with the students, which "would look to the public like a retreat." In the retelling of this story, memories diverge and versions differ. Guthman, who was with Katzenbach, says the strategy was decided that morning. Katzenbach says that it took shape in conversations Monday with RFK and the president. As Bobby did speak to his brother shortly after 9:00 p.m. on June 10, that may have been correct. But how to account for Bobby's proposal early that morning to move the National Guard to the campus? In any event, Katzenbach collected the keys to the students' rooms in the dormitories from Frank Rose. He learned then that Wallace had had a white line painted outside the doorway of Foster Auditorium to instruct the deputy attorney general where to stand. That incensed Katzenbach, who resented being manipulated. "I found it annoying to be cast in a supporting role to Wallace," he said. He blamed Rose, unfairly, and asked him to have the line erased. Katzenbach did consider avoiding Wallace entirely – there was no "legal need" to confront him, the students having been considered registered – and leaving it at that. But "Bobby said, I think rightly, that if we denied Wallace his show, the danger of violence would increase."

Katzenbach remembered that the president was "nervous" that Wallace would bar them and there would be no time for the troops to ensure the students were admitted that day. How would it look if the governor chased away federal officials and made them slink back the next day? Said Katzenbach: "That was important to him; delay would look like indecision or weakness. He thought it might be preferable to put the guard in federal service immediately, which would allow us to get the additional troops into Tuscaloosa. I did not really think we had sufficient basis for federalizing the guard yet, although it is one of those decisions where the president proba-bly has considerable latitude in the exercise of his discretion."

As RFK recalled, the situation was fluid. "You know, we decided the day before, maybe that we should not call up the Guard, and so I called him [JFK] that morning. And it looked worrisome, and I said, 'Well, maybe we'll call up the Guard now.' Now that was before the first confrontation, so . . . the first step would have been taken by us rather than him. And the President said, 'Well, let's wait. We won't do it now.' We decided that we won't do it; let's wait on it. And it was the correct thing as it turned out." Later, Bobby remembered that 8:00 a.m. conversation with his brother, not for the president's revulsion over the suicidal Buddhist, but for their freewheeling response to shifting events in Alabama. After all, he noted, they had left the White House on Monday having agreed on one way to manage the situation, and overnight Bobby wanted to handle it another way and had called Katzenbach and told him so. Katzenbach objected. So did the president, who wanted to avoid provoking Wallace. He wanted to allow the governor to save face, no matter how ugly or dishonorable. That's when JFK told Bobby, "Let's just stay with what we decided originally."

By the time both Jack and Bobby left for work Tuesday morning, the plan was set: they would not send federal troops to Tuscaloosa until Wallace stood up and barred the students, an act of defiance that would trigger an armed response from the federal government. The governor would make the first move. The president would respond.

✳

Bobby, having spent the early morning on the telephone with both Katzenbach and the president, and having refereed his querulous children over breakfast, was now on his way to the Department of Justice, trailing Drew's cameras. RFK was casual about the office (though not about the work). Sometimes he brought along Brumus, sometimes he brought his children (Robert Kennedy Jr., a future environmentalist, learned to train falcons on the roof of the building). The dog and children annoyed J. Edgar Hoover, the dour, closeted director of the Federal Bureau of Investigation. He frowned upon Kennedy's informality – one of his many grievances against "that snot-faced kid." Bobby shrugged. He was attorney general and his brother was president; if he wanted to bring his mutt and his brood to work, he would. And so he did that day, of all days.

As Bobby slips into the back seat of the Cadillac parked in the driveway of Hickory Hill, the door held open by his neatly-attired black chauffeur, four of his rambunctious children jump in. They are David, seven, Courtney, six, Michael, five, and Kerry, three years and nine months. On the way from McLean down the George Washington Memorial Parkway and across the Potomac River, the untethered kids bounce around the capacious upholstered interior. Amid the din, RFK reads the newspaper. David reads it, too. A radio newscast reports the previous night's racial unrest in Danville, Virginia.

The Department of Justice sits grandly at 950 Pennsylvania Avenue, NW, between the Capitol and the White House. Dedicated in 1934, it is an ageless blend of neoclassical and art deco. Within its Indiana limestone walls and beneath its red-tile hip roof are interior courtyards bedecked with New Deal murals. Statuary adorns the two-storey Great Hall. When RFK and his children arrive, two of them bound up the marble stairs to the fifth floor. The other two follow the cameraman. Once the kids are in the attorney general's offices, they have the run of the place. One demands a Coke. "It's nine o'clock and you want a Coke?" Bobby asks in mock horror. "How about chocolate milk instead?" Burke Marshall is on the phone to Doar, who is now with Katzenbach. Both were off together early from Tuscaloosa to pick up the students in Birmingham and escort them to the campus. They will leave for the university at 8:00 a.m. (in Alabama). RFK, once again, asks Katzenbach what will happen if they take the students to their dormitories. Whatever the answer, he's satisfied.

Over the whoops and giggles of his marauding children, RFK manages to talk to Katzenbach, musing that "the problem is the great show put on down there . . . and the victims are the students." The show is Wallace. It is now after 9:00 a.m. in Washington and RFK, strangely, is still contemplating federalizing the Alabama National Guard and bringing it to campus by 10:30 a.m. in Tuscaloosa. He wonders to Katzenbach whether that would be wise. Wasn't this question settled an hour or so ago? Hadn't he and the president, on the advice of Katzenbach, decided *not* to do this? Sure they had. But Bobby remains terrified of violence. He worries there won't be federal marshals or soldiers at the auditorium to protect the students from a lynch mob. Riots were as common as grits in the South. He was looking for reassurance from Katzenbach.

As Bobby holds the receiver to his ear, little Kerry stands beside him, affectionate and playful. Blonde hair tied neatly in ribbons, she wears a striped skirt and sweater and smiles mischievously. A conversation follows.

Kennedy: "Do you want to say hello to Kerry?"

Katzenbach: "Yes."

Kerry: "Hi, Nick."

Katzenbach: "Hi, Kerry. How are you dear?"

Kerry: "Are you at our house?"

Katzenbach: "No, I'm not at your house. I'm way down in the Southland. Way down south. And do you know what the temperature is here? Ninety-eight degrees. You tell your father that. Tell him we're all gonna get hardship pay!"

After a minute or so of banter, Bobby wrests the receiver from Kerry, says good-bye to 'Uncle' Nick, and makes more phone calls, including one to Frank Rose, who is watching from a perch near Foster Auditorium. As the tension rises, Bobby looks out the big window pensively. Or he paces. Time ticks on. More calls, more advice from RFK to Katzenbach on what to tell Wallace on the doorstep. "I would give him the spiel about law and the United States," says the attorney general.

Kerry and her siblings are now in full howl galloping around the office, as if they're on a safari. Soon they are playing hide-and-seek. Between calling Katzenbach, conferring with Marshall, and dealing with bemused assistants and secretaries fluttering around him, Bobby guides Kerry to her concealed brothers. "You're hot!" he cries. "You're cold! No, hot! No, cold!" Her brothers, giggling, cower under his desk.

In Alabama, Katzenbach understood RFK's anxiety and why his children are with him that day. They're a distraction. "I think it was hard on Bobby and Burke to be in Washington and have to deal at a distance with all the uncertainties," he wrote in 2008. "Clearly, a lot was at stake, and for someone as active as Bobby, it is hard not to take hands-on responsibility. The mess in Mississippi had to be on his mind all the time. His concern came through in every call." Everyone was haunted by the riot of September 30 and October 1, 1962, at the University of Mississippi in Oxford. It had been a nightmare for the Kennedys, who lost control of the situation. When they had had to send in federal troops to restore order, the soldiers took hours to arrive. JFK was incensed. As Katzenbach noted, Kennedy had criticized General Abrams harshly for the Army's tardiness, and Abrams was determined things should go right this time. Over time, Katzenbach and others came to see Ole Miss as much more of a victory than it seemed then – ultimately the Kennedys faced down the governor and integrated the university – but it had been a bloody mess. Fortunately for them, the Cuban Missile Crisis erupted three weeks later and washed it all away. Now, eight months on, the university was integrated and the campus was at peace; the last soldier had left Oxford on Monday. The Kennedys had learned their lesson, which is why they had spent weeks considering every possibility in Tuscaloosa.

While Katzenbach was on the road from Birmingham to Tuscaloosa with the students, Bobby called him on the car's two-way radio. The radio didn't work well, however, and Katzenbach went to a shopping center and called him collect (marveling that he had reached him with a dime in a Ma Bell payphone and not through the wizardry of the Signal Corps). RFK told him the president had a proclamation that he wanted Katzenbach to give Governor Wallace. The White House had made arrangements for Katzenbach to receive it en route; before facsimile machines and the Internet, it was presumably dictated over the telephone to a federal associate in Alabama, typed up, and given to Katzenbach. He understood its purpose. "The proclamation had no legal significance that I was aware of, but there was no harm in issuing it," he recalled. "I think the president felt out of it and wanted to play a part. Why not? I would have felt exactly the same way."

It was one of forty-seven proclamations that JFK issued in 1963.

They ranged from announcing National Farm Safety Week on February 14 to declaring Sir Winston Churchill an honorary citizen of the United States on April 9. On Monday, for example, Kennedy had issued a proclamation called Modifying Adjusting Imports of Petroleum and Petroleum Products. Though such proclamations are usually ceremonial, the president has the power to confer presidential pardons or make federal lands national monuments. Some have been epochal, such as George Washington's Proclamation of Neutrality of 1793 and Abraham Lincoln's Emancipation Proclamation of 1863. Often, though, presidents issue proclamations when they cannot do much else. That was Kennedy's situation June 11. His purpose was to deter, discourage, cajole, frighten, or neutralize a grandstanding governor. It did not matter that the proclamation had no legal weight and would be ignored. A president makes a declaration like this one because he wants to be seen to be president. It's about perception. If Wallace was doing a song and dance in Tuscaloosa, Kennedy wanted his part as lyricist and choreographer.

Accordingly, just before 11:00 a.m. in Washington on Tuesday – in the ten minutes between his meetings with John Cabot and David Bruce – Kennedy approved the wording of Proclamation 3542: Unlawful Obstructions of Justice and Combinations in the State of Alabama. Ted Sorensen, who drafted it, had discussed the wording that morning with Bobby, who objected to a clause suggesting "a serious risk of domestic violence in Alabama." While it was true, Bobby thought the phrase was provocative and would attract unwelcome attention. He asked Sorensen to drop it. Now, when to issue the proclamation? In Robert Drew's film, the camera catches Burke Marshall's watch. It is now 10:55 a.m. in Washington, 8:55 a.m. in Alabama. On the telephone to Sorensen, RFK instructs: "I wouldn't screw around. I would just get this thing out."

The proclamation used the standard arcane language – a succession of assertions, each a paragraph long, beginning with "whereas" – to make the case for the presidential directive to follow. The facts were that the United States District Court for the Northern District of Alabama had issued its order on June 5, preventing the governor from barring the admission of black students to the University of Alabama. That the governor had served notice that he intended to defy the court and would bar their admission. That the president had requested – but had not received – assurances from the governor that he would abandon his course of action. And that the governor, if he acted, would make it "impracticable" to enforce the law by the judiciary. "Now, Therefore, I, John F. Kennedy, President of the United States of America . . . do command the Governor of the State of Alabama . . . to cease and desist. . . ."

After the long, wordy preamble, the command was anticlimactic. Kennedy was saying: "Governor, back off." Having approved the proclamation just before 11:00 a.m. in Washington, the president called in Andy Hatcher, and told him to release it to the press. (To be legal, a presidential proclamation needs the signature of the secretary of state; Dean Rusk signed it between 12:30 p.m. and 1:00 p.m. in Washington, 10:30 a.m. to 11:00 a.m. in Alabama, just as Katzenbach was arriving at the university to hand it to Wallace.)

James Hood, who was with Vivian Malone in the car with Katzenbach and John Doar, remembers stopping on the way to the University of Alabama, just past Vance. As Hood recalls, Katzenbach spoke to the president at the White House. The conversation took place near a church and cemetery. "We got out of the car and walked around the cemetery, and I said, 'You know, Vivian, this is strange.' And she said, 'What's strange about it?' I said, 'We're sitting out in the middle of the cemetery, in 90-degree weather, and the Assistant Attorney General is talking to the President. That doesn't make sense to me.'"

Bobby, the president, and Katzenbach continued to exchange telephone calls. Again, Bobby and Katzenbach discussed what to say to Wallace. This call took place while Hood and Malone waited among the graves under the shade of an old cedar tree; the marshals had driven Katzenbach to the nearby shopping center. The message was the same. "We don't want a charade," says Bobby, on camera. "This is silly. This is play-acting. It is important that they attend the university. It is beyond politics. Ask him to step aside and let the two students who want to attend university attend university." He advises Katzenbach to speak to Wallace with clarity and firmness. "This doesn't make sense. You know they are going to attend the university in the end. I would like assurance that you will step aside now."

The conversation lasted thirty minutes. Katzenbach remembered it this way:

"What are you going to say to the Governor?" Bobby asks.

"I really don't know," says Katzenbach. "Something about his obligation to obey the law. I haven't written anything. Any ideas? Anything you want me to say?"

"The President wants you to make him look foolish."

"Thanks a lot. Any thoughts on how?"

"Nick, you'll do just fine. Good luck."

✳

The little caravan, now a little late, moved purposefully along U.S. Highway 11 to meet the little man at the door. Katzenbach, Doar, and the two students traveled in a white sedan. Two brown sedans accompanied them, carrying, among others, federal officials Macon L. Weaver, U.S. attorney for the Northern District of Alabama, and Peyton Norville Jr., the federal marshal for Alabama. Already they had dropped a plan, crafted the day before, to put the students in different cars, one each with Doar and Katzenbach. They were improvising all morning. The students and their advocates had planned to arrive in Tuscaloosa at 10:00 a.m., but it was taking them longer. However impolite, they need not have fussed about keeping the governor waiting. A patient man, he was prepared to wait. Without an opponent, he would have no moment. Wearing a light gray suit and blue-and-brown tie held fast with a gold tie clip, Wallace arrived on the sunbaked campus at 9:53 a.m. He entered Foster Auditorium, where he had commandeered an office fitted with two air conditioners, which was no small mercy that day. The heat wave suffocating Washington and the southeastern United States that week – the same heat that felled spectators at American University the day before – was blanketing Tuscaloosa, too. Katzenbach said it felt like "130 degrees." At midmorning, the temperature was ninety-five degrees and climbing. It was an undulating, heavy heat, the kind that leaves dark lunar circles under arms, soaks the skin, and mats the hair, creating wells of perspiration between the legs and sending rivulets running down them.

A half century later, the collision of institutional authority and personal vanity in Tuscaloosa looks like a soap opera in sepia. Or, a farce. The Kennedys saw it as that; to them, their adversary on the doorstep was neither honorable nor principled. He was silly, cheap, petty, pugnacious, and a touch maniacal. His suit was rumpled, his lip curled, and his ear was strained, as deaf to their charm as to their scorn, as misguided as his grandiloquent ancestors, and as certain to fail. The Kennedys knew – oh, they knew – that today was inevitable. Wallace wanted this moment, by God, and he would get it. Without it, who knew how it would end? With it, who knew? The man who knew violence – he was once a bantamweight prizefighter – always insisted that he didn't want it. Then again, as Katzenbach wryly observed, Wallace and the southern autocrats always renounced violence, unless it was at their hands, on their terms. As long as blacks remained frightened of whites, they knew there would be no Freedom Riders, no lunch-counter sitters, no street demonstrators. Wallace was standing against all that. He wanted his way and his show. Today he would get both, if fleetingly.

And so at 10:48 a.m. in Tuscaloosa – 12:48 p.m. in Washington, three minutes after the president had sat down with the Republicans and twenty-four minutes after Bobby and Burke Marshall had sat down to lunch – Katzenbach and the students entered the campus, turned off University Boulevard, and pulled up at Foster Auditorium. As arranged, Malone and Hood stayed in the car, where the temperature inside was one hundred degrees. Within the barriers keeping out the public, the auditorium was ringed with Wallace's loyal constabulary – some one hundred fifty pistol-packing high-way patrolmen, green-jacketed forest rangers, and revenue agents. Aside from the police, the officials, and the students, there were only journalists.

More than three hundred reporters, photographers, camera-men, soundmen, and producers had descended on Tuscaloosa, two-thirds of them from out of state. Journalists from Japan, South Korea, the Netherlands, and from eight British newspapers arrived. American newspapers sent their best reporters. The university gra-ciously accommodated them all. It created a makeshift pressroom, installing multiple telephones and newswires, as well as two air-conditioned darkrooms. Operators for Western Union stood by to transmit copy on Teletype. Moving from crisis to crisis on the tor-tuous civil rights trail, developing a battle-hardened camaraderie much like war correspondents in the field, the traveling press corps rarely had it so good, on a story this good.

The media exposure pleased the Kennedys, who knew the importance of journalists as interpreters of events. In *The Race Beat*, their acclaimed account of the media and the civil rights movement, Gene Roberts and Hank Klibanoff write that Doar, Katzenbach, and Guthman had "a keen awareness of, even a near reverence for, the importance of news coverage. Katzenbach . . . felt that the public needed to have its nose rubbed in the awful scent of racism to provoke a reaction that could bring change. Exposure of the segregationists' view, the public disclosure of their private con-victions, Katzenbach believed, was essential to break through to a public that might prefer complacence." In Alabama, in particular,

Katzenbach felt the media would show that the federal government was not there to provoke violence but to prevent it.

Yet almost as much as Wallace wanted his show, the Kennedys wanted theirs, too. If the governor was going to be seen and heard, so was the president. That's why they had agreed to let in Robert Drew's cameras. They were confident that this would turn out well, that they would come out winners. They knew, as Katzenbach said, "it was pretty obvious that President Kennedy didn't have a choice" but to let this unfold as Wallace wanted. If that was so, why not profit from it? The president also knew that he would not be where he was today – preparing to ask the nation to revisit its views on race relations and to unveil a civil rights bill – had the white authorities in city after city not responded to black civil disobedience with brutality. And had the media not been there to report it. The worst – or the best – example of this was Birmingham, where the beastly images had shocked Americans and moved public opinion. It was critical.

When Katzenbach got out of the car, television reporters asked him to wear a microphone. He refused. He was in no mood to take orders from anyone. Wallace, for his part, was wrapped in wires, appearing "from every coat and trouser pocket." The governor wanted to be sure that no one missed a word. No one would. It was all caught on film by Drew and everyone else. Although television did not broadcast the confrontation live, radio did. In Washington, at that moment, Robert Kennedy and Burke Marshall were lunching in an alcove of the attorney general's office at a half-moon table, set with china on a snow-white linen cloth. An assistant came in with a boxy radio, which could have been borrowed from Norman Rockwell's portrait of a family listening to one of Roosevelt's fireside chats. A portable television on wheels with cartoonish rabbit ears followed. Later that afternoon, the attorney general and Marshall watched the delayed broadcast.

✳

For all the anticipation, the stage was disappointing. The school-house door was not, in fact, in a schoolhouse, and it had not one but two (swinging) doors. Foster Auditorium, where the university was registering summer applicants that day, was a gymnasium. Dedicated in 1939, it had been built by the Public Works Administration during the Depression. Ironically, here was Wallace, castigating the federal government from the threshold of a building financed by the federal government. Architecturally, Foster Auditorium was unexciting. A curtain of limestone columns framed the north entrance where Wallace was standing, giving it a faux neoclassical facade. In this heady moment, standing under that colonnade, the governor of "the greatest people to ever trod the Earth" might have imagined himself Napoleon or Hannibal. A sneering Bobby saw him as "Mussolini."

As Katzenbach approached at 10:50 a.m., the governor stood proud and stiff behind a classroom wooden lectern placed six feet from the door. Feet fixed, he was flanked, like a tinhorn dictator, by a praetorian guard of stocky, helmeted troopers. Wallace was silent. He glowered. He shifted. He held his hands behind his back, leaned forward, and stuck out his chest, accentuating his height of five feet six inches and weight of 150 pounds. Katzenbach was accompanied by Macon Weaver and Peyton Norville. Both were alumni of the university who had volunteered for this assignment at risk to their careers in Wallace's Alabama. Katzenbach strode briskly up the brick stairs. Wallace raised his hand imperiously, as if to say, "Stop." Katzenbach kept going "just for the hell of it," until he was four or five feet from Wallace, past the white line. Like the proffered microphone, the line insulted him. He resented being a prop; he would not be told where to stand. Katzenbach was particularly galled to see that Wallace, fresh and dry from that air-conditioned office, his pompadour unmolested, had positioned himself strategically in the shade, while he was left in the sun. That was deliberate, too.

"I have here President Kennedy's proclamation," Katzenbach began, taking it from his pocket. "I have come to ask you for unequivocal assurance that you or anyone under your control will not bar these students. I have come here to ask now for unequivocal assurance that you will permit these students, who, after all, merely want an education in the great university . . ."

Wallace cut him off. "Now you make your statement, but we don't need your speech," he ordered.

"I am making my statement, Governor," replied Katzenbach, who asked again for an assurance that Wallace would admit the two students.

Wallace, listening to Katzenbach, pleased to let him wilt in the sun, then read a four-page "statement and proclamation" of his own. It was a spirited denunciation of "the central government" – he would not dignify it with "federal" – with typically windy rhetoric, such as this "unwelcomed, unwanted and unwarranted intrusion on the campus of the University of Alabama." Like his Inaugural Address, it had been written by Asa Earl Carter, the euphonious Klansman. Ed Guthman, who was in the crowd, thought Wallace saw Washington as "the Kremlin." His proclamation was studded with more "whereas" clauses than Kennedy's, as if he, the governor, had to show that his proclamation was longer than the president's. Then, Wallace's coda: "I . . . hereby denounce and forbid this illegal and unwarranted action by the central government."

For seven minutes the light-suited Katzenbach listened, glistening in the harsh light. Towering above the governor at six feet two inches tall, he leaned into him. His arms were folded at his chest, which could only have made him hotter. His jacket pocket bulged with a walkie-talkie. His shirt was a canvas of creases, his brow a reflecting pool; he frequently mopped his face and bald crown with a white handkerchief. His legs were trembling. He was tired – he had been kept up the night before at his hotel trying to calm a journalist having "a nervous breakdown" who had insisted on talking to him — and he was nervous, knowing the president would be watching. Afterward, Katzenbach was displeased with his performance. "Every time I see it, I think of all the things that I did not say and should have," he recalled years later. "That is, I think, a common experience among lawyers. I have never argued a case without having exactly the same feeling afterward." Katzenbach was too hard on himself. He was doing just fine.

Katzenbach: "I take it from your statement that you are going to stand in the door and that you are not going to carry out the orders of the court, and that you are going to resist us from doing so. Is that so?"

Wallace: "I stand according to my statement."

Katzenbach: "I'm not interested in this show. I do not know what the purpose of the show is. . . . From the outset, Governor, all of us have known that the final chapter of this history will be the admission of these students . . . I ask you once again to reconsider. . . . They will register today. They will go to school tomorrow."

From Wallace, a grim silence, broken by the sound of clicking cameras held by photographers whose heads were wrapped in makeshift bandanas to shield them from the sun. Wallace thrust his chin forward like Il Duce. After an awkward minute or so, Katzenbach turned, walked away, and returned to the car where Vivian Malone and James Hood were waiting. Wallace returned to his temporary office in Foster Auditorium. Their minuet had taken fifteen minutes.

The first act was over. It had ended in stalemate. After an intermission of four and a half hours, the drama would resume. Katzenbach and his deputies had done their work, and Bobby and his advisors in Washington had done theirs. On that decisive day, Robert Kennedy was co-president. He was resourceful, tactical, and indispensable. He not only oversaw every logistical detail of the confrontation in Tuscaloosa, he also urged his brother to pivot quickly and adroitly to seize the moment. More than anyone else in the president's circle, he pushed to redefine the question of race — and would keep pushing, hard, that afternoon and evening.

Tuesday, June 11, 1963
CHAPTER 12

Early Afternoon

"WALLACE HAS REFUSED to step aside," declared a radio news reporter broadcasting live from the campus. "The moment of confrontation has ended for the moment. Wallace has stood his ground. He has refused to let them in. Governor Wallace has fulfilled his pledge to stand in the schoolhouse door."

It was now 1:05 p.m. in Washington, 11:05 a.m. in Tuscaloosa. Only minutes before, JFK, closeted with the senators, had noted that "it [the confrontation] ought to be just about happening now." Without live television coverage, no one was watching. After the news broke, Bobby called him immediately. The president, putting down the telephone, said, ". . . so now we are going to have to call up the National Guard and we assume that he may step aside then, otherwise we may have to push him and this Judge may have to arrest him, which we don't want to do unless we can help it." In Tuscaloosa, Katzenbach and Doar followed their plan. Katzenbach returned to the car, put his head through the window, and told Malone they were going to walk to her dormitory. To get there, they had to wade through a cordon of surprised rangers, who made no move to stop them. Katzenbach and Malone walked across the south parking lot of Foster Auditorium and entered Mary Burke Hall, a new residence. They were met at the door by the house-mother, who greeted them with words Katzenbach would never forget: "Oh, you must be Vivian!"

She invited Malone to lunch. First, Malone went to see her room on the fifth floor and freshen up. When Frank Rose learned that Malone was going to eat shortly, he "went absolutely crazy," Katzenbach recalled. He telephoned Katzenbach at the dormitory, warning that there was going to be "a riot if you do this." But Katzenbach felt that not arranging for James Meredith to eat shortly after he entered the University of Mississippi had been a grave mistake. He didn't want to repeat that here. "Look," he told Rose, "she's gonna be eating in that dormitory, she might as well start with lunch."

Malone had steeled herself for whatever happened that day, donning a suit of psychological armor that protected her from taunts and insults. For her, that lunch was the most poignant moment of the day. She was on her own now and eating alone would confirm how solitary her life as a student there would be. "Vivian was prepared to brave it," recalled Katzenbach, who escorted her to the cafeteria but watched from the entrance. "She did, all by herself, no marshals in sight. She went through the cafeteria line and then sat at a table alone. No sooner had she done so than two young women got up and joined her. No matter that they were summer students from north of the Mason-Dixon Line. Tears were in my eyes." At about the same time, John Doar took James Hood to Palmer Hall, his dormitory, a mile away. They had driven over in a border patrol car. Hood lunched across the street at Paty Hall, after most of the students had eaten. Like Malone, Hood had no trouble settling in. Other than the occasional barb, the students were well received that day. "She's very attractive," one of Malone's housemates told the *New York Times*. "I don't think we'll have any trouble with her. She was calm. She wasn't nervous or close-mouthed."

The students were now in their dormitories but, technically speaking, they were not registered in the university (though by one account, they had enrolled by special arrangement in a courthouse in Birmingham that morning). Governor Wallace was in his cool makeshift office in Foster Auditorium, retrenching. Doar and Katzenbach were at their headquarters on campus, regrouping. The university was still not integrated. That would mean sending in soldiers.

✷

If there was a crisis in Alabama, you would not know it in the White House. While Evelyn Lincoln or Kenny O'Donnell would not stamp "crisis" on the president's agenda and clear his schedule of all unrelated appointments or obligations, surely they might have arranged fewer or more focused meetings on June 11. They did not. Throughout the morning and afternoon, Kennedy continued to meet diplomats and dignitaries and make public appearances. He had not abandoned the senior class of the Capitol Page School or the American Committee on Italian Migration; he had seen John Cabot, David Bruce, Iain Macleod, and the Republicans. While he had to meet the politicians to discuss civil rights, today's preoccupation, his other business that day was less pressing. He would have meetings in late afternoon and early evening with experts on space and on Indonesia, with the director of the United States Information Agency, even with a visiting French contemporary historian. Given cascading events, an anxious president might have canceled them all. Kennedy also found time to swim, lunch, and nap. It was business as usual. Presidential appointees were announced, press releases issued, telephone calls made and returned.

On Monday, for example, Kennedy appointed more than one hundred postmasters in small communities across the country. In one fell swoop, he announced, among others: Harry W. Van Hook in Mount Pulaski, Illinois, Norma L. Beckwith in Jones, Michigan, and Kenneth E. DePriest in Lobelville, Tennessee. On Tuesday, the president named Dr. George E. Taylor, professor of Far Eastern History and Politics at the University of Washington, to a three-year term on the Board of Foreign Scholarships. The board supervised the educational programs administered by the Department of State. Taylor's appointment merited a two-page press release and a personal letter from the president.

It was not that Kennedy was keeping up his schedule simply to keep up appearances, as he had in the Cuban Missile Crisis. Then, as he convened his advisors to respond to Soviet nuclear missiles in Cuba, he had continued to campaign in the midterm congressional elections. He didn't want to arouse suspicion. But Tuscaloosa was not Cuba, Berlin, Vienna, or the other flash-points of his presidency. It was a domestic crisis. It was con-tained. It was manageable. If the administration moved "smoothly and without undue excitement" in handling Wallace, as the *New York Times* noted, it was because it had been through this twice before. A president learns a few things. The Freedom Riders and Ole Miss had taught the White House hard lessons in patience and planning.

Still, Alabama *was* a crisis, if only for the fact that how it would end was unknown – and unknowable – when Katzenbach and Wallace walked away from each other. Kennedy had been watching it play out and pondering whether to address the nation that eve-ning. By midday, though, he had not yet decided and had made no preparations. Wouldn't the prospect of a speech of this importance be reason enough to rearrange his affairs for the remainder of the afternoon? Wouldn't he have to prepare, even rehearse, as he did other major speeches? Not today.

Kennedy was a quick study and a master juggler. His self-confidence had not served him well in the Bay of Pigs and Vienna, but it did now. Historians suggest that his self-assurance came from an intense, tumultuous life which he nearly lost more than once to illness. It also came from winning every election he fought, and the presidency, too, against the odds. It came from going to war as a young lieutenant, losing his boat, and saving his crew. (As Ed Guthman noted, apart from Sorensen and RFK, almost all the senior New Frontiersmen, including himself, Katzenbach, Doar and Marshall, were war veterans. They were the youngest group to come to power since the beginning of the republic, and it made them impatient with mediocrity and distrustful of convention.) Kennedy could delegate authority to a superb staff – fractious as it was – as he presided over it without a chief of staff. Sometimes he even gave his associates latitude to manage issues at the same time, unbeknownst to each other. And always he trusted the graceful Ted Sorensen to find the words.

But the biggest reason for Kennedy's equanimity – even insouciance – was his brother, who was presiding over the day's shifting events like a field marshal. On a day when things might have been coming apart for the administration, when the president might have had cause for anxiety or doubt, they weren't and he didn't.

*

With Katzenbach and Wallace having returned to their corners, the president was ready to federalize the Alabama National Guard. He had little doubt it was necessary, as he had told the senators, but he wanted to hear from Bobby, who was waiting to hear from Katzenbach. While Malone was upstairs in her dormitory in Room 515, Katzenbach had returned to the car to talk to Washington. He shooed away reporters trying to eavesdrop on his conversation, got into the broiling front seat, and tried to use the radio. Again, it was erratic. In a garbled transmission to Burke Marshall, who had asked what Wallace was doing, Katzenbach answered unintelligibly. "I was sure he [Wallace] was thinking of something," Katzenbach told Marshall. "All this response did was confuse everyone in Washington. I should have known better, but I was angry at being put in the sun." Marshall didn't understand what Katzenbach was saying, but urged the president to federalize the guard immediately. Bobby wanted more definitive word. With a clearer connection established, he asked Katzenbach whether anything had changed in the last few minutes and whether the soldiers were still necessary. They were, replied Katzenbach.

At 1:20 p.m. (11:20 a.m. in Tuscaloosa), the confrontation was rebroadcast on television. His meeting over, the president joined Evelyn Lincoln in her office, adjoining his, to watch on a portable television set. In Drew's film, a crowd gathers around the wheeled television in the attorney general's office. Wallace's pint-sized figure fills the flickering screen. "My actions don't constitute disobedience," Wallace says, reading his prepared statement. As all eyes fix on the snowy image, a window washer dangles from a rope outside the office, a surreal counterpoint. Everyone is silent. They are seeing this for the first time.

Soon Bobby is on the telephone again with his brother: "I thought it was *good*," he says of Katzenbach and the showdown, drawing out that monosyllabic word as if to savor it. "Didn't you?" RFK tells him troops can be in Tuscaloosa within hours. "Are you issuing the thing?" he asks JFK, referring to the executive order authorizing the troops. The president agrees and sets the machinery in motion. "Kennedy's decision was instantaneous," says Hugh Sidey. "The order would be issued as soon as he finished meeting with the Republicans." At 1:15 p.m., the congressional leaders left the Oval Office. At 1:34 p.m. Kennedy federalized the guard.

Executive Order 11111 was called "Providing Assistance for the Removal of Obstructions of Justice and Suppression of Unlawful

Combinations within the State of Alabama." Shorter than the proclamation issued earlier that day, it was necessary because the proclamation's "commands . . . have not been obeyed . . . and the unlawful obstructions of justice . . . continue . . ." It ordered the secretary of defense "to call into the active military service of the United States . . . all units of the Army National Guard and of the Air National Guard of the State of Alabama . . . for an indefinite period." Unlike the presidential proclamation, the executive order carried the full weight of the office. It was one of 214 executive orders that Kennedy issued as president, fifty-five of them in 1963. Some of them were a delight for him, like one the next day establishing the President's Advisory Council on the Arts. This one was not. As commander in chief, a president has the power to move armies. That day, he just wanted to move a governor.

Now it had come to this. Sending in soldiers was the president's greatest fear and the governor's fondest hope. Wallace's vaudeville show would have a second act. How it would end was clearer than an hour ago, but the situation was still fragile. The delicate equilibrium could dissolve if Wallace were to change his mind, refuse to leave the campus, and resist arrest by the Guard. Things could get ugly if he were dragged away, hauled into court, found in contempt, and thrown in jail. For someone said to be irrational and unpredictable, inciting mob violence was not impossible. Yet there were early signals that Wallace was prepared to walk away. At 1:36 p.m. in Washington (11:36 a.m. in Alabama), Burke Marshall read Bobby a dispatch from a UPI reporter in Tuscaloosa. "Wallace will step aside," read Marshall, his voice thin. "'He will not oppose the armed might of the U.S. government,' says an aide to the Governor." Wallace would "surrender."

Bobby was taking no chances. That morning, in anticipation of sending in the Guard, he had called General Abrams at the Army Reserve Center in Tuscaloosa, the government's command post. The attorney general revered Abrams. In the next decade,

Abrams would become Army Chief of Staff and commander of U.S. forces in Vietnam and the country's best-known soldier. A battle tank would be named after him. On film, Kennedy twice mentions in banter with Marshall the role of Abrams in the storied defense of Bastogne in the Battle of the Bulge in 1944; he knows about sieges. "But I doubt he's ever dealt with something like this," says Bobby. Then, he asks facetiously, "What would Eisenhower do?" The conversation, caught by Drew, shows RFK's obsession with detail. Once again, the question is how to remove Wallace in a way that does not cause unrest on campus, in town, or across the state.

"I thought we need to develop a plan," he tells Abrams. "I am not in favor of carrying the Governor away. I don't want to pick up the Governor. Better if we could shove him aside. . . . I want to make as little show as possible." Then, lawyer that he is, Kennedy asks a series of intricate questions about the guardsmen who will enter the campus. Will they have scabbards? If they have bayonets, do not fix them, he advises. Sidearms? Better than carbines, he says. Numbers? As few as possible, as inconspicuous as possible. To remove Wallace, perhaps six men – two to carry him, four to clear the way. The route? Avoid marching through Tuscaloosa, which might be provocative; he worries about the possibility of Alabamans turning out to jeer and stone federal troops. How far from the campus is the Armory, where they will assemble? When he learns the distance is 4,000 feet, he tells Abrams that the soldiers should avoid parading down University Avenue like the Union Army entering Atlanta. To reduce the chances of an incident, he wants the streets cleared to keep out troublemakers.

Once Executive Order 11111 was issued, the Pentagon informed the Guard in Alabama at 2:05 p.m. in Washington (12:05 p.m. in Alabama) that it had been placed under the control of the federal government. The plan had always been to federalize the Guard rather than use army troops from elsewhere, even Southern bases,

269

ensuring that those carrying out the court order were Alabamans. Although Marshall had worried about the loyalty of the reservists from racist Marengo County, that wasn't enough to dissuade the Kennedys from using the Guard.

The loyalty of the Guard's commanding officers *was* a worry. In a small state, the two senior commanding officers were thought to be too close to Wallace. Abrams turned to the third line officer, Brigadier General Henry V. Graham of the 31st Infantry Division, to lead the operation. Graham, a realtor from Birmingham when he was not on reserve duty, was tall and craggy. Receiving his orders, he flew immediately by helicopter from a base 120 miles from Tuscaloosa. He arrived at 1:40 p.m. When Abrams gave him his assignment, Graham was displeased; the prospect of removing a popular governor was unappealing, particularly if your business was selling real estate in the state's largest city.

Fortunately for Graham and the Kennedys, a deal would be struck with Wallace. Taylor Hardin, a friend of the governor, asked to come to the Army Reserve Center to meet Graham. There he told the general that Wallace wanted to make another statement, after which he would leave quickly and quietly. His troopers would remain in place to keep order, but he would not interfere with the registration of the students. Graham checked with Abrams, who consulted Katzenbach, who was unhappy that the governor was demanding an encore. "I was annoyed at another speech but hugely relieved to know that the Governor was surrendering," he recalled. "I told Abe [General Abrams] that Wallace could have two minutes, no more, and got on the phone to notify Bobby of the arrangements. My relief that a happy ending was in sight was shared by Bobby." Finally, they had the personal commitment they had sought since April: Wallace would walk away.

As Wallace recast events for the press that day, so did the Kennedys. They were acutely conscious of how this was playing out on the television, radio, and in the newspapers. In early afternoon,

Bobby was concerned that this morning's drama would be interpreted as a victory for Wallace. In the long afternoon intermission, he didn't want the governor's intransigence to be seen that way, even temporarily. He got word to Guthman, who was briefing reporters in Tuscaloosa, to put out the story that the students had been registered and that they had not been rejected, as news reports suggested. RFK wanted it understood that Wallace had turned away Katzenbach, but he had not turned away the students. In fact, while the governor had stood at one door, the students had entered through another. They had gone to their dormitories. For Bobby, finally, they had been granted both admittance *and* admission. This was public relations before the Age of Spin. He knew that Hood and Malone had not fully registered at the university like the other 3,800 summer students over these two days. For the sake of appearances, though, Kennedy considered them to be registered. If they were officially in, of course, Katzenbach would not be returning with Graham and the Guard that afternoon.

✳

Four and a half hours after the first act, the curtain rose on the second. At 3:16 p.m. in Tuscaloosa (5:16 p.m. in Washington), General Graham arrived on campus in a green, unmarked command car with three troop carriers, carrying one hundred members of the 31st (Dixie) Division. Against the attorney general's wishes, they were toting M-1 rifles. At 3:30 p.m., Graham approached the auditorium. He was accompanied by four men (not Bobby's suggested six) in green berets, followed by Katzenbach, Peyton Norville, and Macon Weaver. The governor was standing in the doorway, flanked by police and shadowed by the press, just as he had been that morning. Wearing a soft hat and combat fatigues with a small Confederate flag on the breast pocket, Graham walked briskly up to Wallace and saluted. Wallace returned the salute.

"It is my sad duty to ask you to step aside," Graham said, his voice barely audible, "on order of the President of the United States." Katzenbach was appalled. He resented Graham's tone and sentiment. *There was nothing sad about this to him.* "I could have shot him on the spot without bothering with a court-martial," Katzenbach seethed decades later. When Wallace asked to make a statement, drawing a crumpled piece of paper from his pocket, Graham nodded. "Certainly, sir," he replied.

It was done, then. This university and others in the state would admit black students. Vivian Malone and James Hood would register later that afternoon and a black student would enroll at the University of Alabama in Huntsville the following day. It would be integration today and integration tomorrow. Wallace had lost, though not entirely. In the South, losing was its own reward. It was the defiance that mattered, and Wallace's stand at the schoolhouse door would make him a four-term governor and a spoiler in national politics, inspiring four renegade presidential campaigns that exploited race through a coded vocabulary. "When it comes to the niggers," Wallace had boasted to an assistant after his appearance on *Meet the Press* on June 2, "I'm the expert." Early that week, Wallace had shown Robert Drew's filmmakers around the Governor's Mansion in Montgomery, pausing before a portrait of William Lowndes Yancey, a leading nineteenth-century secessionist. "I'd rather live a short life standing for principle than live a long life of compromise," Wallace says, quoting Yancey. Turning to his Northern visitors, he adds quizzically, "Of course that may not mean much to you folk."

To Graham, Wallace said that "but for the unwarranted federalization of the Alabama National Guard, I would at this moment be your Commander-in-Chief. . . ." In saluting Graham, he acted as if he still were – even if the Kennedys had commandeered his army. How many divisions had this pope? At this moment, none. Now Wallace was left on the doorstep with nothing but words. He again attacked the tyranny of Washington, insisting that "Alabama is winning this fight against federal interference, because we are awakening the people to the trend toward military dictatorship in this country." Then, soliloquy over, he bolted to the waiting cars, short legs pumping, drove off to the airport, and flew back to Montgomery. It was 3:33 p.m. (5:33 p.m. in Washington).

✳

Some suggested then – and some suggest now – that the showdown with Wallace was a charade. "Wallace's 'stand' was carefully scripted, orchestrated, and arranged in co-operation with federal authorities . . . ," wrote John Lewis, the legendary civil rights activist and veteran congressman, in his memoir in 1998. David Brinkley, the television anchor who launched *The Huntley-Brinkley Report* in 1956, was also on the civil rights trail that spring. In his memoir in 2003, he wrote that George Wallace stood in the doorway and "by prearrangement with Attorney General Robert Kennedy, whom he had met earlier in the day, stepped aside and let the students in." Neither is correct. It was not scripted, arranged, or orchestrated. Bobby was in Washington that day. Not only had he and the governor not met since April, they had not even talked. Howell Raines, who covered the civil rights movement before becoming editor of the *New York Times*, has argued that the showdown in Alabama was "rigged to the extent that Wallace had sent his pledge of capitulation through General Graham." In that sense, he was right. There was an agreement, in early afternoon, for Wallace to speak briefly and leave quickly.

But was the whole thing "rigged," particularly the first confrontation? The transcripts of Kennedy's meetings with congressional leaders and the telephone conversations with his brother, as well as the raw documentary footage of Kennedy and his associates at work on these two days, are unequivocal. It comes to this: Wallace made assurances and the Kennedys made plans, yes, but neither knew how it would turn out. It is true that Wallace insisted on making his stand and that the federal government let him. The Kennedys knew that he had to save face, that he promised there would not be violence, and that he took steps, beginning with sealing off the campus to outsiders, to ensure that. Critically, though, no one knew if there would be violence because no one was sure how the erratic Wallace would act – or react. Minute by minute, hour after hour, Drew's film reveals the punctilious planning at the Department of Justice over days, even weeks, in a climate of anxiety that ironclad assurances from Wallace would have immediately dissipated. Wallace never offered those assurances. He said there would be no violence, yes. He even had his representatives approach the Klan to ward them off, and they agreed, for now. But he never said that he would walk away until the last hour. He wanted to reserve that option on Tuesday morning and fuel speculation that he was prepared to go to jail as a martyr to segregation.

Years later, when Katzenbach pressed Raines to explain his assertion made in 1984, Raines said that Katzenbach had been his "source." Katzenbach wryly rejoined that that made him (Katzenbach) competent to talk about it, and he did. "It wasn't scripted one bit," Katzenbach insisted in 2008. "There was no arrangement at all. We did not know, we just guessed, hoped, estimated at such time, and when he [Wallace] turned down the first effort, we went back . . . But there was nothing scripted until that afternoon, if you call that scripted."

With the governor gone, the students could register. Three minutes later, James Hood walked up the steps of Foster Auditorium and went inside. Hood's sister called it the longest walk of his life; he feared what might happen – a taunt, a rock, a bullet – as they waded slowly through the crowd of journalists, troopers, and students. Malone followed a minute later. "Hey, there, we've been waiting for you," exclaimed a cheerful administrator to Malone in the well-staffed, empty gymnasium. The remaining formalities were handled quickly and politely. She and Hood each paid their $500 for the summer term. Both students had changed their clothes from that morning. Hood wore a blue suit and a snap-brim hat and carried a brown leather briefcase, like an executive on Madison Avenue. Malone wore a two-piece pink ensemble. They said nothing at first when reporters asked how they were feeling, but Malone smiled. Fifteen minutes later, they returned to their dormitories, where Graham found Hood later that afternoon. "He [Graham] came in and wanted to assure the President that everything was okay, so I told him it [was] all right. And he called the President from my room and told him that he was in my room, that everything was okay. And the President said, 'All right.'" Recalling the chaos at the University of Mississippi, Graham took no chances with Hood's safety that night. He bunked on a sofa in the lobby of the dormitory.

In Washington that afternoon, Bobby and his staff had listened to the afternoon confrontation on the radio. When word came that Wallace had walked away, they greeted the news calmly, even impassively. No hugs, no handshakes. No sense of triumph. No exhortation or congratulation – only ripples of subdued laughter when the reporter noted that the bystanders cheered when Wallace made good on his promise to retreat. "Whether the cheers are for his stand, or his withdrawal, I don't know," the reporter says flatly. A moment later, the denouement: "It's all over now. The Governor has stepped aside." As RFK listens to the broadcast, in the eye of Drew's lens, he sits at his desk writing notes that he slips into the pages of two books. With the crisis over, he places yet another call to JFK.

"Hello," says Bobby to his brother, in pitch-perfect deadpan.

"Well, they got into the university."

Tuesday, June 11, 1963
CHAPTER 13

Midafternoon

THE CONFRONTATION ENDED at 3:33 p.m. in Tuscaloosa,
5:33 p.m. in Washington. Ted Sorensen joined JFK in the
Oval Office and watched the rerun of a capitulating Wallace with
him on television. "As Wallace left the doorway," he wrote, "the
President turned around and said to me, 'I think we'd better give
that speech tonight.' What speech?" There was no speech – at least
not one Sorensen had written.

With the students on campus and George Wallace in retreat,
the crisis was over. Politically, though, Tuscaloosa was still useful
to the Kennedys. Whether it was a crisis or a charade, scripted or
unscripted, didn't matter. Whether it was predictable or managed
didn't matter. Whatever this highly publicized spectacle had been,
the president and his brother were not going to let it go to waste.
They had won. There was still political capital to be scraped from
the schoolhouse door. How to use it, strategically, to advance their
hardening commitment to civil rights?

The president had already decided to send civil rights legislation to Congress. He had discussed the contents of the bill in meetings at the White House the day before and with the Republicans and Democrats that day. While the civil rights bill, like the test ban treaty, was not comprehensive as its fiercest advocates hoped, it was unprecedented in its scope for its time. It was also risky for a northern Democrat who had won the presidency narrowly in 1960 and faced re-election in 1964, seventeen months away. Angry Southerners in Congress, whose states Kennedy had mostly carried, would oppose the bill and, quite possibly, take revenge on his legislative program, as LBJ had warned.

After the tumultuous spring, there was no denying the juggernaut of civil rights any longer. "The civil rights movement has suddenly turned, following Birmingham, into a Negro revolution," Arthur Schlesinger wrote in his diary on June 2, 1963. "It has been a long time since I have felt things to be so vividly in motion in our country. Old institutions and ideas, which have held firm for so long, seem to be giving way all at once. Of course, this is optimistic; and there will be much ugliness and sadness before we are out of the woods. Yet I feel this is a turning point." That same week *Time* reported that civil rights had now "burst into a feverish, fragmented, spasmodic, almost uncontrollable revolution." If Kennedy had been an observer for most of his two-and-a-half years in office, as some critics argued, he was no longer. That was impossible now. The question for him on Tuesday was not whether he would propose a bill. He would. It was not whether he would be its champion – finding allies, lobbying opponents, marshaling the authority of his office. He would. The challenge was more immediate, and, for his advisors, more contentious: how to put this great question before the nation in a fresh, compelling way, and when.

Kennedy had avoided addressing racism legislatively, and he had appointed some racist judges to keep Southerners happy. But his administration had not ignored civil rights. It had moved to protect the Freedom Riders in 1961 and forced the integration of the

University of Mississippi in 1962. Neither was fast enough and both had come at a political cost in the South where Kennedy's popularity would fall from 60 percent to 44 percent in September. (Outside the South, it fell from 76 percent to 69 percent over the same period.) Kennedy had signed an executive order on discrimination in housing, belatedly, and hired more black men and women in the federal government, inadequately. The afternoon of his Inauguration, watching the parade from a reviewing stand near the White House, Kennedy asked an assistant by his side to find out why there were no black men in the Coast Guard contingent and demanded a report on his desk the next morning. It was probably his first presidential order. In February 1963, Kennedy had spoken about civil rights in a message to Congress. He had discussed it in press conferences, interviews, and speeches, the most recent on Sunday, June 9, addressing the Conference of Mayors in Hawaii, where he had proposed a five-point plan to advance civil rights. It was front-page news in the *New York Times* on Monday.

The administration certainly thought that it had done more on civil rights than any other. Lee C. White, assistant special counsel to the president, who worked directly for Sorensen, wrote a five-page briefing note titled "Kennedy Administration Accomplishments in Civil Rights." The president had sent two messages to Congress on civil rights, it noted, creating a sub-cabinet group and designating senior people in all agencies to monitor interracial problems. It had made high-level black appointments – Robert Weaver, the housing administrator, the highest position ever held by a black American; George Weaver, assistant secretary of labor; Carl Rowan, ambassador; and Andrew Hatcher, associate White House press secretary. It had also appointed the first black commissioner in the District of Columbia and the first black postmaster of a major city. It had hired more blacks in middle and upper management in the civil service than any other administration. It had supported desegregation in education and in interstate commerce; bus, train, and air terminals were now integrated. It had pushed desegregation in remaining pockets of the armed forces and had embraced equal employment opportunity. On voting rights, the Justice Department had brought more than thirty cases before the courts, compared with ten between 1957 and January 1961. It was, for example, challenging the Louisiana State Board of Elections on the constitutionality of a state statute allowing its registrars to determine whether people could vote on the basis of reading and understanding the state's constitution.

The administration had a creditable record – compared to Eisenhower's. Later, its defenders argued that Kennedy could not have proposed civil rights legislation sooner because public opinion in the United States would not have supported major reform in 1961 and 1962, and Congress would not have enacted it. "The point is raised continuously that President Kennedy only realized there was a civil rights crisis the night after Birmingham in 1963, or otherwise he would have tried to obtain passage of legislation in '61 or '62 or '63," Bobby Kennedy said in 1964. "That's ludicrous, really, on the basis of the facts. Number One: Nobody would have paid the slightest attention to him. If he had sent up a more comprehensive bill, it would never have gone very far in any case – as seen by the civil rights bill that we did send up, where nobody rose to great support." Bobby's point was that if JFK could not easily persuade Congress in 1963, after the public revulsion to Bull Connor and Birmingham, where would he have been before Birmingham?

By May 1963, though, it was clear that all this was not enough. There had to be legislation. Enforcing the law, calling in troops, and courting business and community leaders would go only so far. The deteriorating situation demanded a stronger response. Bobby did not need to hear the anguish of James Baldwin and the others in New York City to lament, at Trinity College, the lack of progress on civil rights "reforms, which all of us know in our hearts, should have been made some time ago." If the president himself needed prodding, he would have found it on June 10 in his well-creased copy of the *New York Times*. The day before Kennedy would send troops to Tuscaloosa and then make the strongest statement on race relations of any president since Lincoln, Martin Luther King Jr. scolded JFK for his lassitude on civil rights. Kennedy was better than Eisenhower, King conceded, but he had merely substituted "an inadequate approach for a miserable one." King urged him to cancel his trip to Europe and devote himself to civil rights. He said that the president should revive fireside chats and cast racism in "moral" terms, "in which we seldom, if ever, hear the President of the United States speaking."

It was King's strongest criticism of Kennedy. He did not know – though he would learn later that day – what was afoot in the White House. In 1964, he attributed Kennedy's evolution to the unrest that spring: "Events changed him. I think that events had so dramaticized [*sic*] the indignities and the exploitation and the oppression that Negroes face, that he had sort of a soul-searching development that caused him to feel that he had to take a new position or that he had to take a stronger position, even if he did not have a consensus. . . . I really felt that he had come to the point of seeing the nation, the security of the nation, the unity of the nation, the survival of the nation. He went through what Abraham Lincoln went through."

When Kennedy and his advisors had met the day before at the White House, they talked about managing Wallace, defusing the threat, preparing and presenting the civil rights bill. They also discussed a presidential address. When to speak, what to say – these were the critical questions before the brain trust on Monday, as they had been, intermittently, in the weeks before. All Kennedy's advisors, save one, counseled against a set-piece television address. The bill wasn't ready, they said, the ground wasn't ploughed. The speech should wait. "They felt that it would just involve him personally and that it would be politically disadvantageous in 1964,"

Burke Marshall recalled. "That was in their minds and that was the way it was put." They worried – of course, it was their job to worry – about the loss of support in Congress and in the South. Sorensen shared those reservations and offered his own. "I felt that a major speech on civil rights should await the completion of the legislation and cover its contents," he said in his memoir. "Moreover, the situation at the University of Alabama was not a constitutional crisis, was not directly related to the most controversial parts of the legislation, and seemed an unlikely basis for a major presidential speech."

Sorensen had made the same point the weekend before at a dinner party in Georgetown at the home of Katie Louchheim, the highest-ranking woman in the State Department, long-time Democrat, and prominent hostess. There had been much talk that week among the cognoscenti about the timing of the president's intervention on civil rights; Walter Lippmann and James Reston, two of the nation's most influential columnists, urged the president to seize the moment. That view was shared by Dick Harkness, a senior correspondent at NBC News, who also dined at Louchheim's table that evening with Sorensen. "What should the President do?" Louchheim wrote in her diary on June 8. "How about the boilerplate of Reston [and] Lippmann, suggesting he [JFK] go on television? Ted . . . is already committed to a NO. He [JFK] shouldn't go unless there is a crisis. The 'why educate' or 'impassionedly plead' argument does not go down . . . In the end it is left that Dick wants him on – and Ted wants him off." As Sorensen recalled in his memoir, "no decision had been made [by June 11], and no draft had been prepared." When Bobby told his brother and the others Monday that the Justice Department had a "draft [which] . . . doesn't fit all these points but it's something to work with . . . and [has] some pretty good sentences and paragraphs," JFK replied that "it" might help us get ready "because we may want to do this tomorrow."

Tomorrow was now today. Talking to his brother on the morning and afternoon of June 11 as they monitored events in Alabama, Bobby raised the idea of the speech at least twice. In a conversation around 11:00 a.m., he asked Jack, almost plaintively: "What about the speech? Any thoughts? Do you think it's a good idea? I think we should do it tonight or tomorrow." He raised it again in the afternoon. Bobby was persistent because he felt that his brother had to give it. As he had said in the meeting at the White House the previous day, "You're going to have a lot of people saying: 'Why doesn't the President speak on this?'" But he was alone in urging the president to speak. Larry O'Brien, Kenny O'Donnell, Burke Marshall, and Sorensen all disagreed.

Lyndon Johnson wasn't at the meeting on June 10, but he had his own ideas about presenting and selling civil rights legislation. He had conveyed them to Sorensen in that long monologue over the telephone on June 3 and to Norbert A. Schlei, chief of the Justice Department's Office of Legal Counsel, in a meeting on June 4. Schlei, who was leading the team of lawyers drafting the bill, had gone to the Capitol to discuss it with LBJ in his office there. Why he went is uncertain; perhaps it was to assuage the vice president after Sorensen had told RFK about Johnson's reservations. Johnson reaffirmed his view that not only would the bill fail if it were submitted now – there had not been enough preparatory work – it would also be "disastrous" for the administration's agenda.

Johnson suggested several measures to advance the issue. Rather than a national televised address, Johnson proposed that Kennedy give "a major speech in each of the main southern states on the moral principle in ending discrimination . . . talking generally about full rights of citizenship and equality of opportunity across the board." He should open with a speech at the NASA installation in Mississippi; Johnson suggested that the president invoke Gordon Cooper's recent space flight and assert "that the purpose of the whole effort is to ensure we can live on this Earth under democracy and in freedom." Johnson then wanted the president to declare that inequality "was morally wrong and utterly unjustifiable," urging Southerners "to look into their souls, make the necessary moral decision and give the administration their support in the effort." Nothing much came of Johnson's conversations with Sorensen and Schlei, though both informed Bobby of them.

The problem was that Johnson was not making these arguments directly to the president. Johnson told Schlei on June 4 that he had asked Kenny O'Donnell for fifteen minutes alone with JFK to discuss the legislation. No meeting was arranged, Johnson complained. And when the president had asked at a meeting June 3 on civil rights whether his brooding vice president had anything to add, "at that stage and in that group, he did not feel that a long tirade would be constructive," Schlei wrote. Johnson's thoughts on the issue would be no more than a footnote to this story had he never become president. But in less than six months he was. And he would commit himself to passing Kennedy's civil rights bill, using some of the language (the "morality" of ending discrimination) and some of the salesmanship that he was advocating now.

By midafternoon, a presidential address did not seem likely. Everyone was opposed: O'Donnell, O'Brien, Sorensen, Marshall, and Johnson, too. They saw the speech as an imprudent, misguided impulse, a presidential whim that did not make political or practical sense that day. For O'Brien and O'Donnell, it was about politics. For Sorensen, it was about the pretext (or lack of one). For Marshall, it was about time; there simply wasn't enough of it to prepare a speech of this importance. "How could he [JFK] possibly do that?" he wondered. Only the Kennedys wanted the speech. Marshall thought that the president had decided to give the speech (suggesting it was not a caprice) but wanted to hear out his advisors even as he intended to ignore them. "I really don't think he [JFK] ever intended not to [speak], for a minute," Marshall said. "He listened to the arguments against it, but I think his question was just a question of when rather than whether. The Attorney General thought it ought to be done then, and he urged that on the President on the morning of Tuscaloosa. Now, of course, whether he would do it after the confrontation with Wallace or not would depend on how it went. So, it was a very last-minute thing."

It was also a close-run thing, which could have gone as wrong as the showdown in Tuscaloosa. E. Culpepper Clark, an Alabaman who has written the definitive account of the crisis, says the White House had "six hours" to prepare the speech. So does journalist Nick Bryant. Others believe, from watching Robert Drew's *Crisis,* that the administration had twenty-four hours. In fact, the speech was pulled together frantically and messily in far less time and delivered powerfully if extemporaneously (in part) from an unfinished text.

The truth is that Kennedy did not decide to speak that evening until very late in the afternoon. As Marshall says, he wanted to know first that Wallace had walked away. JFK's worry was that his speech might turn out like the one he gave the night of the riot at the University of Mississippi; he had gone on the air to announce that he was sending troops only to find that they took hours reaching the campus. When violence broke out and two people died, he looked inept and his television appearance premature. If things ended badly in Tuscaloosa, he would have to tell the nation about the arrest of the governor, perhaps riots in the streets, and the occupation of Alabama. Like Marshall, Bobby felt the day before that the president "had pretty much made up his mind that he would speak . . . but not finally." As Bobby recalled, "He and I talked almost all that day." After Wallace had retreated on Tuesday afternoon, the president felt the time was right. "I think he just decided that day," added RFK. "I think he called me up on the phone and said that he was going to do it that night." Jack did place a call to Bobby at 4:50 p.m., fifty minutes or so before the second encounter with Wallace was over. But he did not know yet how things would go, and presumably waited until later in the afternoon to assure his brother that he would make the speech.

✳

There was no speech – at least not one Sorensen knew about. But that had not stopped the president from asking for fifteen minutes of time on the television and radio networks at 8:00 p.m. Such requests were fairly routine for the White House. All Pierre Salinger had to do was instruct the White House operator to connect him with the three networks (ABC, CBS, NBC) and the two leading wire services, Associated Press and United Press International. "She would have them [representatives of all five news organizations] on the line [simultaneously] within two minutes," he said. In many accounts of the events of June 11, Kennedy calls each of the networks "personally" to request airtime. This is how it is presented in *JFK: Seven Days that Made a President*, a fanciful docudrama broadcast on the National Geographic Channel in November 2013. Here a brusque Kennedy turns to a hovering Sorensen in the Oval Office and snaps, "Ted, give me the network." A moment later, the "network" on the line, he grabs the phone from Sorensen and barks: "This is the President. I want to go live on air tonight. Make it happen." It did happen, but not like that. According to Sorensen, it was Salinger, not JFK, who telephoned the networks with the request. If so, Salinger disappeared shortly afterwards. He did not appear to be around for the speech itself, his duties assumed by Andy Hatcher. Whoever called, the networks agreed to the time.

If Sorensen and Kennedy had watched the late afternoon confrontation with Wallace on a delayed television broadcast – as JFK had watched the delayed broadcast from that morning – it meant that the president could not have raised the speech with Sorensen until 5:30 p.m. or later. While Sorensen said his conversation with

JFK took place "after 4:30 p.m.," it was surely after Wallace had left the campus at 5:40 p.m. (in Washington). In fact, Sorensen had not two days, one day, or six hours to write the speech. He had *two hours*. Even for the master wordsmith, who was known to work all night drafting, revising, and polishing, this was forbidding. "I made some noises about limited time," Sorensen recalled. "RFK, who had arrived with Burke Marshall, said, 'Don't worry, we have a lot of good material over at the Justice Department that we can send to you.' I worried anyway."

Bobby, who was meticulous about everything that day, was untroubled by the late hour, at least initially. While he kept pressing his brother to speak, he knew that JFK would not make up his mind before he knew the university was integrated. Anticipating the showdown in Tuscaloosa, Kennedy would not give an address on civil rights in May or early June (although there was talk in the White House of Kennedy speaking the evening of June 10, before the confrontation with Wallace, to explain the government's position and the steps it was taking).

✳

If RFK was unconcerned about time, it was because he thought the president could give the speech from notes, if necessary. He also was confident, as he had assured Sorensen, that there was enough material gathered by the Justice Department to put something together. In their joint oral history recorded in 1964, Bobby and Burke Marshall mention "a draft" of the president's speech, which they found "unsatisfactory." They don't identify its author or its origin, though at one point RFK suggests that Sorensen wrote it. But Sorensen maintained that he had written no speech before the president asked him to prepare one. In fact, as far as Sorensen knew, no draft had been written by anyone because, until that hour, there was no firm decision to make the speech. That there was no draft is a view shared by Robert Schlesinger, Arthur's son, in his engaging book on presidential speechwriters, *White House Ghosts*, which examines the civil rights speech.

But Bobby and Marshall were not wrong. There was a draft of a presidential speech, though Sorensen may never have seen it. If he did see it, he did not use it. Anticipating this contingency as he had every other one that week, two days earlier Bobby had asked a gifted new speechwriter to draft a civil rights speech. The speech-writer, Richard Yates, had been working for the attorney general for two short weeks. On the evening of Sunday, June 9, he shut himself in a room, plied himself with coffee and cigarettes, banged out a text, and polished and delivered it on Tuesday morning. The draft is short, eloquent, and stark, six pages of double-spaced typescript. The date "6/11/63" is penciled on the top, with the name of the author in cursive.

The theme of the speech is the plight of the black American and the country's obligation to address it. The tone is critical. "I come before you tonight at a time of profound national unrest," the text opens. "No abrupt calamity, no series of harsh surprises has brought about this state of affairs; on the contrary, it is the result of a slow and malignant disease that has been allowed to grow within the tissues of our society for many generations. Negro Americans were freed from slavery a hundred years ago. Yet in all of that century . . . in all that time . . . our Negroes have yet to be truly freed. They have yet to be freed from the bondage of injustice, from the grip of social and economic oppression, from the mindless, desperate hammerlock of emotional prejudice." This is the plight of the black person, it argues, who "has remained enslaved within our shores. It has damaged our own national conscience, our very ability to take pride in calling ourselves Americans." This is a matter of national urgency, it said. Oxford and Birmingham are "only symptoms of the trouble – outward manifestations of the inner disease. And the infection is by no means localized."

The speech offers a bleak picture of the Black American in 1963. Home is a slum dwelling in a ghetto, for which he pays exorbitant rent to an unscrupulous landlord. He suffers demoralization from chronic unemployment, or low-wage, unskilled labor. His children go to an overcrowded, understaffed school, which, though not officially segregated, might just as well be; they find in their lessons so little hope for their own future that they will drop out of high school, joining their parents "on the seemingly endless treadmill of poverty and neglect and despair." This isn't America, says the speech. It isn't acceptable in the greatest free country in the world. "Let no glib specialists confuse the issue by seeing it as a tangle of legal problems, or political problems, or economic problems, or social problems. It is all of these, but above all – and very clearly – it is a moral problem. Something is wrong, in the full sense of the word – something is wrong North, South, East, and West in our country, and it must be made right."

What to do? The speech considers executive action, congressional intervention, or another exercise of governmental authority. "In the past two-and-a-half years, more progress has been made in securing civil rights for all Americans – through executive action, litigation, persuasion and private initiative – than in any comparable period in our history." It mentions the use of troops in Mississippi, and federal marshals in other places to address desegregation. Written before the events of Tuesday morning and afternoon, it does not mention Alabama. It notes executive orders and lawsuits on voting rights, housing, and equal employment in industries working on government contracts. In response to the malaise, it announces the civil rights bill.

But legislation, the speech notes, is not enough. It argues that it is delusional to think that "government edict" alone can bring about "a truly significant improvement." The most forceful program of this or any administration is not enough. "The festering surface eruptions of an internal disease cannot be cured with bandages," it says, seeking a different treatment of this "malignancy in our national life." Treatment, it says, must begin with understanding, empathy, and enlightenment in the nation's communities. Then, the final appeal: "I want to ask you, all of you, to look into your hearts – not in search of charity, or of tolerance, for the Negro neither wants nor needs your condescension – no; I ask you to look into your hearts and find the one plain, proud and priceless quality that unites us all as Americans: a sense of justice."

Blake Bailey mentions the speech in his fine biography, *A Tragic Honesty: The Life and Work of Richard Yates*. It appears nowhere else, in any of the leading accounts of the period or this presidency, not even as a footnote to the story of these momentous events. A stapled copy of these undelivered words lies nearly anonymously among Robert Kennedy's papers in the John F. Kennedy Presidential Library. Yet this impassioned, forgotten speech identifies some of the themes and ideas that appear in the president's address that evening.

✳

Richard Yates burst to prominence in 1961 with the publication of *Revolutionary Road*. A dark account of life in suburban New England in the 1950s, it was a finalist for the National Book Award in 1962, competing with Joseph Heller's *Catch-22* and J.D. Salinger's *Franny and Zooey*. (In 2008, *Revolutionary Road* became a successful Hollywood movie, directed by Sam Mendes and starring Leonardo DiCaprio and Kate Winslet. She won a Golden Globe for Best Actress and the film was nominated for three Oscars.) Yates published a collection of short stories (*Eleven Kinds of Loneliness*) in 1962 and wrote a screenplay for William Styron's *Lie Down in Darkness*. At thirty-seven, he was an urgent new voice, a chronicler of midcentury America with a gift for uncompromising, unadorned prose. Styron, Kurt Vonnegut, and Dorothy Parker trumpeted his talent. All agreed that he had a future in American letters. After his death, he was called the greatest post-war American novelist, if the least known.

When Bobby was looking for a speechwriter in 1963, he approached Styron, a friend of both Kennedys. Styron recommended Yates. Like most writers, Yates needed the money; he was indifferent to the job and his new boss. Politically, his man was Adlai Stevenson. "I don't even know if I *like* the fucking Kennedys," he told Styron. Hiring novelists and journalists wasn't unusual for the Kennedys, who recruited talent wherever they could find it. (Bill Attwood and Joe Kraft, both journalists and authors, were speechwriters for JFK in 1960.) Yates started at the Justice Department in late May 1963.

The attorney general wanted "a real writer" who could give him a distinctive voice. His civil rights speeches had been written by committee; as *Newsweek* reported, they "were missing the mark." After his sulfurous encounter with Baldwin and company, Kennedy wanted to give his words edge. Ed Guthman held a competition for the job, asking applicants to draft a civil rights speech the attorney general might deliver, curiously, at "an exclusive girls' college in the East." Yates wrote all night. The college was Trinity, where Robert Kennedy spoke on June 2. It was Yates who wrote: "You may sometimes regret your education, for a free mind will always insist on seeking out reality, and reality can be far more painful than the soft and comforting illusions of the intellectually poor." It was his first assignment for RFK, and it was spectacular. He got the job.

In his abbreviated time at the Justice Department, Yates saw little of Bobby. He met the attorney general only twice. The first was when he was hired and Bobby told his new speechwriter that they were living in "uncertain times" of "great responsibility," declaiming magisterially like a Roman senator in a toga, which left Yates flummoxed. The second was on an airplane, when Kennedy sat down beside him and complimented his work. From June until November, Yates wrote some of Bobby's most memorable speeches, which, Yates boasted, got the loudest applause of RFK's career. But Yates was an alcoholic and Bobby was a puritan, at least in some matters. (The attorney general thought the eighteenth-century novel *Fanny Hill: Memoirs of a Woman of Pleasure* was so dirty that one night that spring he tossed a copy into the Potomac River.) Whatever his reservations about Yates, whatever his moralism, Kennedy was personally kind to him. By November, though, Yates's position was eliminated at the Justice Department. Years after, he still resented that.

Twice divorced, Yates was a manic-depressive, often broke, and often drunk. Celebrated for his realism, his work was morose, loud, and incendiary. A characteristic sense of despondency permeates the speech on civil rights that he drafted for President Kennedy; "disease," "malignancy," "infection," "germs," colonize its pages like "festering" bacteria. It was too bleak for Kennedy to use – if he ever saw it – although Bailey says that Yates fully expected that some of his phrases would find their way into the speech. Hadn't Bobby said they were "pretty good" the day before? Yates was disappointed when he turned on the television on Tuesday night and found none of his phrases were used, though the overarching theme (the black American's condition), the tone (the call for morality), and the news (announcement of the legislation) are the same.

Yates returned to his sad, dyspeptic life. While he enjoyed a fleeting moment of literary acclaim, none of his books ever sold more than twelve thousand copies in hardcover. By his death in 1992, he was destitute and suffering from emphysema. His work was out of print by the next year, and he disappeared from public consciousness – at least until the movie, *Revolutionary Road*, appeared a decade and a half later, catapulting his forty-seven-year-old novel on to the bestseller lists. It was a success he had never known while he was alive. In an even greater irony of this story, Yates spent his last miserable months in Tuscaloosa, teaching creative writing, at the University of Alabama.

✳

In his many recollections of that afternoon – in his memoir, his oral history, and his many interviews – Sorensen never mentioned a draft speech by Yates or anyone else. He insisted that he began from scratch. "I could not draw upon a previous Kennedy civil rights speech file, because there was no such file," he recalled. It was clear that for Sorensen, writing this speech would be entirely different than writing any other speech, let alone one this important. This wasn't tossing off a few words to the Capitol Page School. It wasn't a toast, a telegram, a congressional message, a proclamation, or an executive order. This was a national address on *the* great domestic issue of the day. It would be carried live on all television and radio networks. Millions of Americans would watch and listen.

Normally, a speech of this stature would be weeks in preparation. The Peace Speech, as we know, flowed from consultations with a small but select group and was important enough for JFK to ask Sorensen (as well as Mike Mansfield and Averell Harriman) to review it with him on his flight from Hawaii. But as Taylor Branch, the definitive chronicler of the civil rights movement, says, the idea for this speech came from the president himself "without a trace of the usual gestation within the government." Rick Perlstein, the historian and journalist, thought Kennedy was proceeding "to make what might have been the most portentously rash decision in the history of the American presidency." There wasn't time for deliberation; the making of the June 11 address was the absolute antithesis of the one the day before. JFK had never given a speech this important with this little preparation.

That made it a job for Ted Sorensen. "Sorensen is obviously a genius," declared Schlesinger on June 22. "I do not see how he could turn out the American University and civil rights speeches, the civil rights message [to Congress], and so many other things, and still keep the pump flowing." Schlesinger's role in the White House was vague. He was house historian, resident humorist, liaison to liberals, reservoir of ideas. That week, for example, he was asked to assess Raymond Loewy's proposal to serve as the government's consultant on design, at $45,000 a year. Designing Air Force One was one thing, but everything? "I would be personally uneasy if Michelangelo were to claim that authority, and Loewy, good as he is, is no Michelangelo," he wrote the president. At forty-five, Schlesinger was an impish, bow-tied intellectual who had taught history at Harvard and won the Pulitzer Prize for his interpretation of Andrew Jackson. The president often asked him to draft remarks on lesser subjects or, occasionally, to collaborate with Sorensen on major addresses. That was difficult because Sorensen was not collegial.

Consider the State of the Union Address delivered on Thursday, January 11, 1962. JFK reviewed Sorensen's draft January 8 and found it "too drab and too long." He asked Schlesinger to revise it. Schlesinger asked the president to tell Sorensen that he had asked him to do so. Then he knocked out a new draft overnight, from 1:00 a.m. to 4:00 a.m., and gave it to JFK later on Tuesday. Meanwhile, Sorensen "was stimulated by these developments to work all Tuesday night and turn out a new draft of his own, derived in part from mine," Schlesinger recalled. By Wednesday morning, the president had dueling drafts. Turning to McGeorge Bundy, Kennedy "gave him the classic presidential instruction: 'Weave them together.'" The process took place that day, with Bundy protecting Schlesinger's passages "against Ted's tendency to reject anything he had not written himself."

Kennedy was aware of Sorensen's possessiveness, and so were others. They adjusted to it. Bundy recalled that one of the reasons that Tom Sorensen was brought into the writing of the Peace Speech was that he knew what words, phrases and ideas mattered to his brother Ted and what didn't, should they decide to drop or change the text. "He (Tom) didn't have his brother's sensitivity, but was perfectly prepared to say 'he will fight like hell over this', or 'I don't think he cares about . . .' This got to be a quite smooth and easy process." It was how Kennedy learned to contour to Ted's territorial instincts.

It created competition, however genteel, between Sorensen and others for the president's favor. By 1963, Sorensen had so fashioned himself as Kennedy's alter ego, his self-proclaimed "intellectual bloodbank," that he could not see himself as anything else. No one could approach him, imitate him, or challenge him. It was Sorensen, more than anyone else in the galaxy of stars in the White House, who shaped the thoughts and words of the Kennedy administration. This isn't to say that Sorensen was a ventriloquist and Kennedy his dummy. Kennedy was too confident for anyone to put words in his mouth, and Sorensen was too gifted to serve an unlettered president; soaring prose on a leaden tongue always comes out wrong.

Sorensen's speeches – laced with originality, flavored with wit, garnished with anecdote, buttressed by fact and figure, spliced with turn of phrase, and delivered by a practiced, compelling speaker – were the apogee of modern presidential oratory. It is why so much of what Kennedy said endures today. There are other presidents who clicked with their speechwriters, such as Raymond Moley and Franklin D. Roosevelt, or Peggy Noonan and Ronald Reagan. No wonder in his comprehensive survey of modern presidential speechwriters, Robert Schlesinger calls the New Frontier "the Age of Sorensen." No one spoke and dazzled like Jack Kennedy. No one wrote and thought like Ted Sorensen. Together, they were magic.

What made Sorensen's speeches distinctive? He believed in brevity, using as few words as possible; clarity, choosing the right word or expression, *le mot juste*; coherence and consistency, putting things in logical order; alliteration and repetition, using literary devices to make it memorable; and quotation and anecdote, citing historical references. Kennedy liked the last element so much that one commentator said his campaign speeches may have "erred on the side of overestimating the literacy and intelligence of the American people." Perhaps. His acceptance speech ("The New Frontier") in 1960 before the Democratic National Convention, which plays repeatedly in an alcove of the John F. Kennedy Presidential Library, is unabashedly replete with nineteenth-century historical reference. However, Sorensen and Kennedy also used elevated but simple language cast in short sentences and telling words. Ultimately, of course, it is ideas that distinguish Kennedy's speeches. Without them, the prose would be hollow.

In his memoir, Sorensen reflected on the power – and lack of power – of speeches: "Saying so doesn't make it so. A speech can stir men's hearts by describing what is; sometimes it can stir their hearts by describing what should be; but rarely can a speech by itself change their fate by determining or changing what will be. It does not have the power of law. It seeks to persuade people to change their views, but it may represent only the view of the speaker or his powerless speechwriter. Rare is the speaker who has the power to make others listen, and, if they listen, to act, and if they act, to do so in the manner he advocates."

Beyond the speeches, Kennedy and Sorensen's greatest collaboration was *Profiles in Courage*, the story of American legislators who made decisions that put their political careers at risk. It was published in 1956 and won the Pulitzer Prize for History in 1957. (That week in 1963, it was optioned to television for a series of one-hour programs.) Drew Pearson, the columnist, claimed it was written by Sorensen, not Kennedy, whose name appeared on the cover. Kennedy threatened legal action and Pearson withdrew the allegation. Some biographers also suggest that Sorensen wrote it. Certainly Jackie felt that Sorensen claimed too much credit. "I couldn't look at Ted Sorensen for about two years after that," she said in 1964, recalling her husband in hospital filling yellow legal pads with his writing. "You know, Jack forgave so quickly, but I never forgave Ted Sorensen. I watched him like a hawk for a year or so."

In his achingly honest memoir, Sorensen allows that it may have been "partly true" that he had privately boasted or directly hinted that he'd written *Profiles in Courage*. He insists that their work was a partnership. JFK wrote the first and last chapters and Sorensen prepared a first draft of the other chapters, to which Kennedy later made revisions. Kennedy was recovering from near-fatal back surgery when he began the book in 1954. He spent six months in hospital, and Sorensen says he drafted chapters (assisted by Jules Davids, a professor of history at Georgetown University, who provided important research and ideas). Sorensen says JFK acknowledged his contribution fully and gave him all the royalties ($100,000 in 1964, according to Jackie, or $766,000 in 2014). In his memoir, Sorensen ponders the meaning of authorship: is it the one who did much of the research and some of the phrasing, he asks, or the one who determined "the substance, structure and theme of the book; read and revised each draft; inspired, constructed, and improved the work?" In another circumstance he probably would have been considered a co-author. Still, he insists that he was treated fairly, though there is a sense that he willed himself to say that long ago and continued to say it, regardless of any residual doubt. "I never felt – not for a moment – that I was wrongfully denied part of the credit, much less a share in the Pulitzer Prize."

The episode soured Bobby on Sorensen, too. In 1964, Bobby said that JFK "liked Sorensen very much," before adding, "Ted Sorensen, for a period of time, was far more interested in himself than he was in the President – which went back a number of years – but I think they got that straightened out and [Sorensen] was much better in the last few years. . . ." Jackie was still scathing. "Someone said he loved himself and finally he loved another person, which was Jack. And he also had such a crush on Jack. I can remember when he first tried to speak like him or dare to call him

Jack, and he'd sort of blush. And I think he wanted to be easy all the ways Jack was easy." As a young man – she called him "the boy" – Sorensen had "a big inferiority complex." Years after the White House, Sorensen's relationship improved with both Bobby and particularly Jackie, and their suspicion fell away. Their remarks at the time, though, reflected an unsympathetic view of Sorensen that was shared by his colleagues, such as Richard Goodwin, who refused to work with Sorensen in the White House.

One detractor was Ralph Dungan, who worked with Sorensen in the Senate and the White House. He described Sorensen in 1964 as arrogant, brusque, and self-absorbed. Sorensen, who was stung by the description, replied in his memoir that he had heard the complaint before and "there must have been some truth in it." As Schlesinger noted, Sorensen wanted to do it all, which made him disinclined to share access to Kennedy or assignments from Kennedy. He was what he was: ascetic, detached, remote, a man with a smile that was always wintry and a glare that was always distant, laughter as spontaneous "as a bank vault swinging open," as one contemporary put it.

In a conversation in 1963 with Walter Heller about Kennedy's aloofness, Dungan pointed to Ted's office and said: "That man never knows one week to the next where he stands." Surely Sorensen knew where he stood with Kennedy. But that did not stop him from working all day and all night, earning his annual salary of $21,000 (in 1961), $5,000 more than he was paid in his last year working for Senator Kennedy. He rarely left his "high-ceilinged, multi-windowed, spacious" office with its own restroom and three secretaries outside. Sustenance came from the White House Mess, where on Monday he ordered toast (10¢), a cup of coffee (5¢), and a cup of tea (5¢). Later he had a club sandwich (55¢), a glass of milk (20¢), and ice cream (20¢). He was always tired. "My clearest memory was that of exhaustion," he says of those years. "I was too busy even to smell the flowers in the White House Rose Garden."

Sorensen was embarrassed watching himself yawning in Robert Drew's film during the "historic session" on June 10, but he had not slept much that week. After all, he had written the Hawaii speech and the Peace Speech, and was drafting the speeches for Kennedy's trip to Europe later in June. He was so busy before these two days that he told Schlesinger on June 4 that he couldn't go to Europe to take soundings in advance of the president's visit, as Kennedy had suggested they both do. On the night of June 9, Sorensen had flown from Hawaii and probably did not sleep. Fifty years later, the *New York Times* erroneously reported that on Tuesday morning "he went home, only to be summoned back at mid-afternoon. . . ." Sorensen did not go home. In fact, he never went home – not then, not ever, not really. And certainly not that day, during a crisis.

No wonder the poor man suffered from stomach ulcers and recurring exhaustion, which put him in hospital for several days in late September 1962. Friends sent him flowers, get-well wishes ("This is the first time I have known any weakness in the flesh to really get you down," wrote Hugh Sidey), and books. One was *Seven Days in May*, the thriller about a military coup in the United States, in which Sorensen was reportedly the inspiration for one of the characters around the president. Sorensen was discharged the day after the riot at Ole Miss. His health remained fragile in June 1963. In the eight weekdays between June 1 and June 12, his daily schedule (amended in pencil) shows four doctor's appointments and three visits to the White House Dispensary. When he told a friend his stomach was bad that spring and summer, he blamed anxiety. "Now that they have told him he had tensions," said the friend, "he began recognizing them."

By June 1963, Sorensen and Kennedy had been together over ten years. The president was his "hero"; he confessed that Kennedy was all that mattered to him. "Sorensen's great mistake as a human being, I would say, is that he pitched over everything for John F. Kennedy," observed Dungan. "And it's a great tragedy in many ways.

I think it further distorted his own personality and screwed up his own personal life . . ." For Kennedy, it is true, Sorensen sacrificed all. He joined Kennedy when he was twenty-four and left him at thirty-five. That decade defined him forever.

Work animated him, drained him, and nearly ruined him, as it did his marriage. When Kennedy began running for president in the late 1950s, Sorensen accompanied him virtually every weekend for three years. The reverential Sorensen did not complain. One journalist noted, "It's almost as if Ted says to his family: 'Look, you have my love, but this man has my life.'" After eleven years of marriage, Ted and Camilla separated in 1960. They divorced in 1963.

※

As there was more than one Kennedy, there was more than one Sorensen. An introverted, obsessive striver, he was a proud father, a witty correspondent, a fierce friend, and, after the failure of his marriage, a surprising lothario. Before Camilla moved to Wisconsin with his three sons in August of 1963, he attended the boys' 6:00 p.m. Little League games, crowing that the two older ones were pitching and one was batting over .500. Occasionally, they accompanied him to the White House.

He was quirky and funny, in his way. His files are full of postcards, letters, and thank-you notes, sent and received. There was, for example, a spirited correspondence with his haberdasher, Bill Swartz, owner of Swartz & Sons Inc. of 600 S. Pulaski Street in Baltimore. ("The sun never sets on SSS suits," it boasted.) When Swartz writes Sorensen on February 11, 1963, to express his disappointment that his usually discriminating client doesn't want a tailcoat "at a price so cockeyed low that it would have been inadvisable not to grab it," Sorensen apologizes: "Sorry to have been a turncoat on the topcoat . . ." On March 11, Sorensen orders a pair of all-wool, lightweight, gray summer slacks. Swartz, as much Sorensen's doctor as his tailor, encourages him to take an evening off and join him at a concert: "I urge you to come not because I'm interested in your handsome puss, but for sound medical reasons . . . getting away from that hellhole for an evening (b'lieve me I mean it)." When Swartz sends him two pairs of slacks, Sorensen cracks: "I accept your judgment that all-wool trousers would be twice as hot as a blend – and I also realize that you are twice as good a musician as I am, twice as funny a letter writer and twice the age of all my sons combined – but is that any reason to send me twice as many pairs of pants as I ordered?" Enclosing payment for the total amount, he adds: "I appreciate your sending me something cool – inasmuch as 'the sun never sets on SSS suits.'"

When Bobby wrote Sorensen in early 1963, asking for his contribution for a joint gift, Sorensen drafted a wry reply playing on some of JFK's somber phrases he'd written during the Cuban Missile Crisis: "For the first time I think Khrushchev got the better deal in Cuba – at least I wish he had. However, it looks like you and I are eyeball to eyeball over this, and I just blinked – by signing the enclosed check for $50.00. Although this sudden deployment of strategic funds has upset the precarious balance of my status quo, I realize the greatest danger is to pay nothing. I must accept this obligation if my courage and commitment are ever to be trusted again by friend or foe. But I will never again write a speech which has the President saying: 'The cost of freedom is high – but Americans have always paid it' – because there is always some hawk like you who believes him. Talk about Pearl Harbor in reverse. Next time it's another Munich for me. It shall henceforth be my policy to regard any letter of assessment launched from the Department of Justice as a clear and present danger to the security of my budget – and this mental blockade will continue until adequate assurances are given, and verified by on-site inspection, that you have *not* dismantled the box or withdrawn those cigars for your own use."

Although Sorensen did not strike friends as naturally funny ("He wasn't Mr. Clown," says one who knew him long after the White House), humor became Kennedy's calling card, and Sorensen provided it. In the 1960 campaign, he created a Humor File that he carried across the country. Humor honeyed almost every speech. "We avoided the tasteless, the cruel and the obscure," recalled Sorensen. "We had one rule: if someone be offended, cut it." Family was fair game. At an event on May 9, 1963, for example, Eunice Shriver cheekily advised her brother: "You should put more fire in your speeches." The president shot back: "And you should put more of your speeches in the fire."

Sorensen found time, as well, to answer personal requests, including one from the young Robert L. White of 16 Park Drive in Baltimore, who asked him to autograph an enclosed card. Sorensen answers him: "Rather than sign this card . . . I thought you might like to have this letter from me which I am signing especially for you. It comes with my best wishes. Sincerely, Theodore Sorensen." From that, White, then a teen, would create the world's largest private collection of Kennedy memorabilia. Sorensen also offered help to petitioners like Howard M. Metzenbaum of Ohio, who wrote praising JFK's approach to nuclear arms and civil rights before asking "if I could be of service." Metzenbaum was of service, eventually, in three consecutive terms in the U.S. Senate.

Among Sorensen's friends was Katie Louchheim, whose gracious home at 2824 O Street in Georgetown he visited often. From her perch professional and social, Louchheim heard what Washington whispered. She filled a thick, gossipy diary of single-spaced pages of typescript – marked by typos, deletions, and misspellings – addressed to a fictional "Dear Gerry." To Sorensen, she was maternal and generous, listening to his romantic woes while fixing him hot milk and honey for his tender stomach. Her view of him was both sympathetic and unsparing. She saw ego and edge. After the black-tie dinner at her house on June 1, dominated by discussion of a presidential speech, she wrote: "In leaving, Ted, who can be juvenile (he brought the young too blonde daughter of the Dixons and actually pouted when she was seated at another table) and so learned and so sure, said, 'I really enjoyed myself. Most dinners are a bore. This was an interesting one, maybe because I did all the talking.'"

One of Sorensen's girlfriends was Sara "Sally" Elbery, with whom he had a strained, episodic relationship. After dating him in Washington, Elbery returned to her native Boston in the fall of 1962. Louchheim described her as "slight, small with those blue eyes that startle you with their blueness." Later, she was the "pert, conventional Irish Catholic who must some day bore him." In the spring of 1963, Sorensen had vowed to get her back. He was certainly trying on June 5 when he spent six dollars on a dozen red roses with a card signed, "All my love, Ted." It was not an easy courtship. "He is very harsh," Elbery tells Louchheim. "He never lets me know how he feels. He used to say such awful things to me. I got so I couldn't stand it. And I was so lonely in Washington." But Louchheim believed Elbery cared deeply for Sorensen. "She understands, must, his dour nature."

Louchheim more than once called Sorensen "juvenile." In April 1963, he had insisted on bringing a date she described as "some uncomfortable pretty young thing who knew no one" to one of her carefully balanced dinner parties. It almost ruined the evening. Louchheim doesn't call Sorensen a "playboy," as she does others in the administration. Earlier that year, though, she commented, "Sorensen has an 18 year-old and Pierre [Salinger] is on the loose. Well, if they will lower the age limit for the power set these things will happen."

Sorensen's other girlfriend that year was Gloria Steinem, a young magazine journalist who would become a leading feminist of her generation. Louchheim found her "bright, capable, indifferent," describing someone whose "straight dark hair falls evenly on her shoulders and forehead." In the fall of 1963 Steinem published *The Beach Book*, a guide to beach culture. She loved the Kennedys. "For the first time in my life I could imagine that something I, or anyone else I knew, wrote might be read in the White House, and I felt connected instead of ashamed of the government," she recalled. Sorensen's work was the basis of her attraction to him and she liked to visit him at the White House. They also shared the memory of wounded childhoods and incapacitated mothers, says Steinem's biographer, Sydney Ladensohn Stern. Eventually, Louchheim observed, Sorensen would have to choose between Elbery and Steinem, this "brainy, beatnik . . . who has the modern career girl characteristics of which he does not approve but whose company he finds stimulating." Steinem recalled they were "misfits from the beginning." Sorensen was attracted to her because she was outside his narrow experience in Nebraska and the strict regime of his work. Steinem, meanwhile, found Sorensen highly judgmental: "If I said 'shit' or 'damn' he would get really upset. If I smoked a cigarette . . . he would get very quiet or very upset – as if it were immoral for women to smoke."

That spring, Sorensen was hurting. "I wonder about this very bright, quite tough and yet tender man," Louchheim wrote, noting that he felt "at home" with her and her husband, Walter, a wealthy entrepreneur. Sorensen talked about his failed marriage (for which he blamed himself in his memoir) and his hopes of remarrying. The problem was that he was married to JFK. "You should not marry until after the campaign," Louchheim advised him in 1963. "Why?" he asked. "It is always this way – campaign or not." Louchheim predicted that it would be hard for him to find the right person: "He is a genius. Not a fond-husband type."

And there was all that work! Louchheim knew of his frequent all-nighters, as if he were an undergraduate cramming for a final. He often left her dinner parties late to return to the White House. For the upcoming visit to Europe, the president would give thirty-one speeches, toasts, and statements in Ireland and Germany alone. With England and Italy, he would give forty-one public remarks between June 23 and July 2. No wonder he told Louchheim that he had slept a total of nine hours in a week. Looking back, Sorensen said that Kennedy gave four of his best speeches in the spring and summer of 1963. He called that period "our hot streak."

✳

Unlike the president, Sorensen had few scheduled appointments on Tuesday, June 11. After the Legislative Leaders Breakfast at 9:30 a.m., he met his assistants, Lee C. White and Mike Feldman, as well as Bill Keel and Paul Southwick. At 1:15 p.m. he had a lunch at the Occidental with one Phil Potter, and at 3:15 p.m. he had an appointment with Dr. Fraser, who was treating him. He may have kept those, but he did cancel a meeting of the National Security Council's Standing Committee on Cuba at 5:00 p.m. Then there were the usual telephone calls that day. Katie Louchheim and Charlie Bartlett had called. Norbert Schlei had called ("important") from the Office of the Attorney General, probably to discuss the wording of the proclamation that morning. Sorensen's brother, Tom, had called "urgently" to ask whether the United States Information Agency, where he was deputy director, should broadcast that night's speech. Hugh Sidey had called to confirm his dinner appointment with Sorensen at 7:30 p.m. Gloria Steinem had called to say she was in town from New York.

There was no time for any of them or for anything else now. The networks were booked, the president was committed, the country was waiting. As the minutes passed, O'Donnell and others in the West Wing worried that the speech would not be ready, that the president would have to go on the air without a full text. Sorensen shrugged and began writing. He had less than two hours.

Tuesday, June 11, 1963
CHAPTER 14

Late Afternoon

IF SORENSEN WAS worrying about the time, the president was not – at least, not yet. Beyond the proclamation
and the executive order he had issued, Kennedy had been managing
events in Alabama coolly and quietly. Crisis? What crisis? At 1:54
p.m., he had gone to the White House Swimming Pool. At 2:16
p.m., he had gone to the mansion, eaten his lunch, and napped, as
usual; he may have spent time with Jackie and the children, whom
he had not seen for almost a week. They had returned to the White
House from Camp David that afternoon, but left again at 4:35 p.m.
for the rest of the day. Kennedy was back in the office at 4:07 p.m.
He had four more appointments before delivering the civil rights
speech at 8:00 p.m. That the text was not written – in fact, not even
started – and might not be ready in time did not alter his schedule.
In between meetings, he conferred with Sorensen and Bobby.

Shortly after 4:00 p.m., Kennedy greeted four guests in the
Oval Office. Two were senior officials at the State Department:
Averell Harriman, Under Secretary of State for Political Affairs,

and Abram Chayes, legal advisor. Were they there to review strategy after the Peace Speech, now more than a day old? Or, as Richard Reeves writes, to discuss Harriman's forthcoming mission to Moscow to negotiate the proposed nuclear test ban treaty? No. The other two visitors suggest something else. One was Wilson Wyatt, former lieutenant governor of Kentucky. The other was Walter J. Levy, a leading expert on oil from New York. The meeting was not about arms and Moscow; it was about oil and Indonesia.

That spring the United States had faced a challenge from President Sukarno, the strongman who had driven the Dutch out of the Dutch East Indies, proclaimed independence for Indonesia, and run the tropical archipelago ever since. Like other Asian leaders of the postwar era, Sukarno was an authoritarian. "Volatile" was the adjective most often used to describe him. He was also wily, corrupt, and bawdy; Jackie called him "a bandit" and David Bruce called him "a bastard," and Bobby said that his brother "hated" Sukarno (though JFK showed no such antipathy.) At a time when the United States was trying to prevent the spread of Communism, Indonesia was important both because it was in Asia and because it was unattached to either ideological camp. In fact, it was a founding member of the Non-Aligned Movement, which was conceived at a conference in Bandung, West Java, in 1955. Indonesia had huge mineral resources and great potential but was riven with ethnic conflict.

Kennedy was fascinated by Sukarno and assiduously courted him. In 1961, he had invited him to make a state visit to the United States. The Kennedys received him at the White House and asked him upstairs for a drink in the Yellow Oval Room before dinner, as they sometimes did. This gesture gave foreign leaders a sense of privileged access, even intimacy, before a state occasion. Hearing that Sukarno was a collector of art, Jackie asked the State Department to send her a catalogue of his collection, which she placed strategically on the coffee table in the living room. When

Sukarno entered, she pointed to the volume and the three sat on the couch – Jack and Jackie on either side of Sukarno – and leafed through the folio. Jackie had not previously looked at it. To her astonishment, she saw page after page of baroque pin-ups of semi-clad women. It reminded her of the contemporary "Vargas girls" painted for *Playboy* and *Esquire* by Alberto Vargas, the popular Peruvian illustrator. "Every single one was naked to the waist, with a hibiscus in her hair," she exclaimed. "You just couldn't believe it, and I caught Jack's eye and we were trying not to laugh at each other." Sukarno kept up a lively commentary. "This is my second wife," he would say (in due course he had eight) and "this was someone else." His "lecherous look" annoyed Jackie and amused Jack.

In the spring of 1963, Sukarno's regime had told Caltex and Stanvac, two American oil companies operating in Indonesia, that it wanted to acquire their refining and distribution facilities. With their contracts running out, the companies were threatening to leave; as of June 15, they were going to order their tankers to bypass Jakarta. There had been a stalemate between the regime and the companies since 1961. Negotiations had failed. Now, given a choice between operating under conditions imposed by the Indonesian government and pulling out entirely, they were going to decamp. The administration worried that the departure of the oil firms from Indonesia, which could not produce or refine oil on its own, would invite economic chaos. The Chinese would rush in and draw Indonesia into the Communist bloc. In search of a solution, the oil executives had appealed to Harriman. While it struck him initially as special pleading, he soon saw their point and took it to Kennedy. Knowing Sukarno, who called JFK "his dearest and best friend," Kennedy thought some creative diplomacy could persuade him to come to terms that would satisfy both parties.

In early June, Sukarno was visiting Tokyo on an extended tour of Asia and Europe. "This is the time to get him," Kennedy said. "Get him in Tokyo while he is having fun; and get him while he is away from his Communist ministers or Communist sympathizing ministers. Let's send somebody out." They agreed that Wyatt, an able politician Kennedy much admired, was "ideal" to name as his personal envoy to Sukarno. Levy, who had advised Harriman twelve years before during his critical intervention in the Iranian oil crisis, would accompany Wyatt. Chayes, an authority on international law as well as departmental procedures and protocol, would go as Wyatt's counsel. But the mission had to be kept confidential. If the Communists in Indonesia (the largest party outside the Soviet Union and China) found out about the American overture, they would try to sabotage it.

First, though, there were matters of protocol. After he met Wyatt and others in the Oval Office on May 18 to discuss the mission, Kennedy asked Michael Forrestal, his Asian specialist, "My God, what am I going to give Sukarno?" He'd already given him books, but he was running out of ideas for something personal. He went into his library and the first book he saw was the collected speeches of Richard Nixon. Eventually, he decided on a collection of his own speeches. He wrote an inscription likening Indonesia to the United States in 1800, saying that it was capable of great things under inspired leadership. The book, edited by Sorensen, was *To Turn the Tide*. Kennedy thought the title appropriate because Sukarno had "turned the tide" in Indonesia. (Kennedy could not give him *Profiles in Courage*, Wyatt remembered, because Bobby had given it to Sukarno on an earlier trip and Sukarno had not liked Bobby. Apparently JFK was untroubled that Sukarno would now have two of his books, as if there was nothing else in the world to give him.) Wyatt would also carry a personal letter from Kennedy to Sukarno expressing his interest in coming to Indonesia when he visited Asia the following year. Eisenhower had bypassed Indonesia on his visit to the region, which offended the proud Sukarno. There was one last thing to charm Indonesia's "President for Life": Wyatt would carry the title "presidential emissary." It was superior to "ambassador," rarely used, and much respected in the developing world.

So, armed with the title, the letter, the book, and a thick intelligence file on Sukarno, Wyatt and company left for Tokyo in late May. From Harriman, some parting words: "Wilson, for the sake of our country, this mission must succeed. I don't know how it can be done. But you know how to use presidential power – and that's what it will take." Wyatt took the advice and the challenge seriously. He prepared carefully for his meeting with Sukarno, who held the key to a successful negotiation.

Much depended on the letter Wyatt brought from the president. In it, Kennedy said the United States could play "a useful role in supporting the vigorous efforts you are making in building the Indonesian Nation, so that it may fully and independently play its important role on the world stage. I have watched with respect and hope the manner in which you have been leading your country in recent weeks to grapple with the problems of its internal economy." Kennedy was flattering Sukarno, who presided over a stunning archipelago stretching three thousand miles from the Indian Ocean to the South Pacific. He was addressing the revolutionary who had wrested this colony from the Dutch and made himself ruler of 100 million people, the world's fifth most populous country in 1963. Kennedy was romancing him. That he was an authoritarian, that he was a plutocrat, that he was a jailor and murderer – no matter. This was the Cold War.

Kennedy concluded his letter with a personal appeal: "Aside from these weightier affairs, Mr. Wyatt has a personal matter to discuss with you on my behalf." When Wyatt told Sukarno of Kennedy's hopes to visit Indonesia, he lit up. The president would have to come for "two weeks," so Sukarno could show him his country – Bali, Sumatra, and Jakarta, of course, where millions would greet him in the streets of the capital, "more people than he has ever seen before!"

Kennedy's charm offensive worked. In three days of intense discussion, Wyatt reached an agreement. The Indonesians got the oil pumps and some facilities with fair compensation; the oil companies got exploratory, development, and export rights for thirty years. The meeting with Kennedy on Tuesday, June 11, postponed from the week before, would allow the president to thank Wyatt and the others personally and present them with formal letters of gratitude. The White House photographer was called in. Kennedy was in his rocking chair, as usual, talking to his guests seated on the couch.

Forrestal, a lawyer in New York whom Kennedy had recruited the year before to join the National Security Council, had promised Wyatt and the others they would see the president. "They all did an extraordinary job," he wrote Kenneth O'Donnell on June 5. "Indeed, I think that perhaps this was the smoothest and quickest bit of preventive diplomacy that I have seen since coming down here. It is something which the Administration can boast about after a few months have passed." Forrestal said that Wyatt "proved himself to be an extremely skillful team leader, courteous, good-humored and sensitive to the peculiarities of Sukarno – but tough. Walter Levy did a masterful job explaining the intricacies of the oil business to the Indonesians, and some of the more outrageous demands of the oil companies to their own executives. In short, he softened up both sides without getting himself in between them."

The agreement in hand, Kennedy hoped that another personal appeal to Indonesia might be a way to recast the Cold War, which was in the forefront of his thoughts. On November 19, three days before Dallas, he summoned his Asia hands to the White House to discuss visiting Indonesia in 1964. As he ran for re-election, he hoped to impress the folks back home with "a hell of a reception" in Jakarta. He knew that his accommodating friend would see to that.

✳

The meeting on Indonesia ended at 4:17 p.m. Thirty-three minutes later, at 4:50 p.m., Kennedy met Edward R. Murrow, director of the United States Information Agency. Of the four meetings that afternoon, this was the only one that was "off the record," which meant little if there were no minutes of meetings in the Oval Office anyway. Most likely, Kennedy had found time on this, the busiest of days, as events were cresting in Tuscaloosa, to ask how the civil rights movement was being seen around the world. At the same time, he may have wanted to know how the agency, the propaganda arm of the government, was playing it. (Years later Tom Sorensen noted angrily that Voice of America "kissed off the Peace Speech" by not making it the lead story on its newscast that day and not giving it much prominence. "It didn't have impact," he said of how it was handled by the USIA. "We didn't do our job. I raised holy hell.") Kennedy may have discussed the prospect of broadcasting his anticipated (though not yet confirmed) civil rights speech on Voice of America, which had been the purpose of Tom's phone call to his brother that afternoon. Or, given Kennedy's curiosity, the president might simply have enjoyed thirty-five minutes of palaver with one of the most interesting people in America.

Before Murrow joined the administration in 1961, he was the foremost broadcaster of his generation. He had had a brilliant career in journalism. As the trusted voice of CBS Radio in Europe before and during the Second World War, he had pioneered broadcast reporting. His nightly reports from Britain attracted millions of listeners in the United States and Canada. He opened every broadcast with the distinctive "This is London," and closed it with his distinctive "Good night, and good luck." Murrow flew on American bombers over Germany and reported the liberation of Buchenwald. After the war, he briefly served as vice president of CBS, director for news and public affairs, before returning to radio broadcasting and news analysis. Between 1951 and 1958, he hosted a television newsmagazine and documentary program called *See*

It Now. Among his guests in 1956 was a shy, conflicted Jacqueline Kennedy who, when asked innocently whether she loved her husband, replied ambiguously. Murrow courageously took on Joe McCarthy, and later the management of CBS, who had challenged his independence. He became an early critic of television for its emphasis on entertainment. In 1960, as his career in broadcasting was coming to an end, he made one last documentary, *Harvest of Shame*, examining the lives of migrant agricultural workers in the United States.

In 1961, Murrow was unhappy at CBS. When Kennedy offered him the directorship of the USIA shortly after taking office, Murrow accepted. He, Adlai Stevenson, and Harriman were the stalwarts of Kennedy's so-called "Ministry of Talent." Washington was a small world. As Murrow entered the Oval Office on the afternoon of June 11, Harriman was just leaving. Both men had had passionate affairs with the same woman – Pamela Digby Churchill – during the war in London. In 1971, Harriman would marry her.

Joining the government was an adjustment for Murrow; the observer was now the participant. When he took the job, he asked to be in on the decisions, and he was. "If you want me on the landings, I have to be on the takeoffs," he told JFK. His tenure was turbulent. Among his first mistakes was asking the BBC not to broadcast *Harvest of Shame* because it embarrassed some farm-state congressmen. He later called his request "foolish and futile." However, in other areas he claimed small victories. He learned to fight Congress for more money for his agency and win. He opposed resuming atmospheric testing in 1961, warning that it would "destroy the advantages of the greatest propaganda gift we have had for a long time. At present, the Soviet decision is causing the Communists great trouble everywhere in the world. It is cutting the legs off the Ban-the-Bomb movements. We have a great asset here which we will waste if we move too quickly." Kennedy delayed tests for several months, and the USIA made the most of Soviet testing.

The president and his brother liked the restrained former broad-caster. "Ed Murrow never spoke, you know, at meetings unless he had something to say," observed RFK. "When he said something, it always made sense. He was damn good."

By the summer of 1962, Murrow wasn't well. A notorious chain-smoker (some sixty cigarettes a day), he had pneumonia during the Cuban Missile Crisis and underwent two lung cancer operations in 1963. On the afternoon of June 11, Kennedy saw a dying man, which isn't to say that JFK did not appreciate a lively chat with him. When Murrow died at fifty-seven years old in 1965, his former col-league and commentator Eric Sevareid called him "a shooting star . . . we will live in his afterglow a very long time."

✳

It was now 5:25 p.m. In ten minutes, George Wallace would walk away from the schoolhouse door in Tuscaloosa (where it was 3:25 p.m.). In fifteen minutes, the students would register. In the half hour between Kennedy's last appointment and his next one, he would decide to go on television and put Sorensen to work on the civil rights speech. He would talk to Bobby, again. As typewriters clacked and the clock ticked, Kennedy was still shuttling between general business and urgent business. Before he focused on the main event, there were other diversions.

At 5:55 p.m., André Fontaine came calling. Fontaine was a celebrated French journalist and historian. Of all the president's meetings that day, this is the most puzzling. Fontaine had visited Sorensen on Monday in his office; perhaps Sorensen found this astute observer of Europe so compelling that he had asked O'Donnell to squeeze him in. Kennedy might have asked Fontaine about General de Gaulle, always an object of frustration and fas-cination. Kennedy had begun secretly learning French, hoping that he could use it one day with de Gaulle, whom he called a "historic figure" and perhaps "the strangest great man of his time." He might have discussed the Multilateral Force (MLF) and NATO with Fontaine. Or, JFK might have been looking for ideas to include in his upcoming European speeches, which is why he had wanted to send Schlesinger and Sorensen to Europe before his visit there.

Unsurprisingly, Schlesinger found the proposed remarks drafted by the State Department vapid. "These speeches could have been given just as easily by President Eisenhower – or by President Nixon," he wrote Kennedy on June 8. "They fail to convey any sense of a fresh American voice or distinctive Kennedy approach." Schlesinger suggested that the president show Europe that America, after a period of somnolence, was capable again of "innovation and vision." He thought that embracing the MLF would be "an error, whatever the merits of the proposal, partly because your audiences don't understand the MLF and couldn't care less about it . . . and because our position should be one of inviting an Atlantic dialogue rather than insisting on American solutions." Schlesinger added, "The authoritarian paternalism of de Gaulle cannot long satisfy a spirited and intelligent modern people." Most of all, Schlesinger wanted Kennedy in Europe "to convince the Europeans that the United States has a vision of the future which is attractive and convincing and one in which they have a central and strong role."

For Kennedy, Fontaine would have been a good sounding board, as well as a voice of perspective on Europe. In 1965, in his *History of the Cold War*, Fontaine evokes a world on the hinge of history in 1963. When he met Kennedy in the Oval Office that afternoon, he may have found grounds for his developing argument that Kennedy had made a historic appeal the day before and that the Cold War was ending. It did not end, but Fontaine did not revise his view when his book came out in English in 1969. He noted the symmetry between Kennedy's two speeches over two days: "What he asked of his countrymen was they go beyond their prejudices and admit that Russians and Negroes were human beings like themselves, with whom they had to learn to live."

✳

It was now 6:20 p.m. The president was scheduled to speak in one hundred minutes, but he had one more appointment before he could focus on what he would say. At 6:30 p.m., Kennedy met James Webb, head of the National Aeronautics and Space Administration. If Fontaine or Murrow were expansive and diverting company, Webb was windy and tiring. Not that Kennedy could avoid him. Space had become an emblem of the New Frontier since JFK had told a joint session of Congress on May 25, 1961, that "this nation should commit itself to achieving the goal, before this decade is out, of landing a man on the Moon and returning him safely to Earth." Now, two years later, America was on its way to what would become one of Kennedy's seminal achievements, extending well into the next generation. After his historic flight, the laconic Gordon Cooper had returned to a rapturous welcome – an address to both houses of Congress, a televised news conference, a medal in the Rose Garden, drinks with the Kennedys upstairs in the residence, and a visit to Broadway to see the season's appropriately titled musical, *Stop the World – I Want to Get Off*. His achievement in space, like all those missions since 1961, was trumpeted by the administration at home and abroad as proof of the country's vigor. However, Kennedy's commitment to the space program was less about science than politics. Much as he grandiloquently likened modern astronauts to ancient mariners, the president was more interested here in Nikita Khrushchev than Christopher Columbus. In the Cold War, landing a man on the moon was about demonstrating American scientific superiority.

The problem was that a moon shot was expensive – some $35 billion over ten years – and Congress was starting to balk. The

House Select Committee on Astronautics and Space Exploration was threatening to cut $500 million from the administration's 1964 budget request of $5.7 billion for space research and exploration. It was the first time since 1960 that Congress had seriously challenged the program's budget, which was a comparatively paltry $339 million in 1959. At the same time, the Senate space committee was holding hearings on the future of the space program. On Monday, June 10, it had heard testimony from five scientists. Philip H. Abelson, the prominent editor of *Science* magazine, argued that the accelerated pace of the lunar program was hurting national security and delaying more important efforts to conquer cancer and mental illness.

Webb, for his part, argued that this was "a contest with the Soviet Union." It was about patriotism and prestige. In a speech on Sunday, he had said that yielding to the Russians on this field would cost the United States credibility. The opposition in Congress was why he was seeing Kennedy that day. With him was Representative Joseph E. Karth of Minnesota, a supporter of the space program and chairman of one of three subcommittees examining it. (The indispensable Larry O'Brien doesn't appear on the president's official agenda, but his name is penciled in, meaning he was also there.)

Kennedy had appointed Webb in February 1961 on the recommendation of Lyndon Johnson, who had been given responsibility for the space program. Webb, a lawyer and former Marine Corps pilot, had held a string of senior government positions in Washington before returning to private business in Oklahoma. He told Johnson that he didn't want the job, as had nineteen other Americans who had been approached. Webb thought the position should be filled by a scientist or engineer. He was neither. But Webb knew that Kennedy valued his experience. "There are great issues of national and international policy involved in this space program," Webb recalled JFK saying, insisting that this seasoned administrator had the right stuff. "I want you to handle it because those are the policies that interest me in my job as President." Webb could not refuse.

According to Bobby, though, Jack complained "frequently" that, had he known how important NASA would become, he would never have appointed Webb. The agency was relatively small when Webb took over, but within three months, after the Russians went into space, Kennedy accepted Webb's proposal to expand NASA and make the moon its mission. In Bobby's opinion, Webb was "awful . . . talked all the time and was rather a blabbermouth. The President was very dissatisfied with him. . . . The President always disliked people who said in fifty words what they could say in seven words. It made him impatient."

If Kennedy thought Webb a blowhard, he hid it well. In a letter written on June 11, Webb thanked Robert Lewine, president of the National Academy of Television Arts and Sciences, for inviting him to appear on the Emmy Awards. Kennedy happened to be watching, he noted. "You might be interested in knowing that the President called me the next day on another matter," Webb crowed, "but opened the conversation by saying he thought I looked great on TV the night before." Webb had access to the Oval Office. If there was something important to discuss, Webb called Kennedy directly. "He would always answer the phone . . . ," Webb recalled. "I could walk in the White House without an appointment and tell the appointment secretary, 'Slip me in between the next two appointments. I'll just take one minute.' I was not just an administrator of some low level program."

Tuesday was one of those days. Webb and Karth had been penciled in on the typewritten schedule for late afternoon, after Kennedy's meeting with Fontaine. While they would discuss the space program and a big managerial change at NASA, to be announced the following day, there was also the matter of John Glenn's goodwill visit to Japan. Kennedy had been reading the cables from former Harvard professor Edwin Reischauer, the esteemed U.S. ambassador to Japan, who had just hosted Wilson Wyatt. He described the astronaut's warm reception in Tokyo. Although Glenn's trip was paid for by the U.S. government, Kennedy suspected that the cost of bringing along his wife and their children was not. He thought that Glenn, who was also vacationing in Japan after helping on the Cooper flight, should not be out-of-pocket. Webb was to tell Glenn that the president "expressed the desire that I stretch a point from normal practice and reimburse the transportation cost for Mrs. Glenn and your family from Houston to Tokyo and return. . . . Both he and I feel that this is a worthwhile investment, and the effectiveness of your appearances were substantially enhanced by the fact that you were accompanied by your wife and children." And so, on this busiest of days, as his frantic foot soldiers were hurriedly gathering ideas and assembling the words he would speak that evening, here was the chief executive officer addressing a star employee's travel expenses with one of his senior administrators.

Of course, there was more important business to discuss with Webb. One issue was whether Kennedy would get his full budget for the space program. Opposition was growing; in two days, Dwight Eisenhower would tell a Republican breakfast that spending $40 billion (Eisenhower's figure) on a lunar program was "nuts." Despite the threat from Capitol Hill, though, Kennedy was optimistic. On Sunday, Charles Bartlett had written, "There is no sign of a broad disposition to clip the rate of spending that in turn retards the rate of progress toward the Moon." Bartlett, who had spoken to the president several times that day and the day before, would not have made such a prediction in his syndicated column if Kennedy had not been confident that Congress would fully fund his space program.

Webb also wanted to discuss the cancellation of the Mercury manned program, which had sent four astronauts on four separate flights into orbit around the earth. NASA was now moving to another phase, Project Gemini, which would send two-man crews into space, followed by Project Apollo, which would land men on the moon in 1969. Webb planned to make the announcement Wednesday before the Senate committee. The end of Mercury, which was not unexpected, had brought the resignation of the program's director, D. Brainerd Holmes. It would be seen as a rift between Webb and Holmes, who had been with the program for two years. That news would break the following day as well. Webb was there to warn the president. But he would have to be quick and to the point, which wasn't his style. He had twenty minutes.

✳

By 6:50 p.m., Webb and Kennedy were done, and so was the president's afternoon of eclectic appointments. This time of day – late afternoon and early evening – was much favored by acolytes and associates, who found it the most propitious time to have a word with Kennedy. Jerome Wiesner, the science advisor, "always used to peek through his door," said Jackie. "He [JFK] said it used to drive him crazy. Every time the door would be open, Wiesner's head would peek in and out . . . and he'd say, 'All right, come in or else go away,' and it was usually something unimportant." Walt Rostow called it "Liberty Hall," that moment at the end of the working day "to do just as you please," in Oliver Goldsmith's words. "He was unlikely to have appointments then. You had the feeling there were almost an infinite number of doors leading into that office," Rostow said, by-passing the unyielding O'Donnell. In any event, his day was now over.

Since returning to the office just after 4:00 p.m., Kennedy had congratulated his special envoys on their mission to Sukarno, conferred with the director of his propaganda agency, discussed the challenges of contemporary Europe with one of its leading journalists, and addressed the future and the funding of the space program with its director. Other than his meeting with Murrow, none of these conversations over the previous three hours would have helped him collect his thoughts on civil rights. In taking all his appointments, even adding to them, Kennedy seemed undaunted by the looming speech. He was confident that there would be *something* to say in an hour and ten minutes – even if he did not yet know its shape or content. No matter. Sorensen was scribbling away down the hall and Bobby and Burke Marshall were on their way over. In the meantime, with all the time in the world, the president would take a swim.

Tuesday, June 11, 1963

CHAPTER 15

Evening

IT. WAS NOW around 7:00 p.m. Ted Sorensen had been writing for an hour. Burke Marshall and Bobby had said they would send over material from the Justice Department, but it was unclear what. Statistics on black Americans? The draft speech by Richard Yates? No bulging file of presidential remarks on civil rights sat on Sorensen's desk. Then again, as he noted in 1966, the subject was not entirely *terra incognita* for Kennedy. The speech "drew on at least three years of evolution in his thinking, on at least three months of revolution in the equal rights movement, on at least three weeks of meetings in the White House," he wrote in *Kennedy*. There were drafts of a new message to Congress as well as the one in February. There were also the president's remarks to the Conference of Mayors in Hawaii. All would be helpful up to a point. Tonight's address would demand a different approach. The pretext was Tuscaloosa (today's confrontation), the context was Birmingham (the unrest there and elsewhere that spring), and the subtext was Washington (to make the case for legislation). Events would give the speech relevance and form. The melodious Sorensen would give it sense and sound.

Sorensen reached back beyond the past three years to remarks that he had written for Kennedy during the presidential campaign in 1960. But beyond that, he mined his personal involvement in civil rights, which had animated him as an impressionable youth in Nebraska. He recalled some of the themes of a well-received address he gave as a high school student at a public speaking competition at Nebraska Wesleyan University in the early 1940s. "We have said the Negro could study and pray, but not in our schools and not in our churches," he had said. "We have said that he could work, but not through our unions. We have said that he could vote, but warn him away from the polls. We have said he could live but not on our level, and we have said he could be free, and then subjected him to discrimination and poverty . . . [and when] an American soldier on the German Front . . . wounded and decorated, returned home . . . he did not find his American liberties. . . . Why? Because his skin was not white." There were echoes of that speech, which he seemed to recall from memory, in the one Sorensen was writing that evening: "Are we to say . . . that this is a land of the free except for the Negroes; that we have no second class citizens except Negroes; that we have no class or caste system, no ghettos, no master race, except with respect to Negroes? . . . When Americans are sent to Vietnam or West Berlin we do not ask for whites only."

In tone, there are also echoes of the speech written by Yates, even though no one acknowledges referring to the draft he had submitted that morning to the attorney general. Both writers used harsh language. Sorensen noted that phrases in his draft – "the cesspools of discrimination," "a social revolution is at hand," "the pace is shamefully slow" – were all softened. The White House was sensitive to offending the white majority who were unused to hearing hard truths. Yates told Americans they were sick; Sorensen said they were callous. Both assessments were too much for the president, who used gentler language in presenting his legislation and explaining its purpose. Comparing the first and final drafts of the speech in his memoir, Sorensen is defensive about Bobby's insensitive assertion that the version the attorney general saw when he arrived at the White House was "unsatisfactory." Ultimately, Sorensen said his words were changed very little: "My speech was toned down, but its substance remained."

✳

Back at the Justice Department, Bobby was still absorbing what had just happened in Alabama. At 5:40 p.m. – he recorded the precise time – he dashed off a note to his exuberant three-year-old daughter, who had, in her own way, been a part of the day's momentous events:

> Dear Kerry,
>   Thank you for coming to the office this morning. It was an historic day not just because of your visit, but because two negroes over the objection of Governor Wallace were registered at the university – it happened just minutes ago.
>   I hope these events will be long past when you have your pretty little head at college.
>
>   Love and Kisses,
>   Daddy

After completing the note, Bobby began drafting remarks with Burke Marshall. They were an unlikely couple – Marshall so frail, reedy, and self-effacing that when RFK first met him, he refused to hire him because he said they had "nothing in common." He did hire him, and Marshall, Katzenbach and Doar became the paladins of the civil rights movement. Now Robert Drew's cameras find

Marshall sitting at the side of the attorney general's desk, pad and paper in hand, and Bobby in his chair, two lawyers playing with language. Marshall speaks of "the moral issue" that will be the signature of the speech. Whether this term comes from him, or Bobby, or is simply in the air at that moment, is unknown. "We are irrevocably committed . . . morally . . . ethically . . . ," someone intones off camera. The jarring, practical words hang there under the vaulted ceiling. Then, a warning from the same disembodied voice: "There will be a terrific problem getting this through Congress."

Marshall and Kennedy left the Justice Department around 6:45 p.m. for the White House. Bobby invited Greg Shuker and D.A. Pennebaker, who had been filming him since breakfast that morning, to come along. That surprised and delighted them. They had planned to follow RFK back to Hickory Hill at the end of the day. But Bobby knew there would be more action – and better images – at the White House. He also knew that the president would not mind their camera, particularly now, with events going his way. Once again, the Cadillac sweeps through the White House gates. Again, the attorney general opens the door of his behemoth before it stops and darts like a gazelle up the grassy slope toward the mansion. And again, he walks purposefully through the Colonnade directly into the Oval Office.

Bobby recalled later that he, Marshall, Sorensen, and the president gathered in the Cabinet Room to discuss the speech. He says it was around 7:15 p.m. or 7:20 p.m. It may have been later – or earlier – because the Secret Service has JFK leaving his office for the pool at 7:12 p.m. and returning at 7:36 p.m. Whenever they conferred, it was then that Bobby said he found Sorensen's draft unacceptable. It was a stinging judgment – and a little rich, too – given his position. Having urged the president most vociferously to make the speech, having assured him the day before that he had a draft with some serviceable passages, having known that Sorensen would have to write the speech with very little time to do so, he was now saying it wasn't much good. No wonder Sorensen so often bristled.

If the Kennedys reached this conclusion around 7:15 p.m., that meant, at best, that there was still no finished speech some forty-five minutes — or, at worst, just twenty-four minutes — before the president was to go on air. Would he delay or cancel the broadcast? When McGeorge Bundy arrived at Joe Alsop's in Georgetown for dinner, everyone expected to watch the speech at 8:00 p.m. Bundy disappointed them. "There isn't going to be a speech," he announced. "I just left the White House thirty minutes ago, and Sorensen didn't have a draft yet."

No, he didn't. After their meeting in the Cabinet Room, Sorensen took his notes, returned to his office, and turned to his scratch pad for another twenty-five minutes or so. *National Geographic's* creative portrayal finds him at this hour in crisp tie and jacket, working at an immaculate, gleaming mahogany desk, free of paper. He is pecking away on a portable typewriter, its case sitting on the table beside him. Although Sorensen's office was spacious and notably uncluttered, that evening he was writing furiously in rolled shirtsleeves and passing pages to his secretary, Gloria Sitrin, who was typing them as quickly as he could produce them.

Meanwhile, the president, the attorney general, and the assistant attorney general remained in the Cabinet Room, alone, talking. They sat at one end of the table. The president was making notes on sheets of White House notepaper, or as Bobby said, "on the back of an envelope." It was now certain that there would be no complete text; the president would have to improvise at least a part of it. That still didn't seem to bother him or Bobby. Both surely had known when they had decided, impulsively, that the speech would be given that night, obviously not enough time to craft the polished address the occasion demanded. "The speech was good," recalled Bobby. "I think that if he had given it extemporaneously it would have been as good or better." Marshall insists that "it didn't faze him [JFK] a bit" to contemplate going on the air without a full text.

Well, maybe. It is true that, having had those meetings, followed by twenty-four minutes in the pool, Kennedy had left things
to the last moment. It may be that a hanging – or, in this case, a
televised address – concentrates the mind. Perhaps Kennedy had
arranged it that way because he thrived under pressure. After all,
by 1963, he was master of the medium. To the upstart without grey
who had bested Nixon in those critical television debates in 1960,
to the performer who had introduced televised press conferences
and come out smiling, to the historian who had allowed documentary cameras into his office, television was familiar and friendly.

But even Kennedy, the Captain of Cool, was beginning to fret
that evening as airtime approached. If he stammered or stumbled,
if he appeared too hot, he knew that television could undo him.
Sorensen remembered JFK walking the few steps down the corridor to his office a few minutes before 8:00 p.m. to ask about the
speech. That was the only time he did that in the White House.
"'Don't worry,' I replied. 'It's in the typewriter now.' My secretary
was typing up my handwritten draft. 'Oh,' he joked, 'I thought I was
going to have to go off-the-cuff on national television.'"

✳

Ultimately, the writing was Sorensen's. He told Schlesinger afterward that he had written the speech himself and that was true. He
had not used the draft written by Yates. If he had it and read it, he
never acknowledged it. Sorensen's two associates – Lee White and
Mike Feldman – did not help in the drafting. Typically, Sorensen
was doing it himself, though White had been asked to pitch in at
the eleventh hour. Amid the rising anxiety, White received a dis-
tress call from downstairs. "I was not in the President's office when
he made the decision [to give the speech], but I knew about it
quickly, because Kenny O'Donnell called and told me I ought to get
down to Sorensen's office, because Ted had just been given an

almost impossible task to do," said White. "O'Donnell and Sorensen were not the closest of buddies, but Kenny felt that Sorensen was in a tight spot and needed help."

A tight spot and needed help. For the frosty O'Donnell to have summoned White from upstairs to assist the cerebral Sorensen downstairs, there must have been trouble in the throbbing White House literary factory. Now even O'Donnell was nervous. "Of course, two people can't write a speech," recalled White, "especially when Ted was dictating to his secretary . . . and she was typing the copy as he dictated." White described Sorensen's speech as "a powerful start" but coming along slowly at this advanced hour. In his oral history recorded less than a year later, he saw a far more agitated Kennedy than others observed that evening: "The President was extremely nervous. Normally he's not nervous, but he was awfully damn nervous about this one." White suspected Kennedy may even have had last-minute doubts about making the speech: "First of all, he wasn't sure exactly what was going to come out of the typewriter. Second of all, he didn't know whether this was the right thing to do or not. Third of all, he was . . . scrounging around for more information and he remembered he'd read something in the *New York Times* two days before, could we find that? People were flying around trying to get it."

While White had no direct role in the speech, he said that Louis Martin contributed the passages on the plight of black Americans. ("This was Louis Martin's speech," White told Taylor Branch.) If so, in this madcap moment, Martin never claimed authorship and Sorensen never shared it. It begs the question of the other missing voice that day: amid the gathering chaos, where was the graceful pen and eclectic mind of Arthur M. Schlesinger?

※

Ah, Arthur. Bobby said that the president thought his other word-smith was "a little bit of a nut sometimes . . . a sort of a gladfly who was having a helluva good time in Washington . . . who didn't do a lot, but he was good to have around." Christine Camp, the press assistant, called Schlesinger that "egghead in the East." He organized monthly seminars led by a visiting authority at Hickory Hill, where, on another occasion, the bespectacled professor was pushed into the swimming pool fully clothed. Beyond that, Camp wondered what Schlesinger did in the East Wing and whether he overstated his importance in his elegant encomium to JFK, *A Thousand Days*. Schlesinger wondered, too. His duties were unclear and he fretted about it. "I feel that I lack some sort of specific gravity of the kind that is required for effectiveness in government," he told his diary. "I guess I convey an ineradicable impression of dilettantism – partly because I am spread so thin and partly because at bottom I must prefer it that way." Lee White noted that he had no operational responsibility, which meant that Schlesinger "was in the ballpark but he wasn't in the ball game." On Tuesday, Schlesinger was needed. The trouble was that he wasn't in the ballpark or anywhere near it. He was attending his twenty-fifth class reunion at Harvard College. Before leaving for Cambridge on Saturday, he had prudently left a note for Mrs. Lincoln to pass on to the president. "Gretchen [Schlesinger's secretary] will know how to get hold of me," he wrote, "and I will, of course, be glad to come back at a moment's notice if I can be of any use in Washington."

This was that moment. But no one could find him. His whereabouts defeated even the crack White House telephone operators, whom Kennedy said he would miss most after leaving the presidency. The time was now 7:00 p.m., the interlude between Kennedy's last meeting with Webb and his evening swim. Schlesinger was supposed to be with the Class of '38 attending a concert of the Boston Pops at Symphony Hall. His classmates had included Joseph P. Kennedy Jr., Jack's older brother, a Navy flier killed in the Second

World War; Richard Tregaskis, the war correspondent, author, and novelist; and Teddy White, the journalist and author. Schlesinger and White had gone to the home of J. John Fox, a friend and Boston politico, for a leisurely drink. They had passed on Arthur Fiedler, the popular conductor, and his light classical repertoire. That night the orchestra was playing music adapted from *Raintree County*, a Civil War film starring Elizabeth Taylor and Montgomery Clift, released in 1957.

Schlesinger and his classmates weren't interested in hearing Fiedler's arrangement of the movie score. Instead, he, White, and Fox planned to watch the president's speech on television. Later, rejoining his class, Schlesinger reported that "several people said to me that I had been publicly paged at Symphony Hall." Imagine the comical scene under the coffered ceiling on Massachusetts Avenue that evening as the Boston Pops serenaded the assembled alumni. Between the strains of "The Swamp" and "Cousin Bob's Plantation" comes an announcement over the public address system. It has rich resonance in a concert hall noted for its acoustics. Imagine the harried appeal: *"Attention Mr. Schlesinger! Attention Mr. Schlesinger! Urgent message from the White House. Call the President!"* "At first, I thought it was a joke," recalled Schlesinger, "but it became evident that something had happened."

Word must have reached him somewhere because Schlesinger did call the White House at 7:55 p.m. It was too late. Returning later that evening to Winthrop House, where he was staying, Schlesinger said he found a message asking him to call the president. He learned from Mrs. Lincoln the next morning that Kennedy's call was about the speech. "I suppose that, at the peak of uncertainty, he was collecting opinions as to what he should do," Schlesinger told his diary. "Anyway, it came out right." Yet it nearly didn't. The making of the speech was less symphonic than operatic. No wonder, in that last hour or so, at that peak of uncertainty, the president was looking for help.

＊

Minutes before airtime, the Oval Office was laced with cable and filled with bulky square television cameras on wheels or double-humped newsreel cameras on tripods, looking as regal as camels. Hugh Sidey, the *Time* correspondent, described "a scene of confusion" as Kennedy entered the room to test the cameras. "The monitor is all right," he said, looking at the test picture. "But the camera ought to be brought up." Technicians scrambled to adjust the image. Kennedy scrambled to adjust the text.

While the position of the television cameras was being fixed in his warm, floodlit office, he was in the Cabinet Room now "quietly going frantic," as White put it. At 7:55 p.m., the president still did not have Sorensen's text. His secretary was still typing. Kennedy appealed to Burke Marshall: "'Come on now, Burke, you must have some ideas.' But he [JFK] knew what he was going to say, and I guess it didn't make much difference whether it was typed or not." Kennedy had no speech, because Sorensen was working on the text up to 7:56 p.m., four minutes before airtime. The delay cost Sorensen his peroration, which was supplanted by what Jack and Bobby had been discussing in the previous twenty-five minutes in the Cabinet Room while Sorensen was blackening pages in his office. It also meant that Kennedy would, in fact, give part of the speech extemporaneously. That worried both the brothers more than they had let on earlier. Marshall observed: "Even the Attorney General, who's not bothered by many things, was shaken by the President not having his prepared text."

When the text did arrive, Kennedy had no more than two minutes to look it over. It was a jumble of fragments and different pieces of paper; he made changes in pen, striking words, adding others. Kennedy was already seated at his desk, cleared of objects including his telephone console, the cameras waiting. White and others remember the pages flying out of Sitrin's typewriter in Sorensen's office. They were "shuttled over to the President as he prepared to go on air." In some accounts of this *opéra bouffe*, pages continued to arrive even after he began speaking (though this is not evident from the telecast).

"Three minutes," said a technician, as Kennedy settled into a pillow on his chair and looked over the text he would place on a shallow lectern. He did not use a teleprompter. From the doorway of the office, Andy Hatcher, acting for Salinger, looked on.

"Thirty seconds."

"There was silence," recalled Sidey. "The President's nervous fingers played with the sheets of his speech text."

"Stand by, Mr. President."

"Kennedy's shoulders moved a few inches forward and his eyes narrowed a bit," said Sidey.

This was it, script or not. The red light went on.

"Good evening, my fellow citizens . . ."

✵

The events in Tuscaloosa gave the speech its *raison d'être*. Kennedy mentioned what had happened that day right off the top – without once referring to Wallace. He also mentioned, four times in his opening paragraph, that it was guardsmen from *Alabama*, acting on the orders of a judge in *Alabama*, ensuring that two qualified students living in *Alabama* could go to the University of *Alabama*. The point was to play down the federal government's intervention. This was a state institution petitioned by its own residents, supported by federal power but integrated, in the end, by Alabamans for Alabamans. The speech also praised the student body for acting "peacefully" (in subtle contrast to their riotous counterparts at Ole Miss the previous autumn).

Then, the first of tonight's stirring appeals from the president: "I hope that every American, regardless of where he lives, will stop and examine his conscience about this and other related incidents. This Nation was founded by men of many nations and backgrounds. It was founded on the principle that all men are created equal, and that the rights of every man are diminished when the rights of one man are threatened.

"Today we are committed to a worldwide struggle to promote and protect the rights of all who wish to be free. And when Americans are sent to Viet-Nam or West Berlin, we do not ask for whites only. It ought to be possible, therefore, for American students of any color to attend any public institution they select without having to be backed up by troops."

Here Kennedy was affirming what he had said the day before at American University: that "peace and freedom walk together." He was linking Vietnam – where, he had been shocked that morning to learn, a Buddhist had set himself on fire in the name of religious freedom – to the struggle for equal rights at home. If the United States was supporting freedom in the hamlets of Indochina and the cities of Eastern Europe, it must do the same at home. It must show the same will in Birmingham as it did Berlin.

And what would that freedom be? Why, quite explicitly, the right of black Americans to stay in hotels, eat in restaurants, shop in stores, and sit in theaters, without having to march in the streets. The right to register and vote in elections without obstruction or intimidation. "It ought to be possible, in short, for every American to enjoy the privileges of being American without regard to his race or his color. In short, every American ought to have the right to be treated as he would wish to be treated, as one would wish his children to be treated. But this is not the case." It *ought* to be possible, Kennedy was saying, to imagine a fairer country. He had used "ought" that morning in appealing to the Republicans, and he was using it repeatedly that night in appealing to Americans. *Ought* was a nice and versatile word, at once suggestive and prescriptive. If "ought" (persuasion) failed in bringing about social change, the government would turn to "must" (compulsion). In a sense it already was, in proposing legislation.

Kennedy, echoing Sorensen and Yates, then painted a stark statistical portrait of the prospects of a "Negro" born in America in 1963: half as much chance of finishing high school, one third as much chance of completing college, one third as much chance of becoming a professional, twice as much chance of becoming unemployed, one seventh as much chance of earning $10,000 a year, a life expectancy seven years shorter.

He emphasized that civil rights was not a sectional issue. There was segregation everywhere in America and, as such, Americans should not see it in narrow, confined political terms. It was universal. Nor was it a partisan issue. There was prejudice within both parties. "In a time of domestic crisis," men of goodwill should be able to overcome politics. It wasn't a legal or legislative issue alone either; "law alone cannot make men see right." Here, three minutes into his speech, Kennedy was positioning himself to say what no president had said before. He would challenge the fundamental assumption of the relationship between black Americans and white Americans.

"We are confronted primarily with a moral issue," Kennedy said. "It is as old as the scriptures and is as clear as the American Constitution." By now, the "morality" of race was no longer an abstraction. It began coming up in the national conversation in May, in remarks that the president thought he might have to give after the violence in Birmingham. Morality was in his speech in Hawaii. Morality was in Johnson's memo (though not in his memorable remarks at Gettysburg on May 30). Morality was in the draft of the speech written by Yates. Morality was in Martin Luther King Jr.'s stinging critique of Kennedy in Monday's *New York Times*.

"The heart of the question is whether all Americans are to be afforded equal rights and equal opportunities, whether we are going to treat our fellow Americans as we want to be treated. If an

American, because his skin is dark, cannot eat lunch in a restaurant open to the public, if he cannot send his children to the best public school available, if he cannot vote for the public officials who represent him, if, in short, he cannot enjoy the full and free life which all of us want, then who among us would be content to have the color of his skin changed and stand in his place? Who among us would then be content with the counsels of patience and delay?"

Having framed the moral issue, Kennedy was asking Americans a moral question. It was simple: if you were black, instead of white, would you be satisfied with the status quo? Would you accept the gradualism and incrementalism and promise of change? Of course not.

It had been a hundred years since Abraham Lincoln freed the slaves, Kennedy said, but their grandsons were not fully free. They suffer "social and economic oppression." Which is why "this Nation, for all its hopes and all its boasts, will not be fully free until all its citizens are free." He went on: "We preach freedom around the world, and we mean it, and we cherish our freedom here at home, but are we to say to the world, and much more importantly, to each other that this is a land of the free except for the Negroes; that we have no second-class citizens except Negroes; that we have no class or caste system, no ghettoes, no master race except with respect to Negroes?"

Kennedy was not finished making his case. "Now the time has come for this Nation to fulfill its promise. The events in Birmingham and elsewhere have so increased the cries for equality that no city or State or legislative body can prudently choose to ignore them." He had to persuade Americans that the problem was acute, that it wasn't going away, that it was going to get worse if the nation did not respond. It would tear apart the whole country, not just the South. "The fires of frustration and discord are burning in every city, North and South, where legal remedies are not at hand," he warned. "Redress is sought in the streets, in demonstrations, parades, and protests, which create tensions and threaten violence and threaten lives."

Then, once again, he returned to the big question: "We face, therefore, a moral crisis as a country and as a people. It cannot be met by repressive police action. It cannot be left to increased demonstrations in the streets. It cannot be quieted by token moves or talk. It is a time to act in the Congress, in your State and local legislative body and, above all, in all of our daily lives."

It wasn't enough, said Kennedy, to blame others. Or to say this was a problem of one region. "A great change is at hand, and our task, our obligation, is to make that revolution, that change, peaceful and constructive for all." Here he was acknowledging the new order remaking the country and inviting Americans to shape it. To do nothing was to invite shame as well as violence.

Kennedy was midway through his remarks. He had addressed the condition of black Americans and laid the responsibility on all Americans. He had done it with numbers, words, and example. He had said the country was burning and the fire was spreading. This was the context for what was to follow. Afterward, Eugene Rostow, the acerbic brother of Walt Rostow, told Schlesinger that Kennedy looked "sullen" giving the speech. If so, it was because the subject was grave. Kennedy was telling home truths rinsed of Yates's revulsion. He wasn't doing it as graphically as Yates, in that unsparing language, but was there any way to make a nation's moral failure a success? Schlesinger, for his part, had never seen the president "so personally engaged." This came from the heart.

Kennedy had defined the problem. Now he offered a solution. Next week he would ask Congress "to act, to make a commitment it has not fully made in this century to the proposition that race has no place in American life or law." The judiciary was already doing this in its rulings, he said. The federal government was already doing this, he noted, in hiring black men and women, bringing integration to federal facilities, and selling federally financed housing.

But now Congress had to act – or face demonstrations in the streets. So Kennedy announced that he would send Congress legislation – the bill he had decided to unveil at that meeting on June 1 – to ensure that all Americans were served in hotels, restaurants, theaters, stores, and other commercial establishments. He would seek more lawsuits to end segregation in public education. He would seek greater protection for the right to vote.

"But legislation, I repeat, cannot solve this problem alone," he warned. "It must be solved in the homes of every American in every community across our country." He lauded Americans who were trying to make life better for all, comparing them to the country's soldiers and sailors who were "meeting freedom's challenge on the firing line; and I salute them for their honor and their courage." Here Sorensen's text ends with one closing paragraph.

Kennedy had spoken for eleven minutes and fourteen seconds. He always favored brevity in speeches, but he knew if this one was too brief, it might be dismissed as light and frothy. So Kennedy ignored Sorensen's ending and kept talking. Now he was winging it. He would extemporize for the next two minutes and ten seconds. The tone of the speech changed, as did the rhythm. A telltale sign of the break in the text came when Kennedy put down the pages and folded his hands on the desk before him, then later, clasped them, before jabbing the air with his forefinger. Afterwards, when White told Sorensen that "'no one would know where his words stopped and President Kennedy's took over,' he replied: 'That's not right.' Of course, Ted was right: both he and the President knew." And we do, too, which isn't to say that viewers that evening.

Improvisation brought risks. One was repetition. Kennedy maintained, once again, that this was an American problem, not a southern problem. "This is one country," he said. "It has become one country because all of us and all the people who came here had an equal chance to develop their talents." Kennedy was making it up as he went along. He warned, once more, of an impassive country forcing frustrated black Americans into the streets to demand their rights. And then, as if he were Uncle Sam recruiting an army of the conscientious, Kennedy made another appeal: "Therefore, I am asking for your help in making it easier for us to move ahead and to provide the kind of equality of treatment which we would want ourselves; to give a chance for every child to be educated to the limit of his talents." (The next day, an editorial cartoon in the *Hartford Courant* showed JFK after his civil rights speech, a finger pointed at the audience while declaring, "And I Do Mean You!")

Kennedy continued: "As I have said before, not every child has an equal talent or an equal ability or an equal motivation, but they should have the equal right to develop their talent and their ability and their motivation, to make something of themselves.

"We have a right to expect that the Negro community will be responsible, will uphold the law, but they have a right to expect that the law will be fair, that the Constitution will be color blind, as Justice Harlan said at the turn of the century.

"This is what we are talking about and this is a matter which concerns this country and what it stands for, and in meeting it I ask the support of all our citizens.

"Thank you very much."

※

It was now almost 8:14 p.m. Kennedy had spoken for thirteen minutes and twenty-four seconds. He had changed little in Sorensen's second draft, though he had dropped the ending and substituted his own. "My fellow Americans – we can no longer afford the luxury of bigotry and racial intolerance," Sorensen had written. "This is one nation. We are one people. We have one cause – the cause of liberty for all. Let us live up to that cause in our public action and in our private lives, in our every word and deed, in the months ahead and in all the years to come. With God's help, that cause will succeed."

Instead, JFK spoke the last eight paragraphs off-the-cuff. Lee White found that "was probably the most moving part of the whole thing." Had Kennedy stopped earlier, where Sorensen had, he would have lost little. Was it useful to say that not all children have equal talent, which he'd said before, as recently as Hawaii? Or, that the black community should be "responsible," a call for restraint amid the fire hoses and the dogs? Of course, it didn't matter either way. The speech was a triumph. These were words written in haste, for the ages. It was a knock-down, flat-out masterpiece.

In less than a quarter hour, Kennedy had addressed race a century after Lincoln, in a voice worthy of Lincoln. In a short, pithy address, he had redefined the debate, reshaped his position, realigned the presidency – all in the cause of civil rights. He had done on this night what he had done the morning before: he had seized the bully pulpit and used it to appeal to Americans. In a conversation the year before, Kennedy had told Schlesinger that he thought more highly of American presidents "of concrete achievement rather than political education. People who educate the nation, without achieving all their goals . . . evidently seem to him to rate under people with a record of practical accomplishment . . . even if they do little to transform the intellectual climate of the nation," Schlesinger wrote. That day and the day before, this president had educated the nation. Now he had to achieve some practical goals.

He had taken Governor Wallace's spectacle, wrapped it in the folds of an accelerating social and political movement, and used it to advance his legislative agenda. The civil rights speech was not simply a moment in great rhetoric. It was the moment that a president pivoted. Kennedy was moving from detachment to engagement, from being a transactional president – as political scientists would classify leadership of a certain type a half century later – to a transformative one. No, it couldn't be about talk alone. Ole Miss had taught him those limits. To make his rhetoric real and his commitment whole, he knew he had to throw himself into the legislation. He would.

The address over, Kennedy waded through the forest of coiled wires and thick cables and went upstairs. He arrived at 8:19 p.m. He would not be alone that evening. Caroline and John were back, with Jackie. They had left the White House at 4:35 p.m. and returned at 7:40 p.m., which would not have been a good time to visit Daddy in his office. While the president sat down to dinner, the country digested his address.

＊

Martin Luther King Jr. was watching the president's speech with Reverend Walter Fauntroy, one of his closest associates. When Kennedy finished, King leapt to his feet and cried, "Walter, can you believe that white man not only stepped up to the plate, he hit it over the fence!" King was staggered by the president's words. He dashed off a rhapsodic wire to Kennedy. "I have just listened to your speech to the nation," he wrote. "It was one of the most eloquent[,] profound and unequiv[ocal] pleas for justice and freedom of all men ever made by any President. You spoke passionately for moral issues involved in the integration struggle." King thought the same in 1964. In his oral history for the Kennedy Library, he praised the speech using the same words.

King's elation was shared by other black leaders, who felt that the march on Washington, which they had been planning for August, should now target Congress rather than the administration. "This was the message I had waited to hear from him," said Roy Wilkins, executive secretary of the NAACP. "I fell asleep that night feeling new confidence. For the first time in years, a real change seemed to be at hand."

In Congress, the reaction was predictably mixed. The Southerners loathed the speech. Senator John Stennis of Mississippi, one of the harshest segregationists, said the proposals "are clearly unconstitutional and would open the door for police control of employment and personal associations in almost every field. These bills will be fought to the limit and their invalidity exposed." George Smathers, Kennedy's old friend (a relationship Schlesinger could never fathom), doubted that a bill was necessary. "I could agree with almost everything the President said, but I don't really believe we need additional legislation. There are plenty of laws on the statute books, and the way the courts have been operating, there is no need of additional legislation to give the Negro his every right." His colleague from Louisiana, Allen Ellender, predicted that Kennedy's proposals "will mean violence. He has all the laws on the statute books now if he wants to use them, but he seems instead to want to follow the advice of Negro leaders and agitators." But while the Southerners opposed the bill, there were many moderate voices, particularly among Republicans. Everett Dirksen and Thomas Kuchel, who had seen Kennedy that morning, were open to his change. Kuchel said: "Neither caste nor creed have any part in our American system. If the President maintains vigorous leadership, all Americans and Congress will follow." Senator Jacob Javits of New York, a liberal Republican in a party that still accommodated liberals, supported Kennedy, but regretted that it had been a long time coming: "Better late than never," he concluded.

Some observers saw the importance of the address immediately, as they had the Peace Speech. "His speech . . . will surely rank as one of the landmark public documents," said the *Courier-Journal* of Louisville, Kentucky. "No Chief Executive before him has spoken out as unequivocally on racial segregation." Said the *St. Louis Post-Dispatch*: "President Kennedy's moving appeal to the conscience of America should be regarded as one of the major achievements of the civil rights struggle."

Other newspapers had words of muted praise, though not the *Wall Street Journal*, one of Kennedy's reliable critics. Lamenting

"The Maligned Majority," it said Kennedy had left the impression that "90 percent of the American people are engaged in a bitter and unremitting oppression of the other 10 percent." It chastised his use of expressions like "the caste system," "ghettos," and "master race" and regretted that he had not presented "a more careful and rounded picture." That did a disservice to black Americans, who it said had made great strides, and to the government, which was trying to integrate itself. And what about America's image in the world? "What is anyone to think when the nation's highest voice speaks of the conditions of Negroes as little more than slavery?" As the voice of moderate (not southern) conservatives in 1963, the *Journal* argued that "the President should have made a strong appeal to all groups for moderation and adherence to the law." It argued that the United States had assimilated many ethnic and cultural strains. "The conditions are not so grievous that the whole nation must be worked into a frenzy which can aggravate tensions," it cautioned. "And in order to improve the conditions of an aspiring minority, it should not be necessary to malign the good motives and continuing efforts of the majority." The *Journal*'s reaction showed why Kennedy would not have used the speech written by Yates which spoke of enslavement.

The thousand or so telegrams arriving at the White House that night ran two-to-one in favor of the speech. Not surprisingly, the ones from the South were unfriendly. "You should marry a Negro," advised one. "Go down and live with your friends," suggested another. One offered a juvenile assessment of the governor versus the president: "Wallace is taller than you are."

And what of Kennedy's brain trust? What did they think of the speech? Sorensen, reflecting in 2009, thought, "It had turned out fine." Schlesinger, in Boston that night in 1963, said, "It came out right." That's all? Sorensen was proud of his work, which he called among "his three most important speeches, in terms of concrete impact and consequences." In his diary of June 16, 1963, Schlesinger likened the activism of the spring of 1963 to the labor unrest of the summer of 1937. "Characteristically, one began with 'sit-downs,' and the other began with 'sit-ins.' In each case, ordinary people took things into their own hands, asserted their rights, and out-stripped not only the government but their own organizations. FDR responded by pronouncing a curse on both houses; JFK, in a more clear-cut case, responded by giving [on June 11] what I would regard as the best speech in his administration." (Mysteriously, in his abridged diary edited by his sons and published in 2007, Schlesinger qualifies his praise. There, he calls it "the best speech in his admin-istration *on civil rights*.") There is no doubt, though, that Schlesinger's original assessment reflected his sentiments. In a letter to historian Nathan I. Huggins a week after Kennedy's June 11 address, Schlesinger called it "the best speech of his Administration so far; and I have never heard him deliver anything with more intensity of conviction."

✳

Upstairs, Kennedy was on the telephone. G. Mennen "Soapy" Williams of the State Department, Secretary of the Army Cyrus Vance, General Creighton Abrams, House Speaker John McCormack, and Charles Bartlett, again, His brother-in-law Peter Lawford, the actor who lived in Beverly Hills, California, had called. So had Chuck Spalding, Kennedy's good friend from Pound Ridge, New York. And, of course, there were calls from Bobby, who had returned to the Justice Department after the speech; he telephoned his brother at 8:40 p.m. and again at 9:10 p.m.

Shuker and Pennebaker, having shadowed Bobby with their cameras at the White House, did not film the president's speech in the Oval Office. Instead, in Drew's documentary, Kennedy appears on the small screen. The viewer sees him as the country does. The filmmakers returned to the Justice Department with RFK.

In the back of the limousine, the cameras rolling, Shuker cannot resist. He breaks his own rule in making their unscripted documentary. He asks Bobby a question.

Shuker: "Were you worried [about Wallace]?"

RFK: "Yes, how did you know I was? How could you tell if I didn't show it?"

Shuker: "Well, I think I know you well enough. Those last few minutes, before 10:30 a.m. . . . ."

Bobby and Marshall return to the office. "See you tomorrow," says Bobby, as they part in the corridor. They had been together for days. Now, the battle over, there is no visible relief or show of emotion. No champagne, no toasts. No whoops or cheers. RFK goes up the stairs, alone. The empty hallway is littered with paper, left by the reporters who had been camped out there during the showdown in Tuscaloosa.

At his desk, Bobby is on the phone to JFK again: "I thought you might want to call General Abrams. He did a great job. And Cy Vance . . . Everyone is very excited about the speech."

Bobby himself calls General Abrams: "You did a great job. Damn good. Pleasure working with you." He asks Abrams to thank John Doar, who works for RFK, and "others down there."

Then Bobby is on the phone with Teddy, his younger brother. Bobby is in high spirits: "I think it went well, didn't you? We didn't have to arrest the Governor. What did you think of Jack's speech? We had a big argument over when to do it."

Then he talks to Ethel about dinner plans. "Aren't you excited?" he asks, not entirely sure that she is.

Again, Shuker is emboldened to ask RFK a direct question. "How do you feel?" he asks.

"I feel fine," replies Bobby. "I feel much better than I would have felt if it had not gone well." He turns to Shuker and says elliptically, "The President said once that 'victory has a hundred fathers, defeat is an orphan.'"

Now, suit jacket draped over his arm, he leaves his office. It has been twelve hours since he arrived with his children, longer since he called his brother after breakfast, longer still since he first talked to Marshall and Katzenbach.

Bobby's day was finally ending, leaving one last thought – a verbal shrug – for Shuker.

"Much better having it work out well rather than not having it work out well," he says, disappearing down the corridor.

Tuesday, June.11, 1963

CHAPTER 16

Midnight

NO ONE KNEW more about hatred than Medgar Wiley
Evers. No one knew more about the caste system and the
master race. No one knew more about the disparity between the
races, from education to income, whether measured by sevenths,
quarters, thirds, or halves. No one knew more about the failure of
the law and the difference between the streets and the courts. No
one knew more about second-class citizenship and moral crisis. No
one knew more about all of this because no one was more a slave to
this struggle than this tough, taciturn bastard son of Mississippi.

For nine years, Evers had served as the state field secretary of
the NAACP. He had the most dangerous job in the most dangerous state. As bad as George Wallace's Alabama was in 1963, Ross
Barnett's Mississippi was worse. There was the South, as they said,
and there was Mississippi. Evers knew the murderous anger in the
piney woods and the crawling kudzu. A close friend of his father's
was lynched when Medgar was fourteen years old. "He was supposed to have insulted a white woman," Evers remembered. "His

clothes stayed out in the pasture where they killed him for a long time afterward. You'd see the blood turning rust color."

Threats and epithets were an almost daily repast for Evers. In 1958, when he boarded a bus in Meridian and refused to sit in a segregated rear seat, the local police took him in for questioning. When he got back on the bus and sat in the front seat again, a white man punched him in the face. In 1960, when his statement of protest against a ruling in a civil rights case appeared in a local newspaper, he was arrested, fined $100, and sentenced to thirty days in jail for contempt of court (a conviction reversed by the Mississippi Supreme Court). In 1961, attending the trial of black activists involved in sit-ins, he applauded the defendants in the courtroom. A policeman beat him over the head with a snub-nosed revolver.

Evers was fearless. Mississippi was his life. Impossibly, he loved the place. He loved it even if it did not love him, even if it had disowned him. He was born in Decatur on July 2, 1925, and joined the Army in 1943 at seventeen. He went ashore at Normandy and fought in France and Germany, winning two battle stars. Returning to Mississippi, he faced the contradiction of all black GIs who had fought for freedom abroad and found little at home. He enrolled in Alcorn Agricultural and Mechanical College (now Alcorn State University) in southwestern Mississippi, where he studied business administration and was president of the junior class and a star athlete. He was taken aback when the college president discouraged him and his classmates from registering to vote because "we had no contribution to make to the community. I couldn't forget that." After graduation, Evers sold insurance. In 1951, he married Myrlie Beasley, a younger classmate, with whom he had three children. In 1954, he went to work for the NAACP.

As the organization's first field secretary in Mississippi, Evers defended the rights of blacks in a repressive state. He went everywhere — most dangerously into the loamy cotton fields of the

Mississippi Delta – to recruit members, open chapters, and collect dues. Evers was methodical, reliable, and practical. No radical, he; in this line of work, he couldn't be. Despite court rulings, progress was fitful. Evers persevered with the hard detachment of Vivian Malone and James Hood in Tuscaloosa and James Meredith in Oxford. The danger was everywhere. Wasn't Evers frightened? "I played football in college for four years," he said, "and no matter how many games you play, there is still a certain amount of butter-flies. But the first time you tackle a man, your fear disappears. You're just in it."

In June 1963, Evers was in it. He was the leading civil rights activist in Mississippi, its face, voice, and spirit, though unknown beyond it. For weeks, he had been campaigning to end discrimina-tion in Jackson. It began on May 12 when the NAACP declared it would end "all forms of segregation in Jackson." Black activists would negotiate in good faith, but if that failed, they would use the traditional tools of nonviolent direct action – boycotts, marches, sit-ins – that were forcing change in Birmingham. On May 27, after making some concessions, the mayor rejected a proposed biracial committee, defended school segregation, and banned demonstra-tions. On May 28, Evers and the NAACP launched "the Negro action campaign," with a sit-in at the all-white lunch counter at the local F. W. Woolworth, the ubiquitous five-and-dime chain department store. A crowd assaulted the demonstrators at the counter, dousing them in mustard, ketchup, and sugar. They took it sitting down. Things worsened. Protests grew. Blacks filled the streets. Hundreds of children were arrested and thrown in what Roy Wilkins, the organization's visiting executive secretary, called "con-centration camps." Drawing parallels with the Nazis, he claimed, "The only thing missing was the ovens." On June 1, Wilkins and Evers were arrested and jailed. That day the *New York Times* fea-tured Evers as its "Man in the News." It was rare national exposure for Evers, who was not an orator and lacked the presence, stature, and recognition of King and other national civil rights leaders. Evers was "the quiet integrationist," who vowed, despite the horror, that one day his sons were "going to find Jackson even better than New York City."

Also that day, amid the mass arrests, Evers sent a desperate wire to the White House: "Please. Mistreatment of Negro children and their parents behind barbed wire confines of Jackson concentration camp. City, county and state law officials involved. Medical attention denied. Injured in some places. Urge immediate investigation by the Justice Department of their denial of constitutional rights to peaceful demonstration. Medgar Evers, 102 Lynch Street." (Decades later, Myrlie Evers bitterly remembered that address.)

The threats mounted. There was the Molotov cocktail (which didn't explode) thrown into the carport of their small, low-slung home at 2332 Guynes Street in Jackson. They had bought the brick, board-and-batten house for $9,500 in 1956, the year it was built in a black middle-class subdivision surrounded by white neighborhoods. It was the only house on the street without a front door; a side door was safer. Given the constant danger, that mattered. "I remember distinctly one individual calling with a pistol on the other end, and he hit the cylinder [against the receiver], and of course you could hear it was a revolver. He said, 'This is for you,'" Evers recalled. "And I said, 'Well, whenever my time comes, I'm ready.'" In the second week of June, he had picked up the telephone at home several times to hear, "We're going to kill you."

On June 8, in the afternoon, Evers parked his car downtown at his office and stepped between it and an idling police car, which the driver then threw into reverse and tried to back into him. Evers jumped like a jackrabbit, which amused the officer. "This is what you must face to get free in Mississippi," Evers remarked. On June 10, a well-placed white friend told Evers that he had learned someone would try to kill him. He advised Evers not to drive alone and to protect his home. The NAACP knew of the threats but refused to help him. "We have better things to do with our money than to pay someone to protect him," it said. Evers shrugged. At thirty-seven, he was weary. Perhaps martyrdom appealed to him. He did tell Myrlie to be sure to turn off the headlights before leaving the car in the driveway and to get out on the right-hand side, away from an overgrown lot across the street that could hide a man with a rifle. Evers noticed unidentified white men showing up at the black rallies; he suspected that he was being followed in his car. Myrlie saw a growing fatalism about him. When she pressed him to buy a new suit, he snapped, "I'm not going to need one." She wondered why he wanted to pay an overdue premium on his life insurance policy when they didn't have the money. That June he was exhausted and depressed. When she spoke of having a fourth child, he said he didn't want to be responsible for bringing another life into a hateful world. "This seems such a hopeless situation," he moaned.

❋

On the morning of Tuesday, June 11, Evers awoke listless. "Myrlie, I don't know what I am going to do. I'm so tired I can't go on, but I can't stop, either." As he left the house, he stopped to embrace the children. "I love you all so much," he told them. In the driveway, his car door open, his wife watched as he gazed across the street at the lot with its menacing cover of honeysuckle bushes and tall grass. She pretended that she didn't see his moment of hesitation. He returned to the house. "Did you forget something?" she asked him. "No, I just wanted to say that I love you." Myrlie found that odd. That afternoon, he called home three times, twice to speak to the children, once following news of the confrontation in Tuscaloosa. "That was totally, *totally* out of character," Myrlie recalled incredulously. Medgar rarely called. She asked him if he was loafing.

President Kennedy was speaking that evening, he told her. "Be sure to let the children stay up tonight and watch the President make his speech. I will see you then." Both she and her daughter, Reena, were struck by his tone that Tuesday. "I knew he sensed something, but he also knew something," Myrlie said. Had he received a new death threat he wasn't telling them about? "You could tell that Daddy was different, almost resigned to something," remembered Reena. After midnight, when Evers dropped off a colleague at his home, he remembered how "he just held my hand and held it and held it."

That evening, Myrlie moved the television into her bedroom, where Reena, eight, and Darrell, nine, lay on the floor, away from the window. Van, three, was nearby. "When President Kennedy appeared," she said, "all three children fell silent, knowing despite their youth that he was going to be talking about them." When he talked about the right to vote and to receive equal service, "I felt he was talking directly about our Capitol Street boycott, our voter registration drives, and suddenly I felt very close to the President of the United States. The children listened intently." She was struck when Kennedy, in the heart of the speech, addressed the condition of black Americans. "Who among us would be content to have the color of his skin changed and stand in his place? Who among us would be content with the counsels of patience and delay?" It spoke to her because it spoke of her husband. "I thought of Medgar, watching the address somewhere, and my heart filled with the joy I knew he would be feeling at these words," she said, noting he had said "something very like this" in an unprecedented and much maligned speech he had made on local television three weeks earlier.

Evers was at a mass meeting at the New Jerusalem Baptist Church that evening. What he thought of the president's speech we do not know. Myrlie hoped it cheered him. After all, if you're Medgar Evers, you've living in a netherworld. You dressed as a field hand to gather evidence in the murder of fourteen-year-old Emmett Till in 1955. You inspected the broken body of Mack Charles Parker, pulled from a prison cell, beaten, and shot by a mob in 1959. You accompanied James Meredith to Ole Miss in 1962. You know the fires of frustration; you lit them. You know what "ought to be" in America. And now, here's your president saying what you have been saying for years. Perhaps the words lifted him. They did Myrlie. "It was a moving speech, the most direct and urgent appeal for racial justice any President of the United States had ever made. It moved me and gave me hope and made what Medgar was doing seem more important than ever before."

✳

Darrell was the first to hear the tires of the powder-blue Oldsmobile in the driveway. It was 12:20 a.m. in Jackson. School was out for the summer, and the kids had stayed up late, watching television, arguing over the program. Their favorite was *The Untouchables*. They were eager to see their father. Myrlie was sitting up in bed. She wondered "what Medgar would have to say" about Kennedy's speech. Evers opened the car door and got out, his arms full of sweatshirts emblazoned with "Jim Crow Must Go."

Then, a shot. The children, well trained for this eventuality, crawled toward the bathroom to get in the tub. Outside, Evers staggered and fell, dragging himself for thirty feet. In a life full of premonitions, Myrlie knew immediately what had happened. "I flew to the door, praying to be wrong. I switched on the light. Medgar lay face down at the doorway drenched with blood."

Evers's white shirt had made an easy target for a killer with a .30/06 Enfield rifle, nestled across the street, 150 feet away. The sound was very loud and the bullet traveled far – through his back, out his chest, through the screen and glass of the living room window, through another wall into the kitchen, off the refrigerator, shattering the coffee pot. It came to rest, incredibly, on the opposite counter beside a watermelon. Myrlie screamed in the driveway and called his name. The children gathered around him. "Please,

Daddy, please get up!" He lay in the carport, keys in his hand, sweatshirts scattered. The neighbors rushed over. Myrlie recalled that "someone turned Medgar over and he was breathing heavily, in short spurts, and his eyes were open, but they were set and unmoving. I called and called to him, but if he heard me, he showed no sign." A neighbor's station wagon arrived. Myrlie tried to get in but was held back. "I fought like a demon, physically fighting, to go with him," she remembered. "I had been with him all the time, and I wanted to be with him when he took his last breath."

Evers was going out on his own terms. The neighbors put a blanket over him and prepared to lift him into the back and take him to the hospital.

"Sit me up," he said. "Turn me loose."

※

Medgar Wiley Evers was pronounced dead at 1:14 a.m. at the University of Mississippi Hospital. It was the hollow of the night in the northeast. At 2:00 a.m., the telephone rang in the home of Roy Wilkins in New York City. The shooting in Jackson sent him into a fury. "If there was one moment in my life when I hated whites, that was it," he wrote. Word reached the White House at 3:00 a.m.

Would they wake the president with the ghastly news? Would he say something? Would the White House issue a statement? No. All that would wait until morning. Forty-four feverish hours after he had awoken aloft somewhere over America, he would remain asleep.

EPILOGUE

Jᴀᴄᴋ Kᴇɴɴᴇᴅʏ ᴇɴᴛᴇʀᴇᴅ a new world on June 12, 1963. He had passed through the looking glass. His electrifying two days had crystallized and codified his thinking on nuclear arms and civil rights. His quest for "peace and freedom" would animate those last five-and-a-half months, at once darkening and brightening the evening of his life. It became horrifyingly real to him at 7:00 a.m. when an assistant – probably Andy Hatcher – came to his bedroom to tell him that Medgar Evers was dead. Amid the low monotone of anonymous lynchings, shootings, and drownings of black men in the Southland, this one jangled. In the burst of a deer-hunter's rifle, Kennedy understood the necessity – and the penalty – of his poetic appeal of eleven hours ago. As the *New York Times* put it, the murder "was a ghastly postscript to President Kennedy's pleas for a vast moral awakening to end America's maltreatment of its Negro citizens."

As much as it was postscript, it was prelude. The killing of Medgar Evers opened a long season of assassination in the United

States. His was the first of six political murders over the next nine years. Five of the victims were associated with the events of June 10 and June 11. Gunmen would claim or maim angels and demons on both sides of the racial divide: Jack and Bobby Kennedy, Malcolm X (the Black Muslims), George L. Rockwell (the American Nazi Party), Martin Luther King Jr., and George Wallace. Here, in a dead man's blood, stamped on the driveway of a segregated subdivision in Jackson, Mississippi, was an omen. His murder prefigured the antipathy Kennedy would sow in the South, where his popularity was falling; the skepticism in the North, where anxiety over civil rights was rising; and the battle in Congress, where resistance to reform was hardening. From Washington, Stewart Alsop wrote his editor at the *Saturday Evening Post* in New York: "If anything is predictable, it is this: The race issue is going to be *the* [italics his] overwhelming issue, the one subject everyone is interested in, for the next year at least."

While Kennedy's advisors told him to stay home to deal with civil rights, the president went to Europe later that month anyway. Canceling the visit, said Schlesinger, would have been "a serious mistake. It would suggest that the racial situation is so dangerous that he cannot risk leaving the country." When the president returned in early July after triumphant stops in Berlin and Ireland, he faced two consuming challenges. First, to win passage of the civil rights legislation he had sent to Congress on June 19, eight days after his television address. Second, to negotiate the nuclear test ban treaty with the Russians *and* persuade the Senate to ratify it. If he failed, both of his speeches would be no more than rhetoric, high-minded and well-appointed, ornamental but empty. They would fade as surely as the puffy contrails of *Air Force One*, which had carried him home Monday morning. On Wednesday morning, that seemed a lifetime ago.

Today, more than fifty years later, the power of his two epochal speeches on rights and arms lie not in the words and sentences, pretty as they are. It is that they produced a landmark law and a pioneering treaty. The Limited Nuclear Test Ban Treaty of 1963 took almost four months to negotiate, initial, ratify, and sign. It was Kennedy's greatest achievement in foreign affairs. The Civil Rights Act of 1964 took twelve months to debate and pass. Proposed by Kennedy and propelled by Johnson, it was Kennedy's greatest achievement in domestic affairs.

*

Civil rights was harder. Kennedy was staggered to learn on June 12 that the House of Representatives had defeated his proposal for $445 million for aid to rural areas of high unemployment. "Civil rights . . . was it [the reason] on our side," complained Carl Albert, the House majority leader, in a telephone conversation with Kennedy. "We lost most of the southern boys that we would otherwise have had." (*Time* reported the next week that it was sixteen defecting Republicans, not southern Democrats, who had killed the bill; if so, that was not Albert's perception.) "Christ, you know, it's like they shoot this guy in Mississippi," replied Kennedy. "They shoot somebody, I mean, it's just in everything. This has become everything." Albert feared civil rights was "overwhelming the whole program." For Kennedy, civil rights ("it's just in everything") was a metastasizing cancer. The vote on area development had confirmed his fears. How many times had he told Bobby that civil rights would do in his legislative agenda? Here was the proof! The very next day!

Under Kennedy's cold, rational New England gaze, wasn't Evers, "this guy in Mississippi," just another poor bastard in the wrong line of work? Wasn't life unfair? Yet this murder pierced his aloofness. Hatcher reported, "The President was appalled by the barbarity of the act." Hugh Sidey wrote that Kennedy was "shocked" by Evers's murder. Ted Sorensen said Kennedy "hoped that his speech that night before might somehow start the country down a new path in which that kind of violence would not take place." Kennedy was unaware of Evers before receiving his anguished telegram on June 1 and probably immediately after, too; a typewritten draft of the president's letter of condolence of June 12 to Myrlie Evers twice refers to "Mrs. Evans." But Kennedy knew about Evers now. He told Schlesinger that the patience of black Americans was at an end, that there had to be progress that year. He worried about unity. He did not leave it there; he couldn't, anyway. The murder shook the country. The violence spread. In the two-and-a-half months after Birmingham, there were 758 demonstrations in cities everywhere.

As a veteran, Evers was entitled to burial in Arlington National Cemetery in Virginia, across the Potomac River from Washington. The administration approached the funeral arrangements with typical caution. On June 13, Senator Ernest Gruening of Alaska telephoned Sorensen, asking the president to honor Evers by lowering flags and sending Lyndon Johnson to the funeral. The White House replied that the president could only lower flags for a serving or former government official, and, no, the vice president would not attend the service. In that case, Gruening suggested, could Kennedy send flowers? The president sent Bobby. At the burial, RFK gave Charles Evers, Medgar's brother, his telephone number and told him to call him, day or night, if he needed help.

The next day, June 20, the president invited Charles, Myrlie, Darrell, and Reena to the White House. In the Cabinet Room, awaiting their appointment with Kennedy, Mrs. Lincoln told Darrell that if he sat in the president's chair and made a wish, it would come true. "He hoped and prayed that his father did not die in vain," Charles told Mrs. Lincoln later. In the Oval Office, Kennedy greeted the family warmly. "He took my hand, and shook it and held it," said Myrlie. He paused and asked her how she was. She wanted to say: *I was dead inside, that my life had been snatched away from me, that I wished he could do something about it personally. I wanted to say that my husband had fought for his country and come back home to find he was still not free and had died for his belief that all Americans were entitled to first-class citizenship. I wanted to say that I knew that nothing would be done about it.*

"Fine, thank you, Mr. President," she replied. "You're a brave woman," he said. She thanked him again. Kennedy talked to the children, showing them the coconut husk paperweight on his desk. He gave them the usual vanity gifts (a Kennedy pin and a charm bracelet with a *PT-109* medallion for Reena, a pen and *PT-109* tie clip for Darrell), and signed a copy of the civil rights bill for Myrlie. A photographer took their picture with the president. The family went upstairs for a tour of the residence. From a window, Myrlie saw John Jr. on the South Lawn waving good-bye to his father, who was boarding *Marine One*. Myrlie thought of her son and his father. "I almost broke down," she said.

Downstairs, Arthur Schlesinger had entered the Oval Office as the family was leaving. In his unpublished diary, Schlesinger found Mrs. Evers "exceptionally attractive" and, oddly, the children "cunning." Schlesinger told Kennedy that it was all such "a terrible business." Kennedy said: "Yes, I don't understand the South. I'm coming to believe that Thaddeus Stevens [the radical Republican who wanted to punish the South after the Civil War] was right. I had always been taught to regard him as a man of vicious bias; but when I see this sort of thing, I wonder how else you can treat them."

✳

A few days earlier, Schlesinger had congratulated Kennedy on a great speech on civil rights. "'Yes,' Kennedy responded bitterly, 'and look at what happened to area development the very next day in the House.' He is deeply – excessively – skeptical of the value of speeches *per se*. He then added: 'But of course, I had to give that speech, and I am glad that I did.'" Schlesinger knew that words were no longer enough. "The problem is, of course, that speeches by themselves, no matter how eloquent or deeply felt, cannot do the job," he wrote Mrs. Daniel Koshland on June 18. "The resolution of a problem like civil rights will require . . . positive action by every citizen not only in his own community, but in his own heart. We all hope the President's speech will contribute to that end." When the bill languished in committee that summer and fall, the president had doubts. "We always used to laugh a little about the fact that I'd gotten him into so much trouble," Bobby remembered. In darker moments, the brothers wondered "whether it was the right thing to do."

Suddenly, belatedly, America was somersaulting into the 1960s. Racial injustice was now morally and socially unacceptable; the president had said so. "The present situation is a national disgrace," David Bruce told his diary June 11. "While we blandly urge that cannibalistic Africans should be democratized and every person have a vote, we continue to hold over ten percent of our citizens in a state of humiliation and gross discrimination." To the White House, Kennedy summoned leaders of the clergy, labor, and industry. He even enlisted a skeptical Eisenhower at a meeting June 12. "Day after day, the conferences went on," wrote Hugh Sidey. "John Kennedy's commitment to civil rights progress became total, deeper than any commitment he had made in his two-and-a-half years." As fissures in society turned to fault lines, Kennedy felt the discontent as never before. He was so worried about trouble during the March on Washington on August 28, 1963 – the largest mass protest in American history – that he advised Mimi Beardsley, his lover, to stay away from it.

As civil rights activists marched and Congress debated, Kennedy became anathema in Dixie. Jack Frost could not nip Jim Crow without feeling the sting himself. "I was astonished by the monolithic quality of the bitterness towards Kennedy – or rather the Kennedys – as the President is known in the South," wrote Stewart Alsop.

Schlesinger was worrying about the North, too. In July, he was struck by the gloominess of a liberal friend, James Lanigan, who had returned from Chicago. "He said that civil rights might very well lose the election for Kennedy in 1964; that there was widespread and intense panic in the suburbs; that even good Democrats were appalled by the nightmare of an inundation of their neighborhoods and their schools by Negroes; and that speedy counteraction was necessary. The President has never had illusions about the political benefits of a civil rights fight, but has felt that he had no alternative if he wanted to hold the country together."

Civil rights was getting into everything, especially southern politics. In 1960, Kennedy had carried Texas, Alabama, Arkansas, Louisiana, Mississippi, North Carolina, South Carolina, and Georgia. He lost Virginia and Florida in the South. In 1964, Lyndon Johnson carried Virginia and Florida, and forty-two other states. He lost Alabama, Arizona, Louisiana, Mississippi, South Carolina, and Georgia (which Stewart Alsop predicted in 1963 would go Republican for the first time). It reflected, he said, "a change not in degree but in kind in the white South attitude, the counterpart in the change in the Negro attitude. It could force an absolutely basic political realignment in the U.S., with the ancient, wildly irrational but astonishingly long-lasting Democratic coalition between city machine and rural South shattered once and for all. The political revolt in the white South is just as significant as the social-economic revolt in the black South . . ."

Johnson prophesied his party's eclipse in the South when he signed the Civil Rights Act on July 2, 1964. Between 1969 and 1993, the Democrats held the presidency for only four years (under Jimmy Carter, a Southerner). It would take another dozen years to recapture the White House. They would learn how to win in New England, so rock-ribbed Republican in postwar America that Danny Kaye, in *White Christmas*, could crack about the futility of "digging up a Democrat in Vermont." The Democrats would win in the Midwestern Rust Belt and the Pacific Northwest. In 1963, though, civil rights was poison for the party in the Deep South.

That autumn, three of Kennedy's big bills were stalled: the tax cut, federal aid to education, and Medicare. "The defiance of Kennedy from the Hill has never been more pronounced," wrote Hugh Sidey in 1963. "What was wrong?" Formidable campaigner and innovative electioneer that he was, Kennedy could not cajole legislators as effectively as Lyndon Johnson, that "riverboat gambler" JFK never used to his advantage. The administration was mounting a vigorous campaign to court moderate Republicans to offset the loss of conservative Democrats. For all that, though, there is doubt that *that* Congress would have passed *that* bill. It might well have taken Kennedy until his second term. Sorensen and his contemporaries, for their part, always insisted that it would have passed in 1964, and that the Kennedy White House (led by Nicholas Katzenbach, Burke Marshall and RFK) was far more adept in crafting and selling the bill than historians have generally acknowledged.

Whatever the prospects of the legislation that fall, though, we know this: in the spring of 1963, Kennedy recast the terms of race like no president since Lincoln. In speaking to the nation when he did and how he did, he ignored every advisor but his brother. He acted at a cost to his legislative program, immediately, to his party, eventually, and to himself personally. The antipathy to civil rights would sow a climate of hatred in the South that would await him in Dallas. In the face of all of this, Kennedy was philosophical. "Well, if we're going down," he said, "let's go down on a matter of principle."

If there was a eureka moment when it all became clear to Kennedy on race, no one saw it. "I honestly can't put my finger on any point in time where the President slammed his hand down and said, 'This is it!'" said Lee White. No doubt the brutality of Birmingham shook him deeply. We like to imagine things happening dramatically in life as well as art. Sometimes they do. In the 2013 film *The Butler*, the fictionalized story of Eugene Allen, a black man-servant in the White House, Kennedy has a Hollywood epiphany. Wrapped in a white woolen cardigan, he is upstairs watching the dogs and fire hoses on television. Repulsed, he turns to the butler, whose son in the film was a Freedom Rider: "You know, I never understood what you went through until I saw that. My brother says those kids have changed his heart. They've changed mine, too."

The education of Jack Kennedy on race was less theatrical and more incremental. No longer was civil rights an excursion for him; it was now a long march. "Sometimes you look at what you've done," he told a friend in the summer of 1963, "and the only thing you ask yourself is – what took you so long to do it?" The social unrest, more than anything else, pushed him toward legislation. "He had no other choice," said Mike Mansfield. "His hand was forced. But once he stepped forward, he was for it all the way." Kennedy's racial consciousness did not originate on June 10 and June 11, as if anger and awareness had fallen out of the sky. Yet his swelling commit-ment found its voice there – with a pitch and tone and range that would resound a half century later.

✳

While Kennedy was trying to expand civil rights, he was trying to curtail nuclear arms. The American University speech made this the other cause of his newly agitated presidency. "The Soviet response to the speech changed the atmosphere," wrote Glenn Seaborg, chairman of the Atomic Energy Commission. On July 2, though, Khrushchev announced that he was ready to conclude an agreement banning nuclear tests in the atmosphere, outer space, and under-water, but not underground. On July 16, Averell Harriman left for Moscow, accompanied by Bundy's deputy, Carl Kaysen, and Adrian Fisher, deputy director of the Arms Control and Disarmament

Agency, both of whom helped write the Peace Speech. (They brought no technical experts because Kennedy worried they would thwart an agreement.) Harriman's instructions were to negotiate a comprehensive treaty, or, failing that, a partial one. Put succinctly: "Get an agreement and come home." Harriman exploited his rapport with Khrushchev, whom he had known since the 1940s. Harriman reported that Khrushchev told him "that more than anything else, Kennedy's speech . . . had paved the way for the treaty." Proposals went back and forth between the two capitals, monitored by Kennedy, who for ten days sat in the Cabinet Room conferring on drafts with his advisors, or in the Situation Room, sending and receiving cables. He was following the talks with "a devouring interest."

On July 25, 1963, Harriman initialed a treaty that bound both parties "to prohibit, to prevent, and not to carry out any nuclear weapon test explosion, or any other nuclear explosion . . . in the atmosphere, beyond its limits, including outer space, or under water . . ." The treaty included a preamble and four articles, totaling 800 words. It was the first of its kind in the nuclear age. The next day Kennedy made another appeal on television: "Let us, if we can, step back from the shadows of war and seek out the way of peace. And if that journey is a thousand miles, or even more, let history record that we, in this land, at this time, took the first step." When Harriman returned triumphantly to Georgetown, his neighbors greeted him with "For He's a Jolly Good Fellow." Schlesinger recalled: "One girl brought a tiny baby and said to Averell: 'I brought him because what you did in Moscow will make it possible for him to look ahead to a full and happy life.'"

Persuading the Russians was one thing; silencing the naysayers was another. The loudest were the Joint Chiefs of Staff. Maxwell Taylor, the chair, warned that a comprehensive treaty would allow the Soviets to "make important gains through clandestine testing." After the treaty was initialed in Moscow on August 5, 1963, critics stepped up their attacks. The most formidable was Edward Teller, the nuclear physicist, who argued that ending testing would prevent the United States from developing a shield against ballistic missiles. The administration blunted his criticism and silenced the baying generals, too. On September 24, the Senate ratified the treaty by a vote of eighty to nineteen, easily winning the required two-thirds majority. Among the opponents was Barry Goldwater, who, David Bruce noted, was "currently the reactionaries' white hope, though I think he is, politically, a confused man." As the Republican nominee in 1964, he would lose badly.

Flanked by supporters, Kennedy signed the treaty on October 7, 1963. The ceremony took place in the Treaty Room of the White House at a desk brought downstairs from the Yellow Oval Room. There were big hopes for the treaty: that it would reduce radioactive fallout, contain the arms race, encourage more arms-control agreements, and slow the proliferation of nuclear weapons. The record is mixed. The treaty did reduce radioactive fallout, significantly, which was no small thing, given that renewed testing had doubled the nuclear fallout in the atmosphere in 1962. But because countries continued to test underground, with little public notice, it didn't slow the arms race. There were subsequent arms agreements: the Outer Space Treaty in 1967, the Treaty for the Prohibition of Nuclear Weapons in Latin America and the Caribbean in 1968, the Non-Proliferation Treaty of 1970, and the Strategic Arms Limitation Talks (SALT) in 1972. But nuclear weapons continued to spread; China, India, Israel, and Pakistan developed the bomb. Today, nuclear proliferation remains one of the world's unrelenting concerns.

The Limited Nuclear Test Ban Treaty made testing harder but not impossible. What the treaty did do, though, was to show that it could be done. For the first time, the Soviet Union and the United States addressed limiting nuclear weapons. Getting there had taken two-and-a-half years of posturing and two weeks of nuclear brinkmanship. It had also taken Khrushchev and Kennedy to see the cost of their long, twilight struggle. They had to take on the hard-liners and rejectionists within their camps.

Kennedy called the test ban treaty his proudest achievement. It marked a personal passage for him. "I think Kennedy in the American University speech was really at home with himself," observed John Kenneth Galbraith. "That was the Kennedy of the test ban, not the Kennedy of the Bay of Pigs or the Berlin Wall . . . [where] he was yielding to Cold War pressures." William Sloane Coffin Jr., a prominent clergyman, recalled a bemused Kennedy asking: "Why did it take us so long?" Imagining a carapace of peace, Kennedy talked that summer about visiting Moscow in 1964 and proposed that autumn collaborating with the Russians in space. He remained aware of the evils of Communism, but he began thinking less of winning the Cold War than ending it. As he had told Norman Cousins, whatever the philosophical differences between the two countries, he saw "no alternative – for the good of our peoples and for the good of the human community as a whole – other than to reduce to the vanishing point the danger of war between us." That, he knew, would require "patience, ingenuity, resourcefulness." After all, what choice was there? "Both the Chairman and I have been placed by history and circumstance in a position to help make our planet safe for human habitation," he said. "Nothing means more to me than to work constructively toward that end."

In the end, the Limited Nuclear Test Ban Treaty was a beginning. Who knows where it may have led, had both Kennedy and Khrushchev remained "in a position to make the planet safe"? It was the unfinished business of an unfinished presidency.

✳

Vietnam was the surprise of Kennedy's historic forty-eight hours. Eight months earlier, Cuba and Oxford had set the table for initiatives on nuclear arms and civil rights. But the burning monk was not on the president's agenda on June 11, demanding an appointment between Wilson Wyatt and Ed Murrow. That fiery suicide brought home the dangers of a religious war in Vietnam as well as the contradiction between preaching freedom in Saigon and practicing it in Selma. The biggest casualty of Malcolm Browne's photograph was President Diem. As awareness of the Buddhist revolt – real or exaggerated – grew in the White House, Diem's stock fell. The tone was harsher, more hectoring, in the cable traffic between Washington and Saigon. *Do this, or else*, the Americans told Diem. It got worse for him when Henry Cabot Lodge Jr. became ambassador to South Vietnam that summer. He was less sympathetic to Diem than his predecessor. On June 11, Kennedy saw the photograph and recoiled. The next day, he saw Lodge and reacted.

When they met Wednesday at 10:23 a.m., Lodge said that Kennedy referred to the picture and then "to the overall importance of Vietnam, and to what was going on in Saigon – to the fact that the Diem government was entering a terminal phase." Unless Diem and his family left the country, Lodge thought, "there is no power on earth that can prevent [their] assassination. . . ." Things unraveled for Diem that summer and autumn, as if everyone knew what was coming but him. "His [Lodge's] chief problem may be to convince the regime of President Diem that there has been a shift in American policy," editorialized the *Washington Post* on June 29. "There is no longer a disposition to extend a blank check to the Saigon government. While the United States would not itself do anything to impose a change of regime in South Vietnam, neither would this country feel impelled to defend Mr. Diem from his non-Communist opponents in the event of a coup." On November 1 and 2, Diem and his brother were overthrown and murdered. A conflicted administration had not planned the coup but had not stopped it, either. A remorseful Kennedy told his Dictaphone that he was "shocked" by Diem's murder, and felt responsible.

The question remains: would JFK have seen a hopeless quagmire and withdrawn those 16,500 Americans — waving good-bye to Saigon while declaring "Vietnam for the Vietnamese"? Many thought so had he been re-elected. Others assume that because Johnson's advisors had been Kennedy's advisors, Kennedy would have prosecuted the war too. If we learn anything from watching Kennedy over these two days, though, it is that he was unafraid to ignore his advisors. Of course, he could not have known how tragically the Vietnam War would unfold over the next dozen years (covered brilliantly by Malcolm Browne, who won the Pulitzer Prize for International Reporting in 1964, shared with David Halberstam). Nor that Diem's would be the first of two shocking assassinations that November.

☀

Civil rights, nuclear arms, Vietnam; the world has moved on in the last half century. In a cotton field near Vance, Alabama, where Vivian Malone, James Hood, and Nicholas Katzenbach stopped on their way to Tuscaloosa, Mercedes-Benz builds luxury automobiles. At the University of Alabama, Malone-Hood Plaza outside Foster Auditorium commemorates the integration of the university, which is now 12.2 percent black.

For James Hood, the Capstone nearly became a headstone. He lived in residence, alone, weathering a regime of slurs and threats. As he walked to his first class on the morning Medgar Evers was killed, a fellow student hissed: "Got another one last night in Jackson!" That summer Hood fell out with the university after criticizing its administration. He left on August 11, 1963, he explained, "to avoid a complete mental and physical breakdown." He moved to Michigan to study criminal justice and sociology, and became an educator and administrator there. Twice married and twice divorced, he had five children. He returned to the

University of Alabama in 1995 and earned a doctorate in 1997. He died in 2013.

Vivian Malone stuck it out. She also lived on her own; she had her own bathroom and telephone in her "counselor's suite" because white girls didn't want to share with her. "I would walk across the campus to the Commerce Department, and some of the students would say, 'Here comes the nigger,' and they'd laugh." She smiled and waited for her classmates to smile back, which they rarely did. On the first day of classes, "people got up and moved. But I sat there. It was math class and I happen to like math." Refusing to hide, she ate breakfast, lunch, and dinner in the cafeteria, usually alone, and made a point of going to the snack bar at night, too. She gained thirteen pounds that first summer. Protected around-the-clock, she was unharmed in her two years in Tuscaloosa, even when bombs exploded near her dormitory that autumn. In 1965, Malone became the university's first black graduate, earning a B-average. She married a doctor, had two children, and worked quietly for the civil rights division of the federal government in Atlanta. Unlike other young activists of the early 1960s, she never became deeply involved in politics after Tuscaloosa. She died in 2005.

By the 1980s, the currents of change had deposited George Wallace on the wrong bank of history, where he would remain marooned forever. But his defiance on June 11 would carry him to an unprecedented four terms as governor between 1963 and 1987. Less segregationist than populist, he ran for president in 1964 and 1968 as the candidate of the American Independent Party. Winning Alabama and four other southern states, he drew votes from Hubert Humphrey there and in the North and helped elect Richard Nixon. Wallace ran again in 1972, as a Democrat. At a campaign stop in Laurel, Maryland, in May, he was shot. He remained semi-paralyzed in a wheelchair the rest of his life, but ran for office again in 1976. Eventually, he asked Malone and Hood for forgiveness. In 1996, he presented Malone with an award, admitting that he had been wrong in 1963. Wallace and Hood became friends. When Wallace died in 1998, Hood attended his funeral. "I think he made peace with God," he said.

On June 23, 1963, Byron De La Beckwith was arrested for the murder of Medgar Evers. A white supremacist, Beckwith twice went free in 1964 when all-white juries could not reach a verdict. In 1993, he was arrested and tried a third time on the basis of new evidence, one of several civil rights cases reopened in the 1990s. Beckwith was found guilty in 1994 and sentenced to life in prison, the end of a horrid story that Hollywood retold in *Ghosts of Mississippi* in 1996. In 2001, Beckwith died in prison.

After Beckwith's second trial, Evers and her children fled to California. "I could never get his blood off the concrete," she said. "My eldest son stopped eating. He would take a toy rifle with him to bed." She had been so public immediately after her husband's death that Jackie Kennedy vowed to do the opposite after her husband's death: ("I'm not going around accepting plaques," she said. "I'm not Mrs. Medgar Evers.") Evers studied at Pomona College, worked for the Atlantic Richfield Company, ran unsuccessfully for Congress, and chaired the NAACP. On January 21, 2013, she gave the invocation at the second inauguration of Barack Obama. On June 12, 2013, the City of Jackson formally observed the fiftieth anniversary of Evers's death. His home is a historic site and the airport is named for him. Across the United States, a city college, a naval vessel, schools, bridges, libraries, and parks honor him. In Seattle, a woman whose mastectomy made it painful to wear a bathing suit pressed her right in court to swim topless in the Medgar Evers Pool. She won.

Myrlie Evers, who turned eighty-one in 2014, soldiers on. The past never leaves her. She recalls a surreal moment one afternoon sitting outside her home in the mountainous Pacific Northwest. Unprompted, she said out loud to herself: "'Medgar, I'm tired. I'm tired. It's been fifty years that I've been working.'

"And out of nowhere comes this telepathic message and it was his voice . . . his chuckle . . .

"He said to me: 'I didn't ask you to put in fifty years. You *chose* to do that.'"

＊

Crisis: Behind a Presidential Commitment was broadcast on ABC on October 21, 1963. Robert Drew and Richard Leacock had spent three months creating a documentary of fifty-two minutes from some twenty-six hours of footage. Drew had screened an early cut for Robert Kennedy, who worried that the dialogue in the Oval Office could undermine the civil rights bill that autumn. To satisfy him, Drew muffled some of the conversation. In July, before the film was aired, the *New York Times* criticized filming a president. "To eavesdrop on Executive decisions of serious Government matters while they are in progress is highly inappropriate," it remonstrated. "The White House isn't Macy's window." When the film did come out, the *Times* was no more receptive. It called this candid camera movie "ill-advised," arguing that the executive branch had become "a melodramatic peepshow." It lamented that Drew's film would "stand as a prime example of governmental surrender to the ceaseless and often thoughtless demands of the entertainment world."

But John Horn of the *New York Herald Tribune* called it "an unprecedented television documentary that is a milestone in film journalism." Unprecedented it remains; no president since has allowed cameras to follow him as JFK did. Like the Peace Speech, the film's stature has grown over the decades. In 2011, *Crisis* was named to the National Film Registry of the Library of Congress, one of twenty-five films a year deemed "culturally, historically or aesthetically" significant. "The film has proven to be a uniquely revealing complement to written histories of the period, providing viewers the rare opportunity to witness historical events from an insider's perspective," read the citation. Drew, Pennebaker, Leacock, and Shuker went on to distinguished careers in documentary films.

＊

A semester of tragedy touched the circle of intimates around Joe Alsop's table the evening of June 10. David Ormsby-Gore was killed in an automobile accident in 1985, following his wife, Sissie, who had died the same way in 1967. David Bruce's daughter, Sasha, with whom he had lunched on June 11, after seeing the president, died mysteriously in 1975. That same year, Sir Hugh Fraser was the intended target of an Irish Republican Army car bomb, which detonated prematurely outside his home at 52 Campden Hill Square. "Hugh is grey in the face with shock at what has happened; he was blown backwards in his chair while drinking coffee by the blast," Lady Antonia Fraser wrote in her diary. The bomb killed their neighbor. It could also have killed Caroline Kennedy, who was staying with Hugh (then separated from Antonia) that month. "The poor girl must have thought it was aimed at her," Antonia recalled.

Most shocking was the death of Mary Meyer. She was horribly shaken by JFK's assassination and blamed the CIA. Persuaded of a conspiracy, she began making noisy inquiries around town to influential friends. On October 12, 1964, she was shot point-blank as she walked along the towpath of the C & O Canal in Georgetown. A black man – an unemployed drifter with a history of violence – was charged, tried, and acquitted. The murder was never solved. Later, her sister, Tony, and brother-in-law, Ben Bradlee, found Mary's sketchbook, in which she referred to her affair with Kennedy. Inexplicably, they gave it to a friend in the CIA to destroy. Peter Janney, the son of a spy and Michael Meyer's childhood friend, wrote a book on Meyer in 2013 and concludes she was killed by the CIA.

＊

Within days of Kennedy's assassination, Ted Sorensen asked Sara Elbery, his estranged girlfriend, to marry him. It was a mismatch forged in grief and they divorced in 1966. He ran for the Senate from New York in 1970, and was spectacularly unsuccessful. One critic called him "a burned-out case." Like O'Donnell and Salinger, who also sought high public office, he had no gift for elective politics. He married happily a third time, to Gillian Martin, long associated with the United Nations, with whom he had a daughter. He practiced international law in New York, and wrote and edited books, beginning with *Kennedy*, his reverential account of his life with JFK. It appeared the same year as Arthur Schlesinger's *A Thousand Days*, which won the Pulitzer Prize, and it made them friendly rivals again. To critics, it also made them hagiographers. Sorensen never lost his fealty to the House of Kennedy. He was a frequent speaker at the John F. Kennedy Presidential Library in Boston. His memoir, *Counselor: A Life at the Edge of History*, devotes most of its 531 pages to his almost eleven years with Kennedy. Indeed, that remembrance is twice as long as that covering his life before and after combined. It is touching and painfully honest. Blind in his late seventies, he was brave and gallant. "You are looking absolutely beautiful today, Mrs. Fallows," he told a friend's ailing mother, even though he could not see her. Sorensen never lost a sense of humor. "I have more vision than George W. Bush," he liked to say. Deftly deflecting awkward questions, he would smile and warn: "Ask not."

Charles Bartlett, who talked to Kennedy more than anyone else after Bobby on June 10 and 11, moved on after 1963. So did others in Kennedy's circle. In the face of unflattering revelations, they became more judgmental. Not Sorensen. For him, loyalty, like royalty, was a job for life. As Kennedy's star sometimes faded in the subsequent decades, as revisionists found him more satyr than martyr, it was he who would come forth to deny the rumors and discredit the conspiracies. It was as if he thought anything else (his subsequent career in law, his failed foray into politics) was marginal. Perhaps it was. Sorensen lost his "hero" when he lost John Kennedy. It shaded his long, brilliant life until its end, at eighty-two years old, in 2010.

✳

No one was more tormented by the death of John F. Kennedy than Bobby. No longer was he brother-protector and prime minister; with Lyndon Johnson in the Oval Office and J. Edgar Hoover at the FBI, Bobby lost his authority and influence. He desperately asked Johnson, whom he loathed, to send him to Vietnam as ambassador or to make him his running mate in 1964. LBJ refused. Broken and bereaved, RFK remained attorney general until the summer of 1964. That autumn he was elected to the Senate from New York. His stygian gloom lifted. Bobby remained blunt, mordant, and intense. In the last five years of his life, which began with his elegiac address at Trinity College, he became advocate, skeptic, scold, tribune, folk hero. He opposed the Vietnam War, championed African Americans, Chicanos, and Indians, and agonized over poverty in his frantic presidential campaign, which ended with his murder in Los Angeles on June 5, 1968. On November 20, 2001, RFK's birthday, (he would have been seventy-six) President George W. Bush re-dedicated the Justice Department Building in his memory, endowing it with "a great American name."

✳

More than a half century after his death, John F. Kennedy remains stubbornly topical and strangely alive. The fiftieth anniversary of his death on November 22, 2013, brought a raft of articles, books, documentaries, and feature films. Television presented lapidary documentaries and live coverage of ceremonies from Dallas. "Why

We Can't Stop Grieving," declared one newspaper. "Is there an expiration date on a haunted past?" Fortunately for filmmakers, historians, and journalists, probably not.

If a renaissance artist could capture the events of June 10 and June 11, 1963, on a two-hinged panel, a busy panorama of presidential activity would sprawl across the canvas. Here we would see Kennedy as foreign minister, reviewing a secret mission in Indonesia. Here we would see him as the invalid promoting physical fitness, the seducer who signs a law on pay equity for women, the lieutenant who bypasses his generals on the test ban treaty. He is dry, urbane, and ironic, cool under the scorching sun and anxious under the harsh television lights. Along the way, he tosses flares into the future. The brightest are nuclear arms and civil rights, of course, but others will illuminate the evolving landscape: pay equity, daycare, space exploration, lower taxes, open immigration, organized exercise.

In Kennedy's crowded hour, he begins to see things differently. He asks Americans to do the same. On Monday he embraces the humanity of his enemies. On Tuesday, he seeks equality for the black underclass. On the great issues of his generation, he asks Americans to abandon their prejudices. He does it through the magic of rhetoric and the marble of law. In its time and place, it is nearly subversive. Presidential speeches are often no more than promissory notes, as worthless as junk bonds. At their best, they carry the full faith and credit of the man who makes them in the confidence that something will come of them. Here, something did.

No longer contouring to events, Kennedy was now shaping them. For the first time in his whiplashed presidency, he came to inhabit his office. In finding a moral purpose, he *became* president. By June, though, his time was running out. For all his hopes and dreams, he would have to settle for a few good innings in a short, shimmering season. No one in the stands would ever forget it, especially his lyrical journey to peace and freedom in the spring of 1963.

NOTE ON SOURCES

Two Days in June is an intimate reconstruction of events of more than a half century ago. In telling this story, I have tried to use sources that were previously unavailable or unexamined; in particular, I have mined the memoirs, diaries, and oral histories that have appeared in the last half dozen years or so. At the same time, I have also drawn on contemporaneous accounts in books, reports, yearbooks, magazines, and newspapers.

In retracing President Kennedy's steps over June 10 and June 11, 1963, I began with the White House Diary. This is the official record of what Kennedy did every day of his presidency. It lists his appointments, his public appearances, and more quotidian activities, such as when he lunched and swam. The diary was kept by Kennedy's secretary, Evelyn Lincoln, and Kennedy's appointments secretary, Kenneth O'Donnell. It was usually compiled the next day. In that sense, it is a daily record (what he did) rather than a daily agenda (what he planned to do). The diary, though, is often unreliable. It does not include every meeting, everyone who attended them, and all of Kennedy's comings and goings. As an archivist at the John F. Kennedy Presidential Library (JFKPL) put it, the White House Appointment Books (which they are formally called) "give a deceptive image of completeness."

A more accurate record of Kennedy's movements (though not his meetings) are the Secret Service logbooks. Agents followed Kennedy everywhere, in and out of the White House, logging when he left and when he arrived. Because agents kept the logs in the moment, rather than making their entries later, they are more trustworthy than the White House Diary. Both the diary and the logbooks are in the JFKPL.

Some meetings in the Oval Office are labeled "off the record" which, because there are no known minutes of *any* meetings, is meaningless in

differentiating one meeting from another. There are 265 hours of recordings of meetings and telephone conversations, however, in Kennedy's White
House. For June 10 and 11, there are some transcripts of some meetings,
but no actual recordings to check them against. Because the archivists
warn that the transcripts are unverifiable, I have used them cautiously.

So, how to know what went on in the meetings between the president and his advisors or visitors on June 10 and June 11? For this, I turn
to diaries, letters, memoirs, oral histories, obituaries, interviews, and
contemporaneous press reports. The most useful are from those who
were in the White House, the Justice Department or the administration
on these two days: Arthur Schlesinger Jr. (*Journals* and *The Letters of
Arthur M. Schlesinger, Jr.*); Nicholas deB. Katzenbach (*Some of It Was
Fun*); Lee C. White (*Government for the People*); Ted Sorensen
(*Counselor*); Glenn T. Seaborg (*Kennedy, Khrushchev and the Test Ban*)
and Benjamin C. Bradlee (*Conversations with Kennedy*). Both Sorensen's
(*Kennedy*) and Schlesinger's (*A Thousand Days*) accounts are also criti-
cal. For a sense of Washington, see the memoirs of Lansing Lamont
(*You Must Remember This*).

Then there are the unpublished materials. They include Arthur
Schlesinger Jr.'s papers held in the Brooke Russell Astor Reading Room
of the New York Public Library. Opened in 2011, they offer a remarkable sense of one of the great historians and public intellectuals of the
second half of twentieth century America. Two other superb collections
are the papers of David K.E. Bruce at the Virginia Historical Society in
Richmond, and the papers of William Attwood at the Wisconsin
Historical Society in Madison.

Outside the administration, a sharp observer was Charles Ritchie,
Canada's Ambassador to Washington in 1963. In 1983, he recalls
Kennedy's Washington in *Storm Signals: More Undiplomatic Diaries,
1962-1971*. More revealing and more voluminous, though, are his unpub-
lished diaries, opened in 2011. They are held in the Thomas Fisher Rare
Book Library at the University of Toronto.

Other unpublished sources are the diaries of Katie Louchheim, which
were brought to light by Sally Bedell Smith in her groundbreaking book,
Grace and Power. They are in the Library of Congress in Washington, as
are the papers (letters, notes, drafts, and memoranda) of Joseph and
Stewart Alsop. Both are essential to understanding these two days. To
reconstruct other meetings, I drew on the diaries of Ambassador John
Moors Cabot, which are on microfilm in the Kennedy Library.

A critical resource for any student of the Kennedys is the archive of
some 1,600 oral histories in the Kennedy Library. Many interviews were

conducted in the 1960s and 1970s, when oral history was a new tool of research. The collection has limitations. Subjects are not covered in interviews or are covered superficially. Interviewers are often friends or former colleagues who do not ask hard questions. Some key players were not interviewed at all; some provide only statements.

Used prudently, though, the oral history archive is a treasure trove. For me, it was the key to reconstructing Kennedy's meetings with Andrew Biemiller, John Moors Cabot, and Wilson Wyatt. Other interviewees, such as Max Freedman, McGeorge Bundy, Carl Kaysen, Adrian Fisher, and William Foster, explained how the Peace Speech came together. On civil rights, Robert Kennedy's oral history was particularly useful. Much of it was published in 1988 in *Robert Kennedy in his Own Words*.

The most important oral history is Jacqueline Kennedy's. She recorded eight hours of interviews with Arthur Schlesinger in a series of conversations in the spring of 1964. The recordings were to be sealed until 50 years after her death (in 1994), but Caroline Kennedy decided to release them in 2011. Jackie's wit, insight, and recall illuminate the Kennedy White House. The transcripts were published as *Jacqueline Kennedy: Historic Conversations on Life with John F. Kennedy*, introduced and annotated by Michael Beschloss, the presidential historian. The book includes a CD of the conversations, picking up the ambient sound of ice clinking in glasses and cigarettes inhaled, even interruptions by a young John Jr. Jackie was grief-stricken when she recorded the interviews, and did not expect them to be released for some time. Her harsh impressions of people (such as Ted Sorensen) moderated as she aged. Still, her interviews remain a rich, indispensable source.

I interviewed some of the Kennedys' contemporaries. They include Charles and Martha Bartlett, who introduced Jackie and Jack in 1951; Lansing Lamont, who covered Kennedy's Washington; Ben Bradlee, who saw JFK regularly; Lady Antonia Fraser, who dined with JFK on June 10; and Charles Ritchie, whom I knew in his later years. All were revealing.

Among the period sources, the most helpful were the *New York Times*, *Washington Post*, *Newsweek*, *Time*, *Life*, *Look*, and *U.S. News and World Report*. Among books were Jim Bishop's *A Day in the Life of President Kennedy*, the only such treatment, as well as the elegant profiles of Kennedy in the White House by Hugh Sidey (*John F. Kennedy, President*) and William Manchester (*Portrait of a President*). For the texts of speeches, telegrams, proclamations, and other official pronouncements, I used *Public Papers of the President of the United States: John F. Kennedy*.

✳

In researching *Two Days in June*, the single most important resource was *Crisis: Behind a Presidential Commitment*, the 52-minute cinéma vérité documentary made by Robert Drew in 1963. (It can be watched online or on DVD, along with other films Drew made on JFK). For *Crisis*, Drew and his associates filmed in Washington, Tuscaloosa, Montgomery, Birmingham, and New York City. In 1998, Robert Drew gave 600 boxes of film and video from *Crisis* (and other documentaries) to the Academy of Motion Picture Arts and Sciences in Hollywood, California. It was the largest collection the Academy had ever received. The film is now in the archives of the Pickford Centre for Motion Picture Study. In February 2013, I spent four days at the Pickford Centre. I sat at a 1970s console, assisted by an archivist, watching the black-and-white film on 16-mm reels. Some footage had picture and no sound, some had sound and no picture. The archivists believe – though they are not absolutely certain – that I am the first to see the uncut footage since they received it. The film captures these two days (and those before), giving this story mood, tone, and atmosphere.

Beyond trailing through archives and personal collections, where I found letters and diaries, I also saw JFK's Lincoln Continental at the Henry Ford Museum in Dearborn, Michigan; *Marine One* at the Ronald Reagan Presidential Library in California; and *Air Force One* at Wright-Patterson Air Force Base in Ohio, where I was accompanied by Dr. Jeffrey S. Underwood, the historian at the National Museum of the United States Air Force. At the JFKPL, I saw the semi-tropical murals of the White House Swimming Pool, which were removed from the walls when the pool was closed.

The Kennedy Library remains the greatest repository of materials on the life and presidency of John F. Kennedy. Beyond the oral history collection, logbooks, telephone records and the president's diary, it is here, in the papers of Jack Kennedy, Robert Kennedy, Ted Sorensen, and so many others that we find letters, memoranda, cables, interviews, photographs, and film. It was here, in the papers of RFK, that I came across the draft of the civil rights speech written by Richard Yates. There are items missing in the collection, such as Robert Kennedy's 1963 appointment books. Not all transcripts of all conversations have been released (for example, the meeting between Iain Macleod and the president on June 11). Nor have all oral histories been released.

Still, the Kennedy Library is the ark and covenant of the Kennedy story, which no serious student can ignore.

INTRODUCTION

George F. Will mused about Kennedy's "incompetent first year" in the *Washington Post,* August 12, 2011. He revisits the Kennedy legacy in the *Washington Post,* November 20, 2013. The quotation from Charles Bartlett comes from "Portrait of a Friend" in *The Kennedy Presidency: Seventeen Intimate Portraits of John F. Kennedy.* The figures from nuclear arms are from Andrew Bacevich (*Washington Rules*).

Monday, June 10, 1963

CHAPTER 1 - DAWN

In the telegram to Ted Sorensen from Dolores Martin, her name is spelled Delores; in her newspaper obituary that appeared in the *Honolulu Advertiser* on November 22, 2002, it is spelled Dolores. Martin was one of the leading proponents of statehood for Hawaii, and Democratic National Comitteewoman from 1956 to 1964.

Today, Kennedy's *Air Force One* sits in a World War II hangar inside a security perimeter at Wright-Patterson Air Force Base, near Dayton, Ohio, the largest such installation in the country. The plane glows majestically in the refracted afternoon light. Because it was remodeled by Kennedy's successors, there is little left of the décor and appointments of 1963. The route from Honolulu to Washington (though not conclusive), passenger manifest, weather report, and times of sunset and darkness come from the files on *Air Force One* (particularly the papers of Godfrey McHugh, JFK's Air Force aide) in the John F. Kennedy Presidential Library (JFKPL). The letters and telegrams on Hawaii, as well as the letter from the congressmen on board, also come from those files. For the plane's redesign, see Raymond Loewy's *Industrial Design* and *Never Leave Well Enough Alone*. The text of Kennedy's speech, like all the texts of his public remarks over these two days, comes from *Public Papers of the Presidents of the United States (PPP) John F. Kennedy, January 1 to November 22, 1963*. Martin Luther King Jr.'s comments are from the *New York Times*, June 10, 1963.

On the making of the Peace Speech, see Carl Kaysen, Max Freedman, Glenn Seaborg, McGeorge Bundy, William Foster (OH-JFKPL) and John Kenneth Galbraith in Richard Parker's biography, *John Kenneth Galbraith*.

CHAPTER 2 - MIDMORNING

For the details of Kennedy's Lincoln Continental, see files at the JFKPL. Description of Embassy Row in E.J. Applewhite's *Washington Itself: An Informal Guide to the Capital of the United States*. As a resident of Washington, I walked that route many times.

The commencement program at American University (AU), as well as memos, letters and the student magazine, are in the Archives of American University, as well as material in JFKPL. The formal proceedings were to begin at 10:30 a.m. and finish at 10:35 a.m., when Kennedy was to speak. But Roger Mudd, who anchored the live broadcast on CBS that day, says that Kennedy arrived early and began speaking early. I have followed the minute-by-minute program published by AU, though it may be five minutes off.

June 10 weather from the *Washington Post*; it hit 96 degrees at 4:15 p.m. that day.

The Class of 1963: See the editorial in *Life*, June 21, 1963.

The material on Ted Sorensen comes from his memoir, *Counselor*, as well as Stanley Opotowsky's *The Kennedy Government* and Patrick Anderson's *The President's Men*. Interviews with Faith Shrinsky, e-mail remembrances from Nanci I. Moore and Carl Cook.

CHAPTER 3 - NOON

Kennedy's impatience in Tempest Storm's *The Lady is a Vamp*. On the Equal Pay Act, see the oral histories of Esther Peterson and Andrew Biemiller. On Betty Friedan, see Daniel Horowitz's *Betty Friedan and the Making of The Feminine Mystique*. For books in the 1960s, see Louis Menand, "Books as Bombs," in *The New Yorker*, January 24, 2011.

Robert MacNeil reflects on Washington and the Kennedys in *The Right Place at the Right Time*. See Fletcher Knebel's report on the deteriorating capital ("Washington D.C., Portrait of a Sick City", in *Look* June 4, 1963).

CHAPTER 4 - EARLY AFTERNOON

For details on Robert Drew, see P.J. O'Connell's *Robert Drew and the Development of Cinema Verite in America* and Mary Ann Watson's *The Expanding Vista: American Television in the Kennedy Years.*

While the documentary opens this way, it happened differently in the raw footage. Bobby Kennedy rushed up the grassy slope, into Mrs. Lincoln's office, and asked what the President was doing in the Oval Office. "Equal pay," she said. Bobby, Burke Marshall and an associate then awaited the president in the Cabinet Room, and later, sitting on a low, narrow ledge off the Colonnade, looking like three truant boys.

Carole Radziwill refers to Anthony Radziwill and his uncle's rocker in *What Remains*. Neil Steinberg explores Kennedy and hats in *Hatless Jack*. J.B. West recounts the White House restoration in *Upstairs at the White House: My Life with the First Ladies*. William Manchester (*Portrait of a President*) and Jim Bishop (*A Day in the Life of President Kennedy*) describe Kennedy's daily routine. Bishop's book, which was finished days before Kennedy died, is a fine period piece.

CHAPTER 5 - LATE AFTERNOON

JFK's essay from *Sports Illustrated*, December 26, 1960; he and Jackie appear sailing on its cover. Ben Bradlee's observations about Kennedy in *Conversations with Kennedy* and in Jeff Himmelman's *Yours in Truth* are strikingly perceptive. Jackie never talked to Bradlee again after he published *Conversations*.

The story of the fifty-mile hike is told most vividly by Pierre Salinger in *With Kennedy* and RFK's role is in Ed Guthman's *We Band of Brothers*.

The portrait of the U.S. economy and the tax cut by Joseph Hutnyan in *Encyclopedia Year Book 1964*, Theodore White's *In Search of History*, and William Manchester's *The Glory and the Dream*, Vol. 2.

Dwight Eisenhower's views on JFK are in David Eisenhower's *Going Home to Glory*.

The White House Swimming Pool is described by Pierre Salinger, Jim Bishop (who mistakenly thought the murals evoked Cape Cod), Hugh Sidey (*John F. Kennedy, President*), and Mimi Beardsley Alford in *Once Upon a Secret*. Also, White House Files. Fiddle and Faddle, who were roommates at Goucher College and worked on JFK's presidential campaign, were profiled in *Look* on January 2, 1962.

Kennedy's meeting with Andrew Biemiller (OH-JFKPL) and White House telephone records. Arnold Beichman addresses organized labor and JFK in *Encyclopedia Year Book 1964*. He said JFK probably knew more labor leaders than any president before him, including FDR.

CHAPTER 6 - EVENING

Joe Alsop's dinner party and its guests are drawn primarily from the recollections of Antonia Fraser in an interview with the author in London in May 2013, as well as David Bruce (his diary), Joe Alsop (his letters), and William Attwood (his memoir, *The Reds and the Blacks*). For the life of Lady Fraser, see *Must You Go?* and the *New York Times* Nov. 4, 1966 and November 13, 1979. For her reference to Kennedy and King Charles, see *King Charles II* (London: Weidenfeld & Nicolson). Also David Ormsby-Gore, David Bruce, William Attwood and Hugh Fraser (OH-JFKPL).

Other material drawn from David Auburn's *The Columnist*, Robert Merry's *Taking on the World*, Joe Alsop's memoir, *I've Seen the Best of It*, Bill Patten's *My three Fathers* (in which he richly describes his stepfather's home on Dumbarton Avenue). For Maurice Bowra, see Leslie Mitchell's *Maurice Bowra: A Life* and Isaiah Berlin's *Personal Impressions*.

Shirley MacLaine appeared on the cover of *Life* on June 21, 1963. Arthur Schlesinger's memo to Kennedy in the JFKPL. The portrait of Joe Alsop from letters, diaries, and his memoir. Hervé Alphand from his diaries, *L'étonnement d'être* (1939-1973).

Charles Ritchie's observations are drawn from *Storm Signals* and *Love's Civil War*, as well his voluminous unpublished diaries.

For Mary Meyer, see Peter Janney's *Mary's Mosaic* and Nina Burleigh's *A Very Private Woman,* also Timothy Leary's *Flashbacks*. Marian Cannon Schlesinger's remarks are in her unpublished manuscript on life in Washington in Arthur Schlesinger's papers.

Don Newman, then a young Canadian journalist in Winnipeg, Manitoba, recalls Kennedy's effect on women in his memoir, *Welcome to the Broadcast*. Newman's attractive girlfriend was mesmerized by the President as he smiled and saluted from his limousine when he drove by the couple on his visit to North Dakota in 1963.

JFK's conversation with Martin Luther King Jr., is reported in David Garrow's fine books, *The FBI and Martin Luther King Jr.,* and *Bearing the Cross*.

CHAPTER 7 - NIGHT

Pamela Turnure left three messages for JFK that day, two in early evening. They are in the President's telephone records. For JFK's evening routine, see *Johnny, We Hardly Knew Ye*, by Kenneth O'Donnell and Dave Powers; and Mimi Beardsley Alford's *Once Upon a Secret*. Television listings are drawn from the *Washington Post*, June 10, 1963 and *Newsweek* June 17. Sunset and moonrise from the *Washington Post*, June 10–11, 1963.

Tuesday, June 11, 1963

CHAPTER 8 - EARLY MORNING

The portrait of George Thomas is based on observations from Pierre Salinger, Preston Bruce, Mimi Beardsley Alford, Jim Bishop, J.B. West, Ben Bradlee, and Jackie Kennedy.

The story of the burning monk and the celebrated photograph is told by Malcolm W. Browne in his two books, *The New Face of War* and *Muddy Boots and Red Socks: A Reporter's Life*. He revisits it in "Malcolm Browne: The Story Behind the Burning Monk,"in *Time* on August 28, 2012, and *Reporting America at War: An Oral History*, compiled by Michelle Ferrari in 2003. See David Halberstam's *The Making of a Quagmire* and Peter Arnett's *Live from the Battlefield*. For a sense of Saigon in 1963, I spoke to Thomas Delworth, a Canadian diplomat with the International Control Commission. For William Colby's assessment, see William J. Rust's *Kennedy in Vietnam* and John Mecklin's *Mission in Torment*, as well as Frederick Nolting and Henry Cabot Lodge, Jr. (OH-JFKL).

The percentage of Buddhists in Vietnam in 1963 is unclear. Historian Robert Topmiller notes (in a paper in *The War that Never Ends: New Perspectives on the Vietnam War*) that a 1961 survey conducted in Saigon found that more than 80 percent of the city's population considered themselves to be Buddhist. He said the Asia Foundation estimated that the same percentages would apply to South Vietnam in general, although probably only about 40 percent of the population actively practiced Buddhism.

Where and to whom Kennedy exclaimed "Jesus Christ!" the morning of June 11 is mysterious. The exclamation is said to be in Robert Kennedy's oral history but I could not find it. Historians and journalists often use Kennedy's phrase (Godfrey Hodgson referred to it in his obituary on

Malcolm Browne in *The Guardian* on August 29, 2013) and cite the same sources. Although I could not authenticate it, I have used his reaction because the photograph did shock JFK, he mentioned it later that day and the next, and he often said "Jesus Christ!" when angry or surprised.

For the Legislative Leaders Breakfast, see Jackie Kennedy on Ted Sorensen (OH-JFKPL) and Richard Reeves (*President Kennedy*).

The letters, memos, and messages from Charles Bartlett to JFK are in JFKPL. His columns that spring and summer appeared in *The Pittsburgh Press* and *Chattanooga Times,* among other papers. He has not written a memoir.

For Dean Rusk, see his memoir, *As I Saw It*, and Arthur Schlesinger's journals. Kennedy's warm memo to Rusk of May 8, 1963, is in *JFK Wants to Know: Memos from the President's Office, 1961-1963*. Cable traffic between Moscow and Washington is in JFKPL, as is the summary of press reaction to the Peace Speech. Reports on the mail to the White House are in White House Files.

CHAPTER 9 - MIDMORNING

For John F. Kennedy on immigration, his *A Nation of Immigrants*, and Thurston Clarke, *JFK's Last Hundred Days*. "List of Participants" from the American Committee on Italian Migration in JFKPL. Kennedy's statement in PPP, June 11.

Kennedy's meeting with John Moors Cabot (OH-JFKPL). On the MLF, see David Bruce's diaries and David Nunnerley's *President Kennedy and Britain*. Tom Lehrer's ditty is drawn from his popular LP, *That Was the Year that Was*. Arthur Schlesinger's views on Harold Wilson are in his memo to JFK in the JFKPL. Wilson and Kennedy discussing Profumo are in C. David Heymann's *RFK: A Candid Biography*, though Heymann puts their meeting in March 1963. It was April 2. Jackie's comments on Wilson (OH-JFKPL).

The letters of these two days are in the White House Correspondence files in the JFKPL, sorted by date.

CHAPTER 10 - NOON

The transcript of JFK's meeting with Iain Macleod is closed. Douglas Hurd remembers Macleod warmly in *Eminent Parliamentarians: The Speaker's Lectures*, edited by Philip Norton, as well as Schlesinger's journals. The transcript of the subsequent meeting with congressional leaders on civil rights is confusing but it gives a sense of Kennedy at this critical moment of the day. For Louis Martin's thoughts, see Alex

Poinsett's *Walking with Presidents* and "Organizing Civil Rights" in Kenneth W. Thompson's *The Kennedy Presidency.*

Sorensen recounts his conversation with LBJ in *Counselor*, and Robert Caro addresses it in *Passage to Power*. Transcript in Sorensen's files.

CHAPTER 11 – RFK

A copy of Robert Kennedy's speech at Trinity College, released by the Department of Justice on June 2, 1963, can be found at www.justice.gov/ag/rfkspeeches/1963/06/02-1963.pdf. The transcript does not reflect all RFK's remarks. Robert Drew filmed the entire speech but none of it appears in *Crisis: Behind A Presidential Commitment*.

Robert Kennedy's unpleasant visit to Montgomery is recalled in OH-JFKPL with Burke Marshall, in Edwin Guthman's *We Band of Brothers*, and George Wallace (OH-JFKPL).

RFK's appearance on *Press Conference USA* is in Drew's footage. Ben Allen is quoted (as are Nicholas Katzenbach and Vivian Malone) in *My Soul is Rested*, an excellent collection of interviews with veterans of the civil rights movement gathered by Howell Raines.

On June 10 and June 11, 1963, before there were uniform time zones in the United States, Alabama was two hours behind Washington, D.C. – not one, as often thought.

The portraits of Vivian Malone and James Hood – here and in subsequent chapters – come largely from their interviews before Drew's cameras in New York City; articles in *Time*, *Newsweek*, and the *New York Times*; and their appearances in Kennedy Library Forums (Malone in 2003, Hood in 2008). The memoirs of Katzenbach and Guthman were useful. See the Kennedy Library Forum in 2008: Hood, Katzenbach and Sorensen probe the events of June 11, 1963.

The wording of the executive orders and proclamations are in *PPP: John F. Kennedy, January 1 to November 22,1963*.

The visit of Robert F. Kennedy's children to his office is caught in *Crisis*, but more fully seen and felt in the uncut footage. For the press reports of the showdown, see the *New York Times* and the *Washington Post*, June 12, 1963 and *Newsweek* and *U.S. News and World Report* of that week. The definitive account is E. Culpepper Clark's *The Schoolhouse Door*.

CHAPTER 12 – EARLY AFTERNOON

For a list of Kennedy's appointments, see White House Staff Files in the JFKPL.

The discussions in Robert Kennedy's office were filmed by Robert Drew's cameras.

Lee C. White's memo on civil rights is in White House Files. John Lewis, in his memoir of the civil rights movement, *Walking with the Wind*, says the confrontation was scripted. David Brinkley says the same in his memoir, and some news reports that day said the same.

CHAPTER 13 - MIDAFTERNOON

The story of the making of the civil rights speech is drawn from the recollections of Ted Sorensen (*Counselor* and *Kennedy*), Lee White (his memoir), Arthur Schlesinger (his unpublished journals), Burke Marshall and Robert Kennedy (OH-JFKPL) and Robert Drew's footage.

A copy of Richard Yates's draft civil rights speech is in Robert Kennedy's papers in the JFKPL. Other material on the life of Richard Yates comes from interviews he gave late in his life, and particularly from Blake Bailey's fine biography, *A Tragic Honesty*.

Schlesinger relates his experience working with Sorensen in his journals, some unpublished. The portrait of Sorensen, here and elsewhere, comes largely from *Counselor*, as well as his letters, notes, and memos in his files in JFKPL. Ralph Dungan's comments (OH-JFKPL). Here the diaries of Katie Louchheim were illuminating. In understanding Sorensen in his later years in New York City, I was helped by Douglas Roche, a distinguished former Canadian parliamentarian and ambassador for disarmament to the United Nations. On Sorensen's relationship with Gloria Steinem, see Sydney Ladensohn Stern's *Gloria Steinem*, and his files.

CHAPTER 14 - LATE AFTERNOON

The secret mission to Indonesia is recounted in a chapter in Wilson Wyatt's entertaining *Whistle Stops*. Michael Forrestal (OH-JFKPL) is also helpful, as are his letters in the JFKPL. The agreement with Indonesia was covered by the *New York Times* on June 2, 1963, as well as the *Washington Post* June 1 and June 6, 1963. Jackie's views on Sukarno are drawn from her oral history; RFK's are from broadcaster Knowlton Nash's *History on the Run*. JFK commented on Sukarno in a conversation with Mike Forrestal, Roger Hilsman, and Howard Jones, the U.S. Ambassador to Indonesia, three days before he died, in Ted Widmer's *Listening In*.

Robert Kennedy on Edward R. Murrow in (OH-JFKPL); biographical material is drawn from Alexander Kendrick's *Prime Time*. Arthur Schlesinger mused about the U.S. and Europe in a memo to JFK on June 8.

Kennedy's meeting with James Webb (OH-JFKPL), as well as letters and notes in his files at the JFKPL. Both Jackie and Bobby referred to Webb (OH-JFKPL).

Walt Rostow's reference to "Liberty Hall" (OH-JFKPL).

CHAPTER 15 – EVENING

Drafts of the civil rights speeches are in Sorensen's files at the JFKPL. Kerry Kennedy displays her father's handwritten note on June 11 in the 2013 HBO documentary on her mother, *Ethel*. RFK also wrote his son Michael, mentioned in Schlesinger's 1978 biography, *Robert Kennedy and His Times*.

Schlesinger's note to the president about his forthcoming absence is in his files, and he tells the story of that evening in his unpublished journals. The Boston Pops repertoire (*Raintree County*) on Tuesday, June 11 was advertised in the *Boston Globe*, June 9, 1963.

The three minutes before the civil rights speech, when Kennedy sits at his desk in the Oval Office, are described by Hugh Sidey in *John F. Kennedy, President*. From the *Crisis* footage, Sidey appears to be in the Oval Office for the speech.

Kennedy's comments to Schlesinger on presidents are drawn from a letter Schlesinger wrote to his parents on August 12, 1962, in *The Letters of Arthur Schlesinger, Jr.*

Martin Luther King Jr.'s reaction in his telegram to the White House and in OH-JFKPL. In *Counselor*, Ted Sorensen says Walter Fauntroy told him that King thought JFK had hit a home run in his civil rights speech. James Hood and Nicholas Katzenbach also talked about the day in Tuscaloosa.

Schlesinger's reaction is in his diary and letters to Huggins (June 18, 1963). The discrepancy between the published and unpublished diary on the civil rights speech may be nothing more than words lost in transition. Schlesinger's subsequent letters confirm that he thought Kennedy's civil rights speech was the best of his presidency.

CHAPTER 16 – MIDNIGHT

For the portrait of Medgar Evers in this chapter and the next – his life, death, and legacy – I drew on the observations of Arthur Schlesinger (from his unpublished journals) and *A Thousand Days*, the autobiography of Roy Wilkins (*Standing Fast*), Gene Roberts and Hank Klibanoff (*The Race Beat*), and Adam Nossiter (*Of Long Memory*). For Evers, his murder and his aftermath, see the *New York Times* (June 1 and 13, 1963) and the

Washington Post (June 13 and 20, 1963). On Senator Gruening's request to the president, see the memo from Mike Manatos to Larry O'Brien of June 14, 1963, in the White House Files of the JFKPL. For the Evers family's meeting with JFK, see Evelyn Lincoln's *My Twelve Years with John F. Kennedy*. Where there is a discrepancy, however minor, I defer to *For Us, the Living*, Myrlie Evers's memoir, published in 1967, and subsequent interviews.

EPILOGUE

The draft of the president's letter to Mrs. Evers ("Dear Mrs. Evans") is in the White House Files. Ted Sorensen comments on JFK and Evers and his telegram on June 1, 1963, in a Kennedy Library Forum in 1998.

Sally Bedell Smith (*Grace and Power: The Private World of the Kennedy White House*) calls the Limited Nuclear Test Ban Treaty Kennedy's greatest diplomatic achievement, and the Civil Rights Bill his greatest domestic achievement.

On Vietnam, Kennedy dictated his reaction to Diem's assassination on November 4 in *Listening In*. In 1997, when I was a Washington correspondent with the *Globe and Mail* (Toronto), Seymour Hersh kindly gave me a copy of the recording, which was unknown to the JFKPL. The *Globe and Mail* ("Public, Private JFK heard on tapes") was the first to report its contents on December 19, 1997.

BIBLIOGRAPHY

The books listed here are part of a larger body of resources. Many of these titles reappear in the Chapter Notes; those are intended to point to the published works cited fully here. Magazine articles, interviews, documentary excerpts, and other materials are cited in the Chapter Notes and Note on Sources.

Alford, Mimi. *Once Upon a Secret: My Affair with President John F. Kennedy and Its Aftermath.* New York: Random House, 2012.

Alphand, Hervé. *L'étonnement d'être: Journal (1939–1973).* Paris: Fayard, 1977.

Alsop, Joseph, with Adam Platt. *"I've Seen The Best of It": Memoirs.* New York: W. W. Norton, 1992.

Anderson, David L. and John Ernst, eds. *The War that Never Ends: New Perspectives on the Vietnam War.* Lexington, Kentucky: University Press of Kentucky, 2007.

Anderson, Patrick. *The President's Men: White House Assistants of Franklin D. Roosevelt, Harry S. Truman, Dwight D. Eisenhower, John F. Kennedy and Lyndon B. Johnson.* New York: Doubleday, 1968.

Applewhite, E.J. *Washington Itself: An Informal Guide to the Capital of the United States.* New York: Knopf, 1981.

Arnett, Peter. *Live from the Battlefield: From Vietnam to Baghdad, 35 Years in the World's War Zones.* New York: Simon & Schuster, 1994.

Attwood, William. *The Reds and the Blacks: A Personal Adventure.* New York: Harper & Row, 1967.

Auburn, David. *The Columnist.* New York: Faber and Faber, 2012.

Bacevich, Andrew. J. *Washington Rules: America's Path to Permanent War.* New York: Henry Holt, 2010.

Bailey, Blake. *A Tragic Honesty: The Life and Work of Richard Yates.* New York: Picador, 2003.

Beschloss, Michael. *Presidential Courage: Brave Leaders and How They Changed America, 1789–1989.* New York: Simon & Schuster, 2007.

Bishop, Jim. *A Day in the Life of President Kennedy.* New York: Random House, 1964.

————. *Reporter.* New York: Random House, 1966.

Blair, Anne E. *Lodge in Vietnam: A Patriot Abroad.* New Haven: Yale University Press, 1995.

Bradlee, Benjamin C. *Conversations with Kennedy.* New York: W. W. Norton, 1975.

Branch, Taylor. *Parting the Waters: America in the King Years, 1954–63.* New York: Simon & Schuster, 1988.

————. *Pillar of Fire: America in the King Years, 1963–65.* New York: Simon & Schuster, 1998.

Brauer, Carl M. *John F. Kennedy and the Second Reconstruction.* New York: Columbia University Press, 1977.

Brinkley, David. *David Brinkley: A Memoir.* New York, Knopf, 1995.

Browne, Malcolm W. *Muddy Boots and Red Socks: A Reporter's Life.* New York: Times Books, 1993.

————. *The New Face of War.* New York: Bobbs-Merrill, 1965.

Bruce, Preston, with Katharine Johnson, Patricia Hass, and Susan Hainey. *From the Door of the White House.* New York: Lothrop, Lee & Shepard, 1984.

Bryant, Nick. *The Bystander: John F. Kennedy and the Struggle for Black Equality.* New York: Basic Books, 2006.

Bryant, Traphes, with Frances Spatz Leighton. *Dog Days at the White House: The Outrageous Memoirs of the Presidential Kennel Keeper.* New York: Macmillan, 1975.

Burleigh, Nina. *A Very Private Woman: The Life and Unsolved Murder of Presidential Mistress Mary Meyer.* New York: Bantam Books, 1998.

Caro, Robert A. *The Passage of Power: The Years of Lyndon Johnson.* New York: Knopf, 2012.

Carroll, James. *House of War: The Pentagon and the Disastrous Rise of American Power.* New York: Houghton Mifflin, 2006.

Carter, Dan T. *The Politics of Rage: George Wallace, the Origins of the New Conservatism, and the Transformation of American Politics.* New York: Simon & Schuster, 1995.

Claflin, Edward B., ed. *JFK Wants to Know: Memos from the President's Office, 1961–1963.* New York: William Morrow, 1991.

Clark, E. Culpepper. *The Schoolhouse Door: Segregation's Last Stand at the University of Alabama.* Tuscaloosa: University of Alabama Press, 2007.

Clarke, Thurston. *JFK's Last Hundred Days: The Transformation of a Man and the Emergence of a Great President.* New York: Penguin Press, 2013.

Cousins, Norman. *The Improbable Triumvirate: An Asterisk to the History of a Hopeful Year, 1962–1963.* New York: W. W. Norton, 1972.

Dallek, Robert. *An Unfinished Life: John F. Kennedy 1917-1963.* Boston: Little, Brown, 2003.

De Margerie, Caroline. *American Lady: The Life of Susan Mary Alsop.* New York: Viking Penguin, 2012.

Demery, Monique Brinson. *Finding the Dragon Lady: The Mystery of Vietnam's Madame Nhu.* New York: PublicAffairs, 2013.

Eisenhower, David, with Julie Nixon Eisenhower. *Going Home to Glory: A Memoir of Life with Dwight D. Eisenhower, 1961–1969.* New York: Simon & Schuster, 2010.

Evers, Myrlie B., with William Peters. *For Us, the Living.* Garden City: Doubleday, 1967.

Ferrari, Michelle (compiler). *Reporting America at War: An Oral History.* New York: Hyperion, 2003.

Fraser, Antonia. *Must You Go? My Life With Harold Pinter.* London: Weidenfeld & Nicolson, 2010.

Garrow, David J. *Bearing the Cross: Martin Luther King Jr., and the Southern Christian Leadership Conference.* New York: William Morrow, 1986.

_____ . *The FBI and Martin Luther King Jr.: From "Solo" to Memphis.* New York: W. W. Norton, 1981.

Ghaemi, Nassir. *A First-Rate Madness: Uncovering the Links Between Leadership and Mental Illness.* New York: Penguin Press, 2011.

Glendinning, Victoria, with Judith Robertson, eds. *Love's Civil War: Elizabeth Bowen and Charles Ritchie, Letters and Diaries 1941–1973.* Toronto: McClelland & Stewart, 2008.

Guthman, Edwin O. *We Band of Brothers.* New York: Harper & Row, 1971.

_____ , and Jeffrey Shulman, eds. *Robert Kennedy In His Own Words: The Unpublished Recollections of the Kennedy Years.* New York: Bantam, 1988.

Halberstam, David. *The Making of a Quagmire.* New York: Random House, 1965.

Hammer, Ellen J. *A Death in November: America in Vietnam, 1963.* New York: E. P. Dutton, 1987.

Heymann, David C. *RFK: A Candid Biography of Robert F. Kennedy.* New York: Penguin Group, 1998.

Himmelman, Jeff. *Yours in Truth: A Personal Portrait of Ben Bradlee.* New York: Random House, 2012.

Horowitz, Daniel. *Betty Friedan and the Making of The Feminine Mystique: The American Left, the Cold War, and Modern Feminism.* Amherst: University of Massachusetts Press, 1998.

Jacobs, Seth. *Cold War Mandarin: Ngo Dinh Diem and the Origins of America's War in Vietnam, 1950-1963.* New York: Rowman & Littlefield, 2006.

Jacqueline Kennedy: Historic Conversations on Life with John F. Kennedy. New York: Hyperion, 2011.

Janney, Peter. *Mary's Mosaic: The CIA Conspiracy to Murder John F. Kennedy, Mary Pinchot Meyer, and Their Vision for World Peace.* New York: Skyhorse Publishing, 2012.

Katzenbach, Nicholas deB. *Some of It was Fun: Working with JFK and LBJ.* New York: W. W. Norton, 2008.

Kendrick, Alexander. *Prime Time: The Life of Edward R. Murrow.* Boston: Little, Brown, 1969.

Kennedy, John F. *A Nation of Immigrants.* New York: Harper & Row, 1964.

Kraft, Joseph. *Profiles in Power: A Washington Insight.* New York: The New American Library, 1966.

Lamont, Lansing, *You Must Remember This: A Reporter's Odyssey From Camelot to Glasnost.* New York: Beaufort Books, 2008.

Leary, Timothy. *Flashbacks: An Autobiography.* Boston: Houghton Mifflin, 1983.

Lewis, John, with Michael D'Orso. *Walking with the Wind: A Memoir of the Movement.* New York: Simon & Schuster, 1998.

Lincoln, Evelyn. *My Twelve Years with John F. Kennedy.* New York: David McKay, 1965.

Loewy, Raymond. *Industrial Design.* Woodstock, New York: The Overlook Press, 1979.

————. *Never Leave Well Enough Alone.* Baltimore: John Hopkins University Press, 2002.

Longford, Lord. *Kennedy.* London: Weidenfeld & Nicolson, 1976.

MacNeil, Robert. *The Right Place at the Right Time.* Boston: Little, Brown, 1982.

Manchester, William. *Portrait of a President: John F. Kennedy in Profile.* Boston: Little, Brown, 1962.

————. *The Death of a President: November 20 – November 25, 1963.* New York: Harper & Row, 1967.

_____ . *The Glory and the Dream: A Narrative History of America 1932–1972*. Boston: Little, Brown, 1974.

Martin, Lowell A., ed. Director. *Encyclopedia Year Book 1964*. New York: Grolier, 1964

Martin, Ralph G. *A Hero for our Time: An Intimate Story of the Kennedy Years*. New York: Macmillan, 1983.

Mecklin, John. *Mission in Torment: An Intimate Account of the U.S. Role in Vietnam*. New York: Doubleday, 1965.

Merry, Robert W. *Taking on the World: Joseph and Stewart Alsop – Guardians of the American Century*. New York: Penguin Books, 1996

Mitchell, Leslie. *Maurice Bowra: A Life*. Oxford: Oxford University Press, 2009.

Moritz, Charles, ed. *Current Biography Yearbook: 1961*. New York: H. W. Wilson, 1962.

_____ , ed. *Current Biography Yearbook: 1962*. New York: H. W. Wilson, 1963.

Nash, Knowlton. *History on the Run: The Trenchcoat Memoirs of a Foreign Correspondent*. Toronto: McClelland & Stewart, 1984.

Newman, Don. *Welcome to the Broadcast: A Memoir*. Toronto: HarperCollins, 2013.

Nossiter, Adam. *Of Long Memory: Mississippi and the Murder of Medgar Evers*. Reading: Addison-Wesley, 1994.

Nunnerley, David, *President Kennedy and Britain*, New York: St. Martin's Press, 1972.

O'Connell, P. J. *Robert Drew and the Development of Cinema Verite in America*. Carbondale and Edwardsville: Southern Illinois University Press, 1992.

O'Donnell, Kenneth P., and David F. Powers. *Johnny, We Hardly Knew Ye: Memories of John Fitzgerald Kennedy*. Boston: Little, Brown, 1970.

Opotowsky, Stan. *The Kennedy Government*. New York: E. P. Dutton, 1961.

Parker, Richard. *John Kenneth Galbraith: His Life, His Politics, His Economics*. Toronto: HarperCollins, 2005.

Patten, William S. *My Three Fathers: And the Elegant Deceptions of My Mother, Susan Mary Alsop*. New York: PublicAffairs, 2008.

Perlstein, Rick. *Before the Storm: Barry Goldwater and the Unmaking of the American Consensus*. New York: Hill & Wang, 2001.

Poinsett, Alex. *Walking With Presidents: Louis Martin and the Rise of Black Political Power*. New York: Madison Books, 1997.

Political Profiles: The Kennedy Years. New York: Facts on File, 1976.

Prochnau, William. *Once Upon a Distant War*. New York: Random House, 1995.

Public Papers of the Presidents of the United States: John F. Kennedy, Containing the Public Messages, Speeches, and Statements of the President January 1 to November 22, 1963. Washington: United States Government Printing Office, 1964.

Radziwill, Carole. *What Remains: A Memoir of Fate, Friendship & Love*. New York: Scribner, 2005.

Raines, Howell. *My Soul Is Rested: Movement Days in the Deep South Remembered*. New York: Penguin Books, 1983.

Reeves, Richard. *President Kennedy: Profile of Power*. New York: Simon & Schuster, 1993.

Risen, Clay. *The Bill of the Century: The Epic Battle for the Civil Rights Act*. New York: Bloomsbury Press, 2014.

Ritchie, Charles. *Storm Signals: More Undiplomatic Diaries, 1962–1971*. Toronto: Macmillan, 1983.

Roberts, Gene, and Hank Klibanoff. *The Race Beat: The Press, the Civil Rights Struggle, and the Awakening of a Nation*. New York: Knopf, 2006.

Rusk, Dean, with Richard Rusk. *As I Saw It*. New York: W. W. Norton, 1990.

Rust, William J. *Kennedy in Vietnam*. New York: Charles Scribner's Sons, 1985.

Sachs, Jeffrey D., *To Move the World: JFK's Quest for Peace*. New York: Random House, 2013.

Salinger, Pierre. *With Kennedy*. New York: Doubleday, 1966.

Schlesinger, Andrew and Stephen Schlesinger, eds. *The Letters of Arthur Schlesinger, Jr*. New York: Random House, 2013.

Schlesinger, Arthur M., Jr. *A Thousand Days: John F. Kennedy in the White House*. Boston: Houghton Mifflin, 1965.

————. *Journals 1952-2000*. New York: Penguin Group, 2007.

————. *Robert Kennedy and His Times*. Boston: Houghton Mifflin, 1978.

Schlesinger, Robert. *White House Ghosts: Presidents and Their Speechwriters from FDR to George W. Bush*. New York: Simon & Schuster, 2008.

Seaborg, Glenn T., with Benjamin S. Loeb. *Kennedy, Khrushchev, and the Test Ban*. Berkeley: University of California Press, 1981.

Sidey, Hugh. *John F. Kennedy, President*. New York: Atheneum, 1963.

Smith, Sally Bedell. *Grace and Power: The Private World of the Kennedy White House*. New York: Random House, 2004.

Sorensen, Ted. *Counselor: A Life at the Edge of History*. New York: HarperCollins, 2008.

Sorensen, Theodore C. *Kennedy*. New York: Harper & Row, 1965.

Steinberg, Neil. *Hatless Jack: The President, the Fedora and the History of An American Style*. New York: Penguin Group, 2004.

Stern, Mark. *Calculating Visions: Kennedy, Johnson & Civil Rights*. New Jersey: Rutgers University Press, 1992.

Stern, Sydney Ladensohn. *Gloria Steinem: Her Passions, Politics, and Mystique*. New Jersey: Carol Publishing Group, 1997.

Storm, Tempest, with Bill Boyd. *The Lady is a Vamp*. Atlanta, Georgia: Peachtree Publishers, 1987.

Strober, Gerald S. and Deborah H. Strober. *"Let Us Begin Anew:" An Oral History of the Kennedy Presidency*. New York: HarperCollins, 1993.

Thompson, Kenneth W., ed. *The Kennedy Presidency: Seventeen Intimate Perspectives of John F. Kennedy*. Lanham: University Press of America, 1985.

Walsh, Kenneth T. *Air Force One: A History of the Presidents and their Planes*. New York: Hyperion, 2003

Watson, Mary Ann. *The Expanding Vista: American Television in the Kennedy Years*. New York: Oxford University Press, 1990.

West, J.B. with Mary Lynn Kotz. *Upstairs at the White House: My Life with the First Ladies*. New York: Warner Paperback Library, 1973.

White, Theodore H. *In Search of History: A Personal Adventure*. New York: Harper & Row, 1978.

Widmer, Ted, ed. *Listening In: The Secret White House Recordings of John. F. Kennedy*. New York: Hyperion, 2012.

Wilkins, Roy, with Tom Mathews. *Standing Fast: The Autobiography of Roy Wilkins*. New York: Viking, 1982.

Williams, Michael Vinson. *Medgar Evers: Mississippi Martyr*. Fayetteville: University of Arkansas Press, 2011.

Wyatt, Wilson W., Sr. *Whistle Stops: Adventures in Public Life*. Lexington: University Press of Kentucky, 1985.

Bruce, Evangeline, 132, 140
Bruce, Preston, 176, 178
Bruce, Sasha, 212, 370
Bundy, McGeorge: appointed by JFK,
   107; and Bowra, 140–141; and civil
   rights speech, 325; discusses
   Profumo Affair, 135; efficiency, 196;
   opposes Lodge's appointment, 196;
   and Peace Speech, 22, 25, 27–28, 43,
   201; and Ritchie, 147; role, 293
Burkley, George, 16, 219
Burns, John A., 18
Bush, George W., 59, 372
Byrd, Harry, 219
Byrd, Robert, 57

Cabot, John Moors, 210–212
Cambridge, Maryland, 181
Camp, Christine, 16, 328
Canada: international role, 145, 211;
   relationship with United States,
   145–148
Cannata, Ellen, 206
Capitol Page School, 217
Carson, Rachel, 67
Carter, Asa Earl, 69, 260
Carter, Jimmy, 359
Central Intelligence Agency (CIA): and
   foreign policy, 21; not consulted about
   Peace Speech, 26
Chang, Suzy, 163
Chayes, Abram, 306, 308
China: nuclear arms, 363; and nuclear
   test ban, 52, 53; and Peace Speech, 198
Churchill, Pamela Digby, 312
civil rights: assassinations related to,
   351, 353–354; Eisenhower's endorsement, 118–119; and foreign policy,
   202; Freedom Riders, 75; JFK's
   efforts toward, 6–7, 18, 19–20, 74–75,
   276, 278–279, 358; and organized
   labor, 112, 113–116; proposed bill, 75,
   81, 82–83, 191–193, 224–229;
   protests, 54–55, 72, 180–181, 358;
   setbacks after speech, 355, see also
   civil rights speech; racial equality;
   women's rights
Civil Rights Act (1964): debate, passage,
   and signing, 355, 359; drafting of,
   282; fair employment language, 116;
   introduced in speech, 336; planning
   for, 280–281

civil rights speech: delivery and
   content, 331–339; drafting of, 83, 281,
   284, 286–287, 292–293, 304, 321–325,
   330–331; early (unused) draft,
   287–289, 291, 292, 322; impact on
   Democrats, 359–360; response to,
   339–342, 357–360; timing of,
   276–277, 280–285, 325–326, 360
Clark, Kenneth, 231
Clement, Mary, 218
Clifton, Chester, 103
Clinton, Bill, 16
Coffin, William Sloane, Jr., 364
Colby, William, 188
Cold War: and American physical
   fitness, 97–98; calls for end to,
   52–53; JFK's views, 22, 50, 364;
   simmering, 3–4
Collingwood, Charles, 89
Communism: and Indonesia, 306,
   307–308; JFK's views, 40, 364; U.S
   attitudes toward, 42, 164–165, 200
Congress: civil rights legislation, 75, 82,
   191–193, 224, 277, 279, 354, 355;
   Democratic/Republican split, 191;
   foreign aid legislation, 189, 192,
   203–204; immigration reform, 206,
   208–209; JFK in, 190–191;
   Legislative Leaders Breakfast,
   189–190; pages, 217; reaction to civil
   rights speech, 339–340; stalls JFK's
   bills, 2, 62, 360; tax reform, 106, 108,
   110, 114–115, 192–193
Connor, Eugene "Bull", 75, 232
Cook, Carl, 56
Cooper, Billy, 160
Cooper, Duff, 149, 160
Cooper, Gordon, 2, 282, 315, 318
Cormier, Frank, 17
Cornell, Doug, 17
Cousins, Norman, 25, 50–53, 60, 201
Cowan, Jill, 125–126
Cuban Missile Crisis: Canada's slow
   support, 147; impact on Americans,
   56; impact on JFK, 5–6, 22, 24;
   impact on Khrushchev, 51; internal
   pressures on JFK, 26, 52; internal
   pressures on Khrushchev, 52; JFK's
   and Khrushchev's common goal, 36

Daley, Richard J., 12
Dallas, Texas, 31, 66, 310, 360, 372